Empires of Violence

Empires of Violence

Massacre in a Revolutionary Age

*Philip Dwyer,
Barbara Alice Mann, Nigel Penn
and Lyndall Ryan*

BLOOMSBURY ACADEMIC
LONDON • NEW YORK • OXFORD • NEW DELHI • SYDNEY

BLOOMSBURY ACADEMIC

Bloomsbury Publishing Plc, 50 Bedford Square, London, WC1B 3DP, UK
Bloomsbury Publishing Inc, 1359 Broadway, New York, NY 10018, USA
Bloomsbury Publishing Ireland, 29 Earlsfort Terrace, Dublin 2, D02 AY28, Ireland

BLOOMSBURY, BLOOMSBURY ACADEMIC and the Diana logo are trademarks of
Bloomsbury Publishing Plc

First published in Great Britain 2025

Copyright © Philip Dwyer, Barbara Alice Mann, Nigel Penn and Lyndall Ryan, 2025

Philip Dwyer, Barbara Alice Mann, Nigel Penn and Lyndall Ryan have asserted their right under the Copyright, Designs and Patents Act, 1988, to be identified as Authors of this work.

For legal purposes the Acknowledgements on p. xvi constitute
an extension of this copyright page.

Cover design by Grace Ridge
Cover image: 'Mounted Police and Blacks' depicts the massacre of Aboriginal people at Waterloo Creek by British troops. Tinted lithograph Held at Australian War Memorial - ART50023. 1852. From The Picture Art Collection via Alamy Images

All rights reserved. No part of this publication may be: i) reproduced or transmitted in any form, electronic or mechanical, including photocopying, recording or by means of any information storage or retrieval system without prior permission in writing from the publishers; or ii) used or reproduced in any way for the training, development or operation of artificial intelligence (AI) technologies, including generative AI technologies. The rights holders expressly reserve this publication from the text and data mining exception as per Article 4(3) of the Digital Single Market Directive (EU) 2019/790.

Bloomsbury Publishing Plc does not have any control over, or responsibility for, any third-party websites referred to or in this book. All internet addresses given in this book were correct at the time of going to press. The author and publisher regret any inconvenience caused if addresses have changed or sites have ceased to exist, but can accept no responsibility for any such changes.

A catalogue record for this book is available from the British Library.

A catalog record for this book is available from the Libray of Congress.

ISBN: HB: 978-1-3505-3864-1
       PB: 978-1-3505-3863-4
       ePDF: 978-1-3505-3866-5
       eBook: 978-1-3505-3865-8

Typeset by Integra Software Services Pvt. Ltd.
Printed and bound in Great Britain

For product safety related questions contact productsafety@bloomsbury.com.

To find out more about our authors and books visit www.bloomsbury.com
and sign up for our newsletters.

For Lyndall
Friend, Colleague, Feminist, Scholar

Contents

List of Figures x
List of Tables xi
List of Maps xii
A Note on the Use of Names xiii
Acknowledgements xvi

Introduction 1

1   A Revolutionary Age in a Global Context 13
    Global Colonial Connections 13
    Violence, Massacre and Colonialism 15
    The Massacre on the Colonial Frontier 18
    The Changing Nature of Violence, Warfare and Race 22

2   Ways of Being, Ways of Seeing 27
    Indigenous People of Southern Africa 28
    The Indigenous Nations of the Eastern Woodlands 37
    Aboriginal People on the Southeast Coast of New South Wales and Tasmania 43
    Indigenous Attitudes towards the Land 51

3   Local and Indigenous Ways of Warfare 61
    Indigenous People of Southern Africa 61
    Indigenous American Ways of Warfare 67
    Indigenous Australian Ways of Warfare 74
    Revolt and Rebellion in French-Occupied Europe 81

4 The Logic of Violence and Massacre on the Imperial Frontier 89

A Rhetoric of Hate 89
The Dynamics of Violence and Massacre on the Frontier 95
Atrocities on the Frontier 108

5 Massacre, the State and the Revolutionary and Napoleonic Wars 115

Violence as a State Response 117
Setting an Example: The Politics of Elimination 122
Atrocities and the Dehumanization of the European Other 126
Ideology and the Cleansing Force of Fire 128
A Transition to the Ordered, Modern Massacre 132

6 The Colony of New South Wales 137

Escalating Violence, 1793–1810 137
The Hawkesbury River Frontier, 1794–1810 138
New South Wales, 1802 144
Pemulwuy's War, 1792–1802 146
Fear of the French: The British Claim Van Diemen's Land, 1802–4 149
Risdon Cove, 3 May 1804 152
Violence and Massacre, February–April 1816 159

7 'Determining to Exterminate Them' in 'Terror and Desolation': Massacre in North America 163

The Shawnee of Ohio 164
The Miami of Indiana 170
The Muscogee of Alabama 175

8 'Striking Terror into the Enemy': The Ethnic Cleansing of the Zuurveld 181

The Northern Frontier and the General Commando 181
The Eastern Frontier Wars 185

The Second British Occupation 188
Clearing the Zuurveld, 1812 193
Sealing Off the Zuurveld, the Spoor Law and the Prophet 201
The Fifth Frontier War, 1818–19 205

Epilogue 211

The Killing Continues 213
Global Connections, Violent Attributes 221

Notes 227
Bibliography 287
Index 320

Figures

1. Samuel Daniell: Korah Hottentots preparing to remove, aquatint, 1805 30
2. Joseph Lycett: Corroboree around a camp fire, *c.* 1817 48
3. Anonymous engraving: This is the great freedom which Jourdan promised his fellow citizens, 1796 84
4. Anonymous engraving: Among the kings was the New Frank, polite and gracious, now he is a defender of robbery and fornication, *c.* 1796 86
5. Francisco de Goya y Lucientes: Plate 39 from 'The Disasters of War': 'An heroic feat! With dead men!', 1810 111
6. Augustus Earle, 'Portrait of Bungaree, a native of New South Wales', 1826 158

Table

1 Violent encounters between Aboriginal people and colonists, 1794–1824 219

Maps

1 Indigenous people and clans in the greater Sydney region 47
2 Indigenous American nations in Ohio 165
3 Indiana in the eighteenth century 171
4 The expansion of the Cape Colony before 1778 186
5 The wars on the eastern Cape frontier 189

A Note on the Use of Names

This work comprises the history of a number of Indigenous peoples, as well as geographic names that have since changed.

Most of South Africa had not yet been colonized during the period of this book, despite the Dutch East India Company (*Vereenigde Oost-Indische Compagnie*, shortened to VOC) first establishing a settlement in Table Bay in 1652. The Dutch came into contact with societies which may broadly be described as Khoisan. Though this descriptive term – both a portmanteau word and a neologism – has been criticized, it has acquired a degree of both academic and political acceptability and is now taken as referring to the Indigenous peoples of the Cape. The word 'Khoisan' is a composite of 'Khoikhoi' (or, in alternate spellings, 'Khoekhoe', 'Quenna' or 'Kwenna') and 'San'. Khoikhoi, which means 'men of men' or 'real men' in the Indigenous language spoken by the southwestern Cape Khoikhoi, is the term now used to describe those Khoisan who were primarily engaged in pastoral production. It replaces the pejorative term 'Hottentot' that was used by the Dutch and colonial settlers for many years. 'San', a somewhat unsatisfactory and problematic word, is now used to describe those sections of the Khoisan who were primarily hunter-gatherers. It is considered more politically correct than the word it replaced, namely, 'Bushman', although there are some people today who still prefer to be self-designated as 'Bushmen'.

North America was the homeland of hundreds of Indigenous nations. East of the Mississippi, there were more than 150 different nations, many aligned in powerful and sophisticated confederacies. In this book, we generally refer to the original inhabitants of North America as Indigenous Americans or First Nations people. Where possible, we refer to individual nations by their self-designation, such as Muscogee for Creeks, while elsewhere, for the sake of simplicity, we use common European names, such as Iroquois for Haudenosaunee. The term 'Woodlanders', for example, is a collective reference to the peoples of the northeastern and southeastern regions of the United States, who lived in towns, practiced large-scale agriculture and built ceremonial mounds in the Ohio and Mississippi River valleys.

The penal colony in New South Wales was known internationally as 'Botany Bay', even though the main settlement was several miles north at Sydney Cove. The colony was officially named Sydney in February 1788. Sydney and Sydney Cove are located within the wider expanse of water known as Port Jackson. 'Botany Bay' was the euphemism coined by the British press in 1787 for the proposed colony of New South Wales and was intended as a negative term to mark its penal status. In 1788, the British settlement at Sydney and its environs were located in the heartlands of five major linguistic groups of people, the Darug, the Darkinyung, the Guringai, the Dharawal and the Gandangara, with a combined population estimated at around 5,000. The island of Tasmania, occupied in 1803, was known as Van Diemen's Land until 1856, and was home to nine major linguistic groupings. Across the Australian continent, there were more than 200 Aboriginal people or nations, each with a distinctive language and an estimated total population of one million. In the continent's eastern half, claimed by Britain as New South Wales, there were about 100 Aboriginal people in eleven major regional groups with an estimated population of 500,000. The rest of the continent, 'discovered' by the Dutch in 1644, was still referred to as New Holland until the 1830s.

In Australia and Canada, the word 'Aboriginal' is commonly used to refer to the traditional owners of the land, but in the United States the term is rarely used, and to American Indians, it is considered as dismissive and insulting as the word 'Native' does to Aboriginal people in Australia. For the sake of simplicity, we have decided when talking about the First Peoples of the regions under discussion to refer to Indigenous peoples. We use the term 'local' to refer to communities that are connected to a specific region through ancestry or by living there. We use interchangeably the words 'settler', 'occupier' and 'invader' to describe people who took possession of lands that were not their own, or who came from the European world to live on non-European lands.

For some scholars, the very term 'settler' is problematic. James Merrell, for example, argues that pairing the word 'settler' with 'invader' or 'destroyed' is an oxymoron.[1] We will not go into the semantic difficulties of the term here, but its use in this book in no way suggests that the regions in question were not already 'settled'. The terms 'settler' and 'colonialism' are simply useful theoretical frameworks. In Australia, it is customary to warn Indigenous peoples that this work contains references to people who are deceased, and descriptions of massacres that may disturb some readers.

Acknowledgements

A short while after submitting this manuscript to the publishers, Lyndall Ryan succumbed to her battle with cancer. The rapidity of her demise shocked those who knew and loved her. Lyndall was a woman of integrity, wit and compassion, someone who was widely known and respected in Australian historical circles, especially for her work on the Aborigines of Tasmania, and more recently and more widely for her digital map of massacres against Indigenous peoples in Australia. Her co-authors would like to acknowledge her contribution to this book, her generosity as a collaborator and her ability to find the middle ground when there were apparent intellectual divergences. We dedicate this book to her memory.

The authors would like to thank Grace Karskens for helping clarify the linguistic developments in Australian Indigenous naming. We would also like to thank the four anonymous reviewers who commented on the manuscript for Bloomsbury. Their suggestions greatly helped improve the book. The funding for this book came from an Australia Research Council Discovery Grant. We are indebted to the Rockefeller Foundation for the opportunity to stay at the Villa Serbelloni in Bellagio, Italy, where we were able to put together the makings of a first draft. At Bloomsbury Academic, we are grateful to Maddie Smith for taking on this project, as well as Megan Harris, Paige Harris, and Pritha Suriyamoorthy for guiding us through the production stages of publishing this book.

Introduction

This is a comparative, global study of violence on the colonial frontier, and of the interactions between conquerors and the conquered from around 1780 to 1820. It deals with the expansion of Britain into the world, especially on the Australian and African continents, the westward and southern expansion of the United States, and the expansion of France in Europe during the Revolutionary and Napoleonic Wars. The four regions under study might at first glance appear too diverse to warrant comparison; there are differences in language, institutions, cultures and the very history of conquest and settlement itself. Three regions were subject to settler colonialism, while the fourth was an example of 'administrative' colonialism, an empire in the traditional sense of the word. However, these regions also exemplify what was happening in the world during this period, when the French, the British and the Americans created new empires or expanded old ones, using very similar if not the same violent methods and techniques, and often using very similar if not the same arguments to justify their use of violence.

There were, of course, different forms of colonial rule. In North America, the land was taken by significant numbers of Europeans, even before the end of the eighteenth century, while in Australia and southern Africa, there were never more than a few thousand settlers. In Europe, the colonial enterprise was different again. Once the invading armies had passed through, bureaucrats moved in to rule over the conquered territories in the name of the French Empire. This at least the French had in common with the British colonies, that is, outsiders ruled the conquered territories, with oversight by rulers in a distant metropolis – Washington, London or Paris. For some years now scholars have attempted to think of 'colonial' in the largest possible terms. Comparing these distinctive colonial societies will help bring to the surface the vastly different cultural assumptions, as well as European conceptions of killing and conquest on the one hand, and the Indigenous and local responses on the other. Those contrasts will become clearer in the course of the book.

The subjects treated in the following pages all take place within the larger context of extraordinary social and political change, in the midst of which geo-strategic rivalries took place on a scale not seen since the Seven Years' War (1756–63, also known as the French and Indian War). Those rivalries were mercantilist as well as ideological. New European empires were being created in different parts of the world at the same time, although they were, of course, different kinds of empire, with different historical chronologies. In Europe, with the outbreak of the Revolutionary Wars in 1792, the diplomatic and then the territorial landscape of Europe was completely transformed, eventually leading to the creation of a French empire on the Continent, while it tried to hold on to its old empire in the Caribbean, at the same time as expanding into new regions of the world, such as Egypt. During the Revolutionary and Napoleonic Wars, Britain used its naval supremacy to establish a new colonial empire in the southern hemisphere, reaching into South Africa and Australia, as well as gaining a stronger hold in the Caribbean and in India.[1] In the United States, the early Republic expanded to create a new settler empire in the Old Northwest, moving vigorously into the southwestern Woodlands neighbouring the Mississippi River, displacing First Nations people whose use of the land was ancient. What all these empires had in common was the domination of one group over another in the name of racial and cultural superiority.[2] In Saint-Domingue, for example, the French developed a rhetoric of white racial purity and superiority.[3] During this, as in other historical periods, murder, massacre and violence were the means used to forge new states, new political ideologies and new empires.

The period between 1780 and 1820, often referred to as the Age of Revolutions, invites particular attention because it stands at the crossroads of the modern era.[4] It is a crucial period defined not only by the expansion of empire across a number of regions in the world but also the emergence of a new mentality that would come to characterize the nineteenth-century colonial enterprise.[5] We can confidently call this period a watershed moment in history not only because of the American and French revolutions, with all its implications for Australia and South Africa, but also because of the ways in which the meaning and practise of irregular warfare changed.[6] In Europe in particular, a new element was introduced into the fighting of 'small wars', namely, ideology.

This was also a time when Britain shifted to the east geographically and to the right politically. The geographic shift signalled the increasing importance of the Indian Ocean, and especially India, as an area of imperial expansion, while the political shift signalled an increasing tendency towards greater government control and authoritarianism in colonial government. The loss of the thirteen American colonies did not mean the complete withdrawal of Britain from the Atlantic world: far from it. The Caribbean sugar islands continued to be the most profitable of Britain's overseas possessions, Canada remained loyal, and British trade with the newly independent American states grew rather than declined in value. Nonetheless, there was a noticeable gravitational shift eastward in British imperial interests after 1783, a shift that ensured that the Indian Ocean would play a vital role in the power struggles of the revolutionary era.

The political shift to the right in British imperial policy can be attributed to lessons that were learnt during the American Revolution. The conclusion the British political elite drew from the loss of their American colonies was that tolerance of demands for liberty and political representation could lead to a loss of control. After 1783, British colonies were much more likely to be run along authoritarian lines, frequently by governors who had been in military service. The period after the American colonies broke away from Britain has consequently been referred to as the era of pro-consular despotism.[7] This 'despotism' would characterize British rule in its new possessions in Australia and South Africa as well as its 'possessions' in India, even if the latter was technically run by the British East India Company. The British government thus cast itself as a counter-revolutionary or conservative force. The Revolutionary era in Europe was the moment when Britons were encouraged to embrace a new nationalism that transcended regional or ethnic identities, constructed around loyalty to the monarch, allegiance to the Union flag, and proud and bellicose resistance to France.[8] Britain's decision to found new colonies was thus based on three guiding principles: it would only establish new colonies that met domestic, commercial and strategic needs; it would employ a more despotic approach to colonial governance; and it would acknowledge fewer rights to Indigenous owners of the lands they occupied than had been the case in North America.[9]

Despite the increasing interest in global history, as well as in the history of empire, and despite attempts to view the Revolutionary and Napoleonic Wars as a global phenomenon,[10] scholars across fields and across geographical regions have not always communicated well with each other. This is the first time that researchers specializing in four different regions and four different histories have come together, pooling their knowledge and expertise to uncover the lines of interconnectivity in an attempt to see empire and colonialism within a broader framework of global conflict, modernization, expansion and violence. We are as a result able to tell multiple stories, stories that we feel must be told in light of the continued denial on the part of settler societies that fail to take into account the violent nature of their national histories. That violent past, we argue, can only be judged appropriately when put into a larger comparative context. The creation of empire is violent and involves the deaths of many of those peoples who resist, for whatever reason, either the centralizing state or the encroachment of colonial societies. In the regions under discussion here, women were raped, and many people were killed, kidnapped and enslaved. Subjugated peoples were often treated with the contempt the powerful have for the powerless. Murder and massacre was one of a number of tools at the disposal of the colonizer, which was used to subjugate recalcitrant populations. As we shall see, it was used often.

This study of the imperial frontier writ large focusing on the dynamics of massacre considers questions such as why European settlers felt the need to kill not only the men but also the women and children, killings that cannot be reduced to simple matters of race or revenge killings for the loss of troop, militia or settler lives or livestock. The notion of 'frontier' is hotly contested among historians, and is often indicative of a one-sided, state-centred approach 'predicated on an expansionist perspective'.[11] It implies the advance of the colonizer and the settler along some arbitrary boundary and generally neglects to take into account the local and Indigenous people, who reacted to that advance in many different ways. Other terms such as 'contact zone', 'middle ground', 'shatterzone' or 'borderlands' were contemplated. These terms invoke a more fluid geography and place more emphasis on the resilience of local peoples. The term 'borderlands' is now extensively used in North American and European history, although it seldom appears in the Australian and South African literature.[12] Even though some people think the term 'frontier' conjures up notions of racial superiority and expansionist conquest, others point to its fluidity and its multi-perspectival potential.[13] We believe it can be used while recognizing the resilience of Indigenous peoples. We have thus decided to stay with the term 'frontier' but have attempted to expand the concept to signify not just a simple boundary of advancing colonizers or colonial invaders but also a zone of space which was much more fluid and shifting, a space in which the colonizer and the colonized, the occupier and the occupied, interacted on all sorts of levels over large geographical areas. This is a way of thinking more ethically about how colonial history is written, and one that takes into account the human costs of European expansion. The frontier is a place where different peoples and different cultures confronted and clashed with one another; it was nevertheless permeable and could shift over time. That is why we try to take into account, where possible, the extent to which perpetrators and victims were known to each other and the types of interactions they enjoyed before there was a descent into violence.[14]

Indigenous and local peoples affected by colonization are often talked about in abstract, generalized terms, not as collective identities or as individuals, but so too are the perpetrators of colonial violence. This is in stark contrast to twentieth-century perpetrators of mass killings about whom we know a great deal. Think of the innumerable individual studies on German perpetrators of the Holocaust, and not just high-ranking Nazis. In contrast, we know a great deal less about the killers on the colonial frontier, especially for the eighteenth and early nineteenth centuries. In part, this has to do with the inherent nature of colonial violence as well as the extent to which colonizers and soldiers may have hidden from families and communities the violence committed against local and Indigenous groups. We also have to take into account the lack of survivors from those groups able to pass down stories from one generation to the next either in oral or written form. Colonial violence is, after all, often a story of killing, and it is often perpetrated in the countryside. It is, therefore, largely invisible to people in the colonial metropoles. There is too always the danger of not being able to understand the violence from the perspective of the victim, so that the act of violence itself becomes a tale that lacks empathy.[15] That sense of understanding, however, has to cut both ways. A certain understanding is required not only of the victims but also of the perpetrators of the violence, a position which is sometimes uncomfortable for the historian and difficult for the reader to accept.

It is, however, paramount to understand the colonizing enterprise from the local and Indigenous perspective to recast the conventional portraits of the helpless victims of Europeans, into one of people who attempted to shape the worlds in which they lived by interacting with Europeans in all sorts of constructive and innovative ways. As historians, we realize just how difficult a task this is. Nevertheless, where possible, we have attempted to incorporate Indigenous epistemologies. There are necessarily problems in attempting to incorporate the experiences of Indigenous peoples.[16] Nonetheless, we point out the diverse range of vocabularies used to describe peoples and events, and to describe Indigenous and European understandings of the world. By tacking back and forth between outsiders' and insiders' views, looking at an event from one perspective and then from the other, we hope to offer a deeper understanding of the events being studied. This is always problematic. We are, after all, using the records of one people to decipher the experiences of those of another.

A comparative, global history of violence, warfare, colonization and empire brings with it a number of complications.[17] We are dealing with an enormous variety of local ethnic and racial identities. What happened in South Africa was different to Australia or North America, and what happened in Europe was different again to the colonizing enterprise in the non-European world. Nevertheless, a certain implacable logic drove conquerors to impose their modes of thinking, their modes of exchange and commerce onto local and Indigenous peoples, to take their lands, to rape, loot and plunder, and to eliminate all who resisted their will. The consequences of imperial and colonial expansion, the dispossession and massacre of local or Indigenous peoples, and the use of violence by European imperial and colonial societies – physical, state-directed and symbolic – all occurring at the same time point to a synchronicity that will throw some light on the broader history of the world. We are trying to understand how these four different parts of the world used very similar if not the same forms of violence, while treating the local and Indigenous peoples they conquered as a kind of faceless mass labelled 'savage', 'uncivilized' and 'barbarian'.

To understand the processes and mechanisms behind massacre and violence, it is necessary to understand the attitudes and beliefs of all the parties involved. Chapter 1 examines the different themes that we can draw together across these four regions of the world, including the interconnectedness of colonial personnel, the changing nature of violence, warfare and race, and the meanings of violence and massacre on the frontier. We set out some of our definitions and objectives, placing our work within the existent literature on the topic. The second chapter is devoted to 'ways of seeing' and 'ways of being'. European settlers brought with them both a particular view of the land they invaded and occupied, as well as particular attitudes towards those whose land they dispossessed. They often used these pre-conceived notions to justify the expropriation of land from Indigenous peoples. Explaining those different concepts, especially Indigenous ways of living and their relationship to the land, helps us better understand the violent clash of cultures that occurred, and helps put those differences in a broader context. It also helps us understand European attitudes towards local and Indigenous peoples.

The third chapter in the book examines how local and Indigenous peoples not so much resisted the incursions of foreigners onto their lands, but rather how they normally conducted warfare. In the vast majority of cases, the European invader, military and civilian, killed local and Indigenous peoples with impunity. Those same people resisted everywhere, although not in the same manner. Indigenous Americans soon learnt to incorporate Western weapons into their repertoire but not for example, Indigenous Australians, who did not adapt to changes in military tactics, and did not integrate European firearms into their fighting methods until later in the nineteenth century. Even then, it was unusual. Indigenous warfare was often centred on the raid, or an ambush and its consequent response – a counterraid.[18] Open combat was rarely employed, although there are a few instances of that happening in North America. Indigenous warfare aimed at minimizing losses. We also touch on two related but sensitive issues, what are commonly referred to as 'scalping' and 'ritual torture'. In all cases, and unlike their European counterparts, warfare was never a continuous exercise among Indigenous peoples, but usually a limited affair. In Europe, peasant revolts were often spontaneous, and relatively easily put down, although there were instances of irregular forces, usually dubbed bandits or brigands by the authorities, waging continuous war against invading forces.

Wherever possible, when looking at one region of the world, we have attempted to draw comparison with the other three regions. Every now and then there are forays into British, French and sometimes Dutch colonial experiences in other parts of the world – India, Egypt and Saint-Domingue. Chapter 4 sets the scene, so to speak, by examining some of the factors that allow massacre to occur, such as a rhetoric of hate towards the enemy other, which helps us understand the coloniser's language around wanting to 'extirpate' and 'annihilate' the enemy. This rhetoric of hate is characteristic of the language of the conqueror, found wherever Europeans met non-Europeans, or indeed other Europeans that the conqueror looked down on. It brings us to the question of the relationship between rhetoric and the extreme violence committed by troops, militias and settlers against Indigenous and local inhabitants. The chapter then looks at some of the defining characteristics of massacre in the four regions under study, including cattle theft and the use of massacre in South Africa, the policy of terror practised in North America and Australia, and the dynamics of massacre in the French conquests, including the practice of sacking cities, the use of atrocities and mutilation, and submitting the countryside to a policy of scorched earth. Generalizations about who committed these massacres are not easy to make, but some indication is given with the limited sources available to historians.

The core of the book looks at case studies within our four regions, roughly following a chronological order, looking at Europe, before examining Australia, North America and the struggle for the Zuurveld in South Africa. We begin with the French in Europe which helps put into context violence and the state and the foundations of international law that were applied not only within Europe but to other parts of the world. The 'rules of war' that were developed in the eighteenth century often served as a pretext for the extreme violence that was enacted on local and Indigenous peoples. The extremity of the violence that characterized the civil wars during the French Revolution, when opponents of the regime were demonized, was in part justified by eighteenth-century legal thinking, and in part by a radical revolutionary rhetoric. Attitudes towards opponents of the conquests and the French reforming agenda carried over into the imperial era. Violence and massacre were a state response, part of a policy of terror designed to 'set an example' so that others would not rise in revolt, and a precursor in many respects to the systematic uses of massacre that we encounter in the modern era.

The sixth chapter examines the escalating violence between British settlers and Indigenous Australians in the Colony of New South Wales from 1793 to 1810, focusing on the impact of colonial expansion and military responses to perceived threats. Four case studies examine those violent responses: the frontier war with the Bediagal (or Bidjigal) clan of the Darug people for control of the Hawkesbury River settlements from 1794 to 1810, Governor Philip Gidley King's administration of the colony in 1802–3, Pemulwuy's guerrilla war against the colonists on the Cumberland Plain from 1793 to 1802, and the Risdon Cove massacre in 1804. Put together the case studies produce new insights about the behaviour of colonial governors and the garrison in a new kind of colony in a far-flung corner of the British Empire in a time of global war.

The seventh chapter focuses on North America. There had already been a long involvement between the Spanish and French and Indigenous Americans well before the British landed in the sixteenth century. One might argue that there was very little variation in the interactions between Europeans and Indigenous Americans over the centuries, characterized as it was by warfare, and massacre, regardless of the Indigenous nation, culture or landscape involved. The chapter focuses on three specific examples of this pattern of violence: the Shawnee of Ohio from 1783 to 1787, the Miami of Indiana from 1787 to 1791, and the Muscogee of Alabama in 1813–14. We clearly see how dispossession, race and violence were intertwined in the colonizing process.

After a brief preamble looking at Dutch violence against African peoples before the arrival of the British at the Cape at the beginning of the nineteenth century, Chapter 8 focuses on the British attempts to clear the region called the Zuurveld of Xhosa, in what is a textbook example of ethnic cleansing. The British, like their Dutch precursors, had little regard for human life, shooting indiscriminately as they practised a scorched-earth policy that was probably inspired by tactics used in the Peninsular War. The chapter also illustrates the conflicts and tensions that can arise between Indigenous peoples as they aligned with or fought against the invader. Finally, the Epilogue attempts to draw together some general conclusions about massacre and violence in our four regions of the world, pointing to a number of commonalities regarding the types of violence used in English-speaking settler societies as well as in the French empire from 1788 to around 1820, and the manner in which Indigenous and local communities resisted the colonial encounter.

Empires of Violence is intended to reveal in broader terms the nature and development of colonization at the beginning of the modern era, and during a period in which the wider Atlantic world was undergoing not only a number of political revolutions but also a revolution in the ways in which European colonizers interacted with the local and Indigenous peoples they encountered. It is a reminder that colonization was never peaceful, that resistance was persistent and determined, and that if most of these cultures succumbed to colonization, it was because their capacity to resist was weakened not only by disease but also by the sheer volume of colonizers arriving on their lands. As we shall see, no single massacre or atrocity defines the violence of this period any more than the moments of peaceful coexistence that may have occurred. There were multiple ways for Indigenous peoples and Europeans to interact, that is a given, but this book allows us to focus on the intensification of violence and to shed some light on the darker side of eighteenth- and nineteenth-century colonialism and empire.

Despite the extent and number of massacres covered in this book, the colonial enterprise often continues to be presented in former settler societies, that is, lands that have been occupied by Europeans, as having been of benefit to humankind, at least in some conservative political and historical circles.[19] The nostalgia for empire in post-Brexit Britain is particularly acute with advocates downplaying the depth and breadth of the violence associated with the empire in the nineteenth century.[20] However, the legacy of the Enlightenment and the Revolution leave us with a particularly difficult question: how do we reconcile the idea of reform emerging from the European centre, which entailed notions of equality and humanity that modern readers would recognize, with the killing of Indigenous peoples or other Europeans in the cause of empire? In Europe during the Revolutionary and Napoleonic Wars, the French and British often treated other Europeans as 'barbarous', helping them justify the killing of civilians that could occur. In North America, the British military, sometimes aided and abetted by Indigenous allies, unleashed violence and hatred on settlers whom the British considered rebels and Indigenous peoples invaders. Captain Henry Bird's punishing invasion sweeping down from Detroit, through Ohio and into Kentucky against the rebels in June 1780 is an example.

Massacres in Europe and the colonial world at the end of the eighteenth and the beginning of the nineteenth centuries were not new, but what we clearly see is a new kind of war – in Europe involving mass armies and mass conscription – built upon systems of rhetoric that stigmatized the enemy to the point of having to eliminate the 'other', and a desire by the state to control and channel that violence. Control was a difficult enough goal for the state on the colonial frontier – in Australia, North America and South Africa – but when it comes to revolutionary upheaval – in Europe, Ireland, North America and South America – the state was often responsible for the atrocities committed and massacres were often meant to serve as examples. Massacres were, therefore, subordinated to military, political and economic necessity. In that process, there was an ideological subtext that we try to bring out, an evident desire not necessarily to annihilate whole peoples in the name of an idea, but at the very least to oblige people to comply with new norms through violence. We hope that this book will, along with many others that have been written in recent years, help bring the violence of the frontier to the front of people's minds in former settler societies and in the process, help heal the deep rifts between the colonizer and the colonized.

1

A Revolutionary Age in a Global Context

Global Colonial Connections

We now have some understanding of the process of violence and colonization in different parts of the world at this time, and just how interconnected the European and colonial worlds really were. There is, we argue, much to be gained from focusing on the manner in which a massacre may have unfolded in a single locality. Deep studies of such occurrences can tell us a great deal about colonial policies and practices, local and Indigenous responses, as well as revealing the complex dynamic between the occupiers and the occupied, between the colonizer and the colonized. The premise here is that knowledge of violence was shared. Europeans worked within what has been called an 'imperial cloud', a reservoir of shared knowledge that was accessible to different imperial players.[1] The colonial networks of violence knowledge were extensive among the military personnel that often ran European colonies or who were sent to 'tame' the frontier zones. Military and administrative personnel travelled from the wars in Europe to North America, South Africa, Australia and back again, bringing with them and exchanging their military techniques and knowledge. This exchange of personnel was a feature common to most European colonial enterprises across time.[2] We know, for example, that some of the English involved in the conquest of Ireland in the sixteenth century subsequently moved to new conquests in Virginia, and a new litany of killing.[3]

In a similar vein, some of the senior British officers who served in Ireland in 1798, and who were therefore either witness to or took part in massacres to put down the rebellion there, later served in Spain, India, Afghanistan, Australia and South Africa.[4] Sir John Cradock, whom we will come across later in South Africa, is an example of someone who helped to suppress the Irish Rebellion in 1798 before going on to various other colonial appointments. He was authoritarian, intolerant and hardened by the experience of command in the wars of the Empire.

Likewise, some of the most important figures in the South American wars of independence also fought in Europe during the Napoleonic Wars, conducting terror campaigns against civilian populations reminiscent of the tactics used by French troops against Spanish guerrillas, such as 'flying columns', which gave and received no quarter.[5] French officers who fought in Egypt, Saint-Domingue and Spain were later found committing excesses in Algeria in the 1830s.[6] General Thomas Robert Bugeaud, for example, fought with the French in Spain during the Napoleonic Wars, and then in Algeria, where, along with Louis-Achille Baraguey d'Hilliers, they began to theorize and practice the *razzia* – a raid in which one steals and destroys livestock and provisions – that often had the destruction or starvation of whole 'tribes' as its goal. The practice, at least one historian has speculated, had its origins in the revolutionary destruction of the Vendée region, and in the Napoleonic Wars in Spain.[7] Pierre François Boyer fought in Italy and Egypt in the late 1790s, where massacres were frequently carried out, was part of the expedition to Saint-Domingue, and was transferred to Portugal and Spain, where he earned the nickname 'Pedro the Cruel', for the brutal exactions carried out against the local people there.[8] He too ended up in Algeria in 1830, where he continued to commit atrocities against the local populations. General Bertrand Clauzel was a veteran of Saint-Domingue, Italy and Spain, while General Anne-Jean-Marie Savary was a veteran of Egypt, Italy and Spain. Both subsequently served in Algeria, bringing with them a well-honed approach to colonial warfare.

In New South Wales in 1790, marine Captain Watkin Tench drew on his experiences in the Revolutionary Wars in North America to devise the strategy of the punitive raid at dawn on Aboriginal camps to contain Aboriginal resistance. As an efficient effective form of attack, it was readily adopted by settlers and soldiers alike and by 1820 was the most widely used tactic against Indigenous resistance in the colony of New South Wales.[9] These men embodied the connectivity of the global colonial process; they transferred experiences, attitudes and techniques of violence from one setting onto another.

We come back to the question of the interconnectedness between the European military elites and the colonial empires of which they were a part. The traffic of personnel flowed in both directions so that many bureaucrats and military who had served in the colonies brought what they had learnt back to Europe. It remains to be seen, however, whether there was a transnational sharing of ideas or a sort of 'parallel development' that was occurring during this period.[10] It is obvious that at the heart of the colonizing enterprise, whether English, Dutch, French, Spanish or American, the use of force to either subjugate or eliminate recalcitrant peoples was the norm. One can see a pattern, therefore, in the massacres that took place in North America, South Africa and Australia, where Indigenous peoples were killed and forced off farming or grazing lands, and in Europe where any resistance to French rule was met with an excessive use of force.

Violence, Massacre and Colonialism

Violence is at the heart of this study as we try to understand both the perpetrators and their victims. People throughout the four regions of the world endured ongoing conflict – and by that we include raids, pillaging, massacres and skirmishes – so that an almost constant state of warfare among Europeans and between Europeans and Indigenous peoples existed for most of the period under examination. Descriptions and analyses of specific massacres are not enough to capture the processes behind the killings. In general, case studies or theoretical works that attempt to explain the dynamics of massacre focus on the perpetrators as scholars try to understand their motives, and the psychological processes involved.[11] Massacres and mass killings occur when a group of people or a community wishes to subjugate, eradicate, exact revenge on, or impose power and control over another population, or when it sees another group as a threat to its own survival. It is sometimes done to recover lost prestige and sometimes done to change the existing political or economic order. In the context of colonization, massacres are dispossessive. Local and Indigenous populations that encountered expansionist European powers were stripped of their land and of their means of subsistence and were sometimes eliminated as a people in the process.[12] Massacres on the colonial frontier are generally explained away by racial hatreds, but that only goes part way to explaining the dynamics of killing. Important too is understanding the political, cultural, and social contexts which enable men, sometimes inexperienced in killing, to commit atrocities. We are interested in how 'ordinary' settlers and soldiers become murderers, and how perpetrators legitimated the killing of not just men as potential combatants, but also the elderly, women, and children.[13]

These are questions that scholars who have grappled with the problem of mass killings will be familiar with, but we are focusing specifically on the massacre in a colonial context. The bar for mass killing is set quite high by political scientists, at around 50,000 civilian deaths over a five-year period, whereas the term massacre can be used for far fewer deaths.[14] The sheer brutality of the violence on the frontier instinctively makes historians reach for the term genocide. However, genocide is a legal category and is not necessarily helpful as a basis for the analysis here. As Mark Mazower has argued, the term is both too narrow and too broad a concept for the purposes of historians.[15] The term, moreover, gives rise to controversies about what is or is not genocide, while historians who discuss genocide 'find themselves answering the question as to whether a given event qualifies, and so classifying rather than explaining'.[16] This is often a distraction from a consideration of the events themselves, and even if we answered, yes, it was genocide, we would not have gotten very far with our analysis.

The term massacre is, we believe, more appropriate to describe the violence that ensued from occupier-occupied interactions during the period under study. In the massacre model, state violence is easy to understand; governments and settler societies eliminated people who opposed their primary objective – the acquisition of territory and land. In these circumstances, as was the case in Australia, North America and South Africa, governments and settlers used violence to force people to cooperate and ordered the killing of Indigenous peoples to induce compliance and to have free access to land. There is, of course, a debate about whether colonial governments intended to eliminate all Indigenous peoples – some genocide scholars argue that this was inherent in colonialism[17] – but the intent often varied from one region to another and from one time period to another. The British in North America, for example, were more accommodating than many of the American governments that followed the War of Independence. This is not to say that the term genocide is not applicable to some periods of Australian, South African, North American, and even French history, but that, again for the period under study here, the term cannot be consistently applied across the four regions in question. Rather than get mired in debates about whether the term genocide is applicable or not, we have instead decided to focus on particular examples of killing within the four regions, as well as asking questions about the intentionality of the perpetrators, and the level of participation of various government institutions.

If most massacres were not genocidal in intent, this does not mean that some massacres were not part of a genocidal process. The difference between the two is not immediately clear, but if we use the model proposed by the political scientist, Stathis Kalyvas, we can argue that the pattern of violence on the frontier across the four regions of the world under consideration was consistent with 'indiscriminate violence' – also known as 'reprisals' – rather than with genocidal violence. Indiscriminate violence frequently took place in our four regions of the world, especially in zones where the invader had a predominant presence. Some massacres might have been genocidal in intent, but the distribution of massacres across the regions in question makes this unlikely. The Black Line in Tasmania in 1830 is the exception to the rule.[18] Extermination, in other words, was not always the predominant motive. Some scholars will inevitably contest that claim, but we hope to show that the eliminationist logic of the settler was not yet as consistent as it became later in the nineteenth century.

Over the last two decades or so, a growing body of scholarship on massacre and mass violence has begun to emerge, often focusing on particular case studies.[19] Other investigations focus on the role of massacre in a comparative perspective.[20] At least one scholar has attempted to build a conceptual framework of massacre, as have the authors in this work.[21] These are all welcome additions, although case studies of individual massacres, rich in detail, often lack a larger perspective that would lead to a better understanding of massacre practices over long periods of time and across geographical locations. Larger comparative studies, such as this one, afford a sense of the ways in which massacres evolved historically and were rooted in cultural practices. While our broader comparative study might lack the 'thick description' that often characterizes the examination of individual massacres, it will nevertheless add a badly needed sense of scope to the portrait of massacre.

The Massacre on the Colonial Frontier

Although massacres might appear to be always the same, in reality no massacre resembles another and has to be studied as a unique event in a particular set of circumstances. The vast majority of massacres discussed in this book have largely been forgotten, even when the trauma visited on those societies was significant. And yet the intensification of the phenomenon across the world during this period appears to be linked. One can juxtapose acts of extreme violence committed by the state, as in Europe during the Revolutionary and Napoleonic Wars, or in Ireland during the 1798 rebellion, or indeed in Australia before 1830, with acts of violence committed by individuals working outside of the control of the state, as in Australia after 1830, South Africa, and North America, but often with the state's implicit approval. In Australia, it is likely that the French Revolutionary and Napoleonic Wars made it acceptable for British troops to carry out massacres.

A study of massacre necessitates a definition, a conceptualization to categorize and characterize the phenomenon.[22] The word 'massacre' is still often used in a literary sense to describe the killing of one man by a group of people,[23] just as it is used to describe the indiscriminate slaughter of thousands. The French sociologist, Jacques Sémelin, who has provided the most interesting conceptual framework to date, calls massacre a 'mass crime', the deliberate and brutal destruction of a large number of non-combatants, often accompanied by atrocities that at first appear quite pointless.[24] This definition is nonetheless a little vague and does not take into account either civilians killing other civilians or indeed combatants, or Indigenous peoples killing settlers and combatants. In their seminal work on the subject, Mark Levene and Penny Roberts proposed a broad definition that encompassed the killing of people, and animals, lacking in self-defence.[25]

In Australia, on the other hand, historians generally agree that six or more deaths must be involved to constitute a massacre, at least on the frontier.[26] Six has been proposed because it would have constituted the loss of about one third of what would have generally constituted an Aboriginal hearth, leaving the surviving group vulnerable to further attack, greatly diminished their ability to hunt or gather food, to carry out ceremonial obligations, and to reproduce the next generation. Although this does not take into account the large numbers of people who would have been killed in ones, twos, and threes, for the sake of simplicity a massacre is defined here as a killing, either premeditated or unplanned, of at least six people at any one time. The victims are generally civilians and unarmed. Our focus here is not so much on the number of people killed on the colonial frontier over a specific period of time – something that is in any event impossible to know – but rather on the will of the perpetrators to eliminate other humans.

The purpose of a massacre, it hardly needs to be stressed, is to kill. The reasons why people kill others are almost as varied as the historical and political contexts in which the massacre takes place. Despite this, there are a number of things that most massacres have in common. Groups kill to intimidate, to strike fear into the 'other', so that they become submissive and submit to the will of the group trying to dominate them.[27] In Australia and South Africa, and frequently in North America, 'hunting parties', 'commandos' and militias, consisting of anywhere between a few and hundreds of men, were organized to raid Indigenous towns and villages, usually at dawn when the inhabitants were still asleep. Men, women, and children were killed at random. In Europe, on the other hand, troops were often involved, and often because of the disparity between the forces arrayed, these attacks or raids would take place during the day. Massacres are more likely to occur at the beginning of a conflict – in the case of the frontier, when settlers arrive in a particular locale – and become less frequent over time, as Indigenous groups are eliminated, subjugated as a labour force, or are pushed out of the region. In a colonial setting, a massacre is not an aberration. It is part of a deliberate attempt either to dispossess and destroy people, or to hasten submission and capitulation.[28] In that respect, colonial massacres resemble ethnic cleansing more closely than is often admitted.[29]

Essential of course is to explain why they occurred in some places and not in others, or indeed why at times they spiralled out of control.[30] One argument is that it has to do with the space occupied by the frontier, a zone of extreme violence that existed on the margins of settler/conqueror societies.[31] In the colonial mindset, killing local and Indigenous people was invariably a response to the killing of settlers, militia or occupation troops, or the destruction of property, or the killing or theft of livestock. In Australia and South Africa, the killing of a sheep or a cow was considered a sufficient pretext to kill all Indigenous people in the local area. In Australia, a frontier massacre could take place in response to an Indigenous man killing a settler in reprisal for kidnapping and or killing an Indigenous woman. In North America, invented 'depredations' were sufficient to escalate violence against Indigenous Americans to a 'just war'. In Europe, the types of massacres that occurred were often retaliatory, resulting from the killing of French troops by locals. Vengeance and fear often drove occupiers and settlers to commit excessive acts of violence. Of course, there were all sorts of other ways in which Europeans interacted with local and Indigenous peoples, from trade to attempts at religious conversion to intermarriage and sexual dominance. These interactions often complicated the story of violence which this book tells and are part of the processes that continued to evolve and unfold as the French, British, and American empires continued to expand.

One of the defining features of massacre at the beginning of the modern era is the position and role of the state, sometimes ambiguous and sometimes direct, but always complicit. In regions where vast distances existed between the frontier and the colonial metropole, settlers were often left to battle it out with Indigenous peoples for control of the land so that when excesses were committed, and the authorities eventually found out about them, they often turned a blind eye. Sometimes killing on the frontier occurred without the knowledge or the approval of the state. In North America, militia 'armies' were raised by the government, which commonly paid scalp bounties.[32] The state, or at least its representatives in the military and militias, often instigated violence to extend settler reach in a particular region. In South Africa, the state was virtually absent from the frontier, at least for the period under study. When 'commandos' raided the San peoples in the Cape region, local concerns repeatedly ignored and overrode the state, which in some instances attempted to de-escalate frontier violence. In Australia, on the other hand, government troops, often aided by settlers and convicts, were often involved in killing Indigenous peoples, and did so at the behest of the state, at least before the 1820s. They acted with impunity, usually with the complicity of the colonial state. In those instances, the state's control over vast tracts of land appeared relatively weak as was the state's control over the British who settled those lands. Settler violence, however, was often 'clothed in law', that is, settlers manipulated European laws, especially around property, to justify the dispossession of Indigenous peoples.[33] In Europe too the military acted with impunity, knowing they would never be reprimanded or brought to trial for any excesses committed.

From the very start of the colonial enterprise there was a willingness to kill, alongside a conviction that Europeans had a God-given right to the land they had occupied. This is an 'ideology', broadly defined as a distinctive political worldview. In this instance, it is a belief that local and Indigenous peoples were underserving of the land they inhabited, and that Europeans had a right to possess and dispossess. This was part of an 'ideological pattern' across the four regions of the world we examine that enabled and facilitated the killing of others. We do not discount other factors, some of which we have already alluded to, but we argue that the killing must be understood in interaction with ideology, 'because ideologies play a central role in determining both how people privately think about mass killings and how such violence can be publicly legitimated and organized'.[34]

The Changing Nature of Violence, Warfare and Race

Just as important as understanding the dynamics of massacre is to understand the changing nature of violence. Killing and massacres have always occurred in colonial settings where Europeans vie with Indigenous peoples for the control and exploitation of the land, its people, and its environmental assets. This study of massacre across four continents enables us to interrogate the extent of the violence committed against the original and local peoples of these countries, and to ask whether we are seeing a new form of violence that will develop more fully over the nineteenth century, or whether this is the same violence Europeans always used against conquered peoples. The ritualized aspects of popular violence in Europe – massacres, mutilated bodies, and the parading of body parts – had existed for centuries. Were they simply transplanted onto new geographical sites, or were there fundamental differences? Put another way, is this period the beginnings of the development of a culture of extermination that came to the fore in the nineteenth century and that historians generally associate with colonization? While we have tried to avoid falling into the trap of simply arguing that the massacres that occurred in a colonial context during the Revolutionary Age were a precursor of what was to come, forty odd years of barely uninterrupted killing and warfare across the colonial world were bound to have an impact on the values, attitudes, and the historical references of nineteenth-century Europeans.

Killing on the Colonial Frontier

There are two other essential elements that this book will explore. The first concerns the changing nature of warfare and killing that occurred on the colonial frontier. The master narrative of modern warfare, which is nonetheless contentious, is that the 'absolute wars' of the eighteenth and early nineteenth centuries prefigured the genocides of the twentieth century.[35] Revolutionary warfare in particular is seen as both quantitatively and qualitatively different from preceding wars. David Bell, for example, believes that the massacres carried out by the French against their own people in 1794 mark a new stage in the history of state violence against civilian populations.[36] In that year, around 200,000 people, including 30,000 Republican troops, were killed in the Vendée region of France.[37] Once the 'Vendéens' had been singled out as a political grouping that was counterrevolutionary, then all its members had to die.[38]

We thus see an important divergence between the Revolutionary Age and earlier wars. Moreover, while state violence that occurred in pre-modern Europe was often religiously motivated, the killings that took place on the colonial frontier were profoundly secular in nature.[39] In contrast to massacres carried out in earlier periods, religion is notably lacking among perpetrators as either motive or justification for the period from 1780 to 1820.[40] This was even the case in Ireland during the 1798 Rebellion. What we find instead is that the nature of massacre changes and will continue to evolve throughout the nineteenth century. In fact, many of the atrocities committed were ideologically and racially inspired; there is a connected relationship between the two that involved 'eliminationist' violence. While some settler leaders wanted to eliminate Indigenous peoples, others did not.

Race and fear of the 'other'

This brings us to the second element, which concerns the question of race and whether it was at the heart of the violence that infused the colonial enterprise at the end of the eighteenth and the beginning of the nineteenth century?[41] There is naturally a long history of race and racism leading to the eighteenth century that we will have to pass over here.[42] Enlightenment theories on governance and the hierarchy of the races went hand in hand with imperialist and exclusionary attitudes. As we shall see, there were certainly racist undertones to the rhetoric used to describe both the local and Indigenous people and their ways of life. The word 'savage' was used for the first time in the mid-eighteenth century by Montesquieu in *De l'esprit des lois* (On the Spirit of the Laws, 1748), and were described as those 'who could not unite', in contradistinction to 'barbarians' who could come together in social groups.[43] The 'savage' was meant to be a universal social type who stood at the beginning of 'domestication'. Similarly, there is a long-running debate over whether racial prejudice provided the foundation for Atlantic slavery or whether slavery gave rise to racial prejudice. The historian Sue Peabody argues that ideas of racial difference are best understood as embedded in the social and economic relations in which they occur.[44]

Many Enlightenment thinkers, who were by our own standards racists, attempted to justify slavery and colonialism, and expressed views towards, Jews, Africans, 'gypsies', and Turks that we would consider offensive.[45] Voltaire, Nicolas de Condorcet, Immanuel Kant, and Georg Wilhelm Friedrich Hegel all insisted on the fundamental differences between races. In Condorcet's mindset, for example, the peoples of the world were divided into three categories: those who were waiting for Europeans to appear to learn from their example; those who needed to be delivered from oppression; and those 'savages' who were beyond help, and who would eventually disappear.[46] In other words, Condorcet foresaw the elimination of Indigenous peoples who could not accept or keep up with the European idea of progress. We find a similar line of thinking in the English-speaking world when John Stuart Mill defended colonial wars, including in Ireland, and advocated for the benefits of 'civilization'.[47] In general terms, even those who recognized the evils of slavery and colonialism, and attempted to debunk racial stereotypes, somehow fell into the trap of believing that Black Africans were peculiarly suited to chattel slavery.[48] Either that or they believed that the horrors experienced by the enslaved were compensated for and ultimately justified by the blessings of Christianity.[49] For many eighteenth-century philosophers, religion was the saving grace of slavery and colonialism.

Race was not, however, a causal factor in the decision to carry out a massacre. One historian goes so far as to argue that race never played more than a peripheral role in the killing process, at least for the period under consideration.[50] To use an analogy for a later historical period, antisemitism in early twentieth-century Germany did not lead to the death camps, nor can it possibly explain the behaviour of the men who killed on behalf of the Nazi war machine, but it was certainly one of the factors that led to the conditions necessary where wholesale killing could take place. So too for the colonial frontiers under discussion. To regard others as less than human might help mitigate the act of killing in the conscience of the perpetrator and was often used to justify the killing either before or after the fact, but again, it is not a sufficient explanation for the killing.[51]

There are instead two other complementary elements we would like to introduce when trying to understand the dynamics of violence on the colonial frontier across the world in the Revolutionary Age. One is the notion of the 'other', and the process of dehumanization that invariably occurs when people enter into conflict.[52] In order for the kind of violence we are examining to occur – in which not only men but women, children and the elderly are killed – there must first take place an 'othering' in which the local and Indigenous people are seen as not human and even as subhuman, that is, animal-like. Dehumanization is hardly a new insight; there are any number of examples of this in past centuries, in the four regions of the world under discussion, and in the modern era. However, the rhetoric and language used to describe others as non-human raises interesting questions about views of humanity during the Enlightenment.

The other complementary element that helps us understand the motives of the perpetrators is the notion of 'fear' and misunderstanding. Fear, one might even call it paranoid fear, was and is a powerful driver of violence on the colonial frontier.[53] It is often fear – fear for one's own safety, fear of harm coming to loved ones, and fear of having one's livelihood destroyed – that drove settlers to commit extreme acts of violence.[54] It may also have been the driver behind the Indigenous and local populations attacking settler societies, for the very same reasons. We understand that the term 'fear' is ambiguous and contested,[55] but it is clear cultural misunderstandings often led to a lack of trust on both sides of the cultural divide, and that the resulting fear, coupled with the perception that 'they' were dangerous, led to reprisal massacres.[56] In this mindset, fantastical rumours were believed, and the line between fantasy and reality was blurred.[57] Massacre, in these circumstances, was often pre-emptive, carried out in the belief that one had to get 'them' before they got 'us'.

To better comprehend how these elements played on the minds of Europeans, as well as local and Indigenous peoples, we need to understand how they thought about the land and each other in relation to it, which is the subject of the next chapter. At its core, Indigenous and European colonizers viewed the land as a means of survival, but they had very different customs in how to use the land and its resources. Understanding those customs and attitudes helps underscore the cultural and social differences that led to so much misunderstanding on the frontier, and which in turn helped feed into the cultures of violence that existed in our four regions of the world.

2

Ways of Being, Ways of Seeing

Once European colonizers and Indigenous and local peoples began interacting with each other, different cultural and social expectations produced tensions that often led to violence. It is worth underlining, as we attempt to do in this chapter, what exactly were those preconceived European notions to better understand the ways in which the colonizer behaved towards Indigenous peoples. Just as importantly, we try and understand Indigenous ways of life, Indigenous epistemologies if you will. At the most basic level, Indigenous peoples resisted because their lands were being invaded, but it is much more complicated and nuanced than that. There were all sorts of interactions taking place on the frontier that included negotiation (not always from a position of weakness), trade and even in some instances intermarriage.

This chapter introduces the reader to the Indigenous peoples at the heart of this book, including their social, cultural, spiritual and to a lesser extent their economic frameworks. They were powerful and resilient societies, and in the case of the Xhosa of South Africa and the Iroquois of North America, expansionist polities in their own regions that inevitably collided with European settler societies. As we shall see, their conceptions of the land, or 'country' as Australian Aboriginal people call it, were entirely foreign to European notions of landownership and exploitation; it was unthinkable for Indigenous peoples to own the land. We will start with the peoples of the Cape region before moving on to the matrilineal peoples of northeast of North America where, as an example, 'gift giving' among American Indigenous peoples led to so much misunderstanding, and then to the small-scale patrilineal Indigenous societies in the southeast of the Australian continent.

Indigenous People of Southern Africa

The Khoikhoi and the San

The Khoikhoi were a society of Indigenous pastoralists who entered southern Africa about 2,000 years ago. They probably originated in the region of present-day northern Botswana. Originally, they would have been hunter-gatherers but at some stage they acquired livestock, in the form of sheep and goats, from people to the north of them.[1] They also made the necessary cultural transition from being hunter-gatherers to being pastoralists. This transition would not have been instantaneous as it takes time to put aside the predominant cultural values of hunter-gatherers, which place a high value on sharing, and to take up the predominant values of pastoralists where status is measured by the accumulation of individual wealth in the form of livestock.

The name Khoikhoi has been spelt in a variety of ways – Khoekhoe or Quena are variants – and it means something like 'Men of Men' or 'Real Men'. We may assume that the name implied a degree of superiority relative to those who remained mere hunter-gatherers. About the same time as the Khoikhoi were adopting the pastoralist lifestyle, Bantu-speaking agropastoralists – people who grow crops and keep livestock – were entering southern Africa. The Bantu-speakers were also skilled at metal work and the manufacture of iron tools. Over a relatively long period of time, since at least the second century AD, the Bantu-speaking agropastoralists occupied the better-watered areas where it was possible for them to grow their summer rainfall crops, while the Khoikhoi were restricted largely to those areas that were too dry to grow crops but sufficiently watered to keep livestock. The Khoikhoi dispersed fairly rapidly from their point of origin in Botswana and moved southwards to the Orange River basin. From there, according to a hypothesis first formulated by Richard Elphick in the 1970s and based on linguistic, archaeological and historical evidence, the Khoikhoi moved westwards to the west coast and then southwards to the Cape Peninsula.[2] On reaching the southernmost tip of Africa they moved eastwards along the coast until their progress was barred by encountering the Bantu-speaking groups that had settled in what is now the Eastern Cape. These Eastern Cape Bantu-speakers are known to linguists and anthropologists as the Nguni people. The southern Nguni are today's Xhosa and the northern Nguni the Zulu. The Nguni occupied those regions to the east of the Drakensberg, where they could grow crops. Around about the vicinity of the Gamtoos River in the Eastern Cape the annual rainfall to the west falls below 40 cm per year and crop cultivation becomes unpredictable. It was along this shifting and imprecise isohyet that the Khoikhoi and the Xhosa frontier zone came into being.

At the same time as the Khoikhoi were coming into existence and learning to share the environmental resources of southern Africa with the Bantu-speaking agropastoralists they had to co-exist with the original hunter-gatherer societies of the region. Before the coming of the Bantu-speakers and before the emergence of the Khoikhoi all the human societies of southern Africa had been hunter-gatherers. Quite how extensive the population of hunter-gatherers was in pre-colonial times is hard to estimate though it would be surprising if there were more than 200,000. These hunter-gatherers were widely dispersed throughout southern Africa and spoke a variety of languages that were often mutually unintelligible to different groups but characterized by the use of click sounds. Though the groups were diverse they are often seen as being fairly homogenous by virtue of all being hunter-gatherer societies and possessing the same basic technology. Most hunter-gatherers lived in small bands of between ten to twenty people, extended families in reality. The reason for these small group sizes had to do with the nature of their lifestyle. Groups had to be highly mobile, or semi-nomadic, to survive. They would move so as to be able to exploit the seasonality of environmental resources. Apart from plant food that was gathered (*veldkos*) such as bulbs, roots, berries and seeds, the groups counted on hunting game to supply themselves with meat. As a rule, the women gathered *veldkos* and the men hunted, creating an important gender division in their societies. Their technology consisted of weapons and tools made from stone, wood, bones or shells. They did not manufacture metal. They clothed themselves in animal skins and sheltered from the elements behind temporary structures of scrub.

The groups were highly fissiparous and with weak political structures. People from one group married with those of another and the formation of kin relationships between groups provided a claim for mutual support in times of need. There was no hereditary position of chief or captain and authority was vested in the group rather than in a leader. In times of war groups might merge together for protection and it is likely that skilled hunters assumed temporary leadership positions. But the group was more likely to pay attention to their shamans, or spiritual leaders. As far as we know spiritual power was not gender specific and shamans might emerge from both sexes. A shaman might be gifted with healing powers or spiritual visions, gained through out-of-body travel or trance. Communal dancing brought about the trance state and the insights gained in trance were often portrayed in a visual form through the medium of paintings, or engravings, on suitable rock surfaces. The religious beliefs of the hunter-gatherers were also recorded in stories, fables or songs. Studies of these various sources suggest that there was a widespread belief among the hunter-

Figure 1 *Samuel Daniell: Korah Hottentots preparing to remove, aquatint, 1805.*

gatherer societies in the magical potency of certain animals, particularly the eland, and that in this respect they shared a common cultural universe.[3]

Although each hunter-gatherer group had a distinct name for itself, together they became known, in colonial times, as Bushmen. The Dutch term for this was 'Bosjesmanne' or 'Bosjesman-Hottentoten' as they perceived the Bushmen to be a type of Khoikhoi or, as they called the Khoikhoi, 'Hottentots'. The present term for the 'Bushmen' is San. The term is derived from a Khoikhoi word (Nama to be precise) that is derogatory and means something like 'person of low esteem'. It suggests the pastoralists' natural disdain for the hunter-gatherer. Despite this, however, 'San' has become widely used, particularly among academics, even though many San people today are quite comfortable with the term 'Bushman'.

Though the San were not one people, the Khoikhoi did appreciate that hunter-gatherers were different from themselves. In pre-colonial times relationships between Khoikhoi and San groups ranged from hostility to friendship as the two different lifestyles adjusted to each other. Archaeological research suggests that the intrusion of pastoralist groups into hunter-gatherer territory was accompanied by the withdrawal, in the long term, of hunter-gatherers into the mountainous, more arid and less livestock friendly areas of the country.[4] While this withdrawal may have been in response to violence and force there is evidence that the San and the Khoikhoi were also linked together by trading relationships and relationships of clientship or service. Thus, some San worked as scouts, herders, or soldiers for Khoikhoi groups in exchange for gifts of milk or pottery and they could also exchange honey and the spoils of the hunt for Khoikhoi items if they chose. San medicine and spiritual potency was also highly regarded by the Khoikhoi.[5] On the whole, given the small scale of the populations, the land was big enough to accommodate both groups and the San remained a powerful presence in those areas not directly occupied by the Khoikhoi. The Khoikhoi could buy peace with the San through gift giving but they remained wary of neighbouring hunter-gatherers who were well able to steal their livestock if provoked. In early colonial times in the southwestern Cape one of the Khoikhoi names for a local group of San was the Ubiqua, a name that basically meant 'thieves' and reflects the tense relationship, which sometimes existed between the two groups.[6]

The Khoikhoi habit of regarding the San as being less than 'men of men' because they were not pastoralists was easily understood by the European pastoralist farmers, or trekboers, who also tended to see the San as potential thieves. Indeed, the Dutch word *Bosjesman* or *Bosman*, apart from meaning someone who lived in the bush or forest, was a word applied to a robber, brigand or highwayman in the Netherlands. The perception of the San as 'robbers' was reinforced by the response of the San to the advance of the colonial frontier. As early as 1700, when European farmers began to penetrate the Tulbagh Valley and to cross the Berg River, the San of these regions began to attack the colonists. For the most part these attacks took the time-honoured form of targeting the livestock of the pastoralist enemy. Thus, the cattle and sheep of the colonists were either driven off or killed by the San. Occasionally, farmers or their shepherds were also killed. Pursuing commandos were vigorously resisted and a state of war with the San of the southwestern Cape persisted until about 1715 when a temporary peace was achieved. This peace, it must be said, owed a great deal to the devastating effects of a smallpox epidemic that broke out in 1713 and largely destroyed the traditional Khoisan societies of the southern Cape. Fighting resumed, however, in 1728 and peaked in the so-called Bushman Wars of 1738–40. There was then a lull until about the 1760s when the further advance of the colonial frontier provoked massive Khoisan resistance all along the interior escarpment of the Cape until the end of the century. These were the years of the commando and the years when the massacre of San groups became a common feature of frontier warfare.[7]

The nature and intensity of this struggle encouraged the colonists to view the San as being a type of predator, akin to vermin, like a jackal or a lion. The VOC government was in the habit of offering bounties for the destruction of lions and, at the height of the struggle against the San, a certain frontier *veldwagtmeester* by the name of Petrus Pienaar actually offered to kill Bushmen if he was paid a bounty per head. This offer the government refused, with the explanation that it did not want to encourage the unnecessary spilling of blood, but Pienaar's proposal is an indication of frontier attitudes.[8] The use of the term *schepsel*, or creature, to describe the San was widespread at the time and a sign that the San were considered to be less than human.

The Xhosa

The eastern frontier of the Cape Colony has long been regarded by South African historians as the most important site in the 'epic of South Africa's creation'.[9] This assumption is debateable but owes its origin to a set of ideas borrowed from the American historian Frederick Jackson Turner that seeks to demonstrate that national character evolved in the crucible of the frontier zone – that it was 'the frontier tradition' that shaped the course of South African history.[10] Even though it is clear that the course of South African history has advanced through a variety of different frontiers at different times, the weight of academic consensus has agreed that it is the Cape's eastern frontier that was the most important.[11] This, it is argued, is where all three of the major players in South Africa's history met – Boer, Bantu and Briton.[12] This is where a hundred year war was waged between white and Black, one of the longest continuous colonial, or anti-colonial wars, in history.[13] This is where Blacks were first forcibly colonized, some losing their land, while others entered the colony as labourers. This is where racist attitudes and racial hatreds flourished, setting an imprint on inter-group relations that both presaged and informed the later development of *apartheid*.[14]

While the importance of the eastern frontier in South African history is obvious, its significance may have been exaggerated and the devastating impact of the earlier advance of the colonial frontier northwards into Khoisan societies was a long-neglected area of study. Conquest, land alienation, racial hatred and the subjugation of Indigenous people into an underclass of labourers were all features of the northern Cape frontier before 1780. What is incontrovertible, however, is that the eastern Cape frontier zone was better watered and more fertile than the parched earth of the arid Karoo. They could sustain more livestock and even allowed for the agricultural production of summer rainfall crops. As a result of this more favourable environment more people could be supported and, consequently, competition for these resources involved larger numbers of people. Quite naturally, pastoralists and agricultural societies gravitated to the region, putting pressure on the hunter-gatherer societies that had previously monopolized it.

The south westerly expansion of the Xhosa was restricted by two major factors. In the first place the Xhosa needed sufficient summer rainfall to grow their crops of millet, sorghum and maize. The minimum amount of rainfall for such purposes is about 40 cm per annum. West of the Kei River the annual summer rainfall is usually less than this, the frequent occurrence of droughts making agriculture beyond the 40 cm isohyet less likely to be successful. In years of good rainfall crops might be sown further east, but the harvest could not always be guaranteed, and Xhosa settlement was therefore sparser and more tenuous. So, while the Xhosa habitually grazed their cattle beyond this environmental limit, they did not establish permanent homesteads – implying regularly tended fields – outside of the reliable rainfall zone.

The second limitation to Xhosa expansion was the prior presence of both San and Khoikhoi in the region. In their interactions with these peoples the Xhosa had a distinct advantage. Since they enjoyed greater food security, thanks to having access not only of hunting and pastoralism but to agricultural produce as well, their population was greater than that of their competitors. This demographic strength was enhanced by the presence of stronger political structures in which chiefly authority was more effective than in Khoisan societies in mobilizing large numbers of people for the common purposes of defence, aggression, settlement or food production. Xhosa society was also more hierarchical than Khoisan societies, with certain clans or lineages claiming to have power or status and seniority over others. Kinship networks and marriage alliances were important in creating ties of dependency and obligation throughout Xhosa society and the custom of men marrying more than one wife also ensured that there would be status differences even among the children of a common father. A bride's worth depended on her lineage and was measured in the *lobola*, or bride-wealth paid for her in cattle. As in Khoikhoi society, cattle were a marker of a man's wealth. But unlike in Khoikhoi society, cattle were not the only measure of a man's status. Chiefly descent and membership of a senior lineage were a vital aspect of a man's political authority. Habits of command and obedience thus permeated Xhosa society and all Xhosa acknowledged that they lived under the ultimate authority of a paramount chief, or king, even though regional chiefs enjoyed a great deal of independence.[15]

All of these factors combined to make Xhosa society more powerful and resilient than the Khoisan. The numerically weak and politically fragmented San had been forced into regions that were of marginal utility to the agropastoralist Xhosa. Here some were tolerated for the magical knowledge and healing prowess they possessed, while others were employed as auxiliary scouts, hunters or servants. Still others were treated with the time-honoured hostility felt by pastoralists towards livestock predators. The Khoikhoi, on the other hand, were lovers of livestock, but this was an attribute that caused them to be regarded by the Xhosa as rivals. Linguistic evidence suggests that the Khoikhoi had once grazed their cattle and sheep well to the east of the Kei River. Over the centuries, however, the more powerful Xhosa gained ascendency in the area. Xhosa ascendency did not necessarily mean the extirpation of the Khoikhoi. It is far more likely that the Xhosa exerted a form of political subjugation over those Khoikhoi groups they encountered. While this subjugation was probably accomplished by forcible conquest and displacement – for there is evidence of violent fighting having taken place – the ultimate aim of Xhosa polities was to incorporate subjugated groups into Xhosa society rather than to annihilate them. Political power, ultimately, rested on the ability to command the loyalty of numerous people. Among the Xhosa, as elsewhere, such power implied the ability to enforce obedience, and it is revealing that while the Khoikhoi name for themselves meant 'men of men', their name for the Xhosa meant 'angry men'. Thus, political subjugation was eventually followed by cultural assimilation and intermarriage between members of the societies that were, in many respects, not that dissimilar from each other to begin with. By the beginning of the eighteenth century there were a number of groups living between the Xhosa and the Khoikhoi, such as the Gqunukhwebe, Hoengiqua and Gonaqua, who were of mixed descent.[16]

Where ethnic, tribal and group identities were so blurred it is perhaps fruitless to try to find distinct political boundaries between Xhosa and Khoikhoi society. Even before European settlers arrived at the Cape, the eastern Cape was already a frontier with interaction between two or more distinct societies with different economic, social and political systems. It was also a place of environmental transition between regions suitable for the growing of summer rainfall crops and regions unsuitable for this purpose. Broadly speaking, this frontier lay between the Sundays River in the west and the Fish River in the east. By the time the trekboers, reached this region in the mid-eighteenth century, it was inhabited by both Khoikhoi and Xhosa groups, with some San presence still to be found on the margins. Some of the groups, as has been mentioned, were a mixture of both Khoikhoi and Xhosa. The region became known by the colonists as the Zuurveld after the predominant type of grazing to be found there, open, uncultivated grassland. This name gives a further indication as to why the inhabitants of the region were so peripatetic. Livestock could not graze all year round on sour veld and had to be periodically moved to the sweet veld of other regions. Though river valleys had good mixed grazing elsewhere the grass was harmful to livestock in autumn and winter.[17]

Despite these complicated patterns of co-existence – not unusual in frontiers – early records suggest that this entire region had once belonged to the Khoikhoi before it had belonged to the Xhosa. In 1752, an expedition despatched to the region by the VOC reported that the Keiskamma River was the traditional boundary between the Xhosa and the Khoikhoi.[18] By 1780, however, the most powerful group of the region, the Gonaqua, had been weakened and fragmented, caught as they were between the advancing trekboers and the ever-intrusive Xhosa. Tellingly, by 1780, the strongest Khoikhoi group in the area was not the Gonaqua but the Hoengiqua, a fairly recent creation formed from the broken remnants of numerous southern Khoikhoi tribes and under the authority of a newcomer to the Zuurveld, Captain Ruyter, a Khoikhoi refugee from the Roggeveld.[19]

With all of these different groups attempting to co-exist in the Zuurveld at the same time it is hardly surprising that conflict occurred. Sometimes the conflict was not only between different groups but within the groups themselves, both Black and white. The contestants not infrequently formed alliances that crossed the boundaries of race to defend themselves against rivals from within their own societies, although such alliances were usually of short-term duration. The existence of such cross-racial political alliances, however, should not obscure the fact that between 1780 and 1820 the major issue at stake in the Zuurveld was which of the three major societies – European, Xhosa or Khoikhoi – should predominate. By 1820 the issue had been decided.

The Khoikhoi had disintegrated or been subjugated; the Xhosa had been forcibly expelled from the region to the eastern side of the Keiskamma River while European settlers, under the authority of the British government, had colonized the area. We shall see further on how the struggle was decided and what part massacre played in proceedings.

The Indigenous Nations of the Eastern Woodlands

Politically, three of the best known of the great confederacies in North America were the Haudenosaunee ('People of the Completed Longhouse', or the Iroquois League), the Muscogee Confederacy ('Creek Confederacy') and the pan-Indian Confederacy in Ohio country, which became the largest Indigenous resistance movement in the history of North America.[20] Before Europeans arrived, the Iroquois League controlled the east-west territory from Lake Champlain, which forms the border of the modern-day states of New York and Vermont, west across northwestern Pennsylvania to what is now Toledo, Ohio, at the mouth of the Maumee River below Lake Erie. In the north, the Iroquois League stretched from the St. Lawrence River, which forms the modern-day Canada-US border, south to the Delaware River in Pennsylvania.[21] Above the St Lawrence River sat another, yet distinct, five-nation Iroquoian confederacy, which, if less known to Europeans, was no less vital to Indigenous politics. The Muscogee occupied almost the totality of the modern state of Alabama and western parts of the state of Georgia, with cousin groups such as the Natchez originally running from the modern state of Mississippi as far north as present-day eastern Tennessee.[22] Many geographically smaller leagues than these existed including, for instance, the *Neshnabek* ('Man Sent Down From Above', 'Three Fires Confederacy') of the Ottawa, Anishinaabe and Bodéwadmi ('Potawatomi') of southern Michigan, northwestern Ohio and eastern Indiana.[23]

These sophisticated confederacies operated on a constitutional basis, although it was primarily that of the Iroquois Confederacy that was written down in English and passed along, in this instance by scholars who were themselves Seneca and Tuscarora.[24] All of the confederacies demonstrably operated on the same legal precepts as set forth in the *Kaienerekowa* or *Gayanashagowa* ('Great Law' or Iroquois Constitution in Mohawk and Seneca respectively). Under the Great Law, men and women were equal, with each owing obligations to the community. Arranged into 'Mother' and 'Father' halves, the clan councils of the women (Blood) sat opposite the 'national' councils of the men (Breath), with each side sending 'speakers' to keep the other half apprised of its decisions.[25]

Among the Iroquois, the interaction is described in the imagery of the 'Direction of the Sky' (Breath, being the east-west axis) and 'The Split Sky' (Blood, being the north-south axis), which combine to form the perfectly balanced Four Mothers of the earth and the Four Winds of the sky.[26] The sun is always placed in the Breath realm, so that among the Muscogee, it was called *Hisagitamisi* ('Master of Breath'), and falsely assumed to be the equivalent of the solitary European sky god.[27] In fact, it was just the Breath half of reality, with the Blood half being the *maître du serpent* or, more accurately, the *maîtresse du serpent* (mistress of the serpent).[28] Together, these halves interface in a constantly shifting cosmos, the maintenance of whose proper balance the Cherokee call 'The Harmony Ethic'.[29] Harmony requires continual effort, not just on the part of human beings but also on the collaborative part of all creation. The trees are Mother Earth's lungs, which must function if life is to continue. Waters are the bodily fluids of Mother Earth, which must remain unadulterated, lest she become ill. Similarly, the solar winds are the Breath of Brother Sun, which must blow on Mother Earth for her to bring forth life. The Milky Way is the path that the ancestor spirits of the sky must traverse to embody life here – any life, from birds and fishes to inanimate objects. Human beings are not seen as the purpose, let alone the 'crown' of creation, as in Christian mythology.

The cultures were primarily matriarchal. Women, alone, controlled the food supply.[30] Women, alone, 'nominated', that is, put incumbents into office, from which women alone could impeach any who strayed from their designated obligations.[31] Women decided whom to adopt as citizens and whom to execute, should matters come to that.[32] Only the women could initiate political action, sitting as they did at the 'grass roots' of the people, where they could distinguish *ne gashedenza*, the Iroquoian term for the 'sacred will' of the people.[33] The officials sitting in the collective women's or men's councils came from particular clans and geographical locales, their duty being to forward the words of the people they represented.[34] Women also ran the clans, from which male and female officials were nominated to office, with each clan 'owning' a certain number and category of seats, just as seats in modern congresses and parliaments belong to particular, geographic constituencies. In other words, the women-run clans operated as political parties, putting forward agendas. They were not 'oligarchies', as all too many Western scholars still inaccurately claim.[35]

Settler propaganda regularly but falsely asserted that Woodlanders were 'warlike'. In fact, American-Indigenous political structure made European-style, multi-action, continuous wars almost impossible. Only the Grandmothers could appoint warriors or declare war, but only after they had made three attempts at a peaceful resolution to the problem.[36] At that point, they could either try another trio of 'warnings', or hand the 'black' wampum to the Grandfathers to do with as they pleased.[37] The Grandfathers did not need to follow through with hostilities but might attempt their own peace negotiations.[38] If all else failed, then the Clan Mothers called for war.[39] Their call authorized one engagement *only*, not continuing hostilities. The Young Men did not need to accept the war call, or, having accepted it, right up to the moment that hostilities began, they could decide to go home, with no shame attached.[40] Clearly, the system was built to facilitate peace, which is why the *Gayanashagowa* is often rendered as the 'Great Law of Peace'.[41] Although today some Western scholars continue to attribute the 'Great Law' solely to the Iroquois, all Woodlanders demonstrably acted in accordance with its precepts. The Iroquoian form was simply the one formally recorded by Europeans in articulating the governmental principles practiced by all Woodlanders.

Indigenous confederacies operated day to day at the level of towns, but town governments were not city states. Instead, all towns were organized in cooperative relation to all other towns. Moreover, because they were confederated, they operated by units of two as bound binaries (Blood/Breath) in the Indigenous sense of independent yet interdependent halves cooperating in a continually fluctuating whole. It is a hallmark of Indigenous

Woodland philosophy to perceive reality as operating by halves, so that just about everything, from the social and political, to the economic and spiritual, is deliberately arranged by halves, to replicate the balanced binary of the cosmos.[42] Among the Muscogee, for instance the corresponding town halves were the *Italwalgi*, 'his own towns', and the *Kipayalgi*, 'his opposites', or complements.[43] Each town or town-set had its own paired councils on the local level, which heard issues before anything was passed along to the councils of the whole, which Europeans called 'nations'. Like towns, Indigenous territories did not operate on the European concept of demarcated lands, let alone ownership, although all of the men, keepers of the Breath-based forests, knew exactly what the group's extent of land was.[44]

The Gift Economy

As with most other aspects of Indigenous American culture, the gift economy of the Woodlands puzzled and even infuriated Europeans. The only word Europeans had to describe the free distribution of gifts was 'generosity', just as the only word they had for strangers being welcomed to stay was 'hospitality'.[45] Instead of generosity or hospitality, however, gifting was part of an organized economic strategy to keep the peace. Along with the engineered difficulty in declaring war, Woodlander gift economies removed a major reason for war: acquisition of the goods necessary to life. When all is freely given, there is no point in conflict or taking life to gain something.[46]

This was why, as John Heckewelder marvelled about the Lenape and Mahican, the Clan Mother would prepare 'victuals for the company' of unexpected visitors, 'never grumbling on account of their eating up the provisions'.[47] This was also why, when a Muscogee Grandfather ran across Le Clerc Milfort, lost and hungry in Muscogee Country in 1776, the elder instantly supplied the trespassing Frenchman with succour.[48] The sentiment shared across the Woodlands was that anyone 'so churlish of his eatables as to be inhospitable to one of their own people, especially to a traveling stranger', was 'termed a nobody'.[49] In addition, it was the standing Woodland custom for Clan Mothers to feed war parties passing through their lands, regardless of which side of the dispute their own town was on. In response, the war party was prohibited from attacking the Clan Mothers' towns, a practice still alive and well in the eighteenth century.[50] The gift economy thus deliberately quieted hostilities by supplying all comers.

This tactic was continually applied to Europeans, who did eventually understand gifting dynamics to some degree. The first to do so systematically were the French.[51] After the initial surprise, colonial Englishmen also realized that gifts were expected in return for those given, explaining why, at crucial points, military officers of the British Crown would mollify the Indigenous fighters they needed with supplies.[52] Moreover, by the eighteenth century, the French and British competed with each other over the quality and quantity of the gifts, a practice the British continued into the American Revolution. Thus in 1781, the British Commander at Detroit, Major Arent Schuyler De Peyster, sent a ship full, mostly of alcohol, as a gift to the Lenape and Wyandot of Ohio, who had apprehended rebel spies valuable to him.[53]

Coming to terms with gifting was hard for most Europeans, however, schooled as they were in the exchange economy. The British Commander in North America during the Seven Years' War, Sir Jeffrey Amherst, could never see gifting as an economic system, resisting it instead as extortion, under which he was forced to 'purchase the good behaviour' of his Indigenous proxy fighters, leaving him fuming at his Indian Agent, Sir William Johnson, who managed to spend £17,972 on presents in just one year.[54] Complaining loudly, Amherst pressed his officers to end gifting immediately, although the more culturally sensitive Johnson held out for a gradual secession from the practice.[55] Even Crown attempts at reciprocation failed as often as not, however, because instead of distributing the Crown goods as gifts, individual fort officers in the hinterlands frequently turned around and sold the inventory at egregious mark-ups to anyone who could pay, including settlers, pocketing the proceeds for themselves.[56]

After having won the Revolution in 1783, despite understanding Indigenous gift economies, American officials deliberately redefined gifting as exchange only, and became intent on controlling it as such. Under the US Constitution, the federal government, not the states, had the right to treat with the Indians. When Georgia tested this provision, Congress replied by passing the Intercourse Act of 1790, setting up the system of twenty-eight 'factories', or federal trading posts.[57] Factors, or federally licensed traders, were quite careless with goods that Indians brought in, often not accounting for them or crediting them to Indigenous Americans' accounts. In one instance, rather than send forward 8,000 pounds of animal skins given by Indians, the factor left them rotting in his warehouse for twelve years, at which point, they were worthless.[58]

Worse, these trading posts fooled Indigenous Americans into thinking that they were engaging in give-aways by laying out items just as in gifting rituals, in which the visitors lay their goods on the visitors' table for the host group to choose from, while selecting anything they wanted from the hosts' give-away tables.[59] Of course, Indigenous Americans were neither apprised of the distinction between give-aways and monetized exchange nor informed of the fact that, in selecting items from the hosts' table, they were running up staggering debts that were accruing compound interest. Years would pass before the debts were called. When the arrears came 'due', they were in amounts that no one on either side of the Atlantic could have discharged. In 1798, for instance, the Choctaw were stunned to learn that they owed $12,000. Despite the likely fraudulence of much of the accounting, they were forced to pay it off in land in 1805.[60] The Muscogee fared even worse, receiving a bill in 1803 for $113,512, with the 'Indian agent' promptly arranging a land sale to pay off the debt.[61] Forced land sales were not incidental to the federal trading-post system, but an intended consequence from the outset, as the third president of the United States, Thomas Jefferson, directly stated. In an 1803 letter to his Governor of the Indiana Territory, William Henry Harrison, Jefferson described the scheme of trading posts tricking Indigenous Americans into believing that the United States was engaging in Indigenous-style give-aways with them, to deprive them of their land.[62] Jefferson wrote a second letter in 1803, this one to Andrew Jackson, reiterating land acquisition as the Intercourse Act's intention and usage.[63]

For their part, watching the settlers keep everything and then extract more affronted Indigenous nations, who responded by taking what they needed, should the settlers fail to offer it. In doing so, they were trying to force sharing on the settlers, even as the settlers had forced exchange on them.[64] Such 'borrowing' back and forth among clans was standard economics to Woodlands cultures, with Muscogee traditionalists viewing the 'borrowing' of needed goods 'as reciprocity'.[65] Their actions nevertheless initiated the enduring settler stereotype of the 'thieving redskins', for whose supposed vice a 'diet of lead' was proposed as the only viable remedy.[66]

Aboriginal People on the Southeast Coast of New South Wales and Tasmania

The Aboriginal people of the southeast coast of New South Wales and the island of Tasmania tell several stories about their origins. One ascribes the creation of the first woman, who had a tail like a kangaroo, to a star god who tumbled to earth and was turned into a large rock. Another says they had 'tumbled down to earth' from the night skies and that after death their ancestors in the skies awaited their return. A Tasmanian story says they came by land and that the sea was subsequently formed.[67] The stories are supported by current archaeological research which suggests that Aboriginal people arrived in southeastern Australia and Tasmania at least 65,000 years ago,[68] and that Tasmania became an island when separated from the mainland during the last Ice Age, about 10,000 years ago. However, the coastal groups appear to have settled the Sydney region about 18,000 years ago.[69] No other human groups settled in Australia until the British invaders arrived in 1788.

In the intervening period, the Aboriginal people created small-scale societies based on kin, totem and country and were part of a complex cosmology, known in some societies as the Dreaming, that structured their political, social and spiritual relations with each other and the natural and physical world.[70] Central to their cosmology was the belief that the land or 'country' 'owned' the person who inherited it along with defined obligations as to its care and protection. Although Aboriginal clans were often at war with each other, the causes were not about the ownership or possession of country and the outcome was not about the acquisition of territory. Rather the causes were more about avenging broken protocols or gaining or restoring prestige by kidnapping women.

In the Sydney region of costal southeastern Australia and in Tasmania, the basic social group was the kin group, also known as family or hearth group, ranging between six and twenty people which was connected to a clan of several hundred people descended from a common ancestral being. In turn, the clan could be associated with a larger language group or nation of at least 1,000 people. Kin relationships were different to those practised by the British and were critical to social relations within the clan. For example, brothers were regarded as the same and so were sisters. Thus, a female child called her mother's sister, 'mother' and her father's brother, 'father'. As a consequence, the father's brothers' children were the child's brothers and sisters. A woman speaking of her sister's children would call them daughters and sons. However, this was not the case between a child and an 'uncle' and 'aunt' who were not same-sex siblings to her mother and father. A child did not call her mother's brother, 'father' or her father's sister, 'mother' nor were their children known as 'brothers' and 'sisters'. Rather they were known as 'cross cousins'.[71]

These differences were important in lines of descent and relationships to country – in a patrilineal society a child, its father, the father's brothers and sisters and the father's brother's children all belong to one local group. The child's mother, the mother's brothers and sisters and also the mother's father's brother's children belong to another local group. These relationships had important bearings on whom one could marry. Social relationships between group members and the status of individuals influenced camping arrangements, particularly those of young unmarried males and menstruating women.[72]

Clan membership was attained either through patrilineal or matrilineal descent groups. Patrilineal descent was attained when children belonged to the same clan as the father and matrilineal descent occurred when children belonged to the same clan as the mother's brother. Each local clan was associated with specific totems, usually animals, and thus a person's affiliation with these particular totemic beings came from either their mother's brother or their father depending on the descent rules of the particular community. According to archaeologist Val Attenbrow, who has carried out the most comprehensive study of the Aboriginal people of the Sydney region, clans along the Hunter River 100 miles north of Sydney and south to the Hawkesbury

River were of matrilineal descent and those south of the Hawkesbury were of patrilineal descent.[73] The sketchy information about the social organization of the Aboriginal clans in Tasmania indicates that they followed patrilineal descent and that Aboriginal men also sought female partners from other clans and sometimes from other nations.

Whether matrilineal or patrilineal, the clan was the key political focus of Aboriginal people from both regions and each person knew whom they were eligible to marry. These rules of exogamy also meant that a man or a woman who married might not have shared the same 'first language' or dialect. It was customary for a woman to live with her husband's clan although it was known for the couple to live with her family for some of the time. Even so, when a woman moved to her husband's country, she still maintained her spiritual and emotional ties to her own country and her totemic affiliations were maintained. According to the Australian historian Grace Karskens, the woman returned to her own country to have her babies.[74] Attenbrow suggests that in the Sydney region, 'membership of local descent groups (clans) and probably totemic affiliations were the basis on which marriages were arranged'.[75] However, David Collins, an officer in the First Fleet and historian of the settlement at Sydney Cove, noted that although wives were always selected from another clan, they were also taken in secrecy and in a violent manner.[76] This also seems to have been the case in Tasmania. The warrior Woorraddy from the Nuenonne clan on Bruny Island told how 'a big man' of the Pydairrerme clan of the Oyster Bay (Paredarerme) people 'stole a female child from the Nuenonne clan', possibly to become his wife.[77]

The key difference between the Tasmanians and their Sydney counterparts in relation to marriage, however, is that the Tasmanian Aboriginal people did not appear to practise polygamy. Each clan was led by a headman or elder who had demonstrated his prowess as a warrior in combat with other clans and as a successful negotiator in granting access to the country of the other clans. When Captain Cook visited Botany Bay in 1770 and Adventure Bay in Tasmania in 1777, he believed that the Aboriginal people he encountered were of the same cultural group because his navigation chart showed that Adventure Bay was part of the southern tip of New South Wales. He noted in each place that the women and children remained in the background while the senior men gesticulated to him that as a visitor, he was breaking protocols and should leave at once. He also noted that in each place the people were of dark skin and naked and wore no ornaments, were of middle height and that 'the large punctures or ridges raised on their skin' were the equivalent of clothing.[78]

The Indigenous people whose 'country' included Sydney Cove, the site of the first British settlement in 1788, comprised about 1,500 people associated with about thirty clans, each of thirty to fifty people.[79] Each clan had clearly defined 'country' or territory on the harbour's southern side and largely relied on scale and shellfish and other marine products as well as roots and seeds and small mammals as the mainstay of their diet. The Guringai people on the harbour's northern side supported fewer than 1,000 people of which the best-known clan was the Gamaraigal. The Gweagal clan of the Dharawal in the Botany Bay region south of Sydney was home to several hundred people. The Bediagal clan of the Darug who foraged for small animals and fish along the Georges River from present-day Bankstown to the bay and were more inland. In the region covered by present-day Liverpool, Campbelltown and Appin, the Muringong, Mulgowie and Norongerragal clans of the Dharawal people were located.[80] Inland along the Parramatta River were the Burramattagal, another clan of the Darug, and further west again along the Hawkesbury-Nepean River, known as Dyarubbin, were about 3,000 Bediagal. The people who inhabited the area around Sydney Cove knew all these clans as freshwater people.[81]

On the northern side of Sydney Harbour, the Guringai people had relatives among the Darkinyung-speaking people north of the Hawkesbury River and the Awabakal people at Lake Macquarie whose country stretched to the southern side of the Hunter River as far as present-day Maitland. In turn, the Awabakal had close relations with the Worimi people on the river's northern side.[82] It is estimated that the combined Aboriginal clans in the Sydney region in the 1780s, bounded by the Upper Hunter River in the north, the Nepean River in the west and the Wollondilly River south of Sydney, comprised at least 12,000 people.[83] All the Aboriginal clans on the eastern side of the Great Dividing Range that runs down the eastern spine of Australia formed a distinct cultural area from the Aboriginal clans on the western side of the range. They shared similar language groups in that they could understand each other and at particular seasons of the year would meet for major ceremonies.[84]

Map 1 *Indigenous people and clans in the greater Sydney region*

Performance of ceremony was central to their existence. They were carried out on 'country' that held deep spiritual significance to the surrounding clans and could include important rock art sites. The ceremonial or bora sites were usually in places where several clans could congregate and where food sources were in plentiful supply. The ceremonies could include the performance of song cycles that had developed over a long period of time and acknowledged former battles with warriors from adjoining clans. At each ceremony a new verse would be added, celebrating more recent battles. A ceremony could also be held to mark the end of a major battle or to celebrate a major feast such as the beaching of a whale in winter and as an opportunity to trade shells and ochre, highly prized among all Aboriginal communities, and pay homage to their ancestral beings in the skies. This could include the making of rock art. In the Sydney region alone, there are thousands of rock art sites indicating that it supported a large population. Colonial drawings of their ceremonies, or corroborees in the Sydney region, involved the performance of elaborate songs whose spiritual meaning and significance escaped the early colonists. Spiritually they were tied to their clan homelands by animal and plant totems and by the position of the stars, many of which they identified as their ancestors to guide them through the seasons.[85]

In Tasmania, the nine Aboriginal groups totalling more than 7,000 people were more similar in cultural practices to the Aboriginal peoples of the Sydney region than those on the other side of the Great Dividing Range. The major differences between the Tasmanian Aboriginal people and those in the Sydney region lay in the practice of male initiation rites and the practice of monogamy,

Figure 2 *Joseph Lycett: Corroboree around a camp fire, c. 1817.* Source: National Library of Australia.

rather than polygamy, and the fact that they engaged in more intense seasonal patterns of movement to make best use of food resources. Like their Sydney counterparts, however, the Tasmanians appear to have understood each other's languages arising from formalized seasonal visits to another 'country'. On these occasions, sometimes lasting for several months, the visitors adopted a particular name conferred by the host nation for the duration of the visit. For instance, Truganini, the well-known Tasmanian Aboriginal woman from the D'Entrecasteaux Channel in southeastern Tasmania, was known by the name Lydgugee when visiting relatives in southwest Tasmania.[86]

In the Sydney region the men used spears, boomerangs and waddies, a heavy wooden club, to hunt large mammals such as kangaroos and made bark canoes cut from trees to spear scale fish. The women preferred to make their own bark canoes from which they fished with lines made from animal sinew. They also used digging sticks to prize open shellfish and dig-up yams and made coolamons, or curved trays, from smooth pieces of wood in which to grind native seeds and made grass and kelp baskets to carry shellfish. Family groups of six to twenty people lived in lean-to bark shelters or rock shelters often in sufficient numbers to form a village. They do not appear to have engaged in seasonal migrations beyond their own country, but they did visit adjoining clans for ceremonies which often included access to special foods such as whale meat.[87]

In Tasmania, eight of the nine Aboriginal peoples from which a minimum of forty-eight clans have been identified spent most of the year on the coastline where the rich supplies of abalone and shellfish were seasonally more reliable than scale fish. Women were the divers of shellfish, the grinders of seeds and collectors of kelp along the seashore and hunters of marine birds such as mutton birds. By virtue of Tasmania's cooler climate, their shelters were often more substantial than those of their Sydney counterparts, and ranged from semi-permanent beehive shaped huts on the west coast made from mud and clay and decorated with feathers to the large bark shelters in the central highlands, capable of holding up to twenty people, and the temporary bark wind breaks on the east coast.[88] Men and women constructed bark catamarans to travel across rivers to offshore islands in search of mutton-birds, while the men used fire stick farming to hunt large animals such as kangaroos and emus and smoke possums from trees. On some occasions, entire clans would come together for a ceremonial hunting ceremony. Such an event was taking place at Risdon Cove in May 1804, when the Aboriginal people came across the first British settlement, and in the ensuing melee with soldiers and settlers, many of them lost their lives.[89]

The Aboriginal people in Sydney and Tasmania observed similar cosmologies based on the intertwining of country, kin and totem, practised in ritual, music, art and law so that none formed a truly separate domain. Thus, the men were associated with the sun spirit and the women with the moon, and their customs were based upon totems, with each person at birth being conferred a designated species of bird or animal as a totem, which also included taboos that often-involved avoidance of certain foods or particular relatives. Their spiritual practices appear to have been based on the idea of the good spirit who governed the day, known in Tasmania as Noiheener or Parledee and in Sydney as Baaime. The bad spirit, known in Tasmania as Wrageowrapper and in Sydney as Daramulin, governed the night. These and other spirits were associated with the creation of fire, rivers, trees and the dead.[90]

Baaime and Daamulin are strongly represented in rock art sites throughout the Sydney region and are considered central to the totemic concept of the Dreaming which, according to anthropologist Ronald Berndt, 'spells out a relationship between man and nature, between man and the natural species'.[91] Even so, as Val Attenbrow points out, in southeastern Australia, 'totemism does not appear to have been of such prime concern as it is elsewhere on the continent'.[92] A similar comment could be made about the spiritual beliefs and practices of the Aboriginal people in Tasmania. However, in both the Sydney region and Tasmania, no one could kill or eat their own animal totem; information about totemic beings and their activities is scantily recorded in written histories.

Upon the death of a person in both regions, the relatives usually decorated the body with ochre and clay, wrapped it in leaves with items from their totems such as bird feathers or animal skins and then cremated it in a sitting or lying position either on a specially prepared wooden platform or in the hollowed out base of a tree, amid intense ceremonial to farewell them on their journey to join their relatives in the spirit world. A guardian spirit or 'soul' that lived within their left breast went to live elsewhere beyond their own country. After the body was cremated, female relatives might extract small bones from the charred remains, wrap them in kangaroo fur and use them as amulets to ward off evil spirits. Sometimes the women lit fires in bad weather, or when rivers were in flood, to appease malignant spirits.[93] In Sydney, after a period of mourning, it was not uncommon for a young person to take the name of the deceased.

Perhaps the key differences in cultural beliefs and practices between the Aboriginal people in Sydney and Tasmania lay in the practice of male initiation and marriage. Several rock art sites in Sydney record the spiritual significance of male initiation rites and David Collins, the first colonial historian of the Sydney region, recorded several accounts of male initiation ceremonies that included tooth evulsion and body scarification. His account of a ceremony in 1795 in which young men aged about fourteen were initiated was accompanied by drawings attributed to Thomas Watling.[94] In Tasmania, such rites appeared to focus on body scarification rather than tooth evulsion. In both places, men and women wore body scarification as a way of identifying each person in relation to their age, kin, clan, country and totem. The absence of rock art sites in many parts of Tasmania along with ethnographic accounts of initiation ceremonies has left a yawning gap in our understanding of the practice.

Indigenous Attitudes towards the Land

No Indigenous culture agrees that Europeans had any rights to the lands that were peopled by its original inhabitants and today, in many parts of the world, fiercely resist the old terminologies that still underpin most Western treatments of European expansion. What is called 'exploration' was raiding, 'conquest' was invasion and occupation, 'assimilation' was enslavement or annihilation or absorption into European culture and 'pacification' was massacre or genocide. That said, Indigenous peoples had an entirely different relationship to the land from their European counterparts. If land was something to be possessed by the peoples of Europe, it was a resource to be used collectively for the good of the group among Indigenous peoples. As such, land, or 'country' as Australian Aboriginal people refer to it, was central to their notions of group life. It was an element of group identity rather than simply a means for sustaining this identity.[95]

South Africa

The advance of the frontier of colonial settlement in the Cape during the eighteenth and early nineteenth centuries saw the absorption of territory occupied by three distinct societies that we have already looked at – the San, the Khoikhoi and the Xhosa. As it happened, each of these societies represented one of the first three different stages of human development theorized by Enlightenment thinkers: the hunter-gatherer, the pastoralist and the agriculturalist. Did these different societies, supposedly occupying different stages on the hierarchy of human development, have different attitudes towards land?

There was a widely held European view that the San, being hunter-gatherers, did not improve the land or work it and therefore had no claim to the land. Apart from this perception, but related to it, was the belief that since the San were nomadic, moving across the face of the landscape like wandering flocks or herds, they were devoid of a sense of possession or ownership of the land. Only a people rooted to the land, it was argued, who built houses or grew crops, could be held to own the land. There was also the belief that since the San had no political structures or chiefs, they had no sense of territoriality, and there was no specific tract of land associated with a particular group.

Such perceptions were wrong. It is true that, as with Indigenous Australians, the San did not have a sense that land could be privately owned. This concept was close to unimaginable in a society that made a virtue of sharing resources. Similarly, animals could not be owned. From what we know of San religious beliefs, it is evident that the San saw themselves as being part of the natural world rather than distinct from it and the ability of shamans to assume animal forms or enter animal bodies reinforces this idea. Rituals of respect for the animal dictated both the act of hunting and the act of killing. In the case of the eland, the fattest and most favoured of antelope, the San believed that there was a special potency inherent in it that was released at death. A shaman sought to harness the potency of the dying eland, the !num, to heal or to make rain.[96] Just as animals had power that could be utilized through respectful rituals, so too did the land have power or powers that could be utilized if properly known.

Of obvious importance, in a dry land, were watering points: rivers, springs, underground courses or even rock pools that retained rainwater after the rain. Animals too needed water, and knowledge of where the water points were meant knowledge of where animals could be found. Watering places were therefore essential to a group's survival and an intrusive group could not use another group's water without permission. Groups, in other words, had a sense of territoriality that was frequently centred on a water point. Specific groups had specific territories. Although San groups were territorial they were not restricted to one spot. Being hunter-gatherers, mobility was essential to them, and they were obliged to move to follow the game or to exploit the seasonally changing natural resources. The most important seasonal movement of many San groups of the Cape interior was to follow the game, which moved from the summer rainfall areas to winter rainfall areas in winter and from winter rainfall areas into summer rainfall areas in the summer. The game was in search of good grazing and the San were in search of the game. Since the movement of San was linked to the seasonal availability of resources, they were not strictly speaking nomadic but rather semi-nomadic, as they moved in predictable cycles within finite areas. If during their migrations they entered the territory of another group, they would negotiate this visit, often in exchange for reciprocal rights of visitation to the other group. These reciprocal rights were guaranteed by intermarriage or the creation of kinship ties between the groups. These kinship ties were sometimes established not by actual marriage but through the exchange of names, a ritual that served to create fictive kinship ties. Quite clearly, the land was of the utmost importance to the San who did not regard it as being alienable but as being sacred and essential for the maintenance of their way of life. The land sustained them and the animals through providing plants and water. It could be shared but not taken and the rights of the Indigenous occupants had to be respected.

The Khoikhoi, like the San, were territorial, believing that certain areas were the territory of certain groups. The land was the group's land though and there was no sense of individual or private ownership. When the Dutch began to settle at the Cape and marked out farms for themselves along the Liesbeeck River, the Peninsula Khoikhoi asked what the Dutch thought they were doing as it was their land and where did the Dutch think they should go. The Dutch replied that there was plenty of room and the Khoikhoi should simply move away, an answer that was not satisfying and which was shortly followed by the outbreak of hostilities.

Because the Khoikhoi, like the San, did not grow crops or build permanent homes, the temptation for Europeans was to regard them too as nomadic and having no rights to the land. In fact, like the San, the Khoikhoi were, strictly speaking, semi-nomadic as their cattle and sheep moved seasonally, like game, in search of water and grazing. The Khoikhoi followed, or lead, their livestock in these cycles of trans-humance. Over the centuries the Khoikhoi had learnt how to live with the San but incursions into another Khoikhoi group's territory could spark off warfare or skirmishing. Khoikhoi groups were organized into polities under the leadership of a chief, or wealthy leader, and there was a sense that some groups were more powerful than others and that certain groups held sway over certain areas.

The Xhosa both hunted and herded, but they also needed land to grow their crops – millet, maize and squashes. Maize and squashes were fairly recent introductions to southeast Africa, having been introduced to the coastal areas by the Portuguese through their contacts in America. Maize, being easy to grow and capable of yielding two crops a year, dramatically increased the amount of food available to the Nguni peoples of the coast and contributed to a marked increase in their population by the colonial period. Population increases and the dictates of maize production – a crop that needed virgin soil every few years when farmed without fertilizers – were two of the motors of Xhosa frontier expansion. Another one was the need for Xhosa cattle to find grazing and to move, seasonally, from one area of pasturage to another. This movement, though not dictated by the summer-winter rainfall cycle, was necessary because some pastures were sour, and some were sweet, and the cattle needed a change to remain healthy.

The land belonged to the people, but the king or chief could allocate it to his followers. The basic unit of production in Xhosa society was the homestead, a unit that comprised the hut of the senior male in a family and the hut or huts of his wives. Each wife had her own hut, and the women would tend the homestead's fields. The boys and young men would look after the cattle. Each homestead, or kraal in colonial parlance, was semi-autonomous and usually situated in a spot where there was access to water, grazing, arable land and timber within a reasonable distance. The people in the homesteads owed political allegiance to their chief and were related to neighbours, usually by being members of the same chiefly lineage. When young men were old enough to marry, their chief would grant them land to establish their own homestead. They were thus able to establish their own family. The expectation was that there would be land for every adult male. It was the chief's duty to see to this and the king presided over rituals of fertility and harvest ceremonies. The relatively dense settlement and large population of the Xhosa gave them a demographic advantage over their Khoisan neighbours. This advantage translated into military strength in times of war when adult males were expected to follow their chiefs or war leaders into battle. For the most part, there was little incentive to invade areas of poor rainfall, but disputes could arise over the herding of cattle. It would be the pastoral frontiers of the colony and the Xhosa where conflict occurred.

North America

Indigenous Americans had completely different views of spatial interrelationships from Europeans.[97] In the first place, there was the guiding concept of the sacred Twinship of Blood/earth and Breath/sky, with the term 'sky' indicating outer space, not the blue atmosphere which is part of Mother Earth.[98] The realms were, moreover, intertwined and in a mutually interactive flux. Furthermore, it was not really possible to refer to a point on earth (Blood) without simultaneously noting its direct, celestial counterpart (Breath). The intricate mound complexes across the Woodlands physically manifested this notion by replicating on the ground what was in the sky – assuming that Mother Earth had not already so replicated it, herself, for instance, in the Indigenous Mississippi River's mirroring of the Milky Way Trail.[99] Spatial relationships determined a sense of 'place', so that cosmic spatial range determined one's Breath identity, whereas communal relations determined one's Blood identity, with both halves required for the completion of the Twinship. Clans interpenetrated nations. Thus, asking an Indigene to lay out, two-dimensionally, what his group's national (Breath) but solely earth-based (Blood) boundaries were did not make any sense.

The women of the various Woodlands nations were large-scale agriculturalists who actively culled, hybridized and cultivated two-thirds of the vegetal sustenance currently sustaining the modern world, including fruits such as strawberries and tomatoes, and vegetables, including corn, beans, squashes, potatoes, tomatoes, paprika and sweet peppers and multiple varieties of nuts, all utterly unknown outside of the Americas.[100] For instance, corn only exists because it was hand pollinated and artificially hybridized, well before the Europeans arrived.[101] Sweet corn was not a later European manipulation but an Indigenous creation. Knowledge of it was deliberately kept from the settlers until the invasion of Iroquoia in 1779 brought sweet corn to the attention of the American soldiers, most of whom were farmers. Realizing what they were looking at, they took home some as seed corn.[102]

In addition, Woodlands American farmers – again, all women – invented conservation tillage, primarily in the use of rows of planting mounds about four feet high, in which certain crops were co-planted. The planting mounds were construed as the nourishing 'breasts' or 'bosoms' of Mother Earth feeding her 'children'.[103] The central complex consisted of corn, beans and squash, the 'Three Sisters', called *Dionhéko* ('they sustain us') by the Seneca.[104] Corn was planted at the very top or the nipple of the mound, to gain the sun; beans were planted a couple of weeks later around the base of the corn, to be able to climb her stalk; and squash, often pumpkin, was planted another two weeks later and spaced about every four mounds, to allow its tubers plenty of running space.[105] Seeds of these crops were pre-soaked in 'medicine water', that is, a bath including nutrients made from cattails and natural pesticides, including American hellebore.[106] Sunflowers had their own stands.[107] Tobacco was planted between the mound rows, because it acts as a natural insecticide.[108] This mound-planting system prevented soil erosion.[109]

The acreage cultivated not only addressed the immediate needs of the fields' associated town but also provided surpluses to be used for multi-town festivals and gifting alliances.[110] Festival cycles followed the farming seasons, in planting, hoeing, harvesting and storing dried foods for the winter. Each nation had its own outlay of festivals, but all of them celebrated the most important festival, the Busk, or harvest ceremony, which particularly honoured corn, although beans, squash and berries came in for their share of the honouring.[111] Obviously, these festivities occurred at harvest time, which in the northeastern Woodlands runs from mid-August into October, with harvest falling in the late summer in the southeast. All these careful rounds of activity were not just disrupted but shattered by the European intrusion, which brought its own plough-farming methods. Those methods proved immensely damaging to the Woodland environment.

Australia

Darug attitudes to the land, or to 'country' as they called it, in the Botany Bay region were defined by their social, cultural and political relationships and responsibilities. Known as 'saltwater people', their territory was well marked by physical features, such as cliffs, beaches and watercourses and within it, each clan had clearly defined country. As a hunter-gatherer people, the Darug clans were rarely in their country for more than a few months at a time, but a pregnant woman always returned to country to bear her children. A son might be given a name that was connected with his totem, his clan and the time of year he was born. A daughter would be given a totem name connected to her country and would be 'trained up' to care for it even after she married into another clan or even another nation. In this way, every Darug person had specific connection to their country based on their totem, their age, gender and clan relationship, their birthplace and location in their extended family. This could include obligations to care for their animal or plant totem at a particular time of year as well as physical features of their country such as rock formations and watercourses where they would acknowledge ancestral spirits and 'smoke out' malevolent spirits.

Thus 'caring for country' was both an individual and communal responsibility, making each Darug person integral to the place that 'owned' them rather than the reverse. Their responsibilities could include burning parts of country on a seasonal basis for hunting particular animals and or holding particular ceremonies known as 'singing the country'. Senior clever men and women usually assumed the custodianship of major sites of spiritual significance such as rock art sites or gender specific sites used for initiation ceremonies. From these ceremonies Darug young men and women would learn the law associated with these sites and their relationship to them and how to care for them.

Visitors to 'country' from other nations would be expected to seek permission from the clan owners, but more often they would be invited to country to participate in important ceremonies and feasts. In some seasons the Darug had automatic access to other country. In other seasons they had none at all. When visiting another 'country', however, the Darug would be expected to use the names conferred upon them by their hosts. Trespass could sometimes result in a payback killing or resolved with gifts of ochre, which were held in high ritual value, or the small bones of deceased relatives secreted in a small dilly bag woven from plant fibres, which were believed to have medicinal properties and could assist in healing sickness. Other gifts could include bird feathers, fishnets and firesticks as well as freshly caught possums, kangaroo tails, shellfish, and scale fish. Sometimes clan owners did not visit country for many seasons, perhaps to appease avenging spirits, or to allow a recently deceased relative to 'return to country' in spirit form, or to enable the country to recover from drought or flood so that it could provide food for a later time. Returning to country after a long absence usually involved the practice of 'singing the country' to inform the ancestors of their arrival and then a smoking ceremony to cleanse it of evil spirits.

Thus 'country' was central to Darug understanding of who they were as people and the place they occupied in their universe. Since country owned them, they could not aspire to 'own' another country. For the British, who held quite different concepts of land ownership and sovereignty, the Darug attitudes to country were far too complex to readily understand. So, the British stuck to their original view that the Darug did not use the land in the same way as they did.[112]

One of the clearest distinctions between Indigenous and European settler uses of the land is that Indigenous peoples tended to share the environmental resources, even with European interlopers, but that this generosity was not reciprocated in the same way. This cultural predisposition, along with the custom of 'gift giving' among American Indigenous peoples, led to any number of misunderstandings on the frontier that exacerbated tensions between Europeans and Indigenous peoples. For Europeans in North America, 'gift giving' was another opportunity to exploit Indigenous Americans, leading to the structural forms of violence that were touched on. Reduced to its most simplistic principle, Europeans wanted to own and exploit the land and were also prepared to own and exploit Indigenous peoples in the process. Given these different attitudes, it is hardly surprising that conflict occurred. This is not to say that tensions did not exist between Indigenous peoples – quite clearly, they did – or that they did not ally with Europeans for their own political agendas. This happened frequently in South Africa and North America but not, interestingly, in Australia. We have yet to touch on the nature and the intensity of some of these struggles, which we will approach in Chapter 4, but before doing so, it is worth examining how local and Indigenous peoples approached warfare.

3

Local and Indigenous Ways of Warfare

Indigenous warfare or conflict between peoples in non-state societies could, generally speaking, take one of two forms: a face-to-face confrontation that was normally agreed to in advance and that followed a prescribed ritual; or it took the form of a raid, or an ambush, using surprise, and carried out by either individuals or groups of people, which sometimes took place under cover of darkness.[1] Indigenous peoples across our regions all had this approach to warfare, albeit with variations. The raid seems to have been the main form of warfare. For some, Open combat only seems to have occurred when there was clear superiority in numbers. In all cases, rituals took place before, sometimes during and after combat, either to enlist the support of spirits or to purify and cleanse warriors who had shed blood.

Indigenous People of Southern Africa

Before the European settlement of the Cape the indigenous people were hunters. The procurement of game was an economic and cultural necessity for the San, even if they probably derived most of their food from gathering, and an important supplement for the Khoikhoi and the Xhosa who were loath to kill their own livestock when they could eat the meat of wild animals. Hunting influenced the way people made war and determined that animals – not just domestic animals – were seen as valuable resources. The great herds of game seemed sufficient for all until the white man arrived with his guns and horses and his unbalanced lust for killing for killing's sake. The first clashes between the colonists and the Indigenous people were clashes between white hunters in pursuit of ivory from elephants and hippo, while the demise of the San coincided with the destruction of the eland herds by settler-hunters who turned the huge antelope into dried meat (biltong) and left the San to starve.[2]

Apart from competition for game, however, was the imprint that hunting made on the art of warfare itself. The San were used to stalking game to get close enough to shoot a poisoned arrow into an animal. The animal might then take four days or more to die, while the San ran behind it, waiting for it to drop. These were tactics of stealth, patience and endurance. These same tactics could be employed against the domestic animals of their pastoralist enemies. Overall, face-to-face combat was avoided. The San crept among the herds and flocks, hamstringing some animals and driving the others away for later consumption or destruction, perhaps having quietly killed the shepherd. The point here is that the San waged war like hunters because they were hunters. What triggered them into violence was the trespass of pastoralists or other hunters into their hunting grounds. Hunting was their life. In defending their way of life, however, they were seldom in a position to massacre their foes. It was easier to target their livestock.

Even before the arrival of European settlers the intrusion of Indigenous pastoralists into a world of long-established hunter-gatherer societies caused conflict. The archaeological record reveals that there was friction between intrusive Khoikhoi pastoralists and hunter-gatherers that dated from the introduction of domestic animals into the Cape, first sheep and then cattle, some 2,000 to 1,500 years ago. Early historical period records attest to fighting between hunter-gatherers and the Khoikhoi, sometimes murderous and vicious, and nearly always involving the theft or destruction of Khoikhoi livestock. Livestock made the Khoikhoi vulnerable, whereas the San were much harder to injure. Without horses the Khoikhoi could not always catch the elusive and hard running San. Peaceful co-habitation was obviously in everyone's best interest, and it was often possible given the small size of the groups involved and the vastness of the territory. Without guns and horses, the Khoikhoi did not pose an existential threat to the game that the San depended on. It is hardly surprising that over a period of more than a thousand years there should be some inter-marriage, cultural exchange, and gift giving between the groups, and the certain acceptance of a balance of power. The San, for instance, were known to act as auxiliaries, scouts or soldiers for the Khoikhoi and to accept payment in the form of milk, butter, meat or pots. In exchange the San could provide the products of the hunt, honey and their much-respected magic or medicine.[3] It paid the Khoikhoi to acknowledge the San as the aboriginal inhabitants of the land and to give them gifts or 'protection money'; otherwise, the San could make life very difficult for them.

Similar types of arrangements existed between the hunter-gatherers of the southeastern coast of Africa and the Bantu-speaking groups of agropastoralists who began entering the region during the Early and Late Iron ages, c. 700 to 1100. The ancestors of the Xhosa, who emerged as a distinctive southern Nguni group around the Late Iron Age, would have had centuries of experiencing or negotiating the presence of the San. Furthermore, they would have had to deal with rival pastoralists, the Khoikhoi, who once inhabited much of what became Xhosa territory. The Xhosa were stronger than the Khoikhoi, largely because they were more populous. They were more populous because, in addition to the milk and meat of their cattle, they had the food resources provided by their summer rainfall crops – millet, sorghum and, later, pumpkin and maize. These crops needed about 40mm of rainfall a year to develop, and Xhosa settlement thus tended to stay within this rainfall isohyet. The Xhosa used their superior strength to drive the Khoisan out of the arable, well-watered, crop growing regions but did not resort to massacring the Khoikhoi to do so. The Xhosa regarded people as a potential source of wealth and preferred to exercise a form of political dominance over subjects, extracting tribute from the weak and alliances from the strong. Khoikhoi groups that stayed within or in reach of Xhosa territory inter-married with Xhosa groups, and the result was that there were groups of mixed Xhosa and Khoikhoi descent in the eastern Cape frontier region. The presence of a large number of click sounds and loan words in the Xhosa language is also testimony to a lengthy period of social, economic and cultural exchange between the groups.[4]

It was on the fringes of Xhosa and Khoikhoi society that the time-honoured activity of pastoralists took place – livestock raiding. Young men from a particular group or tribe would win acclaim and enter adulthood by proving their skill at stealing another group's cattle. Though this activity could escalate into war and result in deaths it was usually tolerated and regulated by the elders who ensured compensation would be paid if disproportionate damage was inflicted. Besides, one could always recoup one's losses by a counter raid. This was a type of institutionalized warfare, played for low stakes but high prestige and common to pastoralist societies throughout the world who saw it as a good way to train and control the energies of young warriors.[5] The similarities between this and hunting are obvious, but the objective here was to capture rather than to kill the animal.

Opportunities for stock theft abounded for though the Xhosa did not like to move too far away from their fields and villages they habitually grazed their cattle wherever grazing and water resources were sufficient to do so. In effect this meant that there were always Xhosa herders beyond the 40mm isohyet because cattle could graze where crops could not grow. Similarly, Khoikhoi herders were tempted by the well-watered, sweet pastures of Xhosaland. The fact that the rainfall isohyet shifted east or west from year to year and was sometimes interrupted by devastating droughts meant that there was a shifting environmental frontier in the eastern Cape between the pastoralist and the agropastoralists long before European pastoralists entered this region – known as the Zuurveld – in about the 1770s. If Xhosa pressure became too great in any one year the Khoikhoi could move out of the region altogether and return once the Xhosa had gone back to harvest their crops. Crop failures, however, could mean that Xhosa herdsmen stayed too long in the Zuurveld, escalating tensions with the Khoikhoi.

The damage these pre-colonial pastoralists could inflict on each other, or on the hunter-gatherers, was, however, limited by the absence of guns and horses. Typically, a group could only be massacred if it was surrounded or encircled, if flight was impossible, or if its members could be killed with impunity because they could not get close enough to the enemy to retaliate. Pastoralists could hurt each other by stealing each other's livestock or by killing some of each other's young men. But they could not annihilate each other since a defeated side could usually flee or rebuild its losses by counterraiding. This dynamic equilibrium was to be permanently unbalanced by the arrival of Europeans with their guns and horses.

The colonists thus enjoyed an inestimable advantage with guns and horses, whereas the San, for example, went on foot and had weapons made largely of stone, wood and bone. Their principal weapon was the bow that shot arrows poisoned with plant or snake venom. The estimated range at which these arrows could achieve accuracy was about eighty paces, and they could be fired at the rate of five or six a minute. But the arrows were not designed to knock a target over or to kill on impact; the slow-working poison could take days to take effect. Such a weapon was not designed to dominate a battlefield and for this reason the San preferred to avoid direct contact with their enemies and either launched attacks on the trekboer livestock or waged a type of guerrilla warfare against the most vulnerable members of the trekboer community – the servants. It sometimes happened that a Khoikhoi or slave who was looking after the livestock of their trekboer master would be killed by the San while they were alone or isolated in the veld. Reports of the cruelties that the San were capable of inflicting on such victims may not all be colonial propaganda, for it would be naïve to think that the San would never have retaliated in kind to the atrocities inflicted upon them. Sometimes too empty farmhouses would be destroyed or robbed. But the San always attempted to evade, rather than confront, the well-armed and mounted commandos that came after them.[6]

The San tactics were to attack at night and attempt to drive off as many sheep or cattle as they could and then race towards a mountainous area or region of broken terrain where it would be difficult for the commandos to pursue them. If they had time they would slaughter and eat the livestock at their leisure. If not, they would kill or maim the animals and attempt to escape. In mountainous areas, such as the Sneeuberg, the San would sometimes build rock walls or fortifications, or *sanger*, in front of caves or overhangs which they would defend by firing arrows at their attackers from behind shelter. Sometimes quite large numbers of San would gather for defensive purposes and the commandos would have to retreat. If the colonists chose to advance, they would wear thick leather clothing as protection against the arrows or construct a reed or animal hide screen to shield themselves. More often than not, however, they preferred to let their Khoikhoi or 'Bastaard' servants lead the advance against a fortified stronghold.[7]

It was not always necessary, however, to storm a San *sanger*. If a San raiding party was caught in the open things would go badly for them. The trekboers relied on the superb tracking skills of their Khoikhoi servants to follow the trail of fugitive San and, with the advantage of horses, could move much faster than them. On an open plain the commando members could keep a distance of 100 to 150 paces between them and their targets, and dismount and fire with fatal effect, well out of range of the San's arrows. But the most effective tactic was to launch a surprise attack on a sleeping kraal of San at dawn. Commandos, led by their trackers, and sometimes guided by the smoke of incautiously lit campfires, would quietly encircle a group of San during the night and then fire into their midst at first light. Mostly the group of San hunter-gatherer family groups would be small. Nicolaas van der Merwe's account of his commando's actions in the Roggeveld during the General Commando reveals that the average number of people in each group that he attacked was just over thirteen. Van der Merwe's commando numbered twenty-seven Europeans and thirty-eight Khoikhoi. In such circumstances the commando had an overwhelming advantage in numbers and what followed can only be described as a series of massacres as seventeen kraals, one after another, were destroyed.[8]

Despite the seemingly overwhelming superiority of the colonial commandos, the struggle was not as one sided as it seems. The San remained undefeated until the end of the eighteenth century and the colonial frontier, as we have seen, not only failed to advance much beyond its 1774 limits but, in some areas, retreated. The remarkably long period of military stalemate suggests that the San's guerrilla tactics were extremely effective. As the century progressed, both sides came to gauge each other's strengths and weaknesses. The San soon realized when horse sickness had crippled the offensive capacity of their foes and became especially bold at such times. Periods of drought forced the San to steal from the colonists' livestock to survive, but drought was also a good time to attack because of the difficulties of keeping a commando in the field. Periods of rain, on the other hand, washed away the livestock's spoor and caused the colonists muskets to misfire. The colonists liked to campaign in early spring. There was good grazing for their horses in most areas, and if it was cold, the San often gave away their position by lighting fires. Farmers in the winter rainfall areas would have ploughed and planted their crops and were therefore free to wage war. But in the winter, it was often too cold and wet for such farmers to relish commando duty. Roggeveld farmers frequently had to trek out of their region to escape the extreme cold, and at such times the San broke into their abandoned farmhouses.[9]

Indigenous American Ways of Warfare

In the democracies of the various Woodland cultures, peace as the natural condition of existence was enshrined as an article of faith in the constitutions. Three warnings were required to be given before any hostilities commenced,[10] which helps explain why Indigenous American runners were despatched to settler communities bringing warnings of attack.[11] War was regarded as an aberration, something to be avoided if possible and quickly concluded if not.

Although Western records and histories until recently would make it appear so, men were hardly the only functionaries in matriarchal Woodlands government. To ensure full 'grassroots' inclusion, there were two interactive halves of government: the 'brotherhoods' of the Breath side, called nations; and the 'sisterhoods' of the Blood side, called clans.[12] Each side consisted of Youngers and Elders, with elders always meeting first, although youngers could initially bring issues to their attention. On the Blood side, Grandmothers (elders) and Clan Mothers (youngers) considered all public matters first. On the Breath side, men could not discuss an issue until it was fully considered and forwarded to them by the women.[13] Then, the Grandfathers (civil chiefs) and Young Men, always mistakenly translated by colonists as 'warriors', considered the matter. Decisions were then given to the 'firekeepers', or executives, the chair of the men's grand council and the head clan grand/mother, whose powers were limited to approving, rejecting or tabling the matter.[14] Should public objections arise, an inquiry could be mounted by the Blood side, that is, the women responsible for nominating and authorizing all leaders, which could lead to sanctions and even impeachment of errant public officials, male or female.[15]

These systems clearly go back well before contact, as the earliest Spanish records of the southeast, those of de Soto's entrada, record the powerful Cacica, or female chief of Cofitachequi, located near present-day Camden, South Carolina, invested with institutional power that was already clearly mature.[16] Similarly, the grave of the first Jigonsaseh, or head Mother of the Iroquois who co-founded the League in 1142, was unearthed, laden with pearls, the same jewel marking the office of the Cacica of Cofitachequi in 1540.[17] In fact, the Cacica was probably meeting de Soto with gifts, because word of his depredations had already gotten about, and it was standard operating procedure for the female chiefs to meet a passing war party of any side at a crossroads and supply it with gifts. Legally, once gifts had been given to a war party, that party was forbidden from attacking the head woman's town.[18] Later chroniclers likewise referred to the position of 'la femme Chef' and 'la cacica'.[19] In English, the office was usually rendered 'Queen'.[20]

Importantly, these women alone held the power to call for war to be waged.[21] Among the Iroquois, a woman would raise the cry for war, often in stylized ways that the Jesuits recording the events did not comprehend. In one instance on 10 January 1670, of the Susquehanna calling for an action against the Oneidas, the announcing Clan Mother told all that she had heard a voice emanating from the bottom of her cooking pot and that it was the voice of their war chief. He 'uttered wailing cries, like the cries of those who are being burned'.[22] The Jesuit complained that she 'was believed in all she said', but in the Woodlands, if a captive was to be executed, it was idiomatic to say that he was being 'made soup' of.[23] This Clan Mother's words were thus formulaic for 'the Oneida are coming, so we had better prepare a defence'.

To ensure their continued power over war, Woodlands women physically kept the weapons of war. To call a war, Muscogee women dispensed with the metaphors, but simply brought out the 'weapons and the things needed' and 'lay all of it down one hundred paces' outside of the men's public square, where the Young Men could pick them up – but only if they agreed that war was worth the effort.[24] Even should the Clan Mothers actively appoint Young Men for authorized action, the Young Men were not obliged to agree but were allowed to follow their own inclinations on whether to go or not.[25] As the Baron of Lahontan noted of the Iroquois of the northeast in 1703, the men 'were never rash in declaring War', but 'held frequent Councils before they resolve[d] upon it', taking into careful consideration the sentiments and declared neutralities of their neighbours.[26] In 1793, Le Clerc Milfort recorded likewise of the southeastern Muscogee, that they were unwilling to fight, unless 'an enemy ha[d] forced them to assemble and to take up arms'.[27] Even then, the Young Men entered intensive rounds of fasting and prayer, to prepare themselves for the ordeal.[28] As for the Grandfathers, when war loomed, their task was to quell tempers, not further incite them. Like Miami chiefs, Woodlands Grandfathers were wont to advise the Young Men 'to remain at home and take care of the women and children, and not to trouble themselves with matters that d[id] not concern them'.[29] These transactions explain why the Grandfathers were constantly telling the European commanders that they were 'unable to control' the Young Men, as Shawnee grandfathers informed General Thomas Gage in 1766, and not as some historians assume to this day because the 'village chiefs were increasingly losing control' of them.[30] They had never had war powers over the Young Men.

Under this carefully constructed system, the primary custody of war rested, then, in female hands, a course correction deliberately intended to block the systemic abuses experienced under the old Mound-Builders' hierarchical male-priest-driven governments. Only the Clan Mothers could call for war or appoint warriors, while no more than one engagement was ever authorized – a fact helping to account for the continuing ire of European military commanders with their 'unreliable' Indigenous 'allies'.[31] The Head Clan Mother could furthermore declare peace, at will: 'Her word was law'.[32] Should the Young Men wish to go out again, they needed to propose the option to the Clan Mothers. Thus, in the heat of the 1779 invasion of Iroquoia during the American Revolution, immediately after the Young Men had lost the only European-style 'battle' – a moment fraught with desperation for the Iroquois – the Young Men could not just go out again to fight on. To continue struggling against the US Army, they had first to persuade the women that, even in view of recent events, resistance, not surrender, continued to be the right course of action. The council considering this point was less than rapid.[33] The right of Woodlands women to call, and call off, action remains to this day, as was demonstrated by the Mohawk standoff at Oka, Quebec, Canada, in 1990 and at the Cherokee protest to preserve a major circle mound at the sacred Newark Earthworks of Ohio in 1992.[34]

In the event that an action materialized, there were also strict laws about who could be targeted. Throughout the Woodlands, there was the Law of Innocence, which distinguished between combatants and non-combatants. When the British demanded in 1781 that the Lenape 'kill all, destroy all' of the American rebels for them, the holy man of the Lenape, Hopocan, rebuked the commandant at Detroit: 'Innocence had no part in your quarrels; and therefore, I distinguished – I spared!'[35] Only Young Men who had elected to go to war, or War Women, who had been made men, that is, were 'ceremonial' Young Men (war being a Breath activity), were legitimate targets of lethal action. The Montour sisters, Egonohowin ('Queen' Esther) and 'French' Catharine, were well-known Seneca War Women during the American Revolution, with Egonohowin killed at Newtown in 1779, fighting the American invasion of Iroquoia.[36] All others, including elders, women, children, holy persons and disabled persons, and known neutrals were off-limits, as were any emissaries of peace, a category including the missionaries and even the ambassadors of hated enemies.

Once a battle was over, Indigenous Americans expected hostilities to end. This is another reason that Western commanders were constantly confounded by the supposed 'desertion' of their Indigenous 'allies'. Among Woodlanders, peace was called at the end of the battle, with the losses condoled on both sides in set speeches that dried the tears and parted the clouds, that is, officially ended hostilities and buried the hatchet beneath the roots of the tree of peace. For instance, after the Indian Confederacy lost the Battle of Fallen Timbers over possession of Ohio, the great speaker Tarhe of the Wyandot at the Greenville Treaty Council in 1794 made this traditional condolence speech, forcing General Anthony Wayne to follow suit with his own, truncated version, thus conclusively ending the warfare between the Indian Confederacy and the United States.[37] These speeches were to be accompanied by mutual gifting, with continued war an absolutely unacceptable response to gifts.[38] This is why New Corn, speaker of the Bodéwadmi (Potawatomi), the first group arriving at the Treaty Council, reminded Wayne that they hoped he would 'supply [them] with provision', and why Wayne agreed that he would give the provisions and 'some drink to refresh' and 'make [their] hearts glad'.[39]

Clearly, then, all war mechanisms in the Eastern Woodlands of North America were intended as barriers, rather than as enablers, of warfare. It was only once the Europeans arrived with their imperial conflicts and their metal weapons that Indigenous nations were forcibly drawn into the fray, both as proxy fighters and as resisters.[40] In this respect, it is worth looking at how Europeans and Eastern Woodlanders might have influenced the ways in which war was carried out. At the outset, it is important to dispel some of the myths surrounding Indigenous American scalping and Indigenous American torture to reassess received Western notions on these topics.

Rituals of Violence

We would like to briefly touch on two aspects of American Indigenous warfare, what is referred to a 'scalping' and 'ritual torture', both sensitive topics among Indigenous Americans, historically overplayed in American tracts as an excuse for massacre. In fact, both were far less practiced than settler propaganda would have it. In his exhaustive, seminal study of scalping, Georg Friederici concluded that pre-contact scalping – the removal of a patch of hair-covered skin on the crown of the enemy's head – was confined to small geographical areas and limited ethnic groups in the Eastern Woodlands.[41] Scalping was practised on enemy dead, although not many Indigenous peoples practised it.[42] There is some archaeological evidence that decapitation and scalping of the enemy were part of a repertoire of violence used by Indigenous societies in prehistoric and in pre-contact North America.[43] Scalping practices also varied enormously from one nation to the next, with immense regional differences. Among the Pawnee, for example, it was done for a mixture of reasons: to obtain spiritual power, to ensure the vitality and well-being of the community, and for the men to enhance their status and marriage prospects.[44]

The evidence for Indigenous scalping is nevertheless scant, whereas the European-colonial texts containing them are untested, leaving some question as to whether we can take such accounts at face value. Iroquoian traditions are silent on scalping. Respected traditionalists, including the nineteenth-century Tuscarora sachem, Yutana Nire ('Chief Elias Johnson', 1837–1913) and the twentieth-century Cayuga sachem, Teiohonwé:thon ('Chief Jacob Thomas', Cayuga, 1922–98), heatedly repudiated scalping as a pre-contact practice. Teiohonwé:thon stated that 'contrary to common belief, it was Europeans who introduced scalping' to the Iroquois during the Beaver Wars of the seventeenth century.[45] In 1881, Yutana Nire likewise disclaimed scalping, specifically because the custom appears nowhere in the extensive oral base of Iroquoian tradition.[46]

The Moravian missionary John Heckewelder lived among the Lenape and Mahican for forty-nine years, after having been adopted into the Turtle Clan of the Lenape as Piselatulpe in 1764, when he was seventeen.[47] Learning multiple Lenapean dialects, Heckewelder had a good grasp of Algonkin oral traditions. He described a 'scalp lock' as a little crest of hair left on men's heads, after the rest of their head-hair had been plucked out around the topknot, as was customary across the Woodlands. A plucked head, alone, did not signal hostile intentions. If the man was on his way to war, then an eagle plume was affixed to the heavily moussed scalp lock to signal as much.[48] This treated topknot was what the Lenape in particular, and the Northeastern Woodlanders generally, referred to as a 'scalp'.[49] Absent a topknot, Woodlanders referred to a full head of hair as 'the head'.[50]

The waxed and plumed topknot was preparation for 'scalping', but that does not necessarily indicate what is thought of as scalping today. The idea was for an adversary to get hold of, and quickly cut off, the greased topknot. The possessor did not have to be harmed, let alone killed in the process, for the point was honour, nor murder. In fact, before the European arrival, the primary goal was to push the opposing side off the field and set them running away. Olympics-style contests between factions would be arranged and count as 'warfare', as happened early in League history when the office of Jigonsaseh, the head Clan Mother of the League, was in dispute, to have been settled by a sort of martial arts contest.[51] Instances of an Olympics-style sublimation of warfare go very far back in tradition, in some accounts to the times of the Stone Giants, as in the Winnebago tradition of Hešucka.[52]

The few early examples of scalping came in the context of executions, about which additional historical context is required. To this day, Western scholars insist on terming Indigenous executions 'ritual torture'.[53] Like all cultures, Indigenous Woodlanders had laws which, if broken, had penalties attached. Death was the most extreme penalty, and it was carried out particularly in cases of war crimes. It is hardly surprising, therefore, that the 1609 account from Champlain included head-flaying as part of an execution. Indigenous North Americans, especially on the east coast, were known to torture select captives, a ritual practised mainly against other Indigenous Americans as a way of assuaging the grief and loss caused by the death of relatives.[54] They were also accused of cannibalism, as were Italians, Russians, the Khoisan and Australian Aboriginal people.[55] In North America, there was the occasional, highly ritualized consumption of a tortured enemy's flesh, something that was used in settler propaganda. Again, ritual cannibalism was usually practised on other Indigenous Americans and only incidentally on Europeans. The best-known and most quoted account of the consumption of European flesh described the ritual torture and death of a despised Jesuit missionary, Jean de Brébeuf.[56] Like so many other accusations, though, this account is based on a second-hand reports by the enemies of the Iroquois, and like all propaganda, it utilized 'pre-set images'.[57] The clear purpose of the charge of cannibalism was to put Indians beyond the limits of civilization, which is probably why documented instances of settler cannibalism, such as occurred in Jamestown in 1609, were often ignored.[58]

Woodland peoples followed their own protocol to judge capital crimes, applying the death penalty when it was deemed appropriate. As a Shawnee speaker reminded General William Henry Harrison in 1806, 'You white people also try your criminals' and at a guilty verdict, 'you hang or kill them', so it should hardly have been surprising that Indigenous Americans did 'the same'.[59] Moreover, Indigenous Americans executed people only for serious crimes of murder, and not necessarily even for murder. For example, after the conviction of the killers of her son, the Seneca adoptee, *Dehgewämis* ('Mary Jemison', 1743–1833) asked for, and was granted, that the felons the felons be banished and not executed.[60]

It does not hurt to recall what European executions involved. In North American colonies in the sixteenth and seventeenth centuries, people were drawn and quartered, pressed to death, disembowelled, broken on the wheel, mutilated and dismembered, as well as hung from a slip-knotted cord for a lingering and uncertain death.[61] In Europe, counterfeiters, sodomites, heretics and witches were still being burnt at the stake, while torture was practised even if it was falling into disuse. The English were also not averse to torturing and dismembering captured Indigenous Americans in times of war.[62]

Indigenous Australian Ways of Warfare

According to military historian John Connor, wars of territorial conquest appear to have been unknown to Indigenous people in Australia because each person was associated with particular 'country' that was firmly fixed by their Dreaming connections to family, clan and totem, rather than by political expediency.[63] Thus it was the duty of each Aboriginal person to 'look after' their designated 'country', but they could also have obligations to other areas of country belonging to a relative that had passed away, was absent or was too young or too old to care for it.[64] When the British landed at Sydney Cove in January 1788, the local Indigenous people appear to have considered them by virtue of their pale faces and indeterminate sex, as ancestral ghosts or Berewalgal, as the coastal people called the British, who had returned to pay homage to their 'country'.[65] This led them to largely avoid Sydney Cove for about a year while the Berewalgal completed their Dreaming obligations. But when they did not leave after a year and at least half of the Indigenous community died in a smallpox or chickenpox epidemic a few months later, relations between the two groups moved into a different trajectory. Governor Phillip captured two Indigenous men, Colebee and Bennelong, at the end of 1789, and in retaliation he was wounded in a ritual spear attack at Manly Cove in August 1790, an indication that the local community was now prepared to incorporate the Berewalgal into their own society and cultural practice of mutual reciprocity and gift exchange.[66]

Connor considers that the Indigenous inhabitants of the Sydney region drew no distinction between the concepts of war and peace in that both were an integral part of everyday life and their oral traditions. Traditional warfare was conducted between clans on a continual but limited basis by small groups of men as a way of asserting the superiority of one's clan over neighbouring clans, 'rather than to conquer, destroy or displace' them.[67] So the first war strategies used by the Indigenous people to resist the British invasion were drawn from their traditional war practices of formal battles, ritual trials, raids for women, and revenge attacks.[68]

Formal battles took place when two groups of Aboriginal warriors fought each other to settle grievances between them. Most battles were carefully managed events held at carefully selected venues, with apparent agreement on the number of participating warriors and the kind of weapons to be used, such as long and short hardwood barbed spears, some tipped with stones flakes, as well as *woomeras* (spear throwers), *waddies* (hardwood clubs or fighting sticks) and bark and wooden shields. Hostilities ended when a few participants were killed or wounded. Some of the battles among the Indigenous communities observed by the early colonists required days of preparation while the warriors, numbering between sixty and one hundred on each side, assembled to prepare their weapons. The women psychologically prepared them for battle by ceremonially 'painting them up' and singing stories of former battles. According to Connor, the Indigenous men

> limited the duration of their formal battles by beginning late in the afternoon and ending them soon after dusk. Indigenous women did not take part in the actual fighting of formal battles, but they took part in ceremonies commencing the battle and shouted on the sidelines so loudly that they could be heard over 'the Clashing of Spears and the strokes of lances'.[69]

At the end of the battle, according to historian Henry Reynolds, peace would be restored and after the removal of the dead and wounded, a ceremony or corroboree would be held by both the victors and the vanquished to bring the conflict to a formal conclusion. However, major battles involving hundreds of warriors could only be held when an abundance of food was available.[70]

A few months after the British arrived at Sydney Cove in 1788, a marine officer and two corporals outside the settlement were confronted by fourteen Indigenous men 'painted up' and armed with stones and clubs, walking purposefully in single file and clearly ready for battle. The Englishmen clutched their muskets waiting for attack. But the war party was so focused on its objective that it strode straight past them, as if they did not exist.[71] The officer was relieved to escape a violent encounter but was affronted that Aboriginal people did not consider the British to be part of their mental universe. Indeed, many of the British officers were constantly surprised by their exclusion from Indigenous consciousness.

The first clash between the British and the local Indigenous community was recorded in March 1788 less than two months after the British invaded Gadigal country. A group of male convicts challenged Gadigal warriors to a fight in the bush outside the British campsite at Sydney Cove and ended when one of the convicts was 'dangerously wounded with a spear' and the others were 'very much bruised and beaten'. In this case, the convicts did not carry firearms.[72] The best-known 'battle' took place in March 1797 when the Darug resistance leader Pemulwuy and his warriors challenged a party of soldiers to a fight in the main street of Parramatta. According to one account, Pemulwuy began the engagement by throwing a spear at one of the soldiers who fired his musket loaded with buckshot, hitting Pemulwuy in the head and body. The 'battle was now joined', and in the ensuing shower of spears and volley of musket fire, five Darug warriors were killed, and a colonist was wounded in the arm. Pemulwuy received seven buckshot wounds in the skirmish but managed to survive.[73]

Another form of Aboriginal warfare, the ritual trials, which Connor believes were 'related to formal battles', were a form of trial in which individual Aboriginal men were punished, usually for an assault or murder. The man was expected to stand his ground and accept any wounds he might receive.[74] L. E. Threlkeld, the missionary located at Lake Macquarie south of Newcastle in the mid-1820s, recorded an incident where a sorcerer, who was hired by the Awabakal people from another nation to save the life of a sick child, was accused of her murder. He was 'required to stand with only a wooden shield (*arrabgong*) to protect him, while the disappointed and infuriated relatives of the deceased' hurled their spears at him 'with all the strength and skill for which they are peculiarly distinguished'. In this case he dodged the spears and survived.[75] This kind of warfare was sometimes conducted against individual British men when they were considered to have broken the protocols of Aboriginal society. In 1800, former convict James Wilson was forced to stand ritual trial for killing an Indigenous woman and was fatally speared by a group of her male relatives.[76] It is also probable that Governor Phillip was the subject of a ritual trial when he was speared by Bennelong's countrymen at Manly Cove in 1790.[77]

According to Connor, raids for women in Aboriginal society were also 'acts of warfare' because they transferred 'property from one group to another .... in the same way that fighting for land would be considered warfare in agricultural societies' for Aboriginal women's food gathering and child bearing abilities in Aboriginal society were 'economic resources which were fundamental to the group's survival'.[78] In Tasmania, the Aboriginal warrior Woorraddy from the Nuenonne clan on Bruny Island told government agent G. A. Robinson that before 1820 the Mellukerdee clan at the Huon River were 'a big race of men and had a practice of stealing women from the neighbouring nations', including the Mouheneenner clan at Hobart and the Pydairrerme clan at Tasman Peninsula on the other side of Storm Bay.[79] Of all the known Aboriginal forms of warfare, the abduction of women by British men rendered clans vulnerable to their long-term survival. Known as 'gin raiding' by the British, according to historian Nicholas Clements, in Tasmania it was the common trigger for war.[80]

The final form of traditional Aboriginal warfare was the revenge attack. Connor believes that it usually involved the killing of one person in revenge for murdering another, although in this case the alleged perpetrator could be a woman as well as a man. However, unlike the ritual trial, which took place in the open in the Sydney region, the revenge attack usually took place in the Sydney region at night, but in Tasmania it was usually a daylight ambush, carried out by women as well as men. In 1796, for example, a young Darug girl, orphaned by the frontier war on the Hawkesbury and brought to live at Government House in Sydney, was killed by Aboriginal men and women and her arms severed, because she 'belonged to a tribe of natives that was hostile to the Sydney people' and they 'could not admit of her partaking in those pleasures and comforts which they derived from their residence among the colonists, and therefore inhumanly put her out of the way'.[81] Connor notes that '[t]hese war parties were grimly referred to as "the ones who take you by the throat"'.[82]

At the Hawkesbury in April 1794, a group of Bediagal warriors from the Darug killed and mutilated a British male convict in revenge for the shooting of one of their men.[83] In September, another group, or possibly even the same group, attacked a male colonist and his servant in their hut with spears and clubs and seriously wounded them.[84] The attack appears to have been in revenge for their abduction of a Darug child. By then the revenge attack was a well-known resistance tactic, and the settlers were beginning to respond accordingly. After the same group of Bediagal warriors attacked another colonist's hut a few days later and carried off clothes and provisions, the colonists gathered as many weapons as they could muster and set off in pursuit, killing seven or eight Bediagal.[85] Yet it is clear that the Darug, like all other Aboriginal nations, did not conduct indiscriminate attacks on settlers. Rather they were well-planned responses to particular instances of colonial violence, such as the kidnapping of Darug women and children, or the breakdown in reciprocal arrangements between the Indigenous community and the colonists, including the exchange of food for Aboriginal labour. We should point out that they did not discriminate among colonists; that is, all colonists were held responsible for one person's infringement of Aboriginal laws.

The revenge attack became the best-known Aboriginal war tactic. When used in conjunction with the element of surprise and the use of firesticks and other weapons of war such as stones, spears and waddies, the revenge attack, in particular during the Black War in Tasmania in the 1820s, was both frightening and successful. By 1820, the Aboriginal revenge attack was known by some colonists as guerrilla warfare, a term recently introduced into the English language by British army regiments serving in the Iberian Peninsula where they observed the guerrilla tactics of the Spanish army in their resistance to the French occupation of their country.[86] It is possible that the term was introduced directly to the Australian colonies in 1817 by officers from the 48th Regiment of Foot who served in the Peninsula from 1809 to 1814.[87]

Connor believes that the Bediagal of the Darug nation at the Hawkesbury River were the first Aboriginal clan to develop new tactics to contain the British invasion, by shifting focus from attacking the person to attacking their property. His research indicates that the shift was first apparent along the Hawkesbury River in 1795 when the Bediagal picked the corn that colonists had planted in their yam fields. Every autumn up to 1810, 'corn raids' became a feature of the Hawkesbury frontier with up to 150 Bediagal men, women and children, descending on their former yam fields with blankets and nets to pick and hold the corn. The raids were on such a large scale they not only required 'a high degree of negotiation and co-ordination' but were of such 'sheer size' that they readily intimidated the colonists living on small farms on both sides of the river.[88]

Another tactical innovation by the Darug-Bediagal was their method of attacking farmhouses in search of British foods, such as corn, flour, potatoes, tea and sugar, and hunting items such as hatchets and knives. As they learnt the invaders' language, they became more adept at planning raids on farmhouses to acquire all these goods. In a variation from hunting kangaroo, they would select the farmhouse for attack and then secrete themselves in the bush nearby and wait patiently, sometimes for several days, until the opportune moment arose to attack it. Connor cites the well-known incident at William Knight's farmhouse at Portland on the Lower Hawkesbury, where in June 1805, Bediagal warrior 'Branch Jack' waited with a small group of Bediagal men in the bush nearby for several days until Knight and his servant left the farmhouse before they plundered it for food.[89] By 1820 the tactic was in widespread use by Aboriginal clans across the Nineteen Counties in New South Wales and the Settled Districts in Tasmania.

The final tactic developed by the Darug-Bediagal was a sophisticated use of fire. Connor thinks that it was an important innovation because, although it was widely used in hunting large animals such as kangaroo, it was not used in traditional warfare. His own research suggests that the Bediagal began using firesticks to attack farmhouses from the autumn and winter of 1797 when they used the cover of darkness to burn down farmers' huts.[90] By the summer of 1804 the Bediagal were also using firesticks to burn ripened wheat crops, to force the colonists to vacate their farms. For the British, however, wheat was the staple food for the entire colony, and to protect the crops, the colonial government stationed small detachments of soldiers at several farms on the Hawkesbury to protect them from Aboriginal attack. In 1805, magistrate Andrew Thompson led a party of colonists in a night-time attack on a party of Bediagal near Yarramundi Reach, killing at least eight of them.[91] On the Lower Hawkesbury, where the Bediagal held the military advantage until about 1810, the soldiers could not protect the dispersed farms from attack, forcing some colonists to abandon them.[92]

In 1814, the Dharawal and Gandangara people along the Nepean River in the Appin district southwest of Sydney used firesticks in daylight surprise attacks on recently established farms to destroy wheat crops, drive away sheep and cattle, and burn down remote huts. In these cases, the suddenness of the raid, the realization that it was well planned and that it often took place when colonists were most vulnerable to loss of life and property, led some colonists to consider that these Aboriginal tactics were 'natural' forms of 'guerrilla warfare'.[93]

According to Reynolds, it was Aboriginal access to British food rations, in particular corn, tea, potatoes, and flour that fundamentally changed the nature of Aboriginal warfare. Rather than spending most days hunting and gathering their own food they became increasingly reliant on British food. Yet paradoxically they also devised new resistance strategies to force the colonists from their hunting grounds, including what he calls a form of economic warfare such as breaking sheep's legs.[94] The first recorded account of Aboriginal men spearing cattle in Tasmania, for example, took place in 1810, that is, within seven years of the British invasion of the island and appears to have been an attempt to drive the colonists away rather than from a desire for British food. Indeed, as Sharon Morgan points out, the Tasmanian Aboriginal people initially did not like to eat sheep or cattle and their attacks on colonial livestock to 1820 were not only more common than attacks on people but were also clearly designed to drive the colonists' livestock from their hunting grounds.[95]

Few stand-up battles between Aboriginal people and the British were recorded in the Australian colonies largely because the former quickly understood the power of the British musket; *gooroobeera* was the name given to the colonists as 'those who carry guns'.[96] However, the first known resistance leader, Pemelwuy, not only challenged soldiers to a battle with his warriors in Parramatta in March 1797, he also managed to survive the battle even though he was 'blasted with buckshot'. His reputation as a warrior who was impervious to *gooroobeera* continued for a further five years until he was killed in a special forces operation in 1802.[97]

By 1814, the Darug, Dharawal and Gandangara had perfected the tactic of either taking cover when a musket was about to be fired or rushed 'the man after he had discharged his musket and before he could reload'.[98] The only recorded incident in which Aboriginal men in the Sydney region fired on settlers took place at the Nepean River on 2 March 1816 when a punitive expedition of seven settlers was ambushed by a group of Gandangara warriors. They took the settlers' muskets and 'commenced a terrible attack, as well by a discharge of arms they had captured, as by an innumerable shower of spears', leaving three colonists dead. The four survivors fled back across the river.[99]

Revolt and Rebellion in French-Occupied Europe

The case of European populations resisting the French and then the Napoleonic armies were as diverse as the peoples the French encountered. Resistance was fundamentally different in some respects from Indigenous resistance in settler colonies, but remarkably similar in others. For example, the occupier encroaching on and exploiting lands that did not belong to them, and often kidnapping or raping women and children in the process, invariably led to tit-for-tat reprisals. We also must take into account the more traditional forms of revolt that had always been a feature of peasant life in Europe and that continued during the Revolutionary and Napoleonic Wars. There were, for example, hundreds of subsistence riots during this period that were tied not just to French depredations but also to natural weather occurrences. The

French historian Aurélien Lignereux has inventoried a total of 460 revolts between 1800 and 1813, in the territories annexed to the empire. Another 71 revolts can be added for the year 1814, and that is not counting the 1,000 or so revolts that took place inside France.[100]

Uprisings could involve local peasant communities or urban dwellers who resented the depredations of the French armies, or they could evolve into fully fledged insurrectional movements, as was the case in the Tyrol, southern Italy and Spain. Armed resistance to occupation, that is, large-scale insurrection, was in many respects the exception to the rule, and really only occurred in those few regions.[101] More common was the short-lived village/urban riot or insurrection. It was rare that a combination of factors – topography, assistance from allied troops, access to supplies – enabled insurgencies to succeed.

As we have seen, the usual cause of resistance was French depredations, a direct consequence of the nature of French Revolutionary warfare and its armies living off the land. It is hardly surprising that under these conditions civilians resisted. Circumstances varied enormously, of course, and depended on the region and the length of stay. If troops just moved through and plundered, the reaction was invariably the same; the majority of peasants fled, but some took up arms, engaging in forms of *petite guerre* or irregular warfare, in much the same manner as the Indigenous peoples of South Africa and Australia. In regions where banditry had been common and difficult to control under the *ancien régime*, or where there was a long history of resisting 'foreign' occupation, there was more likely to be organized resistance to the French. This was the case in Calabria, where the Bourbon monarchy had little influence and where bandits fought each other for control of towns and villages.[102] It was one of the regions the French found difficult to conquer; fighting continued for years. What kept the revolt was not devotion to the monarchy or the Catholic Church – although there were elements within the Church who preached revolt – but rather the tradition of the vendetta, and the sheer destitution of Calabrian society.[103] Calabria in many respects falls in the tradition of a peasant revolt, a *jacquerie* as it has been called, aimed at the occupier. In other regions too, brigandage was a violent response to the increasing poverty peasants found themselves in as a result of French depredations.[104] That is why, in some regions, it was difficult to know who the bandits were and who the guerrilla fighters; the lines between them were blurred while the French denounced all armed resistance as a form of 'brigandage'.[105] In Spain, guerrilla bands came to live off the people and were as ruthless in their use of terror as the invaders.[106] In most instances, popular resistance was brigandage and only ceased being so when elites or ambitious adventurers organized their bands into something resembling disciplined militias.[107] We find this occurring in Spain and in the Tyrol. It was in these two regions of Europe that the fighters involved in 'small wars' became 'guerrillas', that is, they became 'partisans' in the modern sense of the word.[108]

In general terms, the pacification or conquest of the land in question could lead to atrocities if the incursions of regular troops, or settlers and pastoralists in other parts of the world, met with resistance on the part of local inhabitants. We will see in greater detail below how the tactics adopted by the French were designed to teach the locals a lesson, so that resistance would melt away or cease.[109] This logic was flawed, since there is little sign that it actually dissuaded people from resisting, but it was nevertheless the logic of irregular warfare which invariably leads to an escalation of violence and brutality on both sides as the parties concerned were frustrated in their ultimate objectives, the one to dominate the countryside, the other to dispel the invader. It inevitably required the occupying army to destroy the enemy – and here no distinction is made between combatant and non-combatant – to achieve a form of collective security, which meant pacifying the population until further resistance was no longer possible.

Apart from the depredations common to the French living off the land, any significant changes to institutional structures could also cause enormous unrest. This was the case for parts of Calabria, Spain and the Tyrol, where attempts to introduce Napoleonic reforms, and in the process to eliminate ancient local privileges, invariably led to opposition and unrest. This was particularly the case for religious institutions. In fact, the one defining feature of European resistance to the French occupier, about which we know little in the rest of the world, is religion. That is, resistance appears to have been strongest in those regions where religion was most practiced. More often, the extreme violence used to suppress uprisings by French troops was enough to quell any

Figure 3 *Anonymous engraving: 'Diß ist die grosse Freyheit welche Jourdan seinen Mitbürgern verspochen' [This is the great freedom which Jourdan promised his fellow citizens], August 1796. Source: Bibliothèque nationale, Paris. One of the very few contemporary illustrations of the depredations carried out in the German lands by French troops, in this case, General Jourdan's campaign in the Rhine.*

sustained resistance. Ordinary men and women living in rural society defined themselves largely in religious terms, so that the presence of an irreligious foreign culture such as the French revolutionary armies was anathema to them.[110] Italy, Spain and the Rhineland were among the most Catholic regions in Europe.[111] Everywhere they went, the 'soldiers of Satan' desecrated churches, and attacked popular shrines.[112] The French were accused of mutilating crucifixes, trampling the host and holy relics on the ground, abusing statues of the Virgin Mary, forcing organists to play revolutionary songs during Church services and performing blasphemous parodies of religious processions, as they had done in France at the height of the Revolution. If that were not bad enough, they also dissolved religious orders, closed monasteries and convents, and sold off Church land.

The popular reaction to these outrages was predictable and understandable. Resistance, both passive and open, was generalized in many parishes. The simple act of taking away church bells – to be melted down for use in the construction of artillery for example – could sometimes only be carried out by the use of military force. At Herschwiesen in the Rhineland, when French soldiers attempted to destroy a shrine, they were attacked by a crowd of 4,000 people.[113] When crowds protested against what they saw as an abuse, they were acting on a belief that the threat they faced was wrong. Local populations turned violent when tradition was stymied. In Navarre and other parts of northern Spain, when Joseph Bonaparte as King of Spain confiscated Church property and sold it off, it hurt the peasants who had until then rented the land from the Church at prices that had sometimes remained unchanged for generations.[114]

Sexual Assault in the Napoleonic Wars

Another theme present among veterans' accounts is the extensive presence of sexual violence committed against girls and women.[115] In Portugal in 1810, for example, the village of Lordelo outside of Porto was attacked and 200 people killed. Women of all ages, from a child of nine to an old woman in her seventies, were raped.[116] They necessarily occurred wherever regular soldiers came to grips with civilians in revolt, and although there is no evidence that rape was carried out in any systematic way, or indeed that it was used by the French imperial regime as a tool of terror to subdue recalcitrant populations as it had been for other regimes and other periods. Rape nevertheless occurred frequently and appears to have been so prevalent that it was probably considered a 'right of conquest', a 'reward' of sorts, and was thus a random act of sexual violence. This sort of behaviour was sometimes endorsed by the army. Some of the ditties distributed and sung by soldiers, for example, were virtual invitations to rape.

Rape nevertheless underlined the powerlessness of the communities concerned and the superiority, physical and cultural, of the conqueror. The following passage from an anonymous book on the first Italian campaign gives an indication of just how widespread the practice was:

> Debauchery is the epidemic evil of all armies. In that of Buonaparté, it was carried to excess. Almost every honest family has had to lament its

dishonour. Age, state, condition, education, nobility, nothing guarantees the honour of the sex from the lust of the soldier. Altars, even sanctuaries, have not sheltered those who have devoted their lives to God. The examples have been frequent and horrible. I have even seen a number of these cannibals cruelly massacre those that had been abducted and dishonoured.[117]

Similarly, the sack of Jaffa by the French in Syria in March 1799 led to a 'traffic of young women' being exchanged for other objects looted in the town. The men, however, soon began to fight over them so that Napoleon ordered his men to bring all the women back to town to the hospital courtyard 'on pain of a severe punishment', where they were promptly executed by a company of chasseurs.[118] Pierre Guingret, while campaigning in Portugal, described how women of all classes were abducted, bought and sold, or exchanged during card games for luxury items. Other, less fortunate women were obliged to 'satisfy

Figure 4 *Anonymous engraving: 'Unter den Königen war der Neufrank, Höflich und erbar, jez ist er ein Vertheidiger des Raubes und der Unzucht' [Among the kings was the New Frank, polite and gracious, now he is a defender of robbery and fornication], c. 1796. Source: Bibliothèque nationale, Paris. Again, one of the rare representations of rape by soldiers of the French revolutionary armies.*

the most unbridled passions' to avoid death, but were often killed anyway.[119] Sergeant Lavaux writes of several soldiers entering a convent in Spain where an unspecified number of nuns were raped and murdered – the whole incident is described in a few lines.[120] In a remarkably frank admission, an officer, Esprit Castellane, recalled a woman being saved by an officer of the general staff who entered a house after the storming of Burgos to find her 'in the midst of fifty soldiers. Each one was waiting his turn'.[121] General Davout wrote of women being 'requisitioned' in Germany to 'satisfy their [the troops'] unspeakable desires'.[122] It was not unusual for men even outside of the 'normal' atrocities that took place during the storming of towns and the systematized marauding to assault women of all ages, including pre-pubescent girls.

There are a number of elements that we can draw from this brief exposé of Indigenous and local approaches to fighting that will serve to put what comes next – the dynamics of massacre on the frontier – into a broader perspective. The word 'warrior' has been mentioned often. It is worth making a distinction between 'warriors' and trained soldiers, and even between 'warriors' and the commandos and militias that they often encountered.[123] Indigenous peoples did not maintain standing armies, nor did they have a hierarchical structure in the Western sense of the term. Instead, they organized themselves on an ad hoc basis with an improvised leadership. This does not mean that they did not plan raids and battles, or that there were not wars of territorial conquest, which certainly happened in South Africa and North America, although interestingly not in Australia. Nor does it mean that they did not adapt to changing circumstances, as we saw with Indigenous Australians shifting their tactics away from attacking people to attacking property. Given the social and cultural character of the warrior, warfare could never be sustained for any length of time. Although there were periods when Indigenous warriors were able to resist and even repel European settlers, it is possibly one of the reasons why Europeans prevailed in the long run. In the next chapter we will examine how massacres occurred on the frontier and what some of the necessary preconditions were.

4

The Logic of Violence and Massacre on the Imperial Frontier

A Rhetoric of Hate

It is somewhat incongruous that massacres were repeated so frequently in so many parts of the world in an era better known for the Enlightenment. How do we reconcile two phenomena that seem so diametrically opposed? On the one hand is the declaration by both the American colonists and the French revolutionaries that all men are born free and equal. Even though there is not yet an implicit understanding that the ideal applies to all men and women, regardless of race, creed or colour, that seed has taken root.[1] On the other hand is the brutal intervention of European invaders, settlers and the imperial-colonial state in the elimination of those who opposed its expansion.

This somewhat schizophrenic situation is best illustrated by the language used by Europeans in South Africa, North America and Australia, against those who resisted their incursions. In South Africa, the Boers classified all non-Europeans as 'heathens' since the Dutch were 'Christians'. The Old Testament was full of examples of how the Israelites had ethnically cleansed the land of Canaan of heathens and how Jehovah had ordered the annihilation of certain tribes of people or the worshippers of false gods. One of the more eloquent of the Boers – *veldwagtmeester* Gerrit Maritz of the Roggeveld – liked to pepper his accounts with biblical language. He once described his rival, Florris Visser, as being a follower of Belial because of his good relationship with the local San.[2] If most Boers eschewed such language, then the Bible provided them with a set of deeply held and barely articulated beliefs that provided them with all the moral authority they needed to subjugate or annihilate those whom they knew to be 'Bushmen', 'Hottentots' and 'Kaffirs', all pejorative terms for what in their opinion were self-evidently inferior people.[3] The most common terms of de-humanization, however, were the words 'schepsels' (creatures, things), thieves, murderers, vagabonds, highwaymen, wild people or 'schelms' (rogues), all of which were more secular than biblical. The word 'Bushman' was thought to encompass within itself all of these conditions, some of which were punishable by death under the Roman Dutch law of the colony.

The average Boer did not, therefore, need to look far to find precedents to justify his treatment of those he regarded as not only being his inferiors but his enemies. If servants could be brutalized, then how much more deserving of death were enemies? Even innocent Khoikhoi could be massacred if they had livestock. This, as we have seen, was part of the dynamic of frontier violence – Khoikhoi were frequently massacred to take their cattle. Evidence suggests that there was a widespread consensus among frontier settlers that it was neither a sin, nor a crime, nor in fact a matter of exceptional import, to kill Indigenous people. There was no need for an elaborate rhetoric of violence when killing was such a banal, everyday act. Later, Afrikaner nationalist historians would explain that the Boers were clearing the land for the white man, but it is doubtful whether those doing the killing at the time had such a sense of purpose or historic destiny.[4]

The British were appalled by the state of violence existing on the Cape frontier when they first arrived in 1795 and, through a series of reforms, attempted, albeit ineffectually, to protect the Khoikhoi and San from cruelty, massacres and *de facto* enslavement by the Boers. There was thus no official British rhetoric of violence aimed at the Khoisan. If anything, officials like John Barrow, the secretary of Governor Earl Macartney, tended to denigrate the savagery of the Boers while pitying the Khoisan and admiring the Xhosa. Missionaries and humanitarians also championed the cause of the Khoisan. It was only when the British government at the Cape became embroiled in the problem of enforcing peace on the Cape's eastern frontier that it put aside the rosy view of the Xhosa expounded by Barrow. Gradually, in the face of determined Xhosa resistance, the British military began to adopt the colonial viewpoint and to portray the Xhosa as treacherous thieves and bloodthirsty savages. By 1809, the Cape's government had come to the conclusion that the only way to ensure peace on the eastern frontier was to remove the Xhosa altogether from the Zuurveld and place them on the other side of a defensible border. They were to become targets for ethnic cleansing, against whom it was permissible to employ 'a proper degree of terror'.

In North America, the words 'extirpate' and 'exterminate' were used by both politicians and land-hungry settlers when referring to Indigenous Americans who defended their lands from encroachment.[5] The meaning of these terms was clear – eradication and destruction – and was synonymous with what today would be regarded as an intent to commit genocide.[6] Some Indigenous Americans were conscious of the meaning of these words. There are sources in English documenting Indigenous discourse that frequently use the terms 'extirpate' and 'exterminate' in reporting Indian allegations. Seneca speakers used *Hanötaká:nyas*, a term that literally translates to English as 'he burns it', but which Seneca anthropologist, Arthur C. Parker (*Gáwasowanaeh*) translated as 'hollocaust [sic]', first recorded in reference to the scorched-earth sweep through Iroquoia carried out by General John Sullivan in 1779.[7] The Muscogee word for the massacre of people is *yvmahketv*, linguistically connected to the wasteful destruction of crops.[8]

The discourse on the European American side is also clear. During the American Revolution, Thomas Jefferson ordered Virginia troops to exterminate the Shawnees in the effort to drive them from their lands.[9] Again in 1776, Jefferson called for the extermination of the Muscogee and their removal west of the Mississippi River, ostensibly because they had fought with the British during the Revolution. In an oft-cited quote, General Henry Knox, the first Secretary of War in the newly founded American Republic, wrote to George Washington, claiming that the American push westwards had resulted in the 'utter extirpation of all the Indians in most populous parts of the Union', boasting that his fellow Americans had been more destructive than the conquistadors of Mexico and Peru.[10] Washington was also responsible for putting into motion an attempt, devastating but ultimately unsuccessful, to wipe out the Iroquois of New York, telling General John Sullivan in the 1779 invasion that his 'immediate objects' in the action were 'the total destruction and devastation of their settlements', so that the countryside might 'not be merely overrun, but destroyed'.[11]

In a letter of 29 December 1813, from his retirement at Monticello, Thomas Jefferson declared of the Northern Alliance under Tecumseh and his brother Tenskwatawa that 'this unfortunate race, whom we had been taking so much pains to save and to civilize, have by their unexpected desertion and ferocious barbarities justified extermination, and now await our decision on their fate'.[12] The 'pains' taken by the US government included the forcible imposition of Christian culture and the consequent dislocation of traditional culture, the seizure of the Old Northwest through warfare from 1789 to 1794, a series of fraudulent treaties foisted on the peoples of Ohio and Indiana, and open war declared upon them under the cover of The War of 1812, purportedly against the British. As for 'the Creek too on our Southern border', Jefferson continued, half of whom aligned with Tecumseh and Tenskwatawa, 'we had done more than for any other tribe'. What the United States had done for the Muscogee was, again, to impose Christian culture while undermining traditional culture, cut a federal road through the heart of Muscogee territory, and amass militia armies to attack it simultaneously from three directions, west from Georgia, east from Mississippi, and south from Tennessee, the better to take all Muscogee land while exterminating the people.[13] After the devastations of the settlers, Jefferson correctly predicted that the eastern nations would 'submit on condition of removal to such new settlements beyond the Mississippi [River] as we shall assign them'. Although Jefferson was too optimistic here by twenty years – Jacksonian Removal would not commence until 1832 – he laid forth in 1813 both the plan and the justification of Jackson's Removal.[14]

In Europe, the language used by the French to describe the Other was as extreme as their English-speaking counterparts. Although there had already existed a nationalist rhetoric against other Europeans, the English in particular,[15] during the Revolution an exterminatory discourse developed among politicians, administrators and some military that was directed at enemies of the Revolution. This rhetoric of extermination, which had its origins in the ideological and religious divisions emanating from the Revolution, may have inspired, or at least helped, justify the horrendous excesses committed by the military in their pursuit of civilian enemies of the Republic. Those killings took place in the context of a civil war, but the political systems that were put in place in conquered territories were born of the belief that French culture was inherently superior to all others, that the Revolutionary and Napoleonic armies were bringing Enlightenment where none existed, and that in doing so they set the standard of civilization. Official reports, as well as the memoirs left behind by veterans of the wars, are replete with unflattering remarks and stereotypes about the people the French had conquered and the countries they occupied. Those described are demeaned – they are 'too dirty' or 'too poor' or 'barbarous' – with epithets that help justify the conquest by a 'civilized' nation.[16] Germans were patronizingly referred to as 'sauerkraut heads' (*têtes de choucroute*), and were considered 'indolent' and 'mean'.[17] Italians were usually described as 'naturally lazy and dirty (*malpropre*)',[18] or as 'degenerate',[19] while the stupidity and the ugliness of the Spanish peasant, a superstitious lot ruled by the clergy, were sometimes compared to Asians, and sometimes to Arabs or Egyptians in a pejorative sense.[20] One French officer did not even count Spain among the countries of Europe but rather described it as an 'African country' 'by its blood, its morals, its language, its manner of living and fighting'.[21] Those who resisted were dubbed barbarians, ferocious hordes, wild beasts, dogs, and furious or bloodthirsty monsters.[22] This is perhaps why some French officers were calling for a 'war of extermination' as the only possible means of assuring complete dominance in the Peninsula.[23] Everywhere the French went, in other words, they were bringing 'good government' to the inhabitants of the lands they conquered. The thing is that notion of 'good government' was strikingly similar to that used by the French in West Africa in the late nineteenth century.[24]

In Australia, by the middle of the nineteenth century, the call to 'extirpate' Indigenous peoples was so common that the brutality of the conversations shocked British visitors to the colony in the 1840s.[25] James Bonwick, who arrived in Hobart in 1841, and who then went on to the Victorian goldfields, has left us with two examples of the colonial mindset towards Indigenous peoples: a former Bushranger is supposed to have confessed to him, 'I'd as leave shoot 'em as so many sparrows'; and citing from the Launceston Advertiser of 1829, 'Let them have enough of Redcoats and bullet fare. For every man they murder, hunt them down, and drop ten of them. This is our specific – try it.'[26] Similarly, the *Colonial Times* reported in 1826, 'The settlers and stock-keepers are determined to annihilate every Black who may act hostilely.'[27] Read too the minutes of the Aborigines Committee, held in Hobart on 23 February 1830. In 1828, the settler John Sherwin had been in the country seven years and was attacked six months prior by forty to fifty Aboriginal people. He was reported to have said that he 'Conceives they must be captured or exterminated. ... Sydney natives, or blood hounds, would contribute to the capture of the Natives in this colony; has heard it proposed that decoy huts, containing flour and sugar, strongly impregnated with poison, should be used'.[28]

This rhetoric of hate is characteristic of the language of the conqueror as colonizer, found wherever Europeans met non-Europeans throughout early modern and modern worlds. As we have seen, the French and the British adopted the same language towards other Europeans as towards non-Europeans.[29] There was an ideological basis to these attitudes; that is, there was a state discourse that portrayed non-French or non-British Europeans in a particular way. Colonial Americans, British and French considered all those who were different to them – Africans, Indigenous Americans, Aboriginal people and even other Europeans – to be inferior, primitive and savage. It is, nevertheless, one thing to describe the Other as 'dirty', 'lazy' and 'ugly' and it is quite another to kill them.

Without wanting to go into the question of the relationship between rhetoric and the extreme violence committed by troops, militia and settlers against Indigenous and local civilians, the implication is clear: if the conquered peoples were unenlightened and incapable of looking after themselves, then that was in itself justification enough for their conquest. We saw in the Introduction to this book that in the modern era of mass killings historians assume that a certain dehumanization of the enemy is required for those killings to occur. The rhetoric of violence and the racial slurs that we saw above were a way of increasing the 'social distance' between the perpetrators and the victims, a process that has been called deidentification – the denial of a common humanity between perpetrators and victims.[30] Deidentification is also meant to eliminate any emotional concern for the welfare of others because they are considered separate from the ingroup. Dehumanization is a more extreme form of deidentification although it is not necessary for mass killings to occur for the perpetrators to see the victims as *entirely* lacking in humanity.

It is easy therefore to conjecture that since the conquered peoples were viewed as less civilized, and even as 'savage', it must have facilitated a tendency towards massacre and atrocities, all the while leaving the perpetrators' sense of cultural superiority supremely intact. However, it is difficult if not impossible to know what impact these 'cultural biases' may have had on troop, militia and settler attitudes towards conquered peoples, and the extent to which they may have influenced their willingness or ability to kill Indigenous and local peoples. The picture is complicated somewhat by the fact that notions of 'human difference' in the eighteenth century were not the same as the racially based criteria of difference in the nineteenth century.[31]

The rhetoric of extermination and extirpation that was prevalent, which appears to have dominated the historical discourse in both settler societies and among the European political elite, is the minimum precondition necessary before an act of violence can occur. The causal connection between rhetoric and action is, however, tenuous. Men safely ensconced in urban centres, removed from the colonial frontier, often espoused the rhetoric of extermination. They were not actively engaged with Indigenous and local people and possibly may not have even met them. There were also men who fought on the colonial frontier and who espoused extermination. That settlers and soldiers felt (racial) disdain for the enemy, there can be no doubt. Once the cycle of violence was engaged, brutalities were committed and a desire to eliminate the enemy ensued.

The Dynamics of Violence and Massacre on the Frontier

In South Africa, Cattle Theft and Massacre

The Cape was supposed to be a small refreshment station for the VOC's ships voyaging to and from the east, but three things happened to change all that. The first was the death of a huge proportion of the Khoikhoi population in the smallpox epidemic of 1713. As a result, and this is the second development, the government calculated that there would be insignificant Khoikhoi opposition to the alienation of their land. In effect, the settlers began replacing the Khoikhoi as pastoralists by becoming pastoralists themselves, that is, by taking Khoikhoi land and livestock. This was in effect an attempt by the VOC to monopolize the cattle trade so that it might supply Company ships with meat. Once their land and livestock had been taken, the Khoikhoi could flee, fight or work for the new owners of the land and livestock. Most became farm labourers whose knowledge of local conditions would be invaluable to the inexperienced colonial pastoralists.[32]

Not content with having taken Khoikhoi land and livestock near the Cape, and this is the third development, white settlers set out to acquire livestock from the Khoikhoi through fraud and force. The first recorded massacres of the Khoikhoi occurred as early as 1702, when a group of colonists travelled miles inland and robbed Khoikhoi groups of thousands of cattle, attacking them with 'violence, murder and death'. Unfortunately, these events happened so far away from Cape Town that the numbers of those killed was not known. In 1705 a certain 'Dronke Gerrit' and his men surrounded a group of Khoikhoi near the Verlore Vlei and fired on them for no reason, burning their huts and stealing all of their cattle.[33] The examples could be multiplied, but by 1714, there were virtually no Khoikhoi with cattle in the vicinity of the south-western Cape. In his search to find meat the man awarded the Company meat contract in 1723, Van der Heijden, travelled with a group of seventy men to the Gonaqua Khoikhoi near Algoa Bay in the eastern Cape and killed so many of them in the process of stealing their cattle and sheep that the survivors claimed never to have seen so many corpses and begged that they too might be killed as they would starve to death having been left with nothing.[34] On one level, this was clearly an example of young men from one pastoralist group setting out to steal livestock from another group – a cattle raid – but it is the excessive use of violence and massacre that is disturbing. It is as though the rules of warfare had been changed.

Cattle theft and massacre were also behind the events leading to the frontier war of 1739 during which colonists, aggrieved Khoikhoi and Namaqua, fought throughout the northern frontier zone, destroying crops and stealing livestock. The war was brought to an end by a piece of treachery and a massacre, when Captain Gibbelaas, in charge of a Boer commando, sat down to parley with some of the rebels but instead killed the negotiators. The tactical benefit of a massacre, of course, is that the victims do not live to fight another day, nor reclaim their cattle. He ordered his men to open fire and killed between thirty and forty of them.[35] A German soldier called Mentzel, who was present, wrote an account of the massacre forty-eight years later:

> Though this was a very weak Commando, some of the soldiers proved that if they were free to do as they pleased, they could be wanton and savage. Some of the most brutal ones seized the small children by their legs and crushed their heads against the stones. Others killed the wounded women and cut off their long breasts, afterwards making themselves tobacco pouches from these as token of their heroism.[36]

Cattle theft and massacre were thus part and parcel of the Cape frontier and were closely entwined. What made massacre a possibility for the settlers, however, and not for their rivals, was that the settlers had guns and horses which they had combined into an institution known as the commando. A commando was basically a group of mounted colonial pastoralists, armed with firearms, together with their loyal Khoikhoi or mixed-race servants. The only difference between commandos and earlier groups of armed colonial robbers and murderers was that a commando was authorized by the VOC to exact revenge on resisting Khoisan or to recover stolen colonial livestock. For this purpose, it appointed an official to a leadership role, usually someone respected in the frontier district, and supplied him with ammunition for distribution amongst his men. It was not unknown for official commandos to degenerate into cattle raiding expeditions, if the circumstances were right. In time, the commando also became an institution that policed and controlled the colonial labour force, ensuring that captives stayed captive and that so-called free labourers did not depart before their period of service was finished.

The commando also ensured, or attempted to ensure, the continuous advance of the pastoralist frontier. An essential dynamic of the early colonial period pastoral economy was that the pastoral frontier had to keep advancing.

If pastoralism was to prosper, if flocks and herds were to grow, then there was a constant need for new grazing and water resources. Ultimately it was the commando that ensured the forward movement of the trekboers by crushing whatever resistance there might be to pastoralist mobility and by contesting for access to new land beyond the horizon. If the Khoisan attempted to stop the onwards march of the frontier by resistance, commandos would attack them. If trekboer cattle and sheep were stolen, or shepherds murdered, the commandos would go in pursuit of the robbers or murderers and kill them. If labourers deserted, the commando would track them down and recapture or kill them. If new labourers were needed, the commando would capture San children. There was, in other words, a direct connection between the dynamics of pastoral production on the Cape frontier, particularly the dynamics of the trekboer economy, and the dynamics of violence and massacre. The commando system guaranteed access to land, labour and livestock and it did this through the utilization of violence and massacre.[37]

This, at least, was the picture on the northern frontier. On the eastern frontier the commando system was not quite as successful, given the superior strength of the Xhosa. Trekboers in the eastern Cape attempted to steal Xhosa cattle, advance into Xhosa territory and extract labour from the Xhosa by force. But they were only partially successful in doing so. The first two frontier wars are examples of the limits of the efficacy of the commando system in the eastern Cape. It would take a regular army, committed to a policy of ethnic cleansing and scorched earth, to remove the Xhosa from the land and to end their resistance. Massacre and violence, facilitated by guns and horses, once again proved to be the necessary accompaniments of conquest.

In North America, the Tactics of Terror

In North America, the policy of terror started not long after Europeans arrived in the sixteenth century and continued unabated into the nineteenth century. We do not yet know how many massacres occurred, nor how many people might have died, because no one has yet attempted to count them. The typical progression in America was complex since there was often contact among Indigenous peoples, missionaries and European hunters/fur traders before the arrival of settlers in any numbers. Both missionaries and hunters took whatever they wanted from the land, typically without permission, while Indigenous Americans would try to set behavioural and territorial boundaries. The fur traders set up forts, making space for the military to arrive to 'protect' the missionaries, hunters and traders. After enough settlers arrived, the military and militia mounted expeditions to break resistance and force concession treaties on Indigenous nations. Here is how an officially dispatched Seneca speaker confronted a Moravian missionary along the Muskingum River in Ohio in 1762:

> Brother! last year you asked our leave to come and live with us, for the purpose of instructing us and our children, to which we consented; and now being come on, we are glad to see you!
>
> Brother! It appears to us that you must since have changed your mind, for instead of instructing us or our children, you are cutting trees down on our land! you have marked out a large spot of ground for a plantation, as the white people do everywhere; and bye and bye another, and another, may come and do the same; and the next thing will be, that a fort will be built for the protection of these intruders, and thus our country will be claimed by the white people, and we driven further back, as has been the case ever since the white people first came into this country. Say! do we not speak the truth?[38]

Terror tactics were employed either to eliminate or to subjugate Indigenous Americans. The early British slaver and 'explorer' John Smith urged the use of 'Spanish' terror tactics to force 'drudgery worke and slavery' on the Indigenous peoples.[39] In 1763, the Pennsylvania Assemblyman John Hughes recommended to Colonel Henry Bouquet that the British army loose ferocious Spanish dogs of war to 'kill the Indians at pleasure', predicting that Bouquet 'would Soon See the Good Effects' of the terror tactic.[40] In his 1779 instructions to General John Sullivan ordering that Iroquoian towns, fields and houses 'not be merely overrun but destroyed', George Washington specifically commanded Sullivan to attack the Iroquois (Haudenosaunee) 'with as much impetuosity, shouting and noise as possible' in rushing the people 'with the warhoop and fixed bayonet', as nothing could 'disconcert and terrify the Indians more than this'.[41] Even as the ink dried on the 1783 Treaty of Paris, the new United States was set on terrifying the Indigenous peoples of the Old Northwest. In one treaty council after another from 1784 to 1795, the national Ottawa speaker Egushawa told of how the 'mighty and powerful' United States assured the Indigenous peoples that 'all the Indian nations compared to them, were but as one child to an hundred warriors! That they held all our nations in their hand, by closing of which they could crush us to death!'.[42]

This was more than simple rhetoric. Massacres were instituted on the frontier to clear the land of its inhabitants. One of the most notorious massacres was the Puritans' wanton destruction of the Pequots of Connecticut at Mystic Hill in 1637. One of the commanders at that massacre, John Mason, recounted the 'battle' in which the Puritan soldiers massacred the unguarded, sleeping town in a dawn attack, while most of the Young Men were absent. This was a standard tactic. In his report on the action, Mason was quite clear that rather than despatch the Pequot by sword, he ordered a fire. 'We must Burn them', he said; 'immediately' entering a wigwam, he 'brought out a Firebrand, and putting it into the Matts' or thatching that shingled the wigwams, 'set the Wigwams on Fire'. Mason described the results: 'And indeed, such a dreadful terror did the Almighty let fall upon their Spirits, that they would fly from us and run into the very Flames, where many of them perished.'[43] As another commander, Captain John Underhill, recorded, the Puritans encircled the town, shooting down and cutting down those who tried to climb over its palisades or rush out of the homes to escape the fire.[44] Underhill claimed that the fire 'blazed most terribly', consuming 'men, women, and children'. Those who managed to escape the inferno ran out 'twenty and thirty at a time, which our soldiers received and entertained with the point of the sword.'[45] Up to 700 Pequot were killed. Accounts differ as to Puritan casualties. There were either one or two killed, one by friendly fire.[46] Historians in the 1970s and 1980s attempted to psychologize the actions of the Puritans, but current scholarship suggest that natural resources and the desire to control the trade networks of southern New England played a crucial role.[47] Others have imbued their actions with a religious zeal that left the perpetrators without any compassion for their victims, because there is no mercy when executing God's vengeance. The Puritans knew their Deuteronomy which required believers to 'avenge His glory' and to 'trample underfoot natural affections'.[48] Whatever the reasons, by 1780, massacre was so commonplace that it hardly registered. On taking Vincennes, Illinois, from the British during the Revolution, General George Rogers Clark could casually order six Ottawa innocently entering the town to be seized and 'Tomahawked in the face of the [British] garrison', helplessly watching from their conquered fort.[49]

In Australia, a Policy of Terror

In Australia, the French have the dubious privilege of carrying out the first massacre of Aboriginal people in Tasmania in 1772. The French explorer Marc-Joseph Marion du Fresne led an expedition of two ships from Mauritius in December 1771, the *Mascarin* and the *Marquis de Castries*, ostensibly to return home a Tahitian, Ahut toru, but in reality, to search for the 'Great South Land'. The two ships anchored at Marion Bay in southeast Tasmania in late February 1772 and, when they noticed some Tasmanian Aboriginal people, sent three longboats ashore, whose men were armed. Protocols were clearly broken on the beach, and when a Tasmanian Aboriginal man allegedly threw a stone at du Fresne, he was promptly shot dead. When the other Aboriginal people fled, the French followed them, shooting. Du Fresne's biographer, Edward Duyker, estimates that between six and ten people were shot dead.[50] Between 1795, when the first massacre was recorded by the British at the Hawkesbury River in New South Wales, to the end of 1830, nineteen massacres were recorded in New South Wales and thirty-two in Tasmania.[51] As the key strategy deployed by the colonial governors, either to suppress the Aboriginal people or to force them to surrender, they were remarkably successful. The majority of the perpetrators were agents of the state, serving British soldiers and police, magistrates and militia, or settlers acting under orders of the state.

In general, European occupying powers carried through policies of terror against Indigenous populations that resisted the occupier. Governor Philip of New South Wales endorsed the collective punishment of Aboriginal peoples for the transgressions of a few, calling for 'a universal terror' to prevent further incidents of violence.[52] A few years later, the same processes were brought over to Tasmania where Governor Arthur introduced a policy of terror to secure the colonists' future on the island.[53] These same methods were used wherever one people attempted to dominate and control another. Terror was usually, although not always, an instrument of the state. It is true that killings of Indigenous people were often undertaken by what might be called servants of the state – the military or militia – but farmers and pastoralists on the frontier also carried out killings, often without the formal knowledge of government authorities.

In Europe, Massacres, Sackings and Scorched Earth

In Europe, massacre has always been a distinctive trait of warfare. In periods of civil unrest, it is more pronounced, especially when religious and political differences come to the fore. They were widespread during the Wars of Religion in Europe in the sixteenth and seventeenth centuries and during the Thirty Years' War (1618–48), but they were also used by the military as a terror tactic against civilian populations in what have since become known as scorched-earth policies.[54] One of the more notorious examples is the French intervention in the Palatinate in 1688–9 during what is called the Nine Years' War between France and the Holy Roman Empire.[55] That strategy failed during the campaign in the Palatinate, but it was used again during the Revolutionary and Napoleonic Wars. The revolutionary Bertrand Barère defended Louis XIV's destruction of the Palatinate when calling for the suppression of rebels in the Vendée in 1794, but so too did Napoleon.[56] Napoleon used 'infernal columns' in Calabria in 1806, although on a reduced scale. Interestingly, there was such an international outcry about French atrocities in the Palatinate that it led to enormous hostility towards France, in part because of a mainly Dutch Protestant pamphlet literature directed against it.[57] There was no such outcry during the Revolutionary and Napoleonic Wars, however, either because the atrocities were not widely known about or publicized or because people had become indifferent to the devastation caused by the wars.

The French were obviously not alone in using this strategy. The British showed themselves to be just as ruthless as the French when it came to scorched-earth practices, which they used to good effect in Portugal, where Arthur Wellesley used the tactic in the winter of 1810 to 1811.[58] As the French advanced into Portugal, the British fell back, instituting a scorched-earth policy and forcing large numbers of people from their homes. They were obliged to live in makeshift refugee camps that had been set up around Lisbon. In this particular case, the British use of scorched earth was not accompanied by the massacre of civilian populations, but it nevertheless had devastating consequences for the civilian populations who got caught up in the strategy, especially as the French turned on the civilian population left behind to feed themselves. French 'foraging parties resorted to torture and murder as a matter of course,'[59] while the civilian population had little choice but to resist. According to one English witness who saw the devastation wrought by the French after they had retreated, they had 'burnt every village and town they went through, and murdered every peasant they could find'.[60]

The French used scorched earth as a strategy when the military believed it was required, but massacre was used much more frequently and was generally an extension of counterinsurgency and pacification operations. That assumes that there was a more-or-less organized resistance to the French occupation. Without wanting to go into a typology of massacre for the Revolutionary and Napoleonic Wars, it is worth underlining the extent to which it was a ubiquitous, constant feature. Massacres were committed, for example, when armed troops killed the wounded or prisoners in the aftermath of battle. This occurred after the siege of Jaffa in 1799 when Napoleon ordered around 4,000 prisoners to be shot or bayoneted to death, and after the battle of Aspern-Essling the reported burning alive of 3,000 wounded Austrian soldiers in a military hospital in the village of Ebersberg in 1809.[61] It also occurred during the retreat from Moscow when hundreds of Russian prisoners were killed: 300 at Viazma, 600 at Smolensk, and 1,200 were shot by Spanish and Portuguese contingents en route.[62]

Massacres were committed by French armies in retreat, sometimes out of revenge and sometimes to deprive enemy combatants of food and shelter. Three episodes in particular stand out during this period: Franconia in 1796, when the Revolutionary army retreated from Germany; Egypt in 1798, when Napoleon's army destroyed everything on its retreat from Palestine into Egypt;

and the retreat from Russia in 1812, when hundreds of villages and towns were destroyed. 'Under the ashes that were still hot', wrote one witness, 'and which the wind blew towards us, were the bodies of several soldiers or peasants. There were also slain children, and young girls massacred in the same place where they had been raped'.[63] It is impossible to know how many were killed during these episodes, but one can infer that when a village was razed, if its occupants had not already fled before the arrival of French troops and in any way resisted, then they too were killed.

Finally, massacres occurred as a consequence of the 'traditional' sacking of towns after a siege.[64] Some of the worst massacres during this period were committed after the storming of towns and include the French taking of Tarragona in Spain in June 1811, which may have resulted in the deaths of anywhere between 2,000 and 15,000 civilians, although the latter is possibly an exaggeration, or the British storming of the Spanish cities of Badajoz in 1811 and of siege and sack of San Sebastián in 1812. It is impossible to know how many civilians were killed during the storming of these two towns, but the figures are probably in the hundreds killed, rather than the thousands often asserted by historians.[65] Again, there is nothing new here. During the Thirty Years War, Albrecht von Wallenstein, commanding general of the armies of the Holy Roman Empire, ordered the execution of the survivors of the siege of Breitenberg in 1628. This too was a tactic designed to intimidate the other garrison into surrendering.

There is no room for doubt that massacres were widespread and deliberate: we have evidence from any number of quarters, including the perpetrators, the victims, and the military and political elite who ordered or witnessed the massacres. Napoleon wrote to General Junot in 1806, who was then operating in Italy, and told him to 'Have five or six villages burnt. Have about sixty people shot: set extremely severe examples … '.[66] When the order to massacre came from above, either from the commanding officer on the ground or from a higher authority in Paris, it was motivated by a desire on the part of the French military and political elite to either 'set an example' and thereby bring recalcitrant populations into line or to impose French administrative norms on those reluctant to embrace them.

That brings us to the question of just who were the perpetrators: Who committed the massacres? Massacres are, fundamentally, a masculine enterprise; the perpetrators are more often than not young men,[67] although there are rare instances in which women also take part in massacres and mass killings. In Spain and Calabria during the Napoleonic Wars, massacres were carried out by armed civilians, including women, against invading troops. In South Africa and North America there were occasions in which Indigenous Americans massacred colonists, although these were always far fewer in number than the massacre of Indigenous Americans. Massacres are often brutal but of short duration, aimed at either eliminating a group of people or intimidating the survivors. The 'survivors' were often the targets of a slower death, left wandering dazed, bereft, without housing or food, to perish, as were 10,000 Iroquois in North America from 1780 on, following George Washington's devastation of Iroquoia, and as happened to the Miamis of modern-day Indiana, after the US Army attacks on them in 1782.[68] Thus invisible to the perpetrators, they are the cadre that famously 'vanish' from existence, their graves unmarked, their existence unacknowledged. In wars, including frontier wars, massacres are usually organized by militias, soldiers or guerrillas. This was certainly the case for Europe and to an extent North America and is a hardly surprising given that the state armed its men on the path to conquest and colonization.

Generalizations about who committed the massacres and who ordered them are often easier to make than finding out details about the perpetrators, or indeed the victims. We have some inkling from memoirs and documents about who perpetrators were,[69] but nothing like the details provided for twentieth-century massacres. It is not so much that, for our period, people felt the need to conceal their intentions or even their role in the massacres but that often orders were verbal. For instance, during the build-up to the Muscogee War of 1813–14, notifications coming to Andrew Jackson from his subordinates make it clear that he had ordered them to find a pretext for swooping down on the Muscogee, even though there is no direct order from him to do so on record.[70] There are a few instances of written orders from French commanders, even Napoleon himself, telling their men to 'set an example' but more often than not, massacres were conducted as a form of reprisal against local populations for killing or harassing invading troops. That is, decisions to kill were made on the ground. On the other hand, troops could go on the rampage and ignore their commanders, as was sometimes the case after a siege was broken. This happened in Spain among both British and French troops. But in regions where the presence of the state was not particularly evident, and where local groups took over the defences of their property, local militia could assemble for the purpose of 'punitive' expeditions.

Local grievances can often begin the process towards massacre, but they invariably require a higher authority either to approve or to turn a blind eye to the killings.[71] This was certainly the case for the South African and North American colonial frontiers, but similar scenarios occurred in other theatres, even if, once again, the circumstances surrounding local conditions can vary. In the case of the Khoisan people on the Eastern Cape frontier of South Africa, for example, Dutch settlers who sent out raiding parties to kill Khoisan often did so without the knowledge of the Cape government, but with the complicit approval of the local Dutch communities.[72] Hundreds of unofficial sorties were organized by individual trekboers along the Eastern Cape frontier during the course of the eighteenth century. The Dutch authorities clearly disapproved of colonists taking the law into their own hands, and tried to curb, and in some cases punish, trekboer excesses against the Khoisan. In general, however, it was in the interests of the Dutch authorities to simply overlook the excesses of the commandos.

In North America, on the other hand, the complicity of the US government is evident. It often countenanced massacre and left its perpetrators unprosecuted. Local militias militias were often used as a convenient scapegoat. It is instructive in this regard to compare the behaviour of the British colonial regime and the incipient US government when dealing with illegal settlers. The British authorities tended to be forceful. As early as 1743, for example, settlers were illegally trying to set up a village near present-day Thompsontown, in western Pennsylvania, deep in Iroquoian territory. The Crown's deputy Indian agent in the region, George Croghan, acting under the authority of the Crown's lead Indian Agent, Sir William Johnson, made a point of arresting the squatters and burning their cabins to the ground, in compliance with a 1721 order of the Crown's governor of

Pennsylvania. Croghan quipped that, if he had not done this, then the Six Nations certainly would have. Even in such a settler-remote area as western Pennsylvania, the Crown's agent stationed near Fort Pitt was still entirely able to enforce a gubernatorial order issuing from Philadelphia on the Atlantic coast – over 500 kilometres away – to corral and control the settlers in remote Thompsonville.[73] There are other examples of colonial governors removing 'squatters' from land that Crown treaties had reserved for Indigenous Americans before the American Revolution. At a time when British troops were stretched thin by the worldwide conflict with France, British authorities were still able to remove a number of illegal squatter settlements in accord with the Treaty of Easton, concluded in 1758 during the Seven Years' War between the British and the chiefs of thirteen Indigenous American nations.[74] When more squatting attempts materialized in 1763, the colonial Governor of Pennsylvania ordered them summarily destroyed, with the illegals again forced back behind colonial lines.[75] At the end of the war, the British Crown issued the Proclamation of 1763, which prohibited settlers from gaining access to lands beyond the Appalachians.[76] It is true that the British removal of the squatters helped fuel the resentment in the backwoods that eventually supported the Revolution in those localities. However, the salient point here is that, despite a genuine lack of finances and personnel, as well as a growing lack of colonial authority beyond coastal areas, British troops successfully dislodged fractious and well-armed settlers on a number of occasions prior to the Revolution.

Soon after the United States was established, the federal government acted exactly as had the Crown with the same success, sending in troops to drag the squatters out of restricted areas, despite the fact that America had no standing army and had been bankrupted by the Revolution. For instance, on 1 June 1785, then-Colonel Josiah Harmar took on an illegal militia, informing the Secretary of War that, per instructions from the Commissioners of Indian Affairs, he had burnt down squatter cabins and destroyed settler crops, forcing the squatters 110 kilometres east of Fort McIntosh, back into US territory.[77] By the same token, when Shays' Rebellion broke out in 1786, the Whiskey Revolt surged in 1794 and Fries' Rebellion arose in 1799, all three tax revolts raised by settler militias were summarily and expeditiously put down by the official US Army, with the assistance of loyal militias. In none of these three militia challenges, two occurring in backcountry, was the federal government too remote from the trouble or too impotent to control the situation.

Clearly, the conventional characterization of the federal government as helpless in the face of unruly militias simply does not wash. In fact, the British and US governments in this period clearly not only could but also did move swiftly and decisively to end disorderly behaviour, regardless of the militias' geographical point of origin or popularity with the public. This leads, first, to the conclusion that settler militias were not as uncontrollable as often thought, so that massacres of Indigenous peoples must have been tacitly countenanced and even quietly intended by the governments. Second, we should distinguish between 'loyal' militias and 'mercenary' militias in assessing militia massacres. (A 'loyal' militia was a group of armed civilians who primarily fought to defend their own community while a 'mercenary' militia fought for money and personal gain.) In both regards, we notice that militia actions conferred both cover and aid on the central government. Not only did militias provide the government with plausible deniability when necessary, but they also simultaneously bolstered imperial aims of expansion.

Atrocities on the Frontier

Massacres were often accompanied by atrocities committed on the body – rape and/or mutilation of the body, both before and after death. This varied from one massacre to the next depending on the circumstances and the men involved in the killing. Atrocities could be carried out by both Europeans and Indigenous peoples as they fought against colonization. In South Africa, North America, Europe and Australia mutilation occurred on both sides of the divide. In Tasmania in the 1820s, and in Bathurst, New South Wales, in 1824, Aboriginal men killed and mutilated European men in reprisal for their kidnapping and raping Aboriginal women. Rape was, however, outlawed by Indigenous Americans, as was frequently recognized by settlers.[78]

On one level, atrocities that included mutilation and the dismembered body can be interpreted as a public, performative act in which the body serves as a kind of stage on which pain and suffering is inflicted. The victim thus becomes part of a perverse morality play, in which the mutilated body serves as a cautionary signifier to others who might be contemplating revolt or resistance, or indeed who dare to trespass on land that is not theirs. In South Africa, the San sometimes tortured and mutilated the bodies of their European victims. In Spain during the Napoleonic Wars, the mutilated body served as a warning to those who collaborated with the French, but it was also used by the Spanish as a warning to those who opposed the guerrillas.

When killers mutilate the body of their victims, either before or after the killing takes place, the type of mutilation carried out can often contain a symbolic dimension. Or at least that is what Natalie Zemon Davis argued for the early modern period in European history, when mutilation often involved religious symbolism. In the instances she was talking about, which occurred during the French Wars of Religion, the removal of an offending body part – a hand, the tongue – was seen as a symbolic purging of the (social) body.[79] Mutilation could also be a means of affirming the killers' identity upon the victims' bodies in which they transgress their own cultural taboos. 'It is another means of destroying the victims before killing them' but it could also mean that the killers gained pleasure from the act.[80]

In Europe, one can find the same latent symbolic value in mutilation for the period under discussion here. In Calabria, insurgents crucified and tortured their victims in ways that can only be interpreted as religious.[81] In Spain, the French profanation of the bodies of condemned insurgents contained a religious symbolism that the local populations would very much have understood. The dismemberment of the body and its display near the site of the killing would have indicated, in a country where the people were deeply religious and where the sanctity of burial and of the tomb were important, that the victim was obliged to renounce any hope of resurrection. The dismemberment of the body was the equivalent of damning someone to the eternal fires of hell. Similarly, in southern Italy, where Calabrians believed that death by suffocation prevented the soul from reaching paradise, French generals were ordered to hang rather than shoot banditti to impress the local population.[82] The French were deliberately using these techniques in the vain hope that they would dissuade local populations from resisting, while local and Indigenous people mutilated their victims as a warning of what to expect if they persisted in staying on their land. To put it another way, what we would now consider to be extreme acts of violence could still contain within them symbolism, sometimes religious, in much the same way as they did during the seventeenth-century Wars of Religion.

The mutilation of bodies also sometimes culminated in scenes of ritual anthropophagy. This was not a new phenomenon. Accusations of cannibalism were thrown about by both sides during the French Revolutionary and Napoleonic Wars; it was a way of dehumanizing the Other and lent urgency to the desire to eliminate the enemy. Accusations of cannibalism had been directed at Indigenous Americans since the time of Columbus, but it was an accusation also used in Europe during the Wars of Religion. The French often accused the Italians of cannibalism during the sixteenth century and continued to do so during the Revolutionary and Napoleonic Wars. It was all part of a process of demonizing the enemy Other, a process facilitated by the enormous cultural chasms that existed between Europeans and the colonized. It is also possible that certain cultural practices were misinterpreted – the Calabrese, for example, were in the habit of licking the blood off the blade of their knives once they had killed their victims – and used to reinforce mistaken notions of anthropophagy.[83]

Leading into and during the American Revolution, Indigenous Americans were regularly mutilated by soldiers and militiamen. In 1770, for instance, American soldiers at Fort Randolf, West Virginia, skinned alive their ally, Chief Colesqua (Shawnee), falsely blaming him for the death of an officer.[84] During the Americans' 1779 brutal invasion of Iroquoia, soldiers mounted hunting parties that went out specifically to skin battle-fallen Indigenous Americans from the hips to the ankles, to make new boots and the leggings commonly called 'leather-stockings'.[85] Treating Indigenous skin like cow, buffalo or bear hides was intended to act out the settler dictum that 'to kill an Indian, was the same as killing a bear or buffalo'.[86] That is, Indigenous peoples were animals that could be skinned, not human beings who felt love, anxiety

Figure 5 *Francisco de Goya y Lucientes: Plate 39 from 'The Disasters of War' (Los Desastres de La Guerra): 'An heroic feat! With dead men!' (Grande hazaña! Con muertos!). Etching, lavis and drypoint, 1810 (published 1863):* https://www.metmuseum.org/art/collection/search/381365.

or fear. It explains why at the end of the Revolution, the military order was found written on trees pealed of their bark: 'No quarters to be given to an Indian, whether man, woman, or child.'[87] One simply did not hesitate to kill dangerous animals of any age.

This brings us to the question of scalping on the American frontier, which seems to have been far more commonplace among Europeans than among American Indians. We touched on this topic in the previous chapter from an Indigenous perspective, but it had an entirely different meaning and application among European settlers. From the late seventeenth century on, there appears to have been a 'sustained commerce in scalps' among settlers.[88] In 1688, the French in Canada offered bounties not only for Indigenous 'enemies' but also for European 'enemies'. Between 1698 and 1700, the French paid Indigenous Americans fifty écus for each enemy scalp, while in 1704, the

British in Massachusetts were offering £15 for the scalp of an Indigenous male over the age of twelve, quickly raising the amount until, by 1724, the bounty was £100. These bounties continued throughout and after the Seven Years' War.[89] Between 1675 and 1760, there were sixty-nine government-issued scalp bounties in the American colonies.[90]

Scalp bounties increased during the American Revolutionary War, as both the British and the Revolutionaries offered sizeable payments.[91] On the British side were people like 'The Famous Hair Buyer General, Henry Hamilton, Esq. Lieut. Governor of Detroit', as George Rogers Clark styled him in a letter to Patrick Henry in 1779.[92] On the Revolutionary side were American bounties, which militiamen never lost sight of, in one recorded instance digging up a cemetery to scalp the freshest of the corpses, thus collecting sixty-four Shawnee scalps for the bounty.[93] A cottage industry in murder broke out, with racially motivated killers enriching themselves. One hero of the American Revolutionary War, whose story continued to charm settlers well into the nineteenth century, was Lewis Wetzel, who excelled at 'stalking and hunting Indians as he would wild animals'.[94] Wetzel was hardly the only such example, but just one of the most prolific, who proudly claimed a scalp count of twenty-seven, although 'it is likely that the number of his victims was considerably higher'.[95]

We can see a number of interrelated factors that, if not precursors to massacre are necessary prerequisites, such as a rhetoric calling for the extermination or the removal of Indigenous populations, the dehumanization of the Other, and an ideology that was either political or economic and that either portrayed Indigenous peoples as inferior or as dangerous. Those preconditions facilitated massacres, but do not mean that they inevitably followed. For that to happen, there had to have been a willingness of the part of the perpetrator – settlers, militias, or troops – to kill or enslave those they feared, hated or considered an impediment to obtaining their own economic objectives. Thus in South Africa, cattle theft went hand in hand with the massacre of Khoikhoi and Khoisan, while in North America and in Australia, massacres were one way of clearing the land of its original inhabitants. As we saw with the massacre of the Pequot, a desire to control the natural resources of New England played a crucial role. Moreover, in South Africa and North

America, Indigenous populations were often seen as potential slaves, or if not exactly as slaves, then as subjugated labourers. The rhetoric of race and difference may have facilitated behaviours and led to justifications for the killing, but at heart this was a struggle over the conquest and possession of land. However, colonization, massacre and the question of coveted lands did not always go together. In Europe during the Revolutionary and Napoleonic Wars, in Ireland and in the Caribbean, it was more a question of controlling territories by obliging their populations to submit to imperial rule. To do that, sometimes a policy of scorched earth was practised, used in other parts of the world as well but perhaps not as systematically as in Europe. In these instances, violence, politics, religion and ideology came into play.

The reasons for massacre then were complex and varied but we should now have a broad understanding of the mechanism of massacre on the frontier, and who some of the perpetrators were. The following four chapters look in detail at the use of massacre and violence in the regions of the world under study. We begin with France because Europe in some respects serves as a template for massacre. It has been practised there by the colonizer for many more centuries, and as a method of conquest and control had been exported to the Caribbean and the Americas as early as the beginning of the sixteenth century. Europe too provides us with a sort of legal framework for the killing of those deemed outside of the normal laws of war.

5

Massacre, the State and the Revolutionary and Napoleonic Wars

The French Napoleonic Empire usually draws comparisons not to that of a nineteenth-century extra-European colonial empire but with the Roman and especially the Carolingian model. Most of the literature dealing with the 'colonial enterprise' during this period looks to the French invasion of Egypt, the attempts to re-establish control over their colonies in the Caribbean, or to the Louisiana Purchase. For the purposes of this study, however, we contend that French territorial expansion during the Revolutionary and Napoleonic Wars within Europe, and the consequent systems of governance and exploitation put in place over annexed territories, bears comparison with colonial experiences elsewhere.[1] This includes the notion of violence within European frontiers, even when taking care 'not to read back into the *ancien régime* the commonplaces of nineteenth-century European imperialism'.[2] One of the reasons for the reticence by scholars of the Napoleonic Empire to use the term 'colonial' is because it is commonly used to denote conquest outside of Europe.[3] Admittedly, there are some historians of the empire who do treat France as a colonizing power. If they do not openly refer to French colonial rule, implying exploitation rather than governance, then they come close to it by referring to neo-colonial rule.[4] Moreover, there are close structural similarities between French colonialism overseas and on the European continent, as well as between other colonial regimes. The assertion then is that the French conquest, domination and integration of large swathes of European land within a larger French Empire should be seen as a 'colonial enterprise' undertaken over a twenty-year period, between 1793 and 1813.

The French Empire was first and foremost a territorial project; the French occupied the Continent not to settle the land but to exploit the resources under their control, that is, to extract men and money to supply the imperial force known as the Grande Armée. Conquest thus fuelled conquest. However, the Empire was also a modernizing, ideological project from which hardly anyone in Europe was exempt. The French had in effect brought with them new ideals and a reforming agenda that they attempted to impose on the conquered peoples of Europe. Even when the French gave up on the vague idea of fostering revolution abroad very early into the Revolutionary Wars, the reforms they introduced challenged ordinary Europeans' position in society and their relations with their social superiors.

As the Empire expanded, the French imposed what became known as the Napoleonic Code, a set of laws that included commercial, civil and criminal codes. It was the great reforming principle, an attempt to fuse disparate lands and peoples through unifying laws. The reforming agenda that followed the French was more about Napoleon modernizing old systems in order better to exploit them, although one should also consider the fact that thousands of 'notables', the elite of imperial and European society, believed in the Empire and the 'civilizing project' that went with it. Those who resisted 'Napoleonic civilization' – especially people in what could be described as the frontiers of Europe, namely the Tyrol, Calabria and parts of Spain – bore the brunt of the Empire's mechanisms of conformity: military government, military tribunals, mobile columns, summary executions and massacres. At the same time, the French were largely secular and rejected the religious principles that had for centuries framed people and the societies in which they had lived. They brought with them a disrespect for the Church and a belief in rational thought that the religious faithful found offensive. And as we have seen, the French too brought with them a disdain for the peoples they conquered, whom they considered to be culturally if not racially inferior.

Violence as a State Response

Military historians of the French Revolutionary and Napoleonic Wars have usually been preoccupied by the changes taking place in warfare so that their focus has been on major campaigns, battles and theorists such as Carl von Clausewitz and Gerhard von Scharnhorst. Although this has certainly begun to change over the last ten years or so, for a long time there had been a lack of reflection on non-conventional warfare, and in particular warfare waged against resisting or recalcitrant civilian populations. In certain regions of Europe, what set the wars apart from traditional confrontations between regular standing armies was the degree to which the people were involved in resisting French incursions. The studies that do exist focus on the origins of guerrilla warfare in particular regions of Europe under French domination, regions like the Tyrol, Calabria and parts of Spain. They largely ignore the complexities of occupying armies interacting with civilian populations, which could range from intermarriage to murder and pillage on a massive scale. As we have seen, one of the methods used by the French to maintain their presence in the conquered regions of Europe was to put down with merciless energy armed resistance to their presence, resulting in the massacre of civilian populations.[5] This is the most obvious difference between conventional and non-conventional warfare. If the former was the political extension of diplomacy to secure limited gains, the latter was the total victory over an enemy considered 'illegitimate' because of the resistance methods used – raiding and irregular warfare.[6] This dynamic of violence was repeated wherever Europeans attempted to expand their empires at the cost of the local inhabitants.

In the course of this colonial enterprise, massacre was used as an instrument of the state, as part of a military and political process of incorporating non-French territories into the expanding French Empire, which was territorially similar in extent to that of Charlemagne. It was, in other words, a conscious policy on the part of French military and political figures at the highest levels, and included such men as Generals Adam Philippe, Comte de Custine, André Masséna, Joachim Murat, Jean-de-Dieu Soult, the Minister of War, Lazare Carnot, and Napoleon himself. The Empire was marked by a determination from the top-down to eliminate resistance to French rule. The letters of Napoleon are replete with examples in which he instructs his subordinates to strike hard against nascent revolts, to show no mercy against civilian populations and to kill to set an example.[7] It was, however, often done under the guise of humanitarianism, or a distorted view of the national character of the occupied peoples in question – and there were plenty of instances in which force was needed to put down insurrections. Under these circumstances, as with the situation in settler colonial societies, military authorities soon ceased making any distinction between combatants and non-combatants, especially when guerrilla-style resistance followed, so that entire populations were targeted.[8] In this, one might argue, the French were no different to any other imperial enterprise.

Historians generally believe that the early modern period resulted in more stable, centralized and increasingly bureaucratic states, which had an impact on the ways in which violence was regulated.[9] The state thus became the arbiter of 'legitimate' force, unlike the medieval period, where monarchies tried but often failed to impose force, and everything else became 'illegitimate'. And as the state 'modernized', expanded and became more stable, it gained increasing control over illegitimate forms of violence, compelling its subjects and citizens to conform, in the process eliminating non-state actors that might threaten the state's existence or stability. This is a traditional narrative that many scholars will be familiar with – violence declined in Europe in the course of the early modern era, and this had much to do with the state assuming a 'legitimate monopoly of power' and in the process compelling its subjects to become more disciplined, and more pliant. The state's external coercion, following Norbert Elias' idea of the 'civilizing process', gave way to self-discipline as these norms were internalized.

The widely held view that violence diminished and declined as history entered the modern era has been challenged, along with the Western-centric, state-centred modernization narrative, where the state first tamed violence within – by disarming and punishing its subjects and then waging war on its enemies – and then tamed violence without by inhabiting and policing the international order by stamping out piracy and slavery.[10] It was never that simple; it was never only about the state imposing its authority.[11] The monarchical, pre-modern, bureaucratic state was required to collaborate with social elites to function. But the point to be taken away here is that, as we have seen, the state was also one of the major vectors of violence in the eighteenth century. One could argue that it had always been and that it would play a much more significant role as vector of violence in the nineteenth and especially the twentieth centuries, but the tools and mechanism developed in the eighteenth century were the antecedents of what was to follow.

There are two intellectual developments in particular that we should look at to understand the evolution of military practice in the second half of the eighteenth century, one born of military 'small war' theory, the other stemming from international law. The first is the development of thinking around 'small wars' in the eighteenth century, something that has until recently remained relatively understudied.[12] There was a surge in interest in small-war tactics in mid-eighteenth-century Europe, but not as we might think of it, as a means of better combatting non-conventional or irregular troops, but as way of utilizing smaller military units within conventional armies. These light units were often referred to as 'free corps'. The 'partisan' was the leader of these light military units of conventional armies, which were closely associated with the collection of forage and booty.[13] In the eighteenth century, the word partisan came to embody the type of small war that Europe's military elites could understand. The Prussian military theorist Carl von Clausewitz, who was one of the major writers on the topic, was probably aware of the use by Washington during the America Revolution of irregular troops or militias to harass and defeat the British and Indigenous Americans.[14] On the other hand, he was certainly aware of the people's uprisings in the Vendée, Spain and Tyrol. They served as an inspiration to a wished for uprising among the German peoples which never really eventuated.

It was during the latter stages of the Napoleonic Wars, and in particular during the Spanish uprising against the French (1808–13), that the 'partisan' or 'guerrilla' metamorphosed into the patriotic 'freedom fighter'. As a result of the Dos de Mayo uprising in Madrid against the Napoleonic coup to seize the Spanish throne in May 1808, the term 'guerrilla' became synonymous with a new type of warfare, and with a new type of fighter. We will have to wait, however, until the middle of the nineteenth century for formal military writings on the lessons to be drawn from imperial wars. Before that, there does not appear to have been all that much reflection among eighteenth-century military theorists about how to combat organized crime bands or groups of insurgents who fought against the state.[15]

For that we have to look to the long history of the international laws of war in the seventeenth and eighteenth centuries. A number of legal-philosophical works over that period attempted to distinguish between what was considered 'legitimate' violence and who were the legitimate targets of that violence. One of the most prominent and influential thinkers in this space was the Swiss writer Emer de Vattel. In 1758, he published *Droits des Gens*, translated into English a couple of years later as *The Law of Nations*. It was possibly the most widely read book on international law in the eighteenth century, its influence extending well into the nineteenth century.[16] The code of conduct called the law of nations aimed at limiting the scope and indeed the frequency of war, as well as preventing wartime atrocities and prohibiting the mistreatment of prisoners of war. This work, along with those of other Enlightenment thinkers, has led historians like David Bell to argue that warfare in the eighteenth century was more contained and more civilized than what followed.[17]

It was not, but it is worth highlighting that Vattel made two important exceptions to the code of conduct on the laws of war. The first was that nations did not need to abide by the laws of war if their opponents failed to do so. Those who did not conform to the laws of war, in the words of the abbé Gabriel de Mably, 'cease to be human'.[18] This rule was, unsurprisingly, applied by the French to their opponents, the Spanish and the English in particular, during the early years of the Revolutionary Wars. The second exception was particularly relevant to the treatment of non-combatants. As we have just seen, by calling opponents 'rebels', 'brigands', 'bandits' or *hors la loi* (outlaws), the state introduced a punitive register that put enemies outside of the law, so that they could be punished using exemplary measures. Vattel, writing about what constitutes an enemy of the state, situated rebels within what he called 'shapeless and illegitimate war, more correctly called brigandage'. He concluded that a nation that was attacked by enemies of that kind was 'not obliged to observe towards them the rules prescribed in formal wars; it can treat them as brigands'.[19] Since this kind of warfare was deemed illegal, it was in keeping with international norms to summarily execute them. The brigand was the eighteenth-century equivalent of the 'savage' and 'barbarian'.[20] We can thus see that the rules of war as outlined by the law of nations contained within it the seeds of its own demise, or at least a loophole which allowed all sorts of atrocities to be committed and justified on behalf of the state. In the law of nations, one could thus already find injunctions to 'destroy' those who violated the laws of nature, thereby making themselves 'enemies of the human race'.[21]

One of the characteristics of the modern state then is that an individual or a group that challenges it can be dubbed an enemy through the use of terms like 'bandit' or 'rebel' or 'partisan', 'guerrilla' and 'terrorist'. The wars Indigenous and local peoples might lead against an oppressive, expansionist state – often dubbed 'small wars', a type of violence found in many parts of the world – were never considered legitimate and everything was done to portray them and the way in which they conducted the war as 'savage' and 'barbarous'. The violence they carried out was a crime or an atrocity. This rhetoric is shaped by assumptions that in the West the state and its elites were civilized and that those who resisted them were not. Not only did this occur within Europe but once Europeans started to conquer and colonize the rest of the world, they began to export their own forms of violence to use on the peoples they colonized.

The hostility towards those perceived to be counter-revolutionary is not quite enough to explain why they were eradicated with such vigour during the French civil war, or indeed during the Revolutionary and Napoleonic Wars. Counter-revolutionaries were central to the revolutionary imaginary. General discourses of extermination underpinned the rhetoric of the revolutionary and soon came to incorporate all groups that opposed their radical reformist agenda, whether domestic or foreign.[22] There were two fronts, one internal, one external, as war and terror became interconnected in revolutionary discourse.[23] No ethical-moral or indeed political position against violence was ever expressed by any revolutionary politician, so that all opponents of the regime became the legitimate targets of revolutionary violence.

There is nevertheless a distinction to be made between what might be called the first and second phases of occupation and assimilation, which could be applied to most European colonial conquests.[24] The first phase usually involved the conqueror laying claim to a geographical space that was not theirs to claim. As a direct consequence of the nature of revolutionary warfare, which entailed living off the land, economic as well as physical depredations, such as rape, often accompanied the official looting. Harsh demands were placed upon locals, both urban and rural, to feed the army.[25] Revolts almost invariably followed, and it often took years to entirely control a geographical space, politically and militarily. That phase could last anywhere between several months and several years, depending on the vagaries of war. The Austrian Netherlands was quickly overrun in 1792, but it was not annexed until 1795. Control of northern Italy was fought over between 1794 and 1800, when it was finally brought into the French orbit.

Setting an Example: The Politics of Elimination

During the first phase of occupation, when French troops were in the process of assimilating a territory into their empire, 'examples' were made of recalcitrant villages and towns, examples that are to be found in every region invaded by the French. It was a conscious policy of terror meant to dissuade other people from resisting the French occupation, a policy that was at times effective.[26] If anti-French revolts were initially reactions to military depredations, once French rule was established, there was often a backlash against the two aspects of the centralizing state that occupied peoples found most objectionable: taxation and conscription.[27] In the latter context, resistance to conscription within the Empire was also a rejection of the French as colonizer, as well as a rejection of the social and cultural reform the Empire was offering.[28] There was also, naturally, resistance to the continued requisition of grain and livestock. The revolts that occurred during this second phase of conquest, when the initial military conquest was complete and the French state began to establish itself, were generally a popular response to what people considered to be inordinate and unreasonable demands made by the state. In some regions, Special Tribunals were set up to deal with small groups of 'bandits', but when whole regions rose up, as was sometimes the case, then those who opposed the centralizing state became the object of, for want of a better term, the politics of elimination. This occurred when Belgium was annexed in 1795, and again in October 1798 when a 'Peasants War' erupted, triggered by the imposition of conscription – known as the Jourdan Law – on a people who had never experienced it before.[29] On that occasion, in December 1798, the town of Hasselt was taken by French troops and more than 1,000 people are reported to have been massacred.[30] In Switzerland in 1798, priest-led Catholic peasants rose up in revolt against French annexation and the creation of the Helvetic Republic. They were massacred. In Italy in 1799, there were massive, pan-peninsular revolts that coincided with French reverses during the war of the Second Coalition.[31] They were somewhat more successful than their northern European counterparts. The Sanfedisti, a 17,000-strong peasant army of the Holy Faith led by Cardinal Ruffo, temporarily drove the French from southern Italy and overthrew the short-lived Parthenopean Republic.

In 1800, Napoleon wrote to General Brune, commander of the Army of the West, exhorting him to 'not spare the municipalities that behave badly. Burn some small holdings and some big villages in the Morbihan, and start making some examples'. A little further on he added, 'It is only by making the war terrible that the inhabitants themselves will unite against the brigands and will finally feel that their apathy is fatal to them.'[32] In July 1806, Napoleon directed his brother Joseph, King of Naples, 'to execute at least 600 rebels' and to 'pillage five or six of the villages that have behaved the worst'.[33] Joseph carried out the order, hanging and shooting 600 'brigands' over an eight-day period.[34] That same year, Napoleon wrote to General Junot to hurry off to Parma, annexed to France in 1801, to put down some riots there. 'It is not with words that one maintains peace in Italy. Do as I did in Binasco (a town in Italy which he sacked in 1796): a large village should be burned. Have a dozen rebels shot.'[35] Binasco was cited by Napoleon on more than one occasion and came to represent a kind of model for dealing with insurgent populations and for imposing French rule.[36] Massacres were, therefore, not only responses to local acts of 'brigandage', they were both political and strategic forms of subjugation, one that had been practised in France during the Revolution.

If fear was used as an instrument of political subjugation, it was also a means of wiping the slate clean so that reforms could be introduced, and the state modernized. We get an inkling of this thinking in Napoleon when he wrote to his brother Joseph, impatient to see the people rise in revolt. 'As long as you have not made an example, you will not be master [of the situation]. Every conquered people needs a revolt. I would look upon a revolt in Naples as a father of a family looks upon smallpox visiting his children. As long as it does not weaken the patient too much, it is a salutary crisis.'[37] The premise was reiterated in other letters to Joseph: 'In a conquered country, kindness is not humaneness.'[38] The fact that people were not prepared to accept French rule, or indeed the spirit of their rule, never occurred to Napoleon or indeed the French occupiers.

When massacres occurred, they were almost never hidden. In fact, it is surprising how openly French officers spoke about it later in their memoirs; there was no shame or dishonour attached to killing civilians who were considered beyond redemption. Massacres were, after all, a public exercise designed to instil fear. They were meant to be talked about among the wider community and were meant to serve as examples so that local populations would more passively submit to French rule. Killing those who resisted was a violent and public confirmation that France was the superior and stronger force. There were, however, occasional attempts to downplay the extent of the killing in the press back home in France and by extension in the wider empire.[39] We can offer four examples, one in Syria, two in Spain and one in Germany.[40]

The first notable example is the massacre of prisoners after the siege of Jaffa in what was then known as Syria. Napoleon was obliged to deny that it had ever occurred and attempted to counteract the rumours that were going around in the French public by promoting an image of himself as a clement ruler. Jacques Miot, one of those who helped carry out the massacre, published his memoirs on the expedition to Egypt in 1804, but Napoleon was supposed to have been so upset with some of the sections on Jaffa that Miot was told to delete the offending items. They only appeared for the first time in an expanded edition in 1814 after the first fall of Napoleon. In this later edition, one can read that as he put pen to paper and started to recall what he had witnessed at Jaffa, his hand began to tremble. This was more than literary flourish designed to warn the reader of what was about to come, but a sign of the trauma Miot must have suffered as a result of the horrors he had witnessed.[41] The important point here is that Napoleon was more concerned about his reputation than he was about having ordered the killing of prisoners of war.

The number of deaths resulting from the insurrection of the Dos de Mayo in May 1808 when the people of Madrid rose up against the French occupation is difficult to determine. We know that somewhere between 150 and 200 French soldiers were killed by Madrileños, and that the likely number of Spanish dead was probably around 1,000.[42] The French ran through the streets killing anyone they found armed. Women and children were supposedly spared on this occasion.[43] At first, the official French newspaper the *Moniteur universel* reported 'several thousand of the country's worst subjects' killed during the repression, but later, to scotch any rumours about the extent of the savagery employed, the newspaper published an article in which it stated that those who had been killed were 'all rebel insurgents and common people who had rioted; not one peaceful man died, and the loss of Spaniards is not as great as it had been previously thought'.[44]

The second example from Spain is the French storming of Tarragona in June 1811, which resulted in the deaths of thousands of civilians,[45] something that was downplayed if not denied by the French press. *Le Journal de Paris*, for example, published a letter from General Louis-Alexandre Berthier on the siege in which he admitted that the troops were driven mad by a desire for revenge but that their officers held them in check.[46] He nevertheless admitted to the massacre of 4,000 people, which one can assume was probably far less than the number of people actually killed.

Finally, on 6 November 1806, French troops under the command of Marshal Bernadotte attacked the Hanseatic city of Lübeck, a neutral city, where Blücher's Prussian corps had found refuge after the defeat at Jena-Auerstädt, and where they endeavoured to make a stand. When Bernadotte's troops entered the town, 'a thousand horrors' were committed on the local population for three days and nights. All the female inmates of a lunatic asylum were reportedly raped.[47] We have two witnesses from the French side written many years later – both very brief accounts – plus an anonymous contemporaneous pamphlet that attempted to bring the massacre to the public's attention.[48] The pamphlet, printed in Leipzig and Amsterdam, went through two editions and was translated into German. Fouché intervened, confiscating the copies and breaking the presses it was printed on.[49]

Three massacres occurred in urban environments, involved large numbers of civilians, exceeded what might have been considered the 'normal' rules of eighteenth-century warfare, but more importantly became known to the greater public in France, a public already weary of the continuous wars. There was then an obvious desire to hide particular massacres from the general public. In the case of Lübeck, it was nominally a neutral city, and the massacre was therefore a violation of international law. The text referring to the massacre at Lübeck was banned not so much for the details of the atrocity itself but because it impugned the public image of the French imperial army. This was not exactly a turning point, but the beginnings of an awareness that atrocities were not always going to be blithely accepted by the public at home.

Atrocities and the Dehumanization of the European Other

Given the number of massacres carried out by the invading French armies, attempts to hide or to moderate reports surrounding what might be considered particularly egregious examples were nevertheless rare. Generally speaking, contemporaries legitimized the brutal repression and atrocities that occurred in the name of civilization and Enlightenment. The French did so generally by marginalizing and dehumanizing civilian populations by excluding them from normal patterns of social interaction. The technique of dehumanizing the enemy is a universal precondition of mass violence, atrocity and massacre, as can be seen in any number of conflicts, both recent and past. One need only note, for example, the tendency for Catholics to dehumanize Protestants during the Wars of Religion, for Nazis to dehumanize Jews or for Hutus to dehumanize Tutsis. As well, although there is no space to develop this theme at any great length here, atrocities committed during the massacres usually, but not always, had some structure to it. That is, the mutilation of bodies was a ritualistic part of the killing process, a means of further humiliating and debasing the enemy, however defined. There are even reports of cannibalism, both real and performed, generally involving the French and their allies as victims.[50] In Padua in 1796, for example, two Italian Jacobins became the victim of the mob and were burnt; pieces of their charred flesh were purportedly cut off and passed around the crowd, including to children.[51] A similar fate greeted Italian Jacobins in Trani in southern Italy, then part of the Kingdom of Naples.[52] They were massacred in the prisons on Easter Monday in 1799, and their corpses were mutilated and dragged through the streets. According to some reports their livers were then sold for meat.

It is difficult to know whether reports of these acts are true, or whether they are to be understood within the context of popular folk memory, but there is little doubt that collective acts of violence were widespread in particular regions of Europe during this time. Let us ponder here two other aspects to these wars: the manner in which the French responded to violent resistance and the manner in which they were depicted by hostile propaganda. In Spain, the French quickly installed exceptional military tribunals in the wake of the occupation to deal with armed resistance among the civilian population. The death penalty was often imposed, with a preference given to hanging, as well as the dismemberment of the body, which was then exposed in public on either trees or gallows near where the victim had once lived. There was not much enlightenment here, even if in Spain the garrotte was considered to be a relatively 'benign', or at least a more humane form of punishment than public hanging, which was thought of as a throwback to the days when torture and the gallows were used by the Spanish Bourbons.[53] More than that, however, the French profanation of the bodies of the condemned contained a religious symbolism that the local populations would very much have understood; through dismemberment, the victim was forced to abandon any hope of resurrection and an eternal life. One finds here a correlation between religiosity and violence. That is, resistance appears to have been strongest in those regions where religious sentiment was strongest, whether Catholicism in Europe or Islam in Egypt and Syria.

Ideology and the Cleansing Force of Fire

In Chapter 4, we saw how rhetoric was used to create differences between those included and those excluded from the revolutionary family, and how excesses in language may have ultimately led to acts of violence. Despite the rhetoric, the use of massacre to suppress recalcitrant populations was hardly a new development and was in effect strikingly similar to the French state's use of massacre as a political and military tool during the *ancien régime* when it was used to enforce obedience from rebellious lower orders.[54] At various periods of European history the use of force by the monarchical state to quell peasant unrest or resistance to the presence of the military was considered entirely acceptable from a political and a military perspective, even if the excesses which the military were sometimes guilty of shocked French and European sensibilities.[55] There was, however, one important distinction between massacres that occurred before and after the Revolution: state violence during the *ancien régime* was carried out on behalf of the sovereign. With the overthrow of the monarchy, violence, massacre and atrocities were carried out on behalf of the nation state and, during the revolutionary phase at least, on behalf of a higher ideal – bringing liberty and the ideals of the Revolution to the oppressed peoples of Europe.

The debate about the relationship between ideology and killing is a fraught one. Over the past few decades, the intellectual pendulum has swung from ideology not being particularly important in the killing process[56] to one in which ideology is now the central focus.[57] One nevertheless has to be careful not to project onto the violent discourses prevalent during the Revolution our understandings of violence that have been shaped by twentieth-century genocides.[58] Admittedly, that is a difficult enough thing to do but if we were to take on board Clausewitz, who asserted that the conduct of war is determined by the nature of societies, 'by their times and prevailing conditions', then it is not unreasonable to think that the prevailing ideology helped shape the nature of warfare during the Revolutionary and Napoleonic eras, which some historians will assert changed dramatically during this period.

The Revolution started out with the best of intentions. The Legislative Assembly laid out a framework for war. It wanted to liberate the oppressed peoples of Europe according to the slogan 'war on the castles, peace on the cottages' (*guerre aux châteaux, paix aux chaumières*). It projected itself as the 'guardian of human rights' and inserted a sort of morality in war where supposedly there had been none before.[59] Very quickly, however, things degenerated, as things tend to do in war. In the logic of the revolutionaries, if they were waging war on the sovereigns of Europe, usually referred to as tyrants, then they could not accommodate any attacks on civilians. The obverse of that thinking is that the crimes committed by enemy troops were perfectly in keeping with the behaviour of tyrants. The enemy then could no longer be characterized by its humanity, and were described as 'assassins', 'robbers' and 'ferocious beasts'. From that moment on, the behaviour of the enemy, or at least the propaganda around it, became part and parcel of the radicalization of the Revolution, which overlapped with an extremist discourse found in speeches, festivals, theatrical performances, songs and so on, and which was an integral part of the war effort. That attitude was essentially applied to anyone who opposed the Revolution and the reformist agenda that was imposed during the Empire. We have gone well past the *ancien régime* precept of simply killing a few ringleaders to set an example. Any form of violent resistance to the French military presence met with an inordinate and excessive amount of violence. Not only was the Catholic Royal Army in the Vendée mercilessly slaughtered but guerrilla groups in southern Italy and in Spain met with the same fate.

The idea of killing for a higher ideal continued during the wars under Napoleon, except this time French troops were bringing not liberty but enlightenment and civilization to the rest of Europe. That process was a bloody one. Take, for example, the destruction of the town of Lauria in August 1806, during which over 1,000 men, women and children were killed.[60] Lauria was a town of about 7,000 people in southern Italy, near the borders of Calabria, that had become the focal point of several local chieftains who, along with their armed bands, numbering about 10,000 men, as well as support from the local population, intended on making a stand against the French troops commanded by General Masséna. To avoid house-to-house combat, which would have resulted in heavy casualties, Masséna ordered the town be set on fire and that no quarter be given; the inhabitants were simply shot or bayoneted, without distinction of age or sex, as they emerged from the houses trying to escape the flames. Within a short space of time, the entire town was reduced to a smouldering ruin.[61] Most of the 'brigands' fled almost as soon as the fighting had begun, but 734 men, women and children were nevertheless killed in this way, according to the French count, although no attempt was made to count the number of inhabitants who died in the fire. A further 341 people taken prisoner were shot or hung over the following days.

According to the official French accounts, which naturally attempted to justify the excessive brutality with which resistance to the French was put down, the locals had been 'worked up into a religious frenzy' by priests and Capuchin monks who had convinced their followers that they were fighting the forces of Satan.[62] Priests and monks were also blamed for inciting locals against the French in Spain,[63] and they may very well have done so, as they did on any number of occasions, but what is important is how this was portrayed by the French. The attack on Lauria, against a civilian population that was in some respects indistinguishable from the enemy, may have been carried out for purely military reasons and may fall within the logic of counter-insurgency tactics being developed at the end of the eighteenth century, but the commanders who ordered the attack dressed the massacre in the rhetoric of an enlightened army fighting the forces of ignorance and superstition.

The pattern one finds at Lauria was repeated throughout French-occupied Europe. It is safe to say that there was not a region or country invaded by the French in which massacres did not occur. In Belgium, in Germany, in Switzerland, the Netherlands, Italy, Spain and Russia whole towns were razed and their inhabitants massacred.[64] This cannot simply be explained away by a breakdown in discipline among troops in the face of local resistance.[65] French soldiers generally became so enraged or frustrated at being attacked by armed civilians over the course of days if not weeks and months, witnessing the mutilated bodies of their comrades at the hands of insurgents, that they would exact revenge against the nearest villages, slaughtering all the inhabitants regardless of sex or age.[66]

Repression and massacres were systematized and occurred frequently, when not at the hands of the invading armies, then at the hands of military commissions, a system exported to the occupied countries from France where they had worked so effectively to bring intractable regions into line during the Consulate.[67] These military commissions that followed in the wake of mobile columns probably killed more people during the early years of the Consulate than during the Terror.[68] Mobile columns were used with ruthless efficiency in Piedmont in 1801 and again in 1802, in Parma and Piacenza in 1805, and in Tuscany in 1808, that is, wherever unruly populations needed to be 'pacified'. In the Kingdom of Naples forty-fifty people were killed at Marcellinara on 29 July 1806, the town of Strongoli suffered the same fate as other towns that resisted; and around forty were killed at Fiume-Freddo at the beginning of September 1806.

Fire was often used indiscriminately to flush out and to kill rebels who were still inside buildings.[69] Fire then was used as an instrument of war, different in some respects to the scorched-earth tactics that we have seen in other instances in the four regions being studied here. Scorched-earth tactics were about depriving the enemy – whether regular or irregular troops – of the means of subsistence. We see this in the Vendée with the institution of 'infernal columns' (*colonnes infernales*), based on the idea of scorched earth. General Turreau, in charge of the Republican forces in the Vendée (the Army of the West), issued an order on 17 January to the commanders of the 'infernal columns', consistent with traditional thinking around scorched earth: 'No village or farm can be burned without first removing all the beaten or sheafed grains and generally all the objects of subsistence.'[70] As for the inhabitants, the orders were clear: 'You will use all means to discover the rebels; all of them shall be killed by bayonet.' Even those who were considered 'suspect' were to be killed. Since there was no clarification about who was deemed a rebel, generals interpreted the order as killing all the inhabitants. A law passed on 19 March 1793 by the National Convention authorized the summary execution of anyone caught arms in hand, although the law was modified a few months later, on 10 May, to apply only to leaders of rebel groups. By that stage the 'infernal columns' had done their job, and tens of thousands of Vendean civilians had been massacred.[71] Those taken prisoner were brought before Special Military Tribunals, thus respecting a form of legality, which often passed the death sentence, and which was immediately carried out.

In July 1794, in the Saar region, for example, the village of Edesheim was burnt down, as was the town of Kusel, to 'serve as an example'. In October 1795, the village of Westhofen was burnt to the ground.[72] At Binasco in northern Italy in May 1796, Napoleon slaughtered an insurgent peasant force and laid the town to waste. He later handed over the town of Pavia to his troops for an orgy of rape, murder and looting.[73] In July, the towns of Arquata and Lugo in northern Italy suffered the same fate.[74] General Boulart, fighting peasants in the Abruzzo, declared that 'from time to time rebellious villages required an expedition to be sent against them to burn three or four'.[75] In Cairo, thousands of people were killed during the suppression of a revolt in October 1798.[76] In southern Italy in the summer of 1806, the French army killed thousands of locals and devastated more than twenty-five villages in an attempt to wipe out all armed resistance. The village of Soveria was completely burnt to the ground by the sixth of the Line and its inhabitants decimated without pity.[77] The same thing occurred at Corigliano, also in 1806, where General Reynier and his men set the town alight.[78] As the inhabitants – old men, women, and children – tried to escape being burnt or asphyxiated, they were shot down by the French. In Galicia in 1809, when the Redondela valley rose up in revolt, French troops received the order to 'put everything to fire and blood' (*mettre tout à feu et à sang*). More than sixty villages, according to one account, were consequently burnt to the ground.[79]

Setting fire to towns with the inhabitants still inside is part of an eliminationist logic, one often found in colonial mentalities, and that was practised around the world. We have then a situation in which the life of the enemy, even a suspect enemy, was worth less than the life of a revolutionary Republican, something that was inherent in revolutionary doctrine. To quote one of the generals who committed some of the worst atrocities in the Vendée, François Joseph Westermann, 'pity is not revolutionary'.[80]

A Transition to the Ordered, Modern Massacre

That massacres occurred will come as no surprise to historians who have explored the themes of occupation and resistance to the French empire between 1792 and 1814, or indeed to historians of colonialism. For the period covered in this book, there is nothing out of the ordinary here; the French armies of the *ancien régime* also massacred. Nor did the French enjoy a monopoly of brutality during this period; massacres were committed by the *ancien régime* armies of other European powers as well, although generally they were not as frequent or as widespread as the French. Despite similarities in the massacres committed during the *ancien régime*, the civil war in France during the Revolution and those that occurred during the course of the wars of conquest, massacre and violence have to be understood on their own terms. During the French wars of conquest, violence was about the need to control. Massacre was a means used by the centralizing state – both revolutionary and imperial – to impose its rule over large areas of land and the people who inhabited it. There were always individual depredations – the files of the military archives in Vincennes are full of indictments against individual soldiers for rape, murder, and pillage – but these were unplanned, the invariable outcome of civilians coming into contact with an occupation army, the undesirable side effects of war.

Massacre, on the other hand, was part of a policy used by the French revolutionary and imperial armies to terrorize the local population into submission. It came about every time civilians resisted the encroachments of the French state. To fully understand that, the military and political violence that accompanied the Revolutionary and Napoleonic Wars has to be seen as part of a larger colonizing process that was determinedly secular. 'Classical massacres', for want of a better term, those carried out by the military during the seventeenth and eighteenth centuries, and which were sometimes encouraged by commanding officers as a form of reward or revenge, were performed in a relatively haphazard fashion, during which individuals were free to do what they wanted. This was often the case for massacres accompanying the sacking of towns. While the massacres carried out during the Revolutionary and Napoleonic Wars were by no means as systematic as twentieth-century massacres, they were increasingly conducted in an organized, rationalized manner. We can still see examples of uncontrolled 'frenzy' that were part and parcel of eighteenth-century warfare occurring during this period,[81] but more and more, massacres followed another logic and were subject to the dictates of a modern army and a modern polity. The people of the city of Córdoba were massacred in 1808 by General Dupont not because they had resisted the entry of the French, on the contrary the city's doors had been opened, but because the region had resisted French encroachments. It was therefore meant to serve as an example. Massacres were becoming more impersonal and were being applied as a response to particular circumstances. The violence committed outside of French territory was not so much about ridding society of an unwanted people – as was often the case in France during the height of the Terror or in the conquered lands outside of Europe – but of bringing them kicking and screaming into the secular fold, of civilizing them. As such, the methods used to control, dominate and eliminate recalcitrant populations during the Revolutionary and Napoleonic Wars mirror the methods already being used in non-European lands against Indigenous populations, and prefigure the methods used in later French colonial wars.[82]

The Revolutionary and Napoleonic Wars were thus, in some respects, a transitionary period between the uncoordinated, retributive massacres of the *ancien régime*, and the bureaucratized, purposeful massacres of the latter nineteenth and twentieth centuries. Can we then conclude that, for the period under consideration, massacre was considered an acceptable political and military expedient used to oblige intractable populations to conform to state control, in both a European and an extra-European context? Massacres during the *ancien régime* were committed for either religious or political-military reasons, that is, an attempt on the part of the state to control people, sometimes their own, or to take possession of another territory. With the advent of the French Revolution, however, we reach a watershed moment in the way violence was used and justified by the revolutionary and then the imperial state. Violence was now carried out for 'ideological' reasons; that is, the justification for massacre carries with it 'humane' overtones: it was about 'liberating' people from their feudal past, about bringing the principles of the Revolution, civilization and Enlightenment to the backward peoples of Europe. Moreover, the French Revolutionary and Napoleonic armies abroad were profoundly secular. In fact, in some regions where there was a religious backlash against the encroachments of the modernizing French state, the repression and the rhetoric surrounding it was pointedly secular.

Despite the massacres committed during the Terror, and during the wars of expansion, the Revolution and the Empire continue to be presented as a benefit to humanity. How does one reconcile the two discordant junctures,

Enlightenment and reform, on the one hand, and mass death, on the other? One cannot, except to say that massacres, mass killing and violence were the means used to forge a new state, a new political ideology and a new empire. At the beginning of the Revolution, the people were laying claim to a prominent place within that new state. The revolutionary state in turn pre-empted the role of the people by using violence as a political tool directed against those who had either rejected the new state – 'counterrevolutionaries', however defined – or who were no longer considered acceptable to those intent on expanding and controlling the existing revolutionary state. All massacres during the Revolutionary and Napoleonic era, at the risk of falling into a gross generalization, were committed for a strategic or ideological reason; that is, they were not simply the mindless killing of others for the sake of killing, and they were not the killing of others to eliminate them as a people, although one could argue that was the intention in the Vendée region. This applies equally to 'accidental' as well as 'intentional' massacres since there was invariably a sense that what they were doing was justified.

Violence in France and Europe at the end of the eighteenth and the beginning of the nineteenth centuries was not necessarily on the rise, despite the number of massacres and the number of deaths through battles, but what we clearly see during the whole revolutionary process is a desire by the state to control and channel that violence, even in a military setting. Massacres were, therefore, subordinated to military but especially to political necessity. In that process, there appears to have been an ideological subtext. There is an evident desire not to annihilate whole peoples in the name of an idea, despite some of the excessive rhetoric displayed by some revolutionaries, but to oblige people to comply with new norms through violence.

We do not know how many massacres were carried out by the French during this period, but the number is probably in the hundreds, especially if we consider the Caribbean. They occurred in every region invaded by the French. It was a conscious policy of terror meant to dissuade other peoples from resisting the French occupation, a policy that was at times effective. When these massacres occurred, they were almost never hidden. They were a public exercise designed to instil fear, meant to be talked about among the wider community, meant to serve as examples so that local populations would more passively submit to French rule, a violent confirmation that France was the superior and stronger force. Worse, there was not only an impetus to eliminate the enemies of Enlightenment, as the peasants who rose up against French depredations were usually portrayed, but there was a desire to hurt and to make the victims suffer and to desecrate the body.

6

The Colony of New South Wales

Escalating Violence, 1793–1810

Governor Arthur Phillip's departure in 1792 left Major Francis Grose, Commanding Officer of the New South Wales (NSW) Corps in charge of the colony. The Corps was raised in England in 1789 as the colony's permanent garrison and the officers and other ranks were expected to make it their home. In the three-year interregnum before the arrival of the second governor, Captain John Hunter of the Royal Navy, the Corps assumed control of the colony. Hunter and his successors, Philip Gidley King and William Bligh, would find it hard to control the officers and their 500-strong corps. Since the garrison was paid in sterling, the officers were in a strong position to take control of the colonial economy by controlling trade and granting themselves several hundred acres of land with unfettered access to convict labour to grow their crops and build their houses. But it was also concerned to make the colony self-sufficient in grain and encouraged former convicts and even serving soldiers and their families to take up land for small farms along the Hawkesbury River, thirty-five miles northwest of the Sydney, with military protection against Bediagal attack.

The Corps would also play a critical role in defending the colony from a possible French invasion. Indeed, the entire period was dominated by wartime fear of the French that reached a climax in 1803–4. The Corps would not only establish new beachheads in Tasmania and the Hunter River to forestall possible French occupation but would also brutally put down what it perceived were two uprisings inspired by the French: the Irish convicts at Castle Hill, west of Sydney; and Aboriginal people at Risdon Cove in Tasmania.

The four case studies explored in this section analyse the colony's violent responses to a possible French claim to parts of New South Wales (NSW), sustained Indigenous resistance and Irish convict dissent. Each case is considered within the rubric of 'distance and fear', a policy of containment which underpins the period. An example is found in the colonial legal ruling that Aboriginal people were not civilized enough to give evidence in court. The ruling confirmed that Aboriginal people were not British subjects enjoying equality before the law but were in a 'savage state' with no enforceable legal rights.[1]

The first case study analyses the frontier war with the Bediagal for control of the Hawkesbury River settlements from 1794 to 1810; the second analyses Governor King's reaction to a an expected French invasion in 1802–3; the third examines the Darug warrior Pemulwuy's guerrilla war against the colonists on the Cumberland Plain 1793–1802; and the final case study examines the methods used by the NSW Corps to address a critical incident in 1804, the Risdon Cove massacre as a response to the fear of French invasion. Put together the case studies produce new insights about the behaviour of colonial governors and the garrison in a new kind of colony in a far-flung corner of the British Empire in a time of global war.

The Hawkesbury River Frontier, 1794–1810

In January 1794, when the British population reached about 4,000, about forty former convicts and some serving soldiers were encouraged by Colonel Francis Grose to occupy the rich alluvial flats at the Hawkesbury River. Although some were in family groups, the sex ratio was about four men to every woman, and they clustered on ten- and twenty-acre farms along the thirty-five miles stretch of the Hawkesbury River frontage from present-day Sackville Reach in the north to Richmond in the south. The area was officially known as Mulgrave Place, named in honour of one of Grose's patron in London, but the settlers called it the Nile of New South Wales because they believed that the rich alluvial river flats would produce abundant crops.[2] Each settler family appears to have constructed a hut, felled some trees to create a patch of ground, planted a crop of maize or potatoes and then caught fish from the river and small mammals and birds for sustenance while awaiting the first crop.[3]

The Australian historian Grace Karskens considers that most Hawkesbury settlers would have had some contact with the local Indigenous communities at Sydney and some of the Darug nation at the colony's second settlement at Parramatta. They would also have employed some of them as labourers and introduced them to 'the rough sociable and exciting pleasures of their popular culture and perhaps attended contests and corroborees themselves. Songs, stories and words must have crossed. Men went hunting together.'[4] However, at Mulgrave Place, the Bediagal clan of the Darug nation were determined to defend their homelands from settler invasion.

In 1794, the Darug nation was estimated to comprise about 1,500 people and was known to the settlers as the 'woods tribes'.[5] Their homelands centred on the Hawkesbury River which they called Dyarubbin and circled Cumberland Plain, which formed the entire Sydney region, from Appin in the south to Broken Bay in the north.[6] However, the Bediagal clan estimated at 500 people certainly considered that the thirty-five-mile stretch of the river between Sackville Reach and Richmond constituted their country. If so, then it would have been one of the most densely populated areas in Aboriginal Australia.[7] As hunter-gatherers, they usually camped in extended family groups of between twenty and sixty people, dug the abundant native yams from the river flats, constructed tunnel traps for catching quail, other birds and small mammals such as bandicoots and native rats, climbed trees to catch possums, caught many varieties of scale fish and shellfish, as well as freshwater turtles from the river, gathered donkey orchids and chocolate lilies, tubers and floating nardoo fern, native cherries and currants, and hunted kangaroos, emus and wallabies.[8] Thus, the river was the central focus of their lives, culturally and economically, and Mulgrave Place area in particular, with its fertile floodplains, chains of ponds and lagoons, was among the most resource-rich areas of the river and an important gathering place for ceremonies. However, the sudden influx of British settlers in the area in early 1794 would make significant inroads on the daily lives of the Bediagal and it was not long before they tried to force the invaders to leave.

Warfare broke out in September 1794, when, according to Judge Advocate David Collins, a settler and his assigned convict servant were attacked and were

> nearly murdered in their hut by some natives from the woods, who stole upon them with such secrecy, as to wound and overpower them before they could procure assistance. The servant was so much hurt by them with spears and clubs, as to be in danger of losing his life. A few days after this circumstance, a body of natives having attacked the settlers, and carried off their clothes, provisions and whatever else they could lay their hands on, the sufferers collected what arms they could, and following them, seven or eight of the plunderers were killed on the spot.[9]

Collins believed that '[t]his mode of treating [the Bediagal] had become absolutely necessary, from the frequency of the evil effects of their visits', but he excused this brutal incident by blaming the settlers: 'there was not a doubt that many natives had been wantonly fired upon; and when their children, after the flight of their parents, having fallen into the settlers hands, they have been detained at their huts, notwithstanding the earnest entreaties of the parents for their return.'[10]

Peter Turbet, the most recent historian of the Hawkesbury frontier, suggests that this particular reprisal killing was 'the largest recorded number of Aboriginal people killed in a single encounter' since the colony had been established nearly seven years earlier.[11] He further points out that the settlers, some of whom were serving soldiers, had been provided with armed weapons in February 1794, and thus they had the means not only to defend themselves from attack but also to respond quickly.[12] Indeed, a month later, Collins reported that the settlers had 'seized a native boy' believing that he was a spy returning to his people, 'a large body of natives', to report the settlers' weakness. They tied him hand and foot and dragged him several times through a place covered with hot ashes 'until his back was dreadfully scorched, and in that state threw him into the river, where they shot and killed him'.[13]

Three months later, in January 1795, Colonel William Paterson, now the acting governor and commanding officer of the New South Wales Corps, stationed a sergeant and ten soldiers at Windsor, in the heartland of the new settlements. In the following month, the Bediagal were reported to have threatened three settlers and wounded two others in revenge for the loss of the little boy.[14] Then in May as the settlers harvested their first crops, they were confronted by a large group of Bediagal men, women and children who, according to Collins, were wearing animal skin cloaks and clothes stolen from the settlers. They picked the corn and carried it away in fishing nets and blankets also stolen from the settlers. When the settlers tried to stop them, the Bediagal men used their spears to kill two settlers.[15] Anxious to protect the settlers and their valuable crops, Paterson despatched sixty-six soldiers and two officers from the New South Wales Corps to the region, with the order to 'kill any [Bediagal] they found and hang their bodies from gibbets as a warning to the rest'.[16] Military historian John Connor, in quoting other contemporary sources, reported that they forced a (Bediagal) boy to reveal the location of his compatriots:

> [T]hat night they made contact with the [Bediagal] in the forest not far from the farm. The roar of muskets filled the night air, followed by the screams of the wounded and dying. The soldiers saw seven or eight of the [Bediagal] fall down in the undergrowth, but when they went out next morning to find the bodies and string them up, they found that the [Bediagal] had carried away their comrades' bodies during the night. The detachment captured a man, five women (at least two of whom were wounded by gunshot) and some children.[17]

According to Collins, it was hoped that in 'detaining the prisoners and treating them well, that some good effect might result', but in the end Paterson decided that 'coercion' would 'more likely to answer his ends' and released the women.[18] This is not altogether surprising. One of the children had died in custody, and one of the women had lost a boy in childbirth. In reprisal, the

Bediagal attacked a farm at Richmond and killed a male settler and his child and wounded his wife.[19]

After that a permanent garrison of two officers and ninety-three soldiers was stationed at the Hawkesbury for the next two years and deployed in three different places along the river. According to William Goodall, the garrison's stores sergeant, '[p]arties of soldiers were frequently sent out to kill the Natives'.[20] For example in December 1795, Collins reported that a large group of Bediagal men had attacked some settlers who had taken up land on the Lower Hawkesbury at Sackville Reach and stripped them of 'every article they could find in their huts' after which an 'armed party was directly sent out, who, coming up with them, killed four men and one woman, badly wounded a child and took four women prisoners'.[21] Although Collins does not say how this incident took place, it would appear that it was a planned night attack on a Bediagal camp.

Over one year, the Bediagal had killed four settlers and wounded five others in five separate incidents. In response, the British had killed at least twenty Bediagal people, and several of their women and children were wounded and captured in three punitive expeditions. This kind of response became the template for other responses in the region. Still, the situation was not entirely to the settlers' advantage. At the Lower Hawkesbury at Sackville Reach, the river was very narrow and surrounded by steep crumbling sandstone cliffs. With less arable land to farm, the settlers were more scattered and isolated from each other and thus more vulnerable to Bediagal attack. Over the next decade they would abandon their farms on several occasions before their farms were permanently secured in 1808.[22]

At the Upper Hawkesbury, however, the war continued. After the Bediagal attacked and plundered another settler's hut near present-day Windsor in April 1797 and burnt his stack of wheat, the governor, John Hunter, signalled that if any of the Bediagal 'could be detected in the act of robbing the settlers, to hang one of them in chains upon a tree near the spot as a terror to the others'.[23] In a despatch to the Secretary of State for the Colonies in London, he said that some of the settlers had been given weapons and foreshadowed that more punitive expeditions were inevitable.[24]

In February 1798, five settler men acting as a lynch mob executed two young Bediagal men, Jemmy and Little George, in revenge for the killing of two settlers by senior Bediagal men, known as Major White and Terribandy. The five settlers were arrested and charged with murder and during their trial the following year, the court heard that settlers in the region were in the habit of abducting Bediagal women and that their compatriots could not get them back 'through fear of Fire-arms'.[25] The five men were convicted of 'wanton killing', but when the court could not decide on a suitable sentence, they were released while awaiting advice from London about their fate. When the judgement arrived two years later, the men were pardoned.[26] Killing Bediagal, no matter how well known to the settlers, was an acceptable practice.[27] According to Connor, the garrison at the Hawkesbury remained in strength at around forty men until 1800, after which fewer than fifteen troops remained, suggesting that they were sufficient to keep the Bediagal in check.[28] After that, the colonists and the Bediagal, 'killed each other in a spiral of retribution'.[29]

From these accounts, Mulgrave Place was divided into two regions. The most significant was the Upper Hawkesbury region from Windsor to Richmond. It was along this ten miles stretch of the river that most of the settlers held their farms and could expect military support to defend them against Bediagal attack. They include two recorded punitive expeditions and other military exploits indicated by Goodall, Paterson and Hunter. When put together with the reprisal attacks by the settlers, they appear to have made significant inroads into the Bediagal population. Indeed, 'once the farms facing the Hawkesbury in the main settlements were consolidated, the [Bediagal] rarely raided them, but they continued to attack the "back farms" which bordered the forest on the edge of the main settlements'.[30]

Bediagal women were still abducted by settlers for sex and their children kidnapped to work as farm labourers and servants. As they grew up on these farms, however, some Bediagal youths became outlaw warriors, wore English hunting jackets, carried firearms and terrorized the neighbourhood. It was only a matter of time before they were shot dead.[31] It appears that Bediagal attacks came to an end on 19 November 1809 'when the main [Bediagal] leaders' met acting Governor Paterson 'and were pardoned in exchange for promising to cease their attacks. ... This seems to have been a consequence of decline in the [Bediagal] population due to disease and warfare'.[32] By then the Bediagal population appears to have fallen to fewer than 100 and the settler population at the Upper Hawkesbury had increased to more than 2,000.[33] In less than fifteen years, the Bediagal population had fallen by about 80 per cent.

The other region, at the Lower Hawkesbury between Sackville Reach and Portland Head, presented a different story. At Sackville, the river turned a sharp corner into a narrow reach and at Portland Head the river wound through a narrow gorge with high sandstone cliffs rising on each side. At both places the soil was unsuitable for farming, and because they were isolated from each other the farms were subject to attacks from the Bediagal hiding in the heavily wooded ridges. The settlers first abandoned the area in 1797 and then again in 1804 after three Bediagal warriors told Governor Philip Gidley King that they raided farms in the region because they had been driven from the river upstream and needed river access.[34] And although King promised them that 'no more settlements would be made down the river', the settlers returned soon afterward. In retaliation in May 1805 the Bediagal carried out further farmhouse raids for corn supplies and used lighted torches to burn down one of the houses.[35] In the last reported raid, it was alleged that a thirteen-year-old Bediagal girl who could speak English visited the farm beforehand and collected intelligence about the settlers' movements, which she then passed on to her people.[36] A combination of Bediagal hostility and the regular Hawkesbury floods continued to limit the number of settler farms in the area. Indeed, as late as 1810 Governor Lachlan Macquarie noted that there were few settlers on the Lower Hawkesbury, and it remained a refuge for some of the Bediagal people at least until 1818.[37]

New South Wales, 1802

In January 1802, the governor of New South Wales, Philip Gidley King, reflected on his long association with the colony. As a young naval officer in the First Fleet in 1788, he established the colony's second settlement at Norfolk Island and, apart from a brief return visit to England in 1790–1, remained there until 1796. Along with David Collins, who served as the colony's judge advocate from 1788 to 1796, King could claim to know New South Wales better than most. As a naval man he envisioned Sydney becoming the centre of Britain's new empire in the South Pacific with jurisdiction over Tasmania, Norfolk Island and Lord Howe Island, as well as New Zealand, Fiji and Tahiti.[38]

By 1802, the British population in New South Wales had reached 8,000 and Sydney was already making its mark as the entrepot for the sealing grounds in Bass Strait and New Zealand. The ships attracted to the region from Britain and the United States brought regular supplies of grain and cattle from the French colony at Mauritius, the Dutch colony at Cape Town, and the British East India Company's settlements at Calcutta and Bombay. Closer to home, regular trade in potatoes, timber and flax was conducted with New Zealanders in the Bay of Islands, and surplus grain was brought from Norfolk Island to Sydney.[39]

From a strategic perspective, however, the colony could best be described as a string of poorly defended settlements of Sydney, Parramatta, the Hawkesbury and Norfolk Island, all of which were reached by water. There was only one British naval ship in the colony, so the colonial government often relied on smaller locally built vessels or hired visiting American ships to transport people and supplies between the settlements. In this vulnerable situation, Governor King was sensitive to Irish convict insurgency and Aboriginal resistance as well as invasion from the French, with whom the British had been mostly at war since the execution of Louis XVI in 1793.[40]

The NSW Corps which had served in the colony as the permanent British garrison since 1790 was also keenly aware of the difficulties defence posed for the colony's extensive territory. Comprising eight companies with a total of about 500 men, the Corps was commanded in the colony in 1802 by Lieutenant Colonel William Paterson.[41] One of the companies, comprising about ninety soldiers under the command of Major Joseph Foveaux and Captain John Piper, was posted at Norfolk Island, two others were located in Sydney under Paterson's command, assisted by Captain Anthony Fenn Kemp, and two more under the command of Major George Johnston and Captain John Macarthur were stationed at the colony's second major town at Parramatta, twelve miles west from Sydney. From there smaller detachments under the command of younger officers such as Lieutenants William Moore, Thomas Davies and John Brabyn were deployed to protect farming settlements at the Georges River ten miles south of Parramatta and the Hawkesbury River, twenty miles to the northwest, thus gaining considerable experience in punitive raids against the Darug Aboriginal people.[42]

Pemulwuy's War, 1792–1802

The Corps' campaign against the Darug along the Georges River reached a high point in June 1802 when Pemulwuy the Darug warrior known to the British since 1790 was finally shot dead and his head cut off. Governor King then despatched it as a trophy to Sir Joseph Banks in London, where it may still be located in the Hunterian Museum at the Royal College of Surgeons.[43] Between 1792 and 1797, Pemulwuy led several raids on farms between Parramatta and Prospect, largely for maize and corn, but he also killed British colonists as payback for attacks on Darug women and children.[44]

In March 1797, Pemulwuy changed tactics. Rather than leading a small group of five to ten men, he now appeared to operate with a much larger and more formidable group of forty to fifty warriors. On one occasion he showed extraordinary bravado in raiding the large government farm at Toongabbie where soldiers were stationed, attacking some of them and taking musket balls and 'other things'.[45] The soldiers and farmers immediately formed a punitive party which 'hunted for the gang right though out the night. Eventually they found their camp in the bush, strewn with maize and musket balls, and pursued the fleeing warriors all the way back to the outskirts of Parramatta'. However, they still couldn't catch them and giving up the chase they retreated to Parramatta the following morning.[46]

According to legend, an hour later, Pemulwuy marched into Parramatta in 'a great rage', leading 100 Aboriginal warriors ranked like a detachment of soldiers. He shouted at the assembled crowd about 'the coercive measures taken by settlers and soldiers to hunt them down like wild animals' and threatened to spear anyone who dared approach him. The soldiers opened fire, spears were hurled and, in the ensuing 'Battle of Parramatta', it is alleged that at least five warriors fell. Even if the battle details are only partly true, as there is no evidence of any soldiers being injured let alone killed, it suggests that Pemulwuy and his warriors were starting to draw on British military methods to develop new ways of fighting. Pemulwuy was 'blasted with buckshot' about the head and carted off to Parramatta hospital, where a fetter was placed round his ankle, and then left to die.[47]

However, he recovered and escaped from the hospital. A month later, with his ankle still fettered, he confronted Governor Hunter on the outskirts of Parramatta. They appeared to part on good terms, but Hunter made no attempt to remove the fetter. Undaunted, Pemulwuy and his band of warriors resumed their guerrilla raids on farms 'in an orbit around Parramatta' by setting fire to sheds and hay ricks, robbing supplies of flour and corn, and assaulting farmworkers. Once again, Hunter sent the soldiers after him, determined this time to capture and then hang him as an example to the other warriors and force their surrender. Nevertheless, Pemulwuy easily eluded the soldiers, and for some months nothing more was heard of him. By then, Pemulwuy 'had acquired an extraordinary reputation for supernatural powers: he was the first of a long line of Aboriginal heroes believed by his people ... to be immune to gunfire'.[48] Like so many Aboriginal warriors in the future, he was often reported to have been killed, only to reappear again. For the New South Wales Corps, whose power rested on muskets, it could hardly have been a more maddening claim and it became 'increasingly urgent to prove the legend false, to demonstrate, logically and rationally, that Pemulwuy was just a man'.[49]

Over the next four years, Pemulwuy conducted a highly successful guerrilla war against the farmers in the region south of Parramatta. Every autumn and spring, he would lead his warriors in raids on farms for maize and corn, usually in daylight, but often at dusk or early morning. Some farms, such as those at Prospect, were forced by the NSW Corps to cluster together for protection, but many others along the Georges River and at Cabramatta were more isolated. The NSW Corps would place two or three soldiers at a farm for a few days, but when they moved on to the next, Pemulwuy and his men would attack, sometimes by setting crops and huts ablaze, at other times maiming sheep and cattle and at others taking the maize crop.[50] The British were in no doubt that Pemulwuy and his warriors were out to 'kill all the white men they meet' and terrible stories of his atrocities, including amputations on colonial men, women and children, abounded. The military reprisals were equally ruthless with their night-time raids on campsites. This was a serious war.[51] Although no casualty statistics appear to exist for the period, there is no doubt that Pemulwuy succeeded in containing agricultural settlement in the region.

After four years of warfare, Governor King was forced to change tactics. Armed with new instructions from London to treat Aboriginal people with 'distance and fear', in May 1801 he ordered all friendly Darug people living on farms in the region to be driven off at gunpoint, and that if they wanted to return, then they must identify the resistance leaders whom he now called 'terrorists' and who committed 'outrages'.[52] Six months later, he declared Pemulwuy an outlaw and offered rewards to the friendly Darug to find him. The tactical change appears to have worked, because seven months later Pemulwuy was shot dead by Henry Hacking, one of the colony's crack marksmen. He also appears to be the man who cut off Pemulwuy's head, and brought it back to King.[53] But King told the Secretary of State for the Colonies, Lord Hobart, that it was the friendly Darug who requested that Pemeulwuy's head be 'carried to the governor' as 'he was the cause of all that had happened'.[54] This is nonsense, for the Darug did not decapitate their own people. Rather Hacking's killing and beheading of Pemulwuy, which remained hidden from public view until 2003, was more like a secret 'special forces' operation.[55] Although a recent claim asserts that Hacking could not have been the perpetrator, the evidence suggests otherwise.[56]

While Pemulwuy was the first successful Aboriginal resistance leader in the Colony of New South Wales, historians have largely ignored his significance, preferring to focus on Bennelong and his relationship with Governor Phillip. It was not until 1987 that Indigenous scholar Eric Wilmot published a biography of Pemulwuy that his vital role as resistance fighter was revealed.[57] His long absence from Australian history is indicative of Australia's refusal to acknowledge the violent impact of the colonizing project on Aboriginal people and that they resisted it from the outset. His absence also suggests that as the leading Aboriginal leader in the Sydney region, negotiations could have been made with him to conclude a treaty. It was clear, however, that neither the colonial government nor the Colonial Office had such a view in mind.

Fear of the French: The British Claim Van Diemen's Land, 1802-4

Between 1800 and 1802, more than 800 United Irishmen, transported for their participation in the Irish Rebellion of 1798, arrived in Sydney. While the British considered them as common criminals, the United Irishmen saw themselves as political prisoners. The Australian historian Alan Atkinson suggests that the United Irishmen sent to New South Wales were 'more inured to violence' than earlier groups of Irish convicts and 'seemed more dangerous' because they were better educated, more politically aware and had a legacy of insurrection.[58]

Governor King despatched most of these men to a newly established government farm at Castle Hill, thirty miles northwest from Sydney, in the belief that, isolated from the major towns in Sydney and Parramatta, they would be less likely to incite rebellion. He then extended sections of the British Sedition Act to the colony and banned any meeting of twelve or more people without his permission. If they failed to disperse after half an hour, they could be hanged, and if any of them was found to have made an 'unlawful oath', they would be punished with 600 lashes. The harsh measures were followed up by a house-to-house search for unlawful firearms.[59]

Just as one of the last ships containing United Irishmen docked in Sydney in April 1802, the French ship *Naturaliste*, under the command of Captain Jacques Felix Emmanuel Hamelin, limped into Sydney Harbour.[60] As one of two ships that formed the scientific expedition under the command of Commodore Nicolas Baudin, it had left France in 1800 during a lull in the war with Britain, to explore among other places, the D'Entrecasteaux Channel in Tasmania, which an earlier French expedition had discovered in 1792.[61] However, during a violent storm en route to Sydney for supplies, the ships became separated. When Baudin arrived six weeks later in the *Geographe*, the ship was so badly damaged that King offered him the purchase of the colonial schooner Casuarina to send the vast collection of specimens back to France. Overall, the expedition remained in Sydney for nearly seven months.[62]

Although relations between the British governor and the French commodore remained entirely cordial during that time, King was convinced that some of the French officers had contacted the United Irishmen.[63] Ever protective of Britain's interests, he was affronted by their questions about the strength of the NSW Corps and about his treatment of the Irish rebels and, in the aftermath of Pemulwuy's execution, his attitude towards Aboriginal people. From his perspective, the United Irishmen were traitors to the British Empire, and Aboriginal people were simply outsiders in the British colonizing project. The French officers took a different view. They saw both groups as members of the universal 'brotherhood of man' and thus part of the Republican ideal encapsulated in the French Revolution. The young zoologist François Peron, for example, talked endlessly about his 'civilized' encounters with Aboriginal people in Tasmania and eagerly displayed to the colony's resident botanist George Caley the list of Aboriginal words the French scientists had collected and portraits they had drawn of the men and women.[64]

King, however, was convinced that the French intended to make a claim to Tasmania.[65] Indeed, his fears were confirmed when, just after the French departed Sydney in November, officers in the NSW Corps told him that they intended to form a settlement in the D'Entrecasteaux Channel.[66] In panic, he ordered the only naval officer on duty in the colony, Acting Lieutenant Charles Robbins RN, to sail to King Island in Bass Strait, which the French said they were planning to visit, plant the British flag in front of their camp and then hand Baudin a letter stating that Britain intended to establish a settlement in Tasmania as soon as possible.[67]

Baudin's response to this tactless exhibition of crude possession confirmed King's fears. Tasmania, Baudin pointed out, was discovered by the Dutch explorer Abel Tasman in 1642, and now that it was shown to be an island rather than part of the mainland of New South Wales, it was open to any European power to occupy it. Further he did not consider that the British had met their obligations to Aboriginal people in Sydney, implying that the Pemeulwuy's beheading was an act of barbarism and that Aboriginal people in Tasmania deserved respect and protection from every European power.[68]

Determined to occupy Tasmania as quickly as possible, in February 1803, King persuaded the young naval lieutenant, John Bowen, aged twenty-three, who arrived in Sydney, to establish a beachhead at Risdon Cove on the Derwent River in the southeastern part of the island. Bowen landed in September with a party of forty-nine, including a lance sergeant and eight privates of the NSW Corps and naval surgeon Jacob Mountgarrett, who also filled the role of magistrate. Bowen proclaimed that Tasmania was part of the British colony of New South Wales.[69]

Despite Baudin's warning to protect Aboriginal people, King gave Bowen no instructions about them. But Bowen may have had some understanding of Britain's new policy of 'distance and fear' for he told King that few of them 'had been sighted since his party's arrival' and 'not apprehending they would be of any use to us I have not made any search after them, thinking myself well off if I never see them again'.[70] His party had invaded the homelands of the Moomairremener clan of the Oyster Bay nation who believed that the strangers were Wrageowrapper, devil men's spirits, and thus to be avoided. They had seen such men before, but they had not stayed long. However, this time there were devil white women and children among them and they appeared to have come to stay.[71]

King, however, was less interested in the Moomairremener than concerned to shore up Risdon Cove from possible French attack. In November he sent a further detachment of soldiers from the NSW Corps under the command of Lieutenant William Moore to the settlement along with two twelve-pound carronades. The settlement's population now reached about 100, with Bowen, Moore and Mountgarrett as the senior officers in charge of about twenty soldiers and some of their families, sixty convicts and some of their families and three settler families.[72] Before his deployment to Risdon, Moore appears to have been stationed in Parramatta where his experience in leading punitive expeditions against Pemulwuy and his warriors might have led to his promotion to lieutenant in 1801.[73]

Three months after his arrival at Risdon in November 1803, a second British settlement was established at present-day Hobart on the other side of the River Derwent. Led by David Collins as Lieutenant-Governor who arrived from London with 400 convicts, the new settlement confirmed Britain's determination to keep out the French.[74] With the Risdon outpost now redundant, Bowen was told by King to surrender his command to Collins and return to Sydney. With no ship readily available, Collins did not press the issue.[75]

In Sydney, King was delighted that the French had been thwarted and told the Secretary of State for War and Colonies on 1 March 1804 that the colony of New South Wales was well prepared to repel a possible French invasion.[76] He had, however, underestimated the Aboriginal people in Tasmania.

Risdon Cove, 3 May 1804

At 2.00 pm on Thursday 3 May 1804, the colonists at the new settlement at Hobart heard cannon fire across the Derwent River at Risdon Cove. The lieutenant governor at Hobart, David Collins, immediately despatched a messenger across the river 'to know the cause'. At 7.30 pm, Lieutenant William Moore, the acting commandant at Risdon, arrived and Collins ordered him to prepare a full report of what had happened. Half an hour later, Moore called on the chaplain Robert Knopwood and delivered a hastily written note from the surgeon Dr Mountgarrett containing the first details of one of the most significant events in the island's colonial history.

> I beg to refer you to Mr. Moore for the particulars of an attack the natives made on the camp today, and I have every reason to think it was premeditated, as their number far exceeded any that we have ever heard of. As you express a wish to be acquainted with some of the natives, if you will dine with me tomorrow you will oblige me by christening a fine native boy who I have. Unfortunately, poor boy, his father and mother were both killed. He is about two years old. I likewise have the body of a man that was killed .... The number of natives I think was not less than 5 or 6 hundred.[77]

Moore told Knopwood that the 'natives' were 'very numerous, and that they wounded one of the settlers, Burke, and was going to burn his house down and ill treat his wife etc. etc.'.[78] While awaiting Moore's report, Collins appears to have declared Risdon off limits to everyone in Hobart, including Knopwood. Nevertheless, in view of the seriousness of the situation, Moore's report delivered to Collins four days later was astonishingly short.

> Agreeable to your desire, I have the honour of acquainting you with the Circumstances that led to the attack on the Natives, which you will perceive was the consequence of their own hostile Appearance.
>
> It would appear from the numbers of them and the Spears etc. with which they were armed, that their design was to attack us, however it was not until they thoroughly convinced me of their Intentions by using violence to a Settler's wife and my own Servant who was returning to Camp with some Kangaroos, One of which they took from him, that they were fired on their coming into Camp, and Surrounding it. I went towards them with five Soldiers, their appearance and numbers I thought very far from friendly; during this time I was informed that a part of them was beating Birt, the Settler, at his farm. I then dispatched Two Soldiers to his assistance, with orders not to fire if they could avoid it; however they found it necessary, and one was killed on the Spot, and another was found Dead in the Valley. But this time a great party were in the Camp, and on a proposal from Mr Mountgarrett to fire one of the Carronades to intimidate them they dispersed.
>
> Mr Mountgarrett with Some Soldiers and Prisoners followed them some distance up the Valley, and had reasons to Suppose more were wounded, as one was seen to be taken away bleeding; during the Time they were in Camp a number of old men were perceived at the foot the Hill near the Valley employed in preparing spears.[79]

The report focused more on the weapons carried by Aboriginal people than on the measures deployed by Moore. Neither did it state how many soldiers and prisoners 'followed' Aboriginal people up the valley let alone estimate the number killed overall.

The following day, 8 May, Collins assumed command of the Risdon outpost, and three days later Knopwood finally crossed the river to christen the little boy Robert Hobart May and 'took a walk to see where the natives had attacked the camp and settlers', but he did not report what he saw.[80] Collins was also shy about providing King with more details apart from noting that three Aboriginal people were 'Killed upon the Spot' and that 'Not having been present myself, I must take It for granted that the measures which were pursued were unavoidable'. However, in keeping with the new policy of 'distance and fear', he considered that their 'vindictive Spirit' would continue because they had since attacked a party of soldiers and convicts gathering oyster shells nearby Risdon and beaten them off with 'Stones and Clubs'. 'We have every reason to believe them Cannibals', he concluded, 'and they may entertain the same Opinion of us'.[81]

Following Pemulwuy's execution, Aboriginal resistance to the British it seems was now considered highly dangerous. Collins ordered the little boy Robert Hobart May returned to his relatives, but the archival record indicates that he remained with a colonist in Hobart and eighteen months later was vaccinated against smallpox.[82] King didn't receive Collins' despatch about the 'attack on the Natives' until 24 August, when the evacuees from the Risdon settlement arrived back in Sydney. It is not known whether he interviewed Moore and Mountgarrett about the affray, but he must have seen the 'native heads' that Mountgarrett had preserved to send to Sir Joseph Banks, and in his response to Collins on 30 September he said: 'I am concerned at the unfortunate event of the party at Risdon Cove being compelled to fire on the Natives, but I hope the measure you had in contemplation to gain their confidence (the return of Robert Hobart May to his relatives) has succeeded.'[83] The *Sydney Gazette*, however, in a brief and highly sanitized version of the affray, had already noted that he was under 'the protection of a Gentleman' at Hobart.[84] At this point the 'attack on the Natives' at Risdon Cove slipped into the official void.

The affray remained, however, very much alive to the colonists in Hobart until the first formal inquiry twenty-six years later. Only then did the full impact become widely known. The inquiry heard that Aboriginal people, most likely the Leenowwenne and the Pangerninghe clans of the Big River nation, numbering about 150, were on a seasonal hunting trip which accounted for the presence of women and children and were unaware of the British arrival at Risdon Cove. The inquiry also revealed that many more Aboriginal people were slaughtered than recorded at the time, with estimates ranging from six to fifty, that the settlement was placed off limits until the bodies were burnt, and that the slaughter was the beginning of the ongoing war between the colonists and Aboriginal people.[85] Further information revealed that Lieutenant Moore was driven to excess by 'a brutal desire to see the Niggers run'.[86]

Nevertheless, fear of a French claim to Tasmania did not subside. On 5 November 1804, a third beachhead was established at Port Dalrymple in Northern Tasmania by Lieutenant Colonel William Paterson, three officers including William Moore and sixty-six soldiers from the NSW Corps, surgeon Mountgarrett and a cluster of settlers and convicts from Norfolk Island. Its purpose was to keep the French out of Bass Strait and stop the Americans from building ships on the islands in the Strait to engage in the sealing trade.[87] A week later, about eighty Aboriginal people appeared at the edge of the camp and their chief was given a looking glass, two handkerchiefs and a tomahawk in apparent payment for trespass. Instead, Aboriginal people, probably from the North Midlands nation, attacked the guards with spears and stones and tried to throw one of the soldiers over a cliff. In the ensuing affray, at least one Aboriginal man was killed and once again surgeon Mountgarrett preserved the poor man's 'very perfect head' for Sir Joseph Banks in London. A few days later, about fifty North Midlands men exacted revenge by spearing a civilian in the back. After that, relations appear to have become friendlier.[88] Even so, there is almost no mention of Aboriginal people in the area after 1806. The NSW Corps it appears left almost nothing to chance.

By the end of 1804, the governor of NSW, in conjunction with the NSW Corps, had secured vast areas of the colony from possible French invasion. They included the settlements in Tasmania and the newly established penal station at Newcastle on the Hunter River. They had also brutally put down an Irish uprising in similar ways to the Rebellion of 1798 and slaughtered a considerable number of Aboriginal people in Tasmania. The war with France it seems had violent implications for Aboriginal people that would have far-reaching consequences over the following decades. Indeed, had Britain not been at war with France, it is doubtful that Tasmania would have been occupied by the British at this time and it is possible that more Aboriginal people would have survived in the longer term.

In January 1808, a leading officer of the New South Wales Corps, Major George Johnston, deposed the governor, Captain William Bligh. In the hiatus that followed, Johnston and Bligh returned to England and Colonel William Paterson, as head of the NSW Corps, returned to Sydney to assume command as lieutenant governor. The British government, realizing that the nexus between a naval governor and a military garrison must be broken, appointed the colony's first military governor, Lieutenant Colonel Lachlan Macquarie, who brought his own regiment to New South Wales, to replace the NSW Corps. Between 1810 and 1821 he ruled the colony as a benevolent despot and became its longest-serving governor.

As an army officer with long experience in India, where he helped bring the forces of Tippo Saib under British control, and as a Scot whose family was dispossessed in the aftermath of Culloden, Macquarie saw New South Wales as the place to create a new kind of society that was more inclusive and egalitarian than any other in the British Empire. When he became governor in January 1810 the colonial population was 11,950. Over the next five years it reached 14,864, mostly from natural increases.[89] Macquarie lost no time embarking on a major infrastructure programme that included new roads, bridges, churches and schools, sought reconciliation with the Irish prisoners by permitting Catholic clergy to conduct services in the colony and conciliation with Aboriginal people living in the Sydney region. After his experiences with Tippoo Saib in India, he believed Aboriginal people in New South Wales, although just 'emerged from the remotest State of rude and Uncivilised Nature', were nevertheless 'perfectly peaceable', 'honestly inclined, and perfectly devoid of ... designated Trick or Trickery' and that it would only be a matter of time before they were fully incorporated into colonial society.[90]

Macquarie arrived in the colony when many of the older generation of Aboriginal people were dead, 'and it was thought that the younger, having witnessed so much terror and violence, were more timid and less encouraged to "come among us"'.[91] He considered that the distance and fear policy, in place for more than a decade, should be replaced with a more inclusive policy of bringing Aboriginal people under his control. But it did not include Aboriginal people giving evidence in court. Even so, he did insist that a colonist accused of killing Pemulwuy's son, Tedbury, should be tried, although from lack of evidence, no verdict was reached. Conversely, however, he insisted that the Aboriginal man Daniel Moowattin, who had lived in George Caley's home since childhood and thus should know the difference between good and evil, when charged with rape, was brought before the court where he was convicted and later hanged.[92]

Four years later, a new frontier war broke out on recently established farms at Appin, nestled between the Nepean and Georges River, on the settlement's southern frontier. Many farms faced on to both rivers, restricting access to the Muringong nation. Once again, the farmers and their servants had set off a chain reaction by abducting and killing Muringong women and children, resulting in the Muringong men killing farmers' wives and children.[93] In retaliation a group of colonists in the area formed a posse to attack a Muringong camp at night where they mutilated and brutally killed several women and children.[94] Unaware of this dreadful incident, Macquarie went out to meet some Muringong chiefs and told them that they must 'desist from all Acts of Depredation or Violence', to which they replied that if they were not 'shot at or wantonly attacked', they would not retaliate.[95] After they were alleged to have killed more farm labourers in July 1814, Macquarie ordered his first official punitive expedition of armed civilians to hunt for the killers. Three weeks later, the party returned apparently without success.[96]

By then Macquarie was making plans to open a school for Aboriginal children, even though the chaplain Samuel Marsden, after raising at least two Aboriginal boys in his home, considered that it was a waste of time to work among them and seek their conversion.[97] Determined to find a fresh approach Macquarie was inspired by the recently arrived missionary William Shelley, who considered that Aboriginal children brought up as a group in the instruction of Christianity and taught to read and write and learn some useful skills would find suitable life partners among themselves and thus have a future in the colony. To this end Macquarie established the Native Institution at Parramatta, a 'radical and thoroughgoing experiment in assimilating

Figure 6 *Augustus Earle, 'Portrait of Bungaree, a native of New South Wales, with Fort Macquarie, Sydney Harbour, in background', 1826. Source: National Library of Australia. Note the breastplate around his chest.*

Aboriginal children so that their future within white society was possible and acceptable (to whites)'.[98]

When few Aboriginal children were offered by their parents to attend the Institution, Macquarie decided to hold a feast at Parramatta for all Aboriginal people on the Cumberland Plain, on 28 December 1814, 'the day of the full moon', corroboree time, and persuade the elders to relinquish their children to him. At the end of the first feast, he acquired four children to join four others who were orphans, but they soon returned to their parents. The experiment only worked with orphaned Aboriginal children. But the feast itself was a huge success and became an annual event for the next two decades. Macquarie recognized its significance as a venue for communicating with Aboriginal people on policy issues and estimating their numbers by distributing blankets, but he was disappointed that the elders did not place complete faith in his civilizing agenda.[99] In a further gesture to 'civilize' some of the adult Aboriginal people in Sydney, such as Bungaree, by granting him a small parcel of land for a farm with about thirty others on the northern side of Sydney Harbour. And in a gesture of his imperial might he presented important, pacified chiefs with engraved metal breastplates.[100] But as in North America, where victorious British forces had conferred similar kinds of breastplates on their Indigenous allies, he also expected them to assist him in pacifying resistant Aboriginal people on the frontier.[101]

Violence and Massacre, February–April 1816

In February 1816, a large group of thirty or forty Muringong and Gandangarra men attacked a farm at Bringelly on another reach of the Nepean River, which formed the southwestern boundary of settlement and stole a servant's possessions. Seeking revenge, the servant called on his mates on nearby farms to help him 'recover the goods' from the Gandangarra camp on the other side of the river. But they walked into an ambush. The warriors closed in on them, wrenched away their muskets and, in a hail of spears, killed four men, speared another in the back and chased the rest back over the river.[102] The following day, sixty warriors crossed the river to attack another farm and, in a hail of spears, forced the occupants, the farmer's wife and her male servant, to seek refuge in the loft where the servant recognized one of the warriors as David Budbury of the Muringong people.[103]

David Budbury's name sent a shudder through the local settlers. Brought up in a settler's home, he spoke English well and knew how to use a musket. He was also known as a 'friendly native' in assisting explorers in finding 'new land' and the police in tracking down escaped convicts. Now he was an outlaw. In fear of his life from a settlers' reprisal party, Budbury sought refuge with a friendly settler who wrote to the governor in defence of his innocence. Indeed, many of the warriors were 'domesticated natives' who knew how to use muskets, although there is no evidence that they actually fired them at the colonists. A week later, they attacked another farm, killing three more servants. In revenge, the local magistrate formed a posse of forty settlers armed with muskets, pistols, pikes and pitchforks, and called on Budbury and other 'friendly natives' to guide them to the warriors' lair. Instead, Budbury led the posse into another ambush. On this occasion none of the settlers was killed, but when a farmer's wife was brutally killed a week or so later, Governor Macquarie decided to invoke British military might against the insurgents.[104]

He published a list of the insurgents' names and forced Budbury to join a major military offensive as an interpreter and guide it to the Gandangarra camps where no distinction would be made between the innocent and the guilty or between men and women. The children, however, would be spared and despatched to the Native Institution.[105] In early April 1816, Macquarie ordered three detachments of his regiment into the field. One, led by Captain James Wallis with Budbury as one of the Aboriginal guides, marched to the insurgents' heartland in Airds and Appin on the southern boundaries of settlement. Budbury soon absconded and Wallis was left to make his own judgement about the whereabouts of his foe. Another detachment, led by Lieutenant Charles Dawe with local colonist Bush Jackson as a guide and assisted by Tindale, 'chief of the Cowpastures tribe', was sent to Cowpastures to track down named insurgents. Although most Aboriginal camps were deserted when Dawe's troops arrived, an indication that Tindale had warned his compatriots in advance, a dawn raid on a camp on the Macarthur estate near Camden based on information by a local stockman yielded two men shot dead and a boy taken prisoner. The third detachment, led by Captain William Schaw and assisted by Aboriginal guides, Bidgee Bidgee and Harry, was sent to the Hawkesbury, to cut off any insurgents escaping to the north.[106]

Two weeks into the operation, Wallis was told that the insurgents in his area were camped at the back of Lachlan Vale, a settler's farm near Appin.

At 1.00 am on 17 April, he led the detachment to the camp in thick bush and found the fires still burning but no Aboriginal people. Knowing they could not have gone far, Wallis ordered a few soldiers to search the thick scrub, and when they heard a child's cry, they formed a line and pushed through the scrub towards a deep gorge of the Cataract River. Then Aboriginal people's dogs started barking and the soldiers opened fire. According to Wallis, most of Aboriginal people 'fled over the cliffs' and met their death in the gorge. Others were wounded or shot dead. The soldiers secured two women, a girl and two little boys, and counted fourteen bodies including two alleged insurgents, Durelle, a well-known Dharawel man, and Cannabayagal, a well-known Gandangarra warrior from the Burragorang Valley.[107]

Following Macquarie's orders, Wallis had the bodies of Durelle and Cannabayagal and of a woman hoisted up on trees on a conspicuous part of a range of hills later known as McGee's Hill. Their heads were cut off and taken to Sydney by one of Wallis' officers, and eventually ended up in the Anatomy Department at the University of Edinburgh.[108] Wallis also arrested two other named insurgents, Bitugully and Yellooming, who were sheltering with a settler in the area and, with the captured women and little boys who had survived the massacre, took them to Governor Macquarie in Sydney.[109] The boys were deposited in the Native Institution, but they soon ran away. The fate of the adult Aboriginal people is unknown.

Was the Appin massacre planned or was it an accident? Wallis' remarkably detailed report of the operation indicates that he knew the area well and in particular the deep gorge in the Cataract River. It is difficult not to draw the conclusion that he knew about the campsite well before the attack and that if Aboriginal people could be trapped, then, rather than seek their surrender, they would be forced to jump into the gorge.[110]

Following the Appin massacre, Macquarie imposed new measures to mop up the remaining insurgents. In this regard, he treated them like other insurgents in other parts of the British Empire. Armed Aboriginal people were forbidden to approach within a mile of any town or farm, and no more than six unarmed Aboriginal people could 'loiter' on any farm while and settlers were forbidden to 'harbour or conceal' any of them or provide 'Aid or Provisions'. He also sent out armed parties in search of the leading insurgents and it seems that by the end of August most of them were killed, or captured, arrested, sentenced and exiled with and their children despatched to the Native Institution.[111]

In November 1816, Macquarie declared an amnesty for the remaining insurgents on the condition that they surrendered before 28 December, the date of the Annual Feast at Parramatta. There is no evidence that any of them did surrender, but the Feast was a great success, with more than 180 Aboriginal people attending. Macquarie conferred on Tindale and Harry 'Reward of Merit' breastplates, and other friendly elders were rewarded with breastplates as 'chiefs'.[112] After twenty-eight years, the War on the Cumberland Plain was over.

7

'Determining to Exterminate Them' in 'Terror and Desolation': Massacre in North America

There was a process leading to massacre in North America that more or less followed the same pattern as in many parts of the colonial world. It began with initiating entry onto Indigenous land and was followed by an initial treaty and the cutting of roads into targeted lands when river access was not possible. This was inevitably followed by the surrounding of Indigenous peoples militarily, the despatch of letters to the United States Congress alleging 'Indian Depredations', the raising of a militia to 'chastise' Indigenous Americans and finally the massacring of the targeted peoples. Over and over again, and with remarkably little variation, these steps characterized the path to massacre in North America.[1] This was regardless of the Indigenous nation, culture or landscape involved. A look at three specific examples of this pattern in the Miami of Indiana, the Shawnee of Ohio and the Muscogee of Alabama demonstrates these steps in action, all leading to the same, unvarying end – mass killings through massacre.

The Shawnee of Ohio

The Shawnee of Southern Ohio, along the Ohio River, were targets of the militias over a longer period than most other Woodland nations. Settlers had had their eye on Ohio since the Seven Years' War, when then-Lieutenant George Washington was despatched to the Pennsylvania and Ohio back country. His main accomplishment there was to provide the British with an excuse to open the Seven Years' War in North America, following his ill-fated attack on the French at Jumonville Glen in western Pennsylvania, after which he surrendered to the French at the Battle of Fort Necessity.[2] While he travelled around in the area, Washington met in council at Chiningue on the Ohio River, originally a Shawnee town.[3] As with many important Indigenous trading towns, more than just Shawnee were present when Washington stopped by, including the famed Ohio Lenape War Chief, Shingask.[4] Also at Chiningue, Washington conversed with a Lenape speaker at a time when the territory was still theoretically under French control.

Washington's trip was close enough to a 'first entry' onto Shawnee lands for these meetings to count in the settlers' minds. By 1783, the United States maintained that, in having defeated the British, they had won the Old Northwest by conquest and, therefore, despatched commissioners to convene a 'peace' conference at the Big Miami River in Ohio. In 1791, the great Ottawa speaker Egushawa described this council as just 'more gracious papers, writing, belts, and messages' intended as intimidation, to require the Shawnee to 'sign what they [the settlers] call a deed', handing over Indigenous land.[5]

On 20 January 1786, despite internecine opposition, a Shawnee delegation arrived under Kekewepellethy, a major War Chief ('Captain Johnny' in the US records), to hear whether peace could be achieved 'consistently with the safety' of Shawnee 'women and children'.[6] The lead Commissioner, United States Army General Richard Butler, was certain that the British were up to something and manipulating the Shawnee delegation.[7] Throughout his journal, Butler indulged such paranoia, not infrequently deviating from the facts as given by Major Ebenezer Denny, also present, and as independently recounted by Egushawa in a 1791 speech.

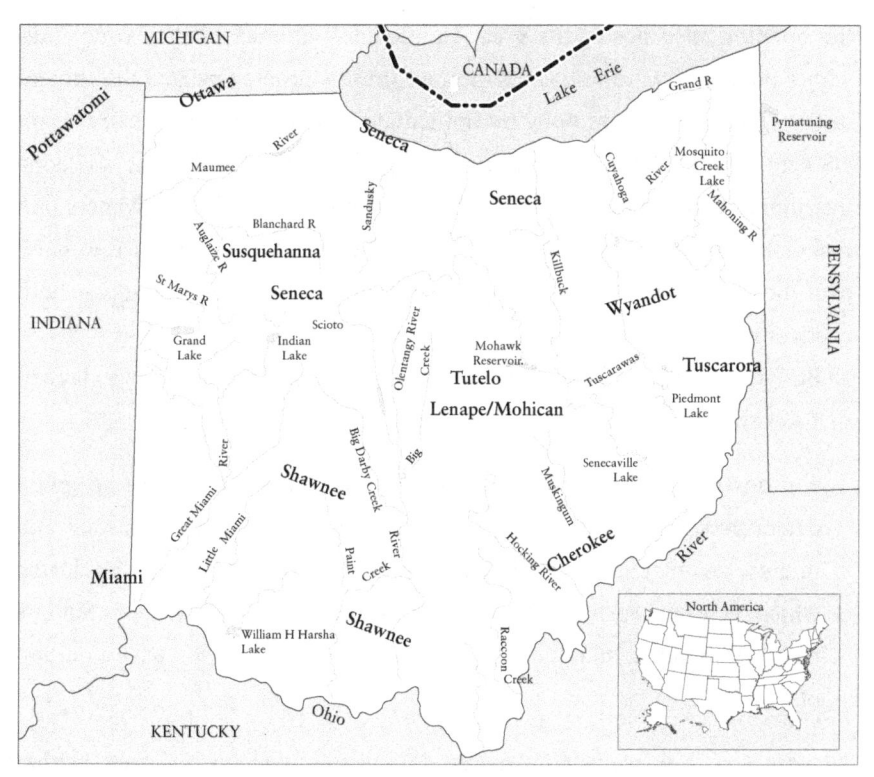

Map 2 *Map of Indigenous American nations in Ohio*

Before the first public meeting, the commissioners scolded the Shawnee for alleged misbehaviour in a clear threat to frighten and bend the delegation to the Commission's will.[8] According to Egushawa, Butler had 'required' the Shawnee delegation to 'sign an acknowledgement', agreeing that the United States' victory over Great Britain had equated to a loss of Shawnee lands.[9] Not easily cowed, Kekewepellethy thundered, 'I tell you brothers, what you say is not true! you never conquered any of us!'[10] Butler again dressed down the Shawnee, displaying a map with the 'boundary line' that the United States 'proposed' as a Shawnee reserve. When the Shawnee refused it, the commissioners moved to 'enlarge the boundary' slightly by encroaching on Wyandot and Lenape lands, a plan likewise rejected.[11]

The commissioners now threatened the Indigenous delegations by reminding them of their perilous 'situation' regarding the United States, using violent language 'to frighten our relations', Egushawa maintained.[12] Next, mimicking the opening speeches of the great Condolence Council of the Woodlands, whose purpose was to initiate calm, the Commissioners obviated the content of the Condolence Ceremony by immediately laying out seven, extravagant US demands.[13] Whether or not this miscarriage of the Condolence was done intentionally, the insult was delivered. Having expected the forgiveness of a real Condolence, Kekewepellethy rebuked Butler and curtly refused to hand over the demanded Shawnee adoptees, regarded by the United States as both captives and hostages to ensure compliance.[14]

Butler's journal ended on Kekewepellethy's refusal, but Egushawa claimed that Kekewepellethy admonished Butler, saying:

> you do this no doubt to insult us, because you know that we are poor, defenceless, and ignorant, and because you are, as you say, strong and mighty, and that you can have all our nations within your hand; by closing which, you can crush us all to death! and that all our nations are as but one child compared to an hundred warriors! and you tell me you have a million of warriors!

Nevertheless, Kekewepellethy roared, 'I will give you no hostages, neither shall you have our lands!' Eyeing the Commissioners, he added, 'I suppose now you will strive in earnest to conquer our lands, and to conquer me! I tell you brothers, that unless you come to your senses, these rivers must run with blood, for we will never submit to be your dogs!' Instead, Kekewepellethy put forward peace 'on proper terms', for 'I will neither give nor sell you my lands; nor shall you take them from me'.[15]

At that, Kekewepellethy threw 'a black string', that is, black wampum, on top of Butler's map.[16] A tense silence ensued. 'None touched the belt', said Denny, but in haughty displeasure, Butler 'contemptuously' flung the black wampum off the table, 'with his cane' and 'set his foot on it', an account that agrees with Egushawa's depiction.[17] 'Indians very sullen', Denny noted.[18] Egushawa quipped, 'This is another mode, my friends, in which the United States have been pleased to evidence their solicitude to live in peace with all nations!'[19]

Accusing Kekewepellethy of 'ungrateful and unwise' deportment in response to the 'bounty and mercy' of the United States, Butler further declared that all peace was off with the Shawnee, and summarily kicked Kekewepellethy and his delegation out of the conference, allowing only road provisions for 'eight days' – Denny said 'six days', and Egushawa, 'ten days provision of flour' – during which time, 'no man' would 'touch' the departing Shawnees.[20] However, after 'that time' had 'expired', Butler declared, the United States would 'take the most effectual measures to protect their citizens, and distress' Kekewepellethy's 'obstinate nation'.[21]

Indigenous and settler records diverge dramatically on what occurred next, with General Butler recording that, rising to leave, he, himself, 'threw down' white and black strings of wampum, a sign of guarded openness to discussion.[22] Butler's minutes claimed that a repentant Kekewepellethy then remained at the conference, begging to resume talks while littering the table with white wampum (full peace) and lavishly praising the United States, to the acclaim of the other Indigenous delegations.[23] However, Denny recorded that vague 'Shawnee begged another meeting' under 'their old king, Molunthy', who pleaded for 'pity on women and children'.[24] Although Melunathe was not the authorized Shawnee speaker at the conference, 'Melunathe, and some other old men, continued at the council fire', said Egushawa, and 'signed the paper the commissioners of the United States presented to them–and for which they have justly suffered!' he added, ominously. The Shawnee proper strongly repudiated Melunathe's treaty, although the name of 'Kakawipilathy' was falsely affixed to the final treaty as a signatory, in the all-too-common dubious behaviour with treaties that Indigenous Americans termed 'pen-and-ink witchcraft'.[25]

Melunathe complied with the demands of Butler, leaving Shawnee 'hostages' with the US Army to ensure 'good conduct' and the return of 'captives', but because Melunathe had no Indigenous standing to negotiate, on 24 March 1786, 'the five hostages deserted' to run home.[26] Nevertheless, on 27 March, the promised settler captives arrived from Melunathe, along with 'professions of friendship' and intelligence on Cherokee war parties in the vicinity.[27] Meantime, Shawnee defences had geared up under Kekewepellethy, who pledged to 'take up a rod and whip' to intruders south of the Ohio River, earning the revered Kekewepellethy and his men the label of 'banditti'.[28]

The militias simply ignored the United States' orders against settlers crossing into Ohio.[29] The usual narrative recounting 'depredations of the

Indians' quickly made the rounds, with Congress voting on 20 October 1786 to raise troop strength to 2,040 men, 'for the support of the frontiers', warning portentously of '1,000 warriors' gathering in the 'Shawanese towns' targeting Kentucky.[30] This was pure hysteria, however, for in 1782, when the Shawnee rushed all of their available men to the support of Upper Sandusky, Ohio, their entire army consisted of 140 Young Men.[31]

By the fall of 1786, all the pieces were in place to mount a successful massacre of the Shawnee. First, Washington's 1752–3 entry had justified 'peace treaty' demands, which had been refused.[32] Second and simultaneously, excoriations of the Shawnee were rampant, even as they were surrounded by forts and fort roads: Fort Harmar lay in western Ohio; Fort Pitt in the northeast; Fort Henry at modern-day Wheeling, West Virginia, on Ohio's southeastern edge; Fort Finney, at modern-day Louisville, Kentucky, directly south.[33] These forts provided excellent platforms from which to launch attacks into Ohio, including those by the Kentucky militias, among the most virulent of all militias. Because the whole area was so well-watered by sumptuous rivers, waterways stood as the primary roads into Ohio.[34]

The 1786 Kentucky militia attack on the Shawnee was purportedly in retaliation for their 'banditti' blocking river access into Ohio, with militiamen seeking special revenge for the 1782 defeat of militia 'Captain' Hugh McGary at a place called Blue Licks. During that fifteen-minute skirmish, McGary lost 72 of his 182 men, as opposed to three casualties on the Indigenous side.[35] Despite Congressional excuses of 'Indian depredations' then, the October 1786 foray by the Kentucky militia was, first, in retribution for Blue Licks and, second, as a direct punishment for Kekewepellethy's having repulsed Butler at the Big Miami Treaty Council.

On 13 September 1786, General George Rogers Clark siphoned off a detachment supposedly attacking the Miami to strike instead the Shawnee of southern Ohio, with orders to 'Spare the white blood', meaning any settler adoptees among the Shawnee.[36] On 1 October 1786, in full knowledge that 'all the warriors had gone' to Indiana to stand with the Miami, Kentucky 'Colonel' Benjamin Logan and his 900 militiamen made a beeline for the Shawnee clan town under Melunathe, the chief who had capitulated to Butler.[37] Two weeks later, Logan returned to Kentucky, having burnt to the ground seven Shawnee towns, in which he unsurprisingly met with 'very little opposition', a fact that did not stop the militia from taking 'scalps' along with 'thirty women and children prisoner'.[38] Indigenous records stated that the first three towns were quickly 'brought to ground' by the militias, the inhabitants killed or taken prisoner.[39] Overwhelmed, the Shawnee were 'retreating in all directions, making for the thickets, swamps and high prairie grass to secure them from their enemy'.[40] Undeterred, the militia 'charged' into the fleeing townsfolk, who 'fought with desperation, as long as they could raise knife, gun or tomahawk', said a subcommander. 'We dispatched all the warriors we overtook.'[41] According to the official Indigenous report of this incident, the last four towns attacked were 'laid in ashes' with the corn 'destroyed' along with 'other produce and everything else they had', before the militia took to its heels, back down 'the Banks of the Great Miamis [the Big and Little Miami Rivers] on their way to Kentucke [sic]'.[42]

The secondary leader of the 1786 Kentucky militia invasion of Shawnee country was none other than Hugh McGary, the incompetent commander who had managed to get seventy-two of his militiamen killed at the 'Battle' of Blue Licks. Assuming the military title of 'major', and even 'colonel' in the records of 1786, although he was generally considered a captain, McGary was not one to forgive or forget but was bent on personal exoneration.[43] McGary perceived Melunathe's populous town as a soft target, meaning that booty and a fair kill-count could be expected, along with scalps for the ubiquitous settler scalp bounties.

Melunathe and his town were, however, expecting protection, not attack, to have resulted from Melunathe's cooperation, so no one evacuated until the militia was actually bearing down on everyone.[44] Still hopeful, Melunathe went forward to meet the militia, 'dressed in an old cocked hat, set jauntily upon one side of his head, and a fine shawl thrown over his shoulders', carrying a peace pipe and a tobacco pouch while displaying 'the thirteen stripes' (the United States flag) and holding out 'the articles of the Miami treaty'.[45]

McGary, 'never particularly sweet, was as much inflamed by the sight of an Indian, as that of a wild bull'. Recognizing Melunathe as one who had been in the lead at Blue Licks, McGary 'scowled upon the old man', demanding whether he 'recollected the Blue Licks'.[46] Not speaking English, Melunathe just smiled, nodded and said either 'Yes' or 'Blue Licks', at which 'McGary instantly drew his tomahawk' to sink it 'in the head of the chief to his eyes'.[47] Immediately, McGary scalped the old man. At protests from a few militiamen, McGary 'raved like a madman', shouting, 'with many bitter oaths, that he would not only kill every Indian whom he met, whether in peace or war, at church or market' but also any militia protesters.[48] Other militiamen heartily approved of McGary's conduct, however, on the grounds that 'an Indian was not to be regarded as a human being, but ought to be shot down as a wolf whenever and wherever he appeared'.[49]

When the dust settled, either seven or eleven Shawnee scalps were turned in for bounties.[50] This disjuncture of official reporting matters, for it indicates, first, the small number of men overtaken in those towns when attacked and, second, the 'legitimacy' of the militia kills. The US government did not like to document that the women, children or 'friendlies' had had their scalps lifted. That one of the scalps had belonged to Melunathe is crucial to understanding the official drop from eleven to seven.[51] Besides Melunathe, the militia seized the diplomat Messquaughenacke and 'tyed him up and Burned him'.[52] A 'friendly' chief, Shade-HewikunweeEwikunwee-Eweecunwee-Hawikanwi, was also murdered.[53] The fourth dead 'friendly' is unknown. Because the United States had been resting its treaty laurels on Melunathe, not to mention using him as a spy against the Cherokee, the fact of his murder before so many witnesses caused some bureaucratic upset. Faced with no choice, in March of 1787, the government court-martialled but promptly acquitted McGary.[54]

The Miami of Indiana

The pretext for an American entry onto Miami land came late in 1778, when militia General George Rogers Clark invaded Indiana to claim the land for Virginia.[55] The capital of the Miami Confederacy, Kekionga (modern-day Fort Wayne, Indiana) sat in the eastern half of the land, at the headwaters of the Maumee River. Immediately as the first settlers got a look at Indiana, they coveted the fertile land, a desire exacerbated by the fledgling American government, which paid its soldiers in 'land warrants', with officers receiving thousands of acres.[56] The British aided the invasion of Indiana at the peace conference in Paris in 1783 that ended the American Revolution. No Indigenous 'allies' attended, while the United States received Indigenous land as the 'Old Northwest' territories.[57] Once the Indigenous allies learnt the full details of this transaction, they flatly refused to recognize it, even as the United States asserted its legal 'right' to seize the territories.[58]

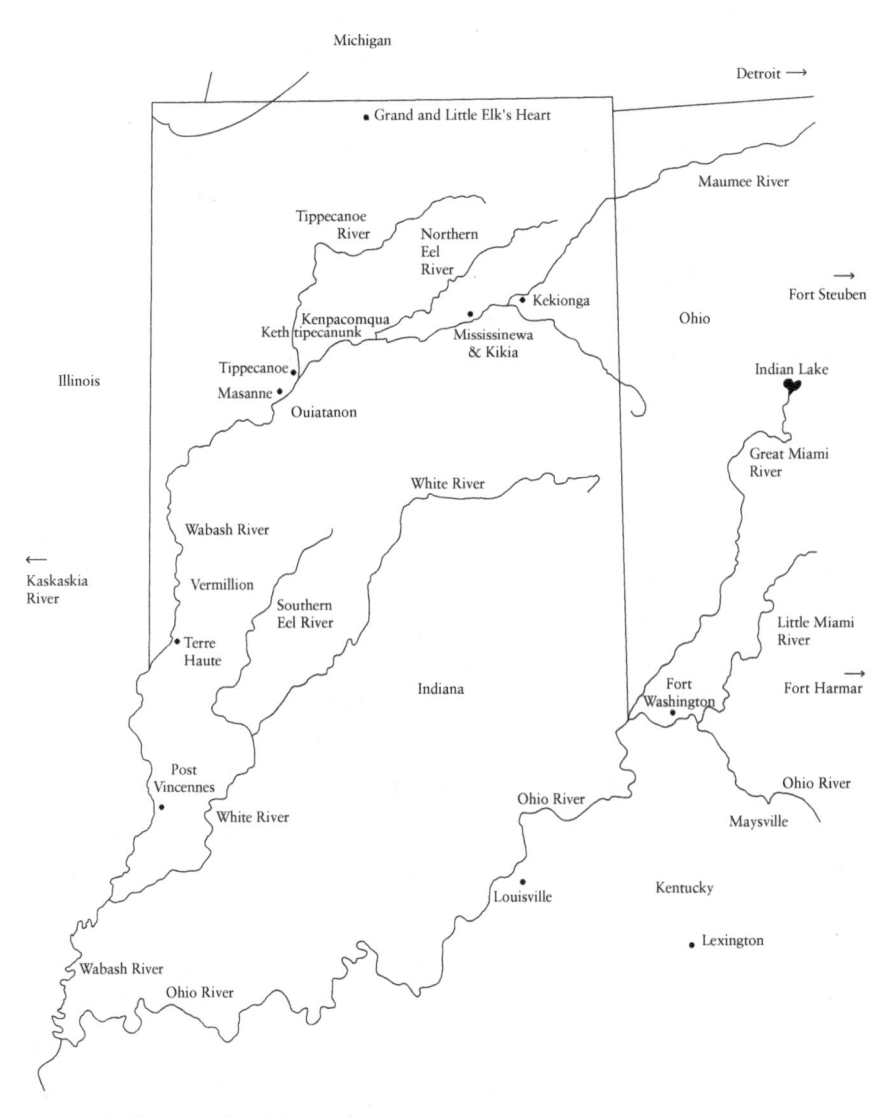

Map 3 *Indiana in the eighteenth century*

In June 1784, Congress sent in Revolutionary War veteran Lieutenant-Colonel Josiah Harmar at the head of 700 troops to 'protect' the settlers in the Northwest Territory.[59] Harmar's tour of Indiana in the summer of 1787 was primarily if covertly for the purpose of land appraisal.[60] On 5 October 1787, Congress appointed another notable Revolutionary War veteran, General Arthur St. Clair, as the federal governor of the Northwest Territory, to establish 'peace and harmony' between the United States and the Miami.[61] Under the command of Major John Francis Hamtramck, 'Post Vincennes', Indiana, was duly established at the western edge of Indiana. Despite Indigenous opposition to any United States takeover of the Old Northwest, in 1788, St Clair determined 'to hold a treaty with the Indians … for the extinguishing [sic] their claims to lands within certain limits'.[62] Not comprehending the confederated governmental structure of the Miami peoples, however, St Clair ineptly treated with Miami underlings and then became irate when they halted proceedings to check with their superiors.[63]

Pressured by the Secretary of War, Henry Knox, to do something, St Clair decided to spin his failures as conclusive evidence of Miami hostility, providing a pretext for war. Consequently, on 23 August 1790, St. Clair gravely informed the Secretary that his 'offers of peace' made on 'principles of justice and humanity' to the Miami had been refused, which stood to 'justify the conduct of the United States' in initiating a war.[64] To whip up the war drive, St Clair began papering the home office with dire tales of 'Indian depredations', in which Indigenous nations of Ohio and Indiana were mingled under the same heading, 'Northwestern Indians', although they were under separate, Indigenous governing structures.[65] By 19 September 1790, St Clair floated to the Secretary of War his plan for Hamtramck's attack on the Miami, 'to exhibit' the United States' 'power to punish them for' their largely imaginary 'hostile depredations', as well as 'for their refusing to treat with the United States'.[66]

In fact, wanton attacks were made against the Indigenous populations. In 1788, for instance, 'Major' Patrick Brown of Kentucky led sixty militiamen into Indiana, there murdering nine so-called friendlies, scalping six of them to cash in on the United States and state scalp bounties.[67] The 1790 Pennsylvania scalp bounty was $100, more than most farmers earned in a year.[68] Lewis

Wetzel (1763–1808) bragged of 'stalking and hunting Indians as he would wild animals', killing 100. He was arrested for wounding a 'peaceful Indian' in 1789 and subsequently released 'because conviction could not be obtained from a frontier jury for the murder of an Indian'.[69]

Upon the Indigenous 'refusal' to negotiate, war was the policy, so when a Miami peace delegation arrived at Post Vincennes on 20 August 1790, Hamtramck 'deceived them by talking peace' while planning war.[70] By 23 October 1790, President Washington agreed to St Clair's 'operation'.[71] Hamtramck marched in from the west, and Harmar from the east, but tipped off and aided by local French settlers, the Miami evacuated ahead of Hamtramck's army.[72] In the east, Harmar attacked Kekionga, likewise evacuated in advance of his march. Joined by the Indian Confederacy, the Miami utterly defeated Harmar, who lost 180 men.[73] The Miami victory was pyrrhic, however, for all told, the Miami lost about 120 'prime warriors'. Moreover, Hamtramck and Harmar cut down all Miami crops and burnt their housing stock, leaving them with the prospect of a grim, cold, hungry winter.[74]

Clearly, a military road was required for complete victory, so preparatory to the next invasion, on 30 August 1791, Hamtramck began to build a road on his western end adequate for 'the passage of the artillery', to link up with a corresponding road coming from the east.[75] Then, starting on 17 September 1791, St Clair ordered a southern road cut north to Kekionga, the route dotted with forts.[76] Not awaiting the road's completion, the Kentucky militia returned in June of 1791, partly to prevent the Miami's recovering from the 1790 attack before staging the next, but also because the militia was incensed at its 1790 trouncing. With the knowledge of St Clair, who was busy preparing his own assault on Kekionga, Kentucky 'Brigadier General' Charles Scott ordered an attack on the eastern capitals, Ouiatanon of the Wea Miami and Masanne of the Kickapoo (Miami-associated). Knowing that the 500 men in these two towns capable of being mustered were off defending Kekionga, Scott fell on the twin cities with 750 militiamen, while despatching between 300 and 400 others to mop up outlying towns. At Ouiatanon and Masanne, Scott killed all the people whom he trapped as they attempted to flee in five, jam-packed canoes.[77]

Scott next peeled off 500 Kentucky militiamen, against 'the important town of Kethtipecanunk', composed of Miami along with intermarried and interracial Miami-French inhabitants.[78] The French-Wea Metís 'lived in a state of civilization', a fact that did not prevent their destruction. Scott killed eight outright and 'literally skinned' a 'war chief' alive.[79] All told, Scott tallied up the housing and crops destroyed, the 'five wounded and thirty-two killed' among 'the enemy', and the fifty-eight taken prisoner.[80] Prisoners usually wound up in slavery. Scott boasted that not a man had been lost by the Americans.[81] Typically, when the other side cannot fight back, this will be the outcome. Because the Miami men were out of town defending Kekionga, just who made up Scott's kill count is unclear. Scott reported only thirty dead, all told, yet just one canoe would hold thirty women and children.[82] Scott must not have included a full head count of the five canoe-kills. Such fudging of the casualty counts was always a signal in militia reports that innocent women, children and the elderly had been murdered.[83]

By the autumn, St Clair's road was completed, so Indiana was now fully passable by US troops, with the Miami clans surrounded on the eastern, western and southern borders of Indiana, preparatory to the Kekionga assault of 4 November 1791, intended to finish off the Miami. The militias, however, faced 2,000 armed, determined men, mostly from Ohio nations, led by the brilliant Miami military strategist Meshikinokwak (1747–1812, 'Little Turtle').[84] The United States suffered 647 dead and 243 wounded, while the Indians suffered 21 dead and 40 wounded.[85] Incredibly enough, St Clair twice represented Kekionga to the US Secretary of War as a United States' victory, in which 'the savages ha[d] got a most terrible stroke'.[86] Once revealed, the truth resulted in St Clair's retirement from the US Army and subsequent court martial.[87] No Miami treaty was promulgated until 1803, when the new Governor of the Northwest Territories forced a series of treaties, the Vincennes Treaties, upon the by-then devastated 'Wabash Indians'.[88]

However brilliant, Meshinokwak's defences at Kekionga should not be misread. Even as the 1791 summer campaigns were being mounted, the Wabash population had already, as St Clair observed, been 'much reduced'.[89] After two years of dedicated attacks, Miami numbers had fallen below sustainable levels in many of the Wabash towns.[90] The Wea and Pepikokia were almost entirely wiped out, with the remaining Miami gutted by two years of warfare and, more importantly, by the utter destruction of their towns, homes and crops. By the time of Removal in 1840, the Miami census was 484, down from 5,660 in 1788, that is, a fall in population of about 91 per cent.[91]

The Muscogee of Alabama

The militia were similarly unleashed against the Muscogee of Alabama from November 1813 through to March 1814, when they sustained the largest recorded instance of killing in US history, with 5,000 Muscogee perishing. A British entry before the founding of the United States again rationalized the US entry into Muscogee territory. Under a 1732 British land grant, James Edward Oglethorpe schemed in 1739 to empty British gaols into America, incidentally cajoling a treaty of sorts out of the Alabama Muscogee for his purpose.[92] Using this as a basis, in 1783 the US government negotiated with a puppet, Hoboi-Hilr-Miko (Alexander McGillivray), falsely elevating and anointing him as the 'Principal Chief' of the Alabama Muscogee to extract land cessions through his settler-accommodating 'council'.[93] The Muscogee might have repudiated Hoboi-Hilr-Miko, but to no avail.

In 1786, following up on the Hoboi-Hilr-Miko opening in the south, as well as the first forced treaties in the Old Northwest, Congress set up two superintendencies over so-called albeit not-yet-seized 'Indian Territories'. The purpose was to remove regulation from states to place all power over newly seized lands squarely into federal hands.[94] Consequently, in 1796, Congress created the office of 'General Superintendent of all Indians South of the Ohio River', appointing a former Continental Congressman, Benjamin Hawkins of North Carolina, a Southern slave-and plantation-owner, as its first superintendent.[95] Hawkins fully appreciated how important acquiring fresh Indigenous land was to keeping the slave plantation economy going. He also understood the ordinary southerner settler's attitude towards Indigenous ownership of the land, recording in 1797 the 'doctrine' of the settlers: 'let us kill the Indians, bring on a war, and we shall get land'.[96]

For all the window-dressing of 'civilizing' the Muscogee through treaties, forced Christianity and the European-style, debt-based economy disguised as 'trade', Hawkins grasped that his main job was to keep Tennessee, Georgia and Mississippi from helping themselves to Alabama by securing it to the United States first. Towards this end, he immediately re-invigorated the 'Creek National Council' after the fraudulent model of Hoboi-Hilr-Miko, ensuring that the council was composed of his own collaborators among the Muscogee, 'chiefs' whom he could manipulate into rubber-stamping whatever proposition he put before them.[97] Like its prototype, this 'Council' displaced and dispossessed the traditional and very sophisticated Muscogee government.[98] Hawkins streamlined Muscogee democracy into a non-representative Council, never recognized as legitimate by traditional Muscogee.[99] This efficiently divided the Muscogee into a wealthy faction, which benefited from the sale of traditional Muscogee land, and the traditional faction, which wanted nothing to do with imposed councils, their regulations or their treaty negotiations. The assimilants lived in the southern third of Alabama, cheek-by-jowl with incoming settlers, whereas the traditionals, 5,000 strong, lived in the northern two-thirds of upstate Alabama. The traditionals entirely rejected the trappings of imposed Euro-Christian culture, preferring their own culture.

Meanwhile, southeastern settlers perceived the federal government as too slow with its ordered, legally constructed land seizures. Hardened by having just been through a bloody Revolution against Great Britain, pro-slavery factions were eager even to break away from the original seaboard states to form their own countries. One of the most important schemes was the Burr Conspiracy, mounted in 1804 and hatched by the sitting Vice President, Aaron Burr, who inveigled both James Wilkinson, the third-senior officer of the US Army and first Governor of the Louisiana Territory in 1805, and Andrew Jackson, who was, in 1804, State Court Judge of Tennessee, the state's top judicial post.[100] In September 1806, two months before the conspiracy collapsed, Jackson hosted Burr at his massive slave plantation, just outside of Nashville, Tennessee.[101] The conspiracy crumbled only because Wilkinson got cold feet at the last moment, betraying the plot to President Thomas Jefferson.[102]

The aftershocks of the Burr Conspiracy helped precipitate the Muscogee massacre. Although Jackson was not named directly in the legal uproar following the conspiracy's exposure, his involvement was known and even blew up in his face when Burr apparently blackmailed Jackson using documents still in his possession.[103] Thus, starting in 1807, Jackson was scrambling to repair his tattered reputation by claiming the championship of the South's Slavocracy, and the best way to do that was to play to the land-hunger of his fellow settlers. He was, himself, both a high-level speculator in the slave trade and a ruthless wheeler-dealer in land speculation, in both of which endeavours he excelled financially, so that he stood to gain handsomely from the acquisition of Alabama.[104] Thus, despite the Burr Conspiracy having been foiled, Jackson decided to carry out its essential aim of land acquisition but as an American militia general acquiring new lands for the South.

The Muscogee tinderbox did not go unnoticed by United States' authorities or by lesser state authorities, with everyone impatient for an excuse to enter fertile Alabama in a 'just war', the legal excuse for large-scale land appropriation under the 'right by conquest', a lynchpin of US 'Indian law'.[105] To be in the best position for the war, on 3 March 1805, the US Congress authorized cutting an east-west road straight through Alabama, from Athens, Georgia, to New Orleans, Louisiana.[106] At first, hardly more than a path, the road could sustain little besides foot traffic, but within six years, it had been rendered a substantial highway, carrying settlers.[107] Between October 1811 and March 1812, almost 3,300 settlers traversed this road to the coveted Tombigbee and Tensaw regions, on the southeastern edge of Alabama, creating Fort Mims.[108]

This entire time, settler propaganda spread stories about the Muscogee, featuring the usual complaints about 'Indian depredations'. In April 1812, the story of Thomas Meredith received wide public attention when, drunk, he was accidentally killed on the federal road.[109] The excitement was quieted by the execution of six Muscogee, including the accused killer.[110] After the Meredith affair faded, a new story arose of 'Six Persons' murdered, with the Muscogee carting off Mrs Martha Crawley.[111] Given the titillating circumstance surrounding a captured white woman, the affair was eagerly seized upon by the public, but faded when, two days later, she escaped, 'half starved and half naked'.[112]

At this point, the Muscogee's civil war provided the event settlers had been looking for, in what persists in being labelled the 'Fort Mims massacre'.

Fort Mims was really just a small, walled, civilian village, sitting on the far southwestern edge of Alabama. It would never have been attacked by the Muscogee but for a failed militia skirmish, somewhat grandly called the Battle of Burnt Corn. A group of sixty Red Sticks had negotiated a few arms from the Spanish garrison at Pensacola, Florida, for use in the Muscogee's civil war of assimilant versus 'Red Stick' traditionals.[113] Hysterical at the thought of Red Sticks with rifles, however, a 180-strong militia waylaid the returning Muscogee, only to be conclusively routed by forty of the sixty Muscogee who, with thirteen rifles among them, beat the militia.[114]

As militia attacks went, this affair was already humiliating enough, but then it led to the disaster of Mims, for the Red Sticks appear to have followed the militia to the fort.[115] Amassing 726 men, they attacked Fort Mims.[116] Contrary to settler propaganda, most of the 130 dead in Mims were soldiers, militiamen or African slaves.[117] On their side, the Red Sticks sustained a significant loss of 202 men.[118] Even though the vast majority of those killed inside the fort were soldiers, slaves or militiamen, propaganda claimed that 350 settlers had died horribly, every one of them defenceless farmers, widows and orphans.[119] Here was the pretext being sought for the 'just war' against the Muscogee. Without Congressional authorization, Jackson personally raised 2,500 militiamen and entered Alabama, starting the Creek War, even as the United States was losing against the British in the War of 1812.[120] Counting Fort Mims, historians of the Creek War typically list eleven 'battles', yet each battle, apart from Mims, was a massacre of Red Stick 'warriors' enumerated immediately before Jackson's invasion.[121] In all, sixty Muscogee towns were levelled, and the inhabitants killed, but the three largest and most illustrative of the attacks were at the Red Stick towns of Tallushatchee, Hillabee and Tohopeka ('Horseshoe Bend').[122]

On 3 November 1813, militia 'Brigadier General' John Coffee of Tennessee, business partner and relative of Jackson, led his 900 men into Tallushatchee.[123] In a sneak-attack at dawn, Coffee's men 'rushed up to the doors of the houses, and in a few minutes killed the last warrior of them' along with 'a few of the squaws and children'.[124] Militiaman Davy Crockett said that 'their squaws and all would run and take hold of any of us they could' with 'seven squaws' crowding 'one man'.[125] When one woman fought back, the 'enraged' militia 'fired on' her, until she had 'at least twenty balls blown through her'. The militia 'now shot them like dogs', while setting fire to a home containing forty-six men to burn them alive.[126]

Not content with this damage, the militia added insult to injury the next day, by returning to the scene of the massacre in search of food. The strewn 'carcasses' of the Muscogee looked 'awful, for the burning had not entirely consumed them', Crockett claimed, but the militia nonetheless rummaged through the remains, finding 'a fine chance of potatoes' in a crawl space of the house in which the forty-six men had burnt. The militiamen proceeded to eat the potatoes, which had been fully roasted in the body fat dripping from the burning men.[127] Between 186 and 200 Muscogee died, with 84 given as captured, whereas Coffee lost 5 men killed with 41 wounded.[128]

Hillabee constituted an even more egregious massacre, especially because its three towns had surrendered five days before they were attacked.[129] Jackson officially accepted Hillabee's surrender on 17 November 1813.[130] On 18 November, militia 'General' James White attacked and sacked the Hillabee towns, massacring their inhabitants. Sixty of the Red Sticks were summarily murdered with 256 taken prisoner.[131] Jackson drafted a report on these Hillabeean 'battles' but never sent it to the US Army.[132]

As January opened in 1814, the Red Sticks still had 4,000 of the 5,000 men with whom they had started out.[133] By the end of January 1814, death had halved that number to at best 2,000 men, and perhaps to as few as 1,800.[134] When Jackson moved on Tohopeka, with help from Cherokee and Muscogee warriors, there were but 1,200 Red Sticks left, including all the women, children, and old folks.[135] These Red Sticks had practically no food and, lacking any ammunition, were using 'war-clubs and bows and arrows'.[136] Jackson rolled in with 5,000 men.[137]

'Determining to exterminate them', Jackson immediately coordinated a three-pronged attack, leaving the Red Sticks no way out but to cross the river.[138] On 28 March, Jackson wrote of his success at Tohopeka in a detailed report tallying 557 killed immediately, with a 'great number' of uncounted more 'killed by the horsemen'.[139] Three hundred more were killed trying to cross the river, for a total of 857.[140] Twenty managed to slip through Jackson's lines, but the militia ran them down, killing sixteen. Meantime, Jackson took 250 prisoners, 248 of them women and children.[141] In the span of five months, Jackson had managed to wipe out 5,000 Red Sticks.[142]

8

'Striking Terror into the Enemy': The Ethnic Cleansing of the Zuurveld

We will have to pass over the long and complicated history of European, that is Portuguese-African, interactions in the Cape dating to the late fifteenth century when it was a refreshment post for ships on the way to the East, to the eventual establishment of a European, that is, Dutch stronghold in the mid-seventeenth century under the Dutch East India Company (*Vereenigde Oost Indische Compagnie*, or VOC). We will briefly touch on the complex history of expansion from the Cape north and then east into the African interior, and the conflicts that ensued between the Dutch settlers and the Indigenous peoples they encountered – the Khoikhoi, the San, and the Xhosa – before examining the British attempt to clear the Zuurveld of Xhosa in 1812.[1]

The Northern Frontier and the General Commando

In the Cape Colony, there were basically two distinct though inter-connected frontier zones, to the north and to the east, during the revolutionary era. The first of these was the so-called Northern Frontier, which was a frontier zone in which Khoisan societies and colonial settlers interacted.[2] It was a zone characterized by the expansion of the trekboers – semi-nomadic Dutch colonial pastoralist, subsistence farmers – into the arid interior of the Karoo, the semi-desert region of the Cape.[3] This expansion was at the expense of the Indigenous peoples of the region, the pastoralist Khoikhoi, and the hunter-gatherer San. These Khoisan societies resisted the colonial advance vigorously and their resistance was met by attacks from colonial commandos – groups of armed and mounted trekboers together with their Khoikhoi or mixed-race servants – who massacred the resisters whilst incorporating any survivors, usually women and children, into the trekboer economy as bonded labourers.

The years 1770 to 1800 correspond to the last years of the rule of the VOC and the first years of the First British Occupation of the Cape (1795–1803), before the British attempted to bring an end to the indiscriminate massacre of San that was taking place on the colony's frontier. These years also correspond to the merciless struggle for control of the environmental resources of the Cape interior, particularly the crucial escarpment of the Roggeveld, Nieuweveld and Sneeuberg mountains that marked the region between the summer and winter rainfall areas. This was an important region as both the hunter-gatherer and pastoralist societies needed to move from one rainfall area to another seasonally to follow the animals they depended on as they moved to replenish water sources and rejuvenated grazing.[4]

The San fought hard to defend their territory and in the process were targeted for extermination by the trekboer commandos. These commandos, groups of armed and mounted men under the command of an officially appointed leader of whom the majority of members were of Khoikhoi, 'Bastaard' (men of mixed slave and European or Khoikhoi and European origin) or 'Bastaard-Hottentot' descent (men of mixed Khoikhoi and slave origin), had originally evolved to protect the flocks and herds of the trekboers from the San or to try to recover stolen livestock.[5] In time, however, their function became more punitive and was aimed at tracking down and destroying groups of San identified as being hostile. At first, commandos were under the control of the VOC to the extent that the government appointed the commando leader – a *veldwagtmeester* or a *veldcorporaal* – and supplied the ammunition to distribute to the men under his command. In theory, the VOC also had to approve of the launching of a commando, and thereby legitimate it, but over time local *veldwagtmeesters* tended to take matters into their own hands and were not always punctilious about reporting on the activities of the ad hoc commandos they raised in immediate retaliation for San attacks.[6]

An important stage in the transition of the commando from being a primarily defensive institution into a primarily offensive one was the establishment of the General Commando of 1774.[7] This commando was organized by the VOC authorities specifically to reduce the San of the interior escarpment 'to a permanent peace and tranquillity' or otherwise to ensure they were 'entirely subdued and destroyed'.[8] In a period of three or four months the General Commando, which was divided into three columns, succeeded in killing a reported 503 San and capturing 239 women and children for the loss of only one commando member killed. These figures alert us to the fact that there was a very high ratio of San killed to San captured and a very low colonial casualty rate. The figures, in other words, suggest that during the course of the General Commando the killing of the San took place in the form of a series of massacres in which the San were virtually unable to protect themselves. The details concerning the captives are also revealing for they suggest that very few men were taken prisoner, whereas women and children under twelve years of age were.[9]

Time would show that these women and children were, contrary to the instructions of the VOC, seldom released, but instead treated as indentured labourers under circumstances often worse than enslavement. The practice of taking San women and children captive would become normalized, as a result of which the commandos had two objectives – to kill male San and to capture women and children when convenient or necessary. Such captives, according to the authorities, were supposed to be treated like other 'free Hottentots' and required to work for the poorer colonists for a 'fixed and equitable term of years'. In practice, however, they were not treated as though they were free but were treated more like the indentured 'Bastaard-Hottentots' who were obliged to have their names and particulars entered in special rolls and to work for their masters until they were aged eighteen (or twenty-five). The surviving rolls date from 1776 to 1803 and list a total of 258 child captives officially recorded during this period. These figures need to be regarded as inadequate, for there were many more San who were captured by colonists during these years of intense commando activity than are recorded here. The General Commando alone took 289 captives – more than the total listed between 1776 and 1803.[10] Colonists justified taking women and children captive since, they argued, it would be crueller to leave them as widows or orphans. Thus, Barend Burger told Donald Moodie in 1836, 'I always considered carrying away children, after a kraal [a traditional village] had been subdued, an act of mercy. I believe the practice to have originated in that feeling rather than in any other.'[11]

Although the General Commando seems to have been a colonial victory in terms of the number of casualties inflicted upon the San and the number of them who were taken captive, it was, in fact, a failure with regard to its objective – to bring the San to a state of 'permanent peace and tranquillity'. The San continued to resist, and commandos became a regular and continuous aspect of frontier life until the end of the eighteenth century. There were, indeed, some years when the colonial borders in the north were in retreat as the trekboers were forced to abandon their farms due to a combination of San resistance and drought.[12] No other commando ever matched the scale of the General Commando but, in many ways, the General Commando was typical of later commandos with a similar ratio of casualties to captives, a high body count of San males relative to a low body count of colonial males, and no category of 'wounded' for the San. Adult males were almost invariably killed, and women and children taken captive.

It is not possible to give an account of all the incidents of massacre that occurred during the 'time of the commandos', even if all such incidents were recorded, which they were not, but we should not doubt that thousands of San were killed by commandos during the eighteenth century before the British managed to impose a temporary peace on the frontier in 1798. What sort of mortality rate did the San suffer? It is very difficult to estimate the numbers of San in the Cape around 1652 or, indeed, around 1780. Most of the San lived outside of the colonial borders and were only listed in the records when they were either killed or captured by commandos. Mohamed Adhikari has estimated that some 10,000 San were killed during the period 1770 to 1800, and although this estimate is not based on archival research, it seems credible.[13]

Whatever the exact figures were the impact on these deaths on San society were catastrophic. Although the rate of slaughter declined after 1798 and under the British authorities who ruled the Cape in the nineteenth century, the damage had been done. In addition to the unsustainable population losses that the San had suffered during the period of VOC rule at the Cape they were also weakened by participating in the British peace initiative of 1798. By accepting gifts of livestock and allowing colonists to enter their territory unmolested they dropped their guard and allowed the colonial frontier to move forward again. The consequences would be fatal for them.[14]

The Eastern Frontier Wars

The second major frontier zone was the so-called Eastern Frontier, long regarded by South African historians as the most important site in the 'epic of South Africa's creation'.[15] This was a zone in which the primary antagonists were the settlers and the Xhosa. The Xhosa were an agricultural as well as a stock-keeping people, a Bantu-speaking branch known to linguists and anthropologists as the Nguni people (the southern Nguni are today's Xhosa and the northern Nguni the Zulu). The favourable rainfall conditions of the eastern Cape allowed for the growing of food crops and had allowed the Xhosa to become populous and powerful.[16] They were the dominant Indigenous group in the region though there were still some Khoisan groups among them, though usually in a subordinate position. When the first trekboers began to encroach on Xhosa territory in the mid-eighteenth century they found the Xhosa to be too strong to subjugate. Initial clashes between the two societies, beginning around 1779, were of a violent yet inconclusive nature, characterized by reciprocal cattle raiding and punitive strikes. With the arrival of the British government and British troops at the Cape in 1795 the balance of power began to shift. British policy was directed towards establishing a fixed boundary between the protagonists and enforcing peace between them.[17] To accomplish this the British eventually came to believe that it was necessary to remove the Xhosa from land deemed to be part of the colony. A policy of land clearance and ethnic cleansing was thus initiated, accompanied

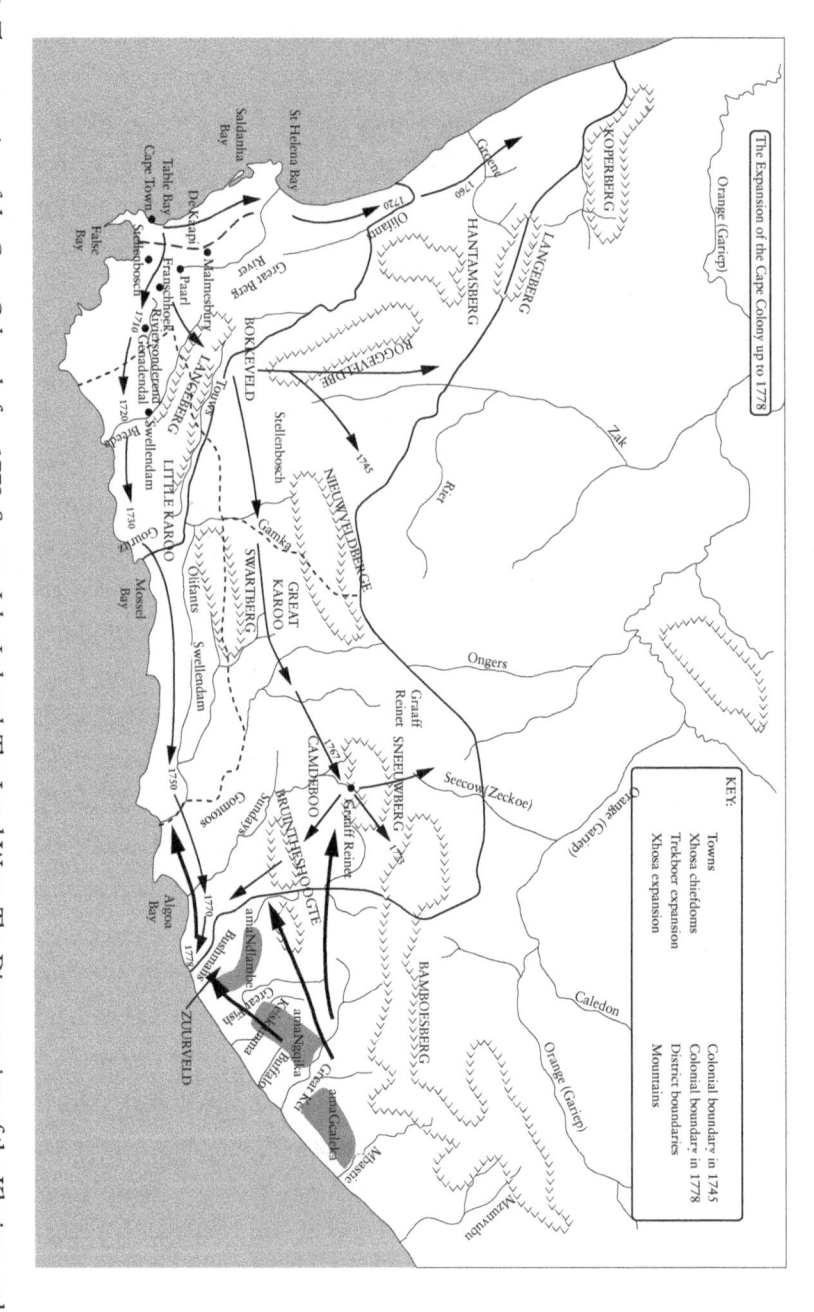

Map 4 *The expansion of the Cape Colony before 1778.* Source: John Laband, *The Land Wars: The Dispossession of the Khoisan and Ama Xhosa in the Cape Colony* (Cape Town: Penguin, 2020).

by tactics of scorched earth and massacre. The Xhosa, sometimes assisted by disaffected Khoisan groups, resisted this invasion with both guerrilla warfare and massed attacks on colonial forces. Despite their resistance by 1820 the Xhosa had been expelled from the Zuurveld – the contested frontier region – and British settlers established in their place.

We will again have to pass over the complicated interactions between the Dutch and British colonists and the Xhosa in 1780–1803 that led to a number of subsequent wars between these antagonists. By the time the British arrived to conquer the Cape in 1795 – thereby preventing it from falling into French hands – there had already been two frontier wars in the region, although some historians suggest that these wars were, essentially, a series of cattle raids and retaliatory raids between the competing sides. The result of these wars was a stalemate. Neither side was able to remove the other, and neither side was able to enforce the return of stolen cattle. The Third Frontier War (1799–1803) coincided with the arrival of the British, and it presented the new government with a challenge. Would it, unlike the VOC or the Xhosa chiefs, be able to impose its will on the frontier zone and enforce a durable peace? The events of the war are complex but perhaps its main feature was that, for the first time, regular troops were sent to the frontier zone alongside the usual ad hoc formations of commandos and colonial militia.[18] The troops seem to have had more of an impact on the Khoikhoi than on the Xhosa, for when the local Khoikhoi saw British troops arriving at Graaf Reinet, accompanied by the Hottentot Regiment, they concluded that the British had come to overthrow the local Boers with the help of the Khoikhoi and rose in rebellion against the Dutch settlers. This was not the effect the British wished to have. To quell the Khoikhoi rebellion, they were forced to promise the Khoikhoi leaders some concessions, such as a grant of land and a reform of labour conditions.[19] British troops did conduct operations against the Xhosa, but the main British goal at this stage was to make peace not to inflict defeat through a costly war.[20]

As it was, the British were too hard-pressed elsewhere in the world to do more than patch up a peace in the eastern Cape. The peace was, in effect, little more than a truce. It largely confirmed the Xhosa in their possessions while the promises that had been made to the Khoikhoi could not be kept because the British were, shortly afterwards, to hand back the Cape to the Dutch. When the British returned in 1806, they found the situation on the eastern frontier much as they had left it in 1803, namely, in a state of dynamic tension. One of the first priorities of the Second British Occupation, therefore, was to settle the unfinished business of frontier security.

The Second British Occupation

Even though the Second British Occupation of the Cape suggested that there might be a more determined effort on the part of the British to solving the eastern frontier security problem, such an initiative was not immediately forthcoming. In 1806 the British Empire could ill afford to send large bodies of troops to the strategically non-essential eastern Cape. The priority was for the new regime at the Cape to assert British control over the colonists and the colony rather than to try to subjugate the Xhosa and expel them from the Zuurveld. Besides, the new government needed to familiarize itself with the situation on the frontiers following the departure of the Batavians, and to do so it was necessary to gather intelligence. Despite these priorities Sir David Baird, the military commander of the forces that had re-conquered the Cape, despatched a large body of troops to Argentina in an abortive, unsanctioned and ultimately disastrous attempt to seize Buenos Aries from the Spanish. It was only in 1807, once Sir David had been replaced by a civilian governor, the Earl of Caledon, that frontier matters were given consideration and a fact-finding mission, in the person of Colonel Collins, was despatched.

As European colonists began to move farther east, they took over land that belonged to local peoples. A series of battles with and massacres against the Xhosa people took place in a region called the Zuurveld.[21] The battles and the massacres were part of what became known as the Cape Frontier Wars. Ultimately, there would be nine Frontier Wars in the eastern Cape, the first beginning in 1779, and the last one occurring in 1878, concluding a period of almost one hundred years of continual warfare.

In 1807 the situation of colonists in the Zuurveld was extremely precarious. Colonial policy at this time consisted of attempting to appeal to the Xhosa

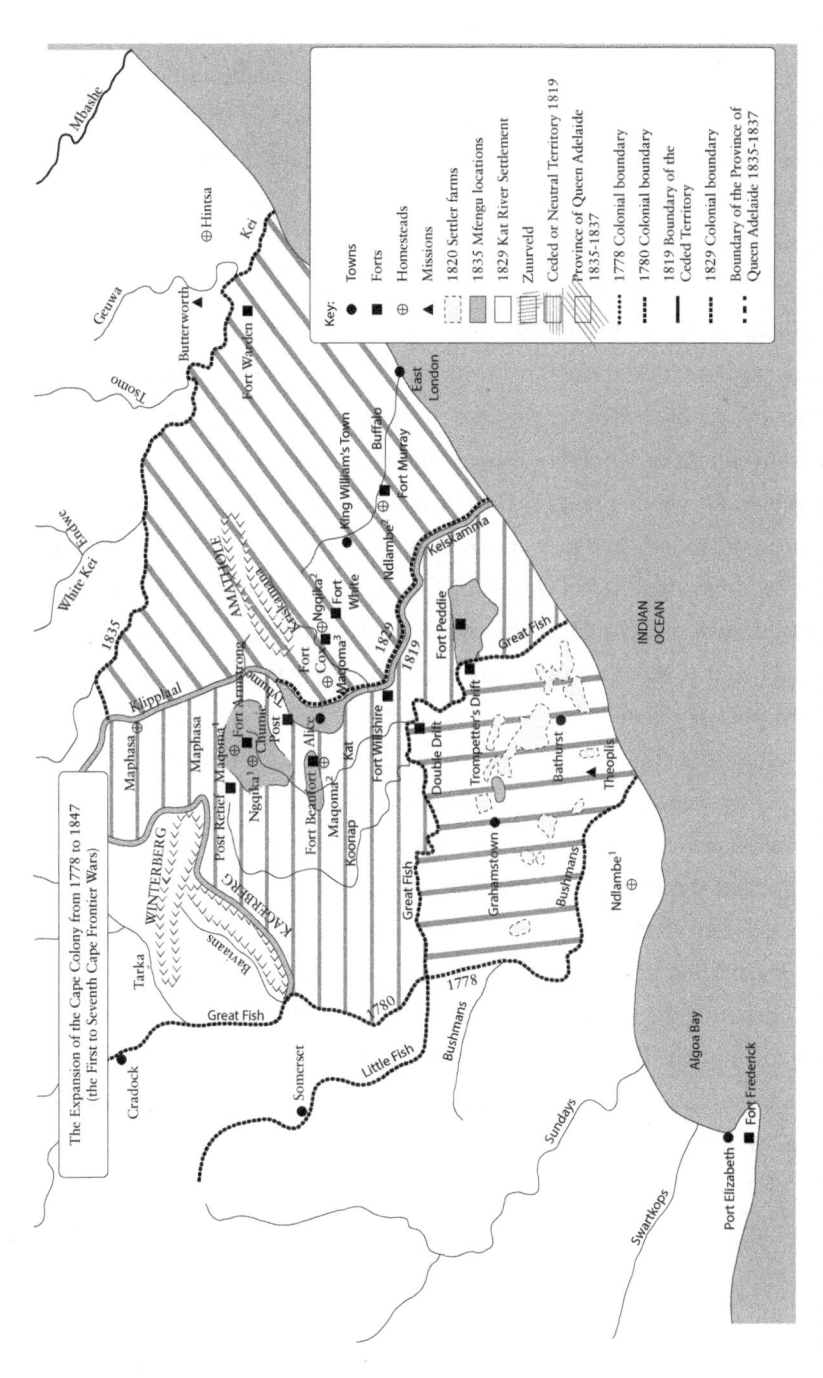

Map 5 *The wars on the eastern Cape frontier. Source: John Laband, The Land Wars: The Dispossession of the Khoisan and Ama Xhosa in the Cape Colony (Cape Town: Penguin, 2020).*

chiefs to restrain those of their subjects who stole or raised colonial cattle and to return stolen stock wherever possible. For the most part Ndlambe, the major Xhosa power in the Zuurveld, realized that it was in his best interests not to antagonize the colonists, or the British authorities, and he tried to co-operate with them. However, despite his pre-eminence in the Zuurveld he proved to be incapable of controlling all his followers, or for that matter, people who were not his subjects.

The British had appointed a royalist American of Dutch descent, J. G. Cuyler, as *landdrost* of Uitenhage, and it was his unenviable task to attempt to keep law and order on the eastern frontier. Cuyler's hands were tied, however, by strict instructions that he was not to permit commandos or colonists to fire on any Xhosa or Khoikhoi robbers unless their lives were in danger. The approved policy was to persuade the chiefs to discipline the guilty parties. This mild and tolerant attitude may, to some extent, be attributed to the genuinely humanitarian sympathies of Governor Caledon. On the other hand, Caledon was acutely aware of the government's weakness, as evidenced by his remark that 'it is better to submit to a certain extent of injury than to risk a great deal for a prospect of advantage by no means certain'.[22]

The situation in the Zuurveld was complicated by the presence of a number of competing leaders and peoples: Ngqika, Ndlambe's nephew, who rivalled his uncle for power among the Xhosa; Chungwa, chief of the Gqunukhwebe, who regarded themselves as being the original inhabitants of the Zuurveld, who had been there long before Europeans arrived; and Hintsa, chief of the Gcaleka and paramount chief of all the Xhosa. As well, there were other quasi-independent groups of Xhosa or Khoikhoi in the Zuurveld who did not answer to any superior authority. This was especially the case in the northern, more mountainous regions of the district, where minor chiefdoms and young men ventured into the Bruintjies Hoogte, Tarka and Buffelshoek regions in search of grazing and independence. Here the presence of colonial farmers was thinner on the ground, and in the face of continuous and increasing Xhosa pressure it was wisest for them to retreat. Xhosa groups were encountered as far west as the Zwartberg. Elsewhere minor Xhosa chiefs found that it was easier than ever before to raid colonial farms in the Zuurveld, and, by 1810, Cuyler reported that cattle stealing from the colonists had become so prevalent as to be institutionalized among the Xhosa. There was, at the same time, an increase in the cultural practice of aggressive begging, whereby groups of Xhosa would visit colonial farms and demand hospitality or gifts before moving on.[23]

None of this did anything to enhance the security of frontier farmers who complained of increasing levels of theft and murder. So bad had the situation become in May 1810 that Caledon sent a force of 200 soldiers and 360 members of the Cape Regiment to the frontier to strengthen patrols and enhance security. This force, however, was not authorized to attack the groups of Xhosa deemed to be in colonial space and was unable to restore the balance of power in the frontier areas as the Xhosa were confident of their own strength. Seen from the Xhosa point of view, it was they who had successfully cleared the Zuurveld of settlers, for the fifth time, by conquest, an act that further legitimated their occupation of the land.[24]

In the meantime, Colonel Collins had returned from his survey of the colony's frontier district and tabled his report in August 1809.[25] In brief, he recommended that 'the steps necessary for the permanent tranquillity of the eastern districts are to oblige all the Caffres to withdraw to their own country; and to remove every inducement to their continuance near the boundary'.[26] These proposals were basically what all previous colonial officials had proposed but which none had been able to achieve. Realistically they looked far from attainable in 1810. Caledon, in forwarding Collins's report to London, stated that he could not 'recommend the measure of dispossessing the Caffres of that country which they at present inhabit, whatever justice may be in our claim to it', and that he recommended 'preserving what we already possess and leaving to a future period what an increased population and a military force unshackled by a foreign war may without risk easily and effectually accomplish'.[27]

Such moderation, or prevarication, was not well received in the colony where there was a degree of desperation among both the colonists and members of the British Army. In 1811, Anders Stockenstrom, the *landdrost* of Graaff-Reinett, reported that cattle raiding was occurring as far west as the Gamtoos Valley and that 1,077 head of cattle had been stolen from his district in the second quarter of the year alone. He ordered virtually all able men in his district out on commando and expressed himself unable to judge why the government still showed so much indulgence to the Xhosa after successive years of robbery and murder. From Uitenhage, *landdrost* Cuyler wrote to report on various murders and cattle thefts in his district, quoting a Captain Abiather Hawkes of the 21st Light Dragoons. Hawkes had written:

> The country on every side is overrun with Kaffirs, and there was never a period when such numerous parties of them were known to have advanced so far in every direction before; the depredations of late committed by them exceed all precedent, and I believe it my indispensable duty to represent to you for the information of His Excellency the Governor and Commander of the forces that unless some decisive and hostile measures are immediately adapted I solemnly declare I apprehend considerable and the most serious consequences.[28]

Cuyler reminded Caledon that he had requested a force of seven or eight hundred strong some years ago to force the Xhosa over the Fish River and let the Colonial Secretary, Henry Bird, know that he had been obliged to ask for commando reinforcements from the district of George.[29]

Even before he had received these complaints Caledon had decided, reluctantly, to act. He had got as far as writing instructions to the frontier *landdrosts* to expect the arrival of additional commandos from Swellendam, Tulbagh and George. These forces, together with regular troops, were to demand the surrender of the recent murderers, the return of all stolen cattle and the removal of the Xhosa across the Fish River. In the event of non-compliance, force was to be used but only once the Xhosa had actually commenced attacking. 'My purpose is to prevent, not to occasion a state of war.'[30] But Caledon did not send these instructions. At the crucial moment a despatch arrived from England confirming the acceptance of his resignation as governor. For some time, he had been locked in a battle for control of the troops in the colony: who was in charge of them, the Governor or Major-General Henry Grey, the Lieutenant-Governor and commander of the military? Caledon felt that he was not receiving sufficient support from his superiors in his battle for supremacy and had offered his resignation at the beginning of 1811. In June, he learnt that his resignation had been accepted.[31]

Clearing the Zuurveld, 1812

In truth, both the colonists and the British government wanted a more forceful, military man as governor. Major-General Henry Grey was appointed as acting governor following Caledon's departure, and he was on the verge of implementing the plan that Caledon had failed to authorize when he himself was superseded by the arrival of the new governor on 6 September 1811, Lieutenant-General Sir John Cradock.

Cradock was, in many respects, an exemplar of the characteristics associated with the Second British Empire. It has been suggested, as we saw in the Introduction to this book, that Britain's loss of its American colonies at the end of the American War of Independence resulted in a change in the nature of the British Empire. As a consequence of the loss of America, attributed among other reasons to having allowed British settlers in America too many liberties, the Empire became more conservative and reactionary. This ideological shift was encouraged by the dangerous example of Britain's main European rival, France, which embraced revolutionary principals after 1789. During the long struggle against France, through the years of the French Revolution and the Napoleonic Wars, Britain became more nationalistic, more patriotic and more militaristic. Christopher Bayly wrote of an era of post-consular despotism as being the preferred form of government in British colonial possessions during the first half of the nineteenth century. Many of the governors, or colonial rulers, were military men, shaped and seasoned by the experience of warfare in the global struggle against France and her allies.[32]

Cradock was just such a man. He had served in the West Indies, helped suppress the Irish Rebellion of 1798, had served in Egypt in 1801 and was then appointed as commander in chief at Madras, where, in 1806, he brutally crushed a rebellion. He went on to command the British forces in Portugal (1808) and then Gibraltar and finally the debacle at Walchern (1809).[33] He was not a man to allow humanitarian scruples to interfere with military objectives. Unlike Caledon, Cradock was granted powers of both governorship and the full command of the armed forces. He immediately approved of plans to expel the Xhosa from the Zuurveld and despatched orders to *landdrosts*

Stockenstrom and Cuyler to this effect on 28 September. By December, 1,033 regular troops, under the command of the Scot, Colonel John Graham of the Cape Regiment, had joined the commandos at the frontier. It was the largest force ever assembled against the Xhosa.[34]

Cradock's instructions to Graham were firm and clear although the language employed tended to obscure the fact that their implementation was likely to result in killing.[35] It was left to Graham to decide what 'measures of example and effect' he would resort to when 'explanations and persuasions' failed. Graham's plan was to divide his force into three parts: a left division, a central division and a right division. They were to advance simultaneously and roughly in line parallel to the Sundays River, driving the Xhosa before them. Ngqika had already been prepared for events by being cautioned to offer the Zuurveld Xhosa no help and to refrain from attacking any refugees who might be forced into his territory. Since some of these refugees were likely to be the powerful and hostile followers of Ndlambe, Ngqika was delicately positioned. For the time being, however, all he had to do was stay out of the forthcoming fight.

The planned attack on the Xhosa and Gqunukhwebe sheltering in the Addo Bush commenced on New Year's Day 1812. Graham's intention was to attack them in a way he hoped would leave a lasting impression on their memories and he instructed his men to fire at 'all men Kaffirs'.[36] The scouring of the Addo Bush lasted five days and produced the somewhat low tally of only twelve Xhosa deaths. The deaths, in fact, were probably suffered by the Gqunukhwebe since one of the casualties was Chungwa. The sick and elderly man had been carried to a hiding place in a thicket by some of his closest followers. There they were discovered by a group of Boers who shot them dead as they lay there. Also, 2,500 cattle were captured and only one colonist, veld cornet Nortje, was stabbed to death.

With the Addo Bush cleared it remained to find Ndlambe and drive him and his followers from the Zuurveld. It was evident that while most of the Zuurveld Xhosa were retreating eastwards, some were heading in a northerly or northwesterly direction towards the Zuurberg. For the time being, the colonial forces concentrated on the coastal and central areas, where Ndlambe was likely to be. Evidence for the events surrounding the pursuit of Ndlambe is rather sparse and heavily reliant on a journal kept by a certain Robert Hart, a Scotsman, who was an officer in the Cape Regiment. The journal itself has not been found but was in the possession of Thomas Pringle, a countryman of Hart's, when Pringle, an 1820 settler, was busy writing his Narrative of a Residence in South Africa in the early 1820s. Pringle, who would later become the secretary to the Anti-Slavery Society in Britain, was a man of deep humanitarian convictions. He wrote that, according to Hart, 'it appears that the Caffers were shot indiscriminately, women as well as men, wherever found, even though they offered no resistance. It is true that Mr. Hart says that females were killed unintentionally, because the boors could not distinguish them from men among the bushes; and so, to make sure work, they shot all they could reach'. Pringle also highlighted another entry from Hart's journal, dated 12 January 1812. 'At noon, Commandant Stolz went out with two companies to look for Slambie [Ndlambe], but saw nothing of him: they met only with a few Caffers, men and women, the most of whom they shot.'[37]

As may be seen from these entries the troops and commando members involved in clearing the Zuurveld of Xhosa in 1812 were shooting indiscriminately and were nonplussed about taking the lives of women. This casual attitude towards human life, and a lack of concern to discriminate between combatant and non-combatant, was most likely encouraged by the tone and contents of Cradock's instructions to Graham. On 30 September 1811, barely three months after he had taken office, Cradock had already instructed Graham that when the time came to 'clear' the Zuurveld of Xhosa, he ought to kill Xhosa prisoners if circumstances made such a course of action necessary.[38] The Xhosa themselves were usually scrupulous about sparing the lives of women and children while fighting but the colonial tactics presaged an unfortunate escalation in atrocities in frontier warfare.

A further escalation in the intensity of the struggle was evident in Cradock's decision to employ 'scorched earth' tactics – no doubt familiar to him as a veteran of the Peninsula War, where such tactics had been used only the year before – and to order the destruction of all the crops, herds and villages of the Xhosa. Cradock's instructions to Graham were that his men should 'totally [remove] every inducement to revisit the regained territory' and it is Hart's journal, again, that provides the details as to what these words actually signified. On 17 January, two parties of 100 men each were sent to 'destroy the gardens and burn the villages. The gardens are very large and numerous; and here also are the best gardens pumpkins, and the largest Indian corn I have ever seen; some of the pumpkins are five and a half foot round, and the corn ten feet high'. On 18 and 19 January, 300 men continued the work of destruction by driving herds of cattle over the crops and vegetable fields of the Xhosa and burning their huts, shooting those whom they could and imprisoning women and children.[39]

The loss of maize and vegetables was particularly severe as it was harvest and the year's food supplies were at stake. As Thompson wrote some years later, 'There is little doubt that the Caffers felt very great reluctance to leave a country which they had occupied the greater part of a century; and the hardship of abandoning their crops was urgently pleaded, since in consequence of this measure, they must necessarily suffer a year of famine.'[40] One such attempt at pleading to remain was made by a son of Ndlambe, who sent a messenger to Commandant Scholtz asking whether the Xhosa could at least stay until the harvest was over. The response was that the messenger was seized and tortured to reveal the whereabouts of Ndlambe. The messenger then led the commando on a wild goose chase for three days, during which time Ndlambe's people escaped. The fate of the messenger is not recorded.[41]

The whole of the coastal region between the Sundays and Fish Rivers was now cleared of Xhosa. So too was the central Zuurveld and the Addo Bush. By March 1812 the entire operation was virtually over and the Zuurveld, an area of about 4,000 square miles, had been emptied of Xhosa. An estimated 20,000 people had been forcibly removed having left behind the bulk of their wealth in the form of cattle and the basis of their well-being in the form of fertile land and unharvested crops. It is perhaps futile to try to estimate the number of Xhosa killed in their eviction from the Zuurveld, given the patchy nature of the records and their often-deliberate vagueness about the number of Xhosa casualties. The nineteenth-century South African historian George Cory commented, 'The struggle lasted barely two months and was accompanied by probably less loss of Kaffir blood than was usual in one of their tribal fights.'[42] Nevertheless, the cost, in every way, was much higher. Also, the British method of waging war was far from comparable to 'a tribal fight'. It was a methodical, ruthless, and seemingly inexhaustible process of destruction.

When missionary John Campbell of the London Missionary Society (LMS) visited the Zuurveld in 1813 he described a landscape of scattered military posts, ruined kraals, deserted gardens and few inhabitants. 'Formerly the whole was covered with Caffre villages, but now there is not a living soul, but stillness every where reigns.' Those Xhosa who contemplated returning to the Zuurveld were aware that they risked death if they did so. Those Boers who sought to re-establish themselves in the contested landscape also believed that they were taking a risk as the region still bore the character of a military zone rather than a permanently pacified possession, even though it was 'exceedingly beautiful, much resembling a nobleman's park in England, being covered with the finest grass interspersed with trees in all directions'.[43]

Graham was aware of the suffering among the Xhosa who had been expelled across the Fish River and sent some maize to them to alleviate their hunger. He also restored some cattle to them, but these Xhosa were now in the territory of, and under the authority of, Ngqika, the rival of Ndlambe. The two chiefs and their followers were now forced into a much closer relationship than either would have liked and were faced with the problem of sharing a smaller and more strictly defined space in such a way as to prevent their difficulties from spilling over the border into the colony. The prospects for a peaceful, long-term solution did not seem promising. Of the two chiefs Ndlambe was both more powerful and more popular. Whereas Ngqika was already tainted, in the eyes of the Xhosa, by his willingness to co-operate with the colony, Ndlambe had unimpeachable credentials in his struggle with the colonists. Ndlambe could also count on the support of Phato, the son of Chungwa, the Gqunukhwebe chief who had been killed in the Addo Bush. Hintsa, chief of the Gcaleka and paramount chief of all the Xhosa, was also an Ndlambe supporter since he had suffered a humiliating defeat at the hands of Ngqika in 1793. For the time being, Ngqika gave Ndlambe permission to settle east of the Fish River, but future conflict between the two seemed inevitable.

Cradock, meanwhile, was proud to be able to report to London that the Xhosa had been expelled from the Zuurveld and that 'in the course of this service there has not been shed more Kaffir blood than would be necessary to impress on the minds of these savages a proper degree of terror and respect'. Lord Bathurst, Secretary of State for the Colonies, was less than enthusiastic on receiving this intelligence, rightly suspecting that excessive force had probably been employed and expressing his scepticism about the possibility of attaining permanent tranquillity in the future. Despite these reservations the British government had come to approve of the outcome of the Fourth Frontier War by 30 November 1812, on which date Bathurst informed Cradock of His Majesty's approval of his and Graham's conduct.[44]

The challenge now facing the British was to keep the Fish River border sealed off in such a manner that, should the Xhosa attempt to return to the Zuurveld, they would find it impossible to do so. Cradock's solution was to build twenty-two military posts along the Fish River, each to be manned by members of the Cape Regiment. He also ordered the creation of a command post to be established at a suitable spot in the Zuurveld not too far from the Fish River. The chosen site was on a derelict Boer farmhouse, abandoned some years before. On 14 August 1812, it was proclaimed that the name of the headquarters would be Graham's Town. Colonel Graham himself left the frontier at the end of the year to be replaced by Colonel Vicar. Two years later the eastern section of the Zuurveld was declared to be a separate division and given the name of Albany, the New York City from which Cuyler had originally come.

The naming, or re-naming of the Zuurveld, could not alter the fact that the district was still vulnerable to Xhosa incursions and that constant patrols were necessary to deter cattle raiders. The Fish River was a body of water that could easily be forded, in many places, at most times of the year. Far from acting as an obstacle its banks and vegetation in fact offered security and protective cover to those wishing to avoid detection. Historian John Milton describes the river as running through 'a remarkable tract of country ... a chaos of great hills, running in long flat ridges, with very steep, smooth sides, divided by extremely deep, narrow, gloomy valleys'. 'I never saw, in any other part of the world', the traveller and botanist Charles Bunbury observed, 'anything resembling the Fish River bush; nor, I should think, does there exist a tract so difficult to penetrate'.[45]

With such natural features it was almost impossible to prevent cattle raiding across the river. As early as 1813 Cradock felt obliged to visit the frontier to encourage the colonial and military authorities to be more active and aggressive in pursuing Xhosa raiders. The situation was as bad in the northern districts where a commando went out under the orders of Major Fraser to 'destroy and lay waste' any Xhosa property discovered as well as to 'shoot all the male' Xhosa encountered following a spate of robberies.[46] There was little to distinguish this commando from many others except that it included the youthful Andries Stockenstrom, then aged twenty-one, was the son of Anders Stockenstrom, the *landdrost* of Graaff-Reinett, who had been killed in the first phase of the war. Some twenty-five years later, Andries would be accused by his enemies of having murdered a defenceless Xhosa boy while on this commando, stating that this was in revenge for the murder of his father. Stockenstrom denied these charges but was brought to trial and was eventually fully exculpated. During the course of the trial, however, he provided many details which are highly illuminating about the nature of such combat and deserving of attention.

Stockenstrom explained that in the course of the commando in pursuit of some hostile Xhosa 'in some jungle or other' (it was in fact on the banks of the Blinkwater River in the Kat River Valley) there was a sudden movement in the bush and a Boer named Charl Pretorius called out 'Fire – there comes an assegai'. Stockenstrom and some other commando members fired blindly into the bush. On closer inspection the commando members found two bundles of assegais [spears], and two dead Xhosa lying on the ground. Stockenstrom stated that he doubted very much whether he had actually fired the shot that killed one of the Xhosa or that he had ever done so, because one could never be sure in bush warfare whose shot had hit the target:

> The only military service which I have to boast of ... is that ungrateful, harassing, degrading species of man-hunting of which, God knows, I have had abundance. That, consequently, in clearing a country, scouring jungles, taking cattle out of almost inaccessible fastnesses, or pursuing an enemy, I must often have been in close contact with the barbarian foe as a matter of course; more than once have I, as a special favourite, been

complimented that my shot was the successful one out of a whole volley, when some unfortunate desperados rushed forward upon us, when I knew the proud compliment was not due, but intended as a piece of flattery. It was a glorious action well deserving of a compliment to shoot a savage under any circumstances; and such it continued until the House of Commons incurred our displeasure by being surprised at it.[47]

When Stockenstrom spoke these words, he was addressing a special Court of Inquiry headed by Governor Napier. It was 1837, after having given evidence to the 1835 Committee of the House of Commons on the treatment of Aboriginal people. He was, in other words, fully aware that it was not a glorious action to kill a Xhosa and he was employing irony, conscious that his auditors were aware of his own reputation as a humanitarian. He made it quite clear, however, that things had been different in 1813:

… but let us not pretend that if the act had been perpetrated that it would have been a solitary one in the history of the Colony. Nine-tenths of those who affect a sudden burst of virtuous horror at the case, which they hope will injure a man who scorns to court the public cheer, know in their Consciences that it was for the express purpose of retaliatory destruction and plunder that warlike expeditions were sent across the Frontier – that to kill, to make an example of, to strike terror into the enemy, was a duty, a standing order – that giving quarter or taking prisoners was never thought of by either party; that this very commando of 1819 [sic] was particularly conspicuous for all those harsh features, and that if I could have extirpated the whole race of Kaffirs exactly in the way described by Klopper, I, instead of being reprobated, should have been lauded throughout the Colony as an example of heroism and filial piety, or, as the Attorney-General has it, 'it would have been good luck to him'. Four thousand Kaffir warriors were killed in your Excellency's last campaign. How came Congo to his end in 1812? How fell Eno's son about 1820? How perished Hintsa in 1835? These were deeds of glory; but there was no obnoxious Lieutenant-Governor to be got rid of.[48]

Stockenstrom's testimony is a clear indication that the eastern frontier wars had degenerated into a 'degrading species of man-hunting' in which the Xhosa was usually the hunted and, as such, seldom shown any mercy. Despite this, however, the Xhosa kept crossing the boundary and it was with the realization that he had not solved the conflict on the border that Cradock learnt, in October 1813, that his resignation had been accepted and that he was to be replaced as governor by Lord Charles Henry Somerset.

Sealing Off the Zuurveld, the Spoor Law and the Prophet

It should not be forgotten that while the issue of keeping the Xhosa out of the colony was the most important aspect of frontier security, the government also had to ensure that both the Khoikhoi of the Zuurveld and the frontier Boers were obedient to authority. The issues were inter-related, as can be seen from the Slagtersnek Rebellion of 1815. The rebellion took place among a small group of farmers in the Baviaans River region to the north of Bruintjies Hoogte. It was provoked by the British insistence that the Boers should respect the Hottentot Code (or Caledon Code) of 1809, and treat their Khokhoi labourers well, and that if they did not, they could be summonsed to appear before a court.[49] When a certain Frederick Bezuidenhout failed to answer such a summons a detachment of Cape Regiment troops was sent to arrest him. He resisted arrest and was shot. His friends, family and neighbours rebelled in sympathy and some of them were later hanged by the British for their resistance. What the rebellion illustrates is that the Khoikhoi were, to an extent, under the protection of British law. Although the LMS missionaries insisted that many cruelties went unpunished and hated the government custom of forcibly enlisting Khoikhoi men in the Cape Regiment as well as obstructing Khoikhoi attendance at their missions, the Zuurveld Khoikhoi, by and large, were pacific. As for the Boers, the Rebellion was limited to the poor and marginal of a distant corner of the frontier and they received no support from the majority of Boers who now clearly accepted British rule. The rebels lost credibility in the eyes of their brethren when they approached the Xhosa for the purpose of forming an alliance against the British. By 1815 those days were gone.[50]

Though Somerset had the responsibility of crushing the Slagtersnek Rebellion, he had not provoked it and was, on the whole, unsympathetic to humanitarian issues. Somerset has the reputation of being the most tyrannical of all the Cape's governors, but his conservatism actually suited the majority of the Boers who appreciated the fact that he loathed missionaries and sneered at anti-slavery initiatives. His was the despotism of a monarch rather than of a general; that is, he did not try to take personal control of the frontier's military operations. He did, however, have definite views on the subject and visited the frontier himself in an attempt to impose his will on events.

Somerset's frontier policy was to try to get Ngqika to take responsibility for 'his' followers. Having toured the frontier zone and been advised about the history of the conflict, Somerset decided that Ngqika, as the senior chief of the Rharhabe, ought to be more assertive in enforcing his authority over his subjects and in ensuring the return of stolen cattle. The trouble was that Ngqika's subjects included Ndlambe and the Zuurveld Xhosa, who were not amenable to Ngqika's commands. Somerset proposed that if colonial cattle were stolen, they would be tracked down to the kraal to which their spoor led and the people of that kraal would be held to be responsible even if they had not stolen them and did not have the cattle. This 'spoor law', as it was called, had obvious disadvantages and provided further occasions for the followers of Ngqika and the followers of Ndlambe to argue with each other. Ngqika was forced to agree to Somerset's proposal through a mixture of intimidation – cannon were brought to the meeting place – and bribery – he was given some trinkets. Somerset assured the chief that he regarded him as being superior to all other chiefs and would bolster his authority.

It was not long before the spoor law worked its divisive ways. In January 1818, a colonial commando rode into Ngqika's territory and demanded of the chief that he return some stolen cattle. When he protested his lack of influence over his followers the commando rode into Ndlambe's territory and exacted reprisal from them instead, much to their displeasure. Ndlambe was, by this stage, under the influence of a charismatic prophet by the name of Makana, or Makhanda, who, because he was left-handed, was also known as Nxele or Links, the Xhosa and Dutch words respectively for 'left'. Makhanda had been influenced by the teachings of LMS missionaries, such as Johannes

Van der Kemp and James Read, who had established mission stations in the Zuurveld. Before the Third Frontier War drove him out, Van der Kemp had preached the gospel of Christ in Xhosa territory itself. The revolutionary message of Christianity, with its doctrines of creation, heaven, hell and resurrection, combined with the violent upheavals of the times, provoked Makhanda into preaching a new message to those who would listen, a hybrid of Christian and African religious traditions with strong millenarian overtones. Makhanda's teaching was that there were two gods, one, Dalidipu, the god of the blacks, and the other, uThixo, the god of the settlers. Dalidipu had a wife whose son was named Tayi. Makhanda was the brother of Tayi. uThiko and the settlers were sinners who would be crushed by Dalidipu's servant, Makhanda. If cattle of a certain colour were sacrificed, the ancestors would rise up and the cattle would be restored. The settlers would be driven into the sea.[51] With these ideas Makhanda succeeded in making a great and favourable impression on Ndlambe, assuming the role of spiritual counsellor, prophet and diviner to the chief.[52]

It is significant, and indicative of the destabilizing and transformative power that Christianity was exerting at this time among the Xhosa, that Ngqika too had a prophet. His name was Ntsikana, and unlike Makhanda, he preached a gentler, more submissive version of Christianity. He is famous for composing the first Christian hymn in Xhosa. His advice to Ngqika was to refrain from responding to Ndlambe's provocations, but in this, ultimately, he failed.[53]

Historians are divided as to what exactly triggered warfare between Ndlambe and Ngqika. The causes are, perhaps, 'overdetermined'. First, there was the deep-rooted antagonism between the two of them. Second, there were the new sources of tension which came from having to live closer together following the Zuurveld removals. Third, there was the divisive and factious influence of the spoor law, and fourth, there was the encouragement of Makhanda. Despite all these good reasons for discord, the historian Julia Wells believes that the two chiefs were pursuing a common and united strategy together against the colonists when suddenly the alliance fell apart and the Ndlambe and other Xhosa suddenly attacked Ngqika because they did not trust him and suspected him of being in alliance with the British.[54] Whatever the reasons, in November 1818 there took place the greatest battle in Xhosa history – the Battle of amaLinde, between the armies of Ndlambe and Ngqika.[55]

Xhosa tradition asserts that the battle was long and bloody. There were no colonial witnesses to the battle. Ngqika's forces were led by one of his sons, Maqoma. Ndlambe's forces were led by one of his sons, Mdushane. The battle lasted all day but eventually went to the Ndlambe, who slaughtered the vanquished wounded left on the battlefield as evening fell. Maqoma, badly wounded, was carried away by his men, and lived to fight another day. Ngqika fled as his enemies burnt his huts, destroyed his kraals and took his cattle. From a refuge place in the Winterberg, Ngqika sent a messenger to Major Fraser, asking for assistance, reminding Fraser that Somerset had promised to bolster his authority against his enemies in times of need. The time had come to honour that promise. The British, indeed, realized that they had no option but to re-instate Ngqika as it would have been impossible to ensure frontier peace, or enforce the spoor law, with Ndlambe in control of the Xhosa. Somerset therefore ordered the newly appointed commander of the frontier forces, Lieutenant-Colonel Brereton to redress the balance of power in Xhosaland by capturing Ndlambe and restoring Ngika to power.[56]

Brereton had no experience of the eastern frontier and no knowledge of Xhosa politics, but he was determined to act boldly and decisively. On 1 December he led a large force of soldiers and commandos across the Fish River to a rendezvous with Ngqika. From there the combined forces marched as far eastwards as the Keiskamma River, firing at any Xhosa they believed to be hostile and encountering the bulk of Ndlambe's people near the Keiskamma on 7 December. After firing cannon into the forests where the Ndlambe had hidden their cattle Brereton unleashed the Ngqika on their enemies. After 'great loss of life' among the Ndlambe as the Ngqika took revenge, Brereton's force came away with 23,000 cattle. Nine thousand of these were given to Ngqika, who was now deemed to be restored to power. Nkqika was indeed very grateful to have seen Ndlambe's followers despoiled, but Ndlambe himself escaped capture. He wasted no time in retaliating.[57]

Barely two weeks after the Brereton raid, Ngqika was obliged to flee for his life into the colony. The raid had impoverished and angered so many Xhosa that Ndlambe and Makhanda had no difficulty in recruiting warriors to his cause which was no less than the destruction of Ngqika and the expulsion of colonists from the Zuurveld. Thus, it was the Brereton Raid that succeeded in provoking what would become known as the Fifth Frontier War.

The Fifth Frontier War, 1818–19

Although there was a general and severe increase in raiding and cross-border incursions by Xhosa groups following the Brereton Raid, the central feature of the Fifth Frontier War was a well-coordinated and widely supported attack on the nascent town and military post of Grahamstown. The attack was masterminded by Makhanda and had the support not only of Ndlambe and some minor chiefs hostile to Ngqika but also of Hintsa. Makhana told his followers that the ancestors of the Xhosa would assist the warriors in the forthcoming battle. The settlers would be driven into the sea and, after he had performed the abuKafula ceremony, the bullets of their guns would be turned into water.[58]

By 21 April 1819, the Grahamstown garrison was under the command of Colonel Thomas Willshire, who had replaced the out of favour Brereton. The latter had been goaded into tending his resignation by Somerset, who let the unfortunate man know that he should have achieved a lot more than simply capturing cattle. Willshire had been in the 38th Regiment from boyhood and was a decorated officer who had seen active service in the West Indies, Portugal (1809) and Spain, fighting in the battle of Salamanca during which he received two wounds and earned the nickname of 'Tiger Tom'.[59] His instructions were to capture Ndlambe and to drive the Xhosa beyond the Keiskamma. In other words, he was to attempt to repeat the success of the 1812 clearance of the Zuurveld but, this time, in the territory beyond the Fish. To achieve this task, he was promised a force of 3,315 men, Boers and soldiers combined. This force was still busy assembling at various points when a Xhosa messenger arrived in Grahamstown on 21 April to inform Willshire that the Xhosa would breakfast with him the next day. With calculated sangfroid Willshire informed the messenger that the Xhosa would find everything well prepared for them.

However, as the messenger departed Willshire, in fact, did very little to indicate that he had taken the threat seriously.

On 19 April Willshire had despatched the mounted section of the 38th Regiment to investigate a report that there was a force of Xhosa near the mouth of the Fish River. The report was actually a piece of disinformation fed to Willshire by a Xhosa spy. By sending away his cavalry, Willshire was left with only about 300 men to defend the town. Hidden in the bush of the Fish River valley were about 6,000 Xhosa warriors. It was they who arrived outside Grahamstown in the morning of 22 April. Willshire quickly organized his defensive positions alongside the stream which bisected the town of some thirty buildings. One end of his line utilized the stone barracks as a strong point and was reinforced by five artillery pieces. The other end was on a rise, fastened onto two artillery pieces. The Xhosa charged down on the town from the high ridge to the east shouting, 'Tayi. Tayi' – the name of the son of God, or Mdalidiphu – as they came.

The ensuing battle was not a close contest, as the casualty figures suggest. The Xhosa warriors were not able to get close enough to their enemy to use their assegais. The fire of British musketry and six-pounders loaded with grape shot and canister – the lead, predictably, did not turn to water – stopped the Xhosa short. Also, at a timely moment, the arrival of colonial reinforcements in the form of 130 Khoikhoi Christians from the Theopolis mission tipped the balance. The Khoikhoi were a party of buffalo hunters, under the leadership of Jan Boesak. Well-armed and mounted they poured accurate fire into the ranks of the Xhosa until the attack broke and the Xhosa retreated. According to Willshire 150 Xhosa bodies were later found about the battlefield but casualties were probably much higher. The retreating Xhosa took their wounded with them, many of whom would die out of sight of the victors. The colonists did not hesitate to kill any wounded Xhosa they encountered. Later estimates suggest that between 1,400 and 3,000 Xhosa might have died. Colonial casualties comprised two men dead – one settler and one Khoikhoi. Five British soldiers were wounded.[60]

For the Xhosa the battle was a conclusive and costly mistake. The Xhosa had had enough experience in fighting commandos and British troops to realize that frontal attacks across open ground by men armed with spears against large groups of men armed with guns, horses and artillery were suicidal. On this occasion, however, the prophecies of Makhanda had induced them into believing themselves to be invincible. Even without these prophecies, however, the Xhosa believed they had a fighting chance. As Makhanda's councillor explained to Stockenstrom some months later: 'We found you weak; we destroyed your soldiers. We saw that we were strong; we attacked your headquarters, and if we had succeeded it would have been just, for you began the war. We failed, and you are here.'[61]

The British were not content to have beaten off the attack and decided to press home their advantage. Reinforcements, borne by sea, arrived from the Cape. Grahamstown was fortified. A powerful attack by over 300 Xhosa on a post on the Fish River called Upper Kaffir Drift was repelled on 8 May. Finally, on 28 July, Willshire advanced across the Fish with a force of over 2,000 men divided into three columns. The warriors of Ngqika and Maqoma provided auxiliary support, happy to visit destruction on Ndlambe's followers. The most difficult task facing the colonial forces was to clear the Fish River bush. This job was largely entrusted to the men under Stockenstrom's command, who took care to search the steepest precipices' and the 'remotest recesses'. In one encounter alone, they shot dead sixty men they had surprised in a deep kloof or ravine. Xhosa cattle were less easy to hide than people and they were rounded up in great numbers. Almost continuous rainfall added to the misery of both hunters and hunted but at least the latter benefitted from the wet weather as it caused the colonists guns to misfire. Those Xhosa who were forced out of the bush found mounted patrols waiting for them on the open plains between the Fish and Keiskamma Rivers, making it a perilous business for them to reach safety.[62]

At last, the Xhosa had had enough and on 16 August Makhanda gave himself up, walking unattended into Stockenstrom's camp, saying, 'People say that I have occasioned the war. Let me see whether my delivering myself up to the conquerors will restore peace to my country.' Stockenstrom handed his captive over to Willshire, who handcuffed Makhanda and had him imprisoned on Robben Island. In the meantime, the pursuit of Ndlambe and Kobe continued, so too did the harrying of any Xhosa groups remaining between the Fish and Keiskamma Rivers. The British had now added Congreve rockets to their arsenal and bombarded the thickets with artillery and rocket fire to flush out the stragglers – mainly women and children. By the end of August, the area between the Fish and the Keiskamma had been cleared and the British prepared for their next move – the invasion of the territory over the Kesikamma.

It was at this stage that a group of Xhosa councillors, including two men of Ndlambe and Makhanda, entered Stockenstom's camp on the Keiskamma and raised the prospect of peace. It was the unnamed councillor of Makhanda who made what is known as 'the Great Speech', in which he accused the colonists of waging an unjust war against a people whom they had forced to take up arms. His majestic and eloquent recapitulation of the history of the struggle for the Zuurveld ended in a request for peace, but a peace that did not involve capitulation to Ngqika and which required the release of Makhanda. Nevertheless, since Makhanda could not be produced, and since British plans for the future definitely involved the recognition of Ngqika as the paramount chief of the Rharhabe Xhosa, peace was not declared and the British juggernaut rolled on.[63]

Willshire's army crossed the Keiskamma on 9 September 1819. The objective, as before, was to capture the Xhosa chiefs, but also to destroy crops and take cattle – and to kill those people who did not retreat. The British columns scoured the forests, crossed the Buffalo River and reached the Kei River. Kobe, at last, surrendered to Fraser and his Cape Regiment. But Ndlambe fled deep into the interior, heading northwards. As the colonial forces approached the Kei they entered the territory of Hintsa, who was most anxious to disassociate himself from Ndlambe. This did not prevent some of his followers from being harried by commandos and by Ngqika's warriors who would have liked to force war upon Hintsa. In these circumstances Hintsa swore that he would do his utmost to live in peace and goodwill with the colony.

Although Willshire would have preferred to have caught Ndlambe, Stockenstrom managed to persuade him that he had achieved his goals. Besides, the colonial forces were exhausted, the Boer commandos drifting back to their farms. Willshire's men had captured over 30,000 cattle from Ndlambe and Willshire could at least boast that he had demonstrated the superiority of British might to the Xhosa chiefs. The British now exerted the rights of conquerors.

On 14 October 1819, Somerset declared the whole of the area between the Fish and the Keiskamma Rivers to be a neutral zone. Not content with having cleared the Xhosa out of the Zuurveld he now decided the 'neutral territory', or 'ceded territory', should be depopulated of both Xhosa and colonists. The fact that this land was where Ngqika's people lived did not deter Somerset from his plan. The only concession made to the chief, the colony's foremost Xhosa collaborator, was that he was allowed to settle in the Tyumie Valley – his birthplace – in the north of the region. Ngqika would die in 1829, a sad and alcoholic man who, nonetheless, was sharp enough to express the irony of his predicament: 'When I look at the large extent of fine country that has been taken from me, I am compelled to say that, though protected, I am rather oppressed by my benefactor.'[64] Although despised by the Ndlambe Xhosa, Ngqika's legacy was not all negative for his sons, Maqoma and Tyhali, would become 'leaders of the new generation of anti-colonial warriors'.[65]

The next stage in the colonization of the Zuurveld was the introduction of 4,000 British settlers into the area. They were granted parcels of land and expected to farm it productively. The first settlers arrived in April 1820, little knowing that, despite the 'neutral zone' to their east, they were effectively in the front line of a disputed territory and serving as a buffer to those behind them. Time would reveal that Somerset's solution may have achieved the colonization of the Zuurveld but had far from achieved peace or stability on the eastern Cape frontier as a whole. The 'neutral zone' was too desirable an area – a million acres of fertile land – to be left empty and, inevitably, it became a site of renewed contention between the Xhosa and the colonists with cattle raids and counter raids criss-crossing the territory.

Cattle loss and land loss did little to reconcile the Xhosa to the colonial presence across the border. Besides, the Xhosa had never agreed to the cessation in the first place. Increased trading opportunities and the increased presence of Christian missions were, arguably, as disruptive as they were beneficial. However, the most unacceptable provocation, which led to the Sixth Frontier War of 1834–5, was the expulsion of Ngqika's son, Maqoma, from the Kat River Valley near Tyume in 1829. This territory had been ear marked by Stockenstrom for settlement by loyal Khoikhoi, many of whom were ex-Cape Regiment soldiers. As so often happened on this frontier, the destinies of the Xhosa and the Khoikhoi were intertwined. When Maqoma went to war he now found he was not just the leader of the Ngqika, but the leader of all those Xhosa who were still smarting from the consequence of defeat in 1819.[66] The British had not kept their promises and, therefore, they could not keep the peace.

It is beyond the scope of this chapter to elaborate on the significance of the arrival of British settlers on the Cape's eastern frontier, a much-neglected topic these days but once of primary concern to South Africans of British heritage and Imperial historians alike. We should, however, note, briefly, that by their very presence the British settlers contributed to provoking the Sixth Frontier War (1834–5) and that for historians like Crais, Mostert, Bank and Lester the Sixth Frontier War marked a watershed in frontier history.[67] It was during this war, according to these writers, that racist ideology became institutionalized as both sides now fought with increased atrociousness. The British settlers adopted the racist attitudes of their Boer neighbours and previously favourable representations of the Xhosa, such as were to be found in the writing of Barrow or the drawings of Daniell, were replaced by savage caricatures, backed by the dubious science of phenology which, in turn, rested on the collection of skulls from battlefield corpses.[68] In this revised version of South African history the villains are no longer solely the Afrikaners but now, primarily, the British colonial government, the British eastern Cape settlers and the British army who sought to force non-whites into a subordinate political, social and economic status. Whatever the merits are of reminding us of the significance of the nineteenth-century British eastern Cape frontier on the development of South African history we should not underestimate the influence of the earlier period of Dutch rule, particularly on the eighteenth-century northern Cape frontier, where the subjugation of the Khoisan was well underway before the British arrived and where massacre and violence were a common feature of the colonial order.

Epilogue

We can now point to a few commonalities across the four regions under study. The raid, or the 'punitive expedition', was the usual practise of warfare, on both sides of the cultural divide. It often took place at dawn or when Indigenous men were away from their villages. Sometimes the order was given to spare women and children, as was the case in Australia in 1816 under Governor Macquarie, but when that was not possible or practicable or desired, they were killed.[1] Terror, after all, was the tried-and-tested means of warfare on the frontier, and that meant killing indiscriminately. When women and children were spared, they were usually enslaved, including in Australia which has a long history of denying slavery. That said, we know that the perpetrators often knew their victims and often lived in close proximity to them for many years before the killings occurred. Violence was intimate and personal. This was the case for the settler massacres of Indigenous peoples on the Australian, South African and North American frontiers, although obviously not the case in Europe. Settlers sometimes held grudges for years about earlier slights, defeats or Indigenous attacks, and waited for an opportune moment to seek revenge.

We can only speculate about the extent to which the perpetrators had become inured to killing non-combatants through their experiences in previous wars. One can assume that if troops had killed non-combatants in a campaign in Europe, then it would not be out of the ordinary to do so against Indigenous populations. In Australia, but not South Africa, troops who had fought in the Peninsular War were transferred among other places to New South Wales. Certainly, the 'imperial careering' that scholars talk about as European military men travelled from one imperial outpost or frontier to the next meant that the men in charge brought with them their own experiences of dealing with recalcitrant local and Indigenous populations. Put another way, extreme violence was the method used to confront unruly people or insurrectionists. But what of settler-civilian killers? In Australia at least, the convicts deported to New South Wales and Tasmania were brutalized by a system in which capital punishment and floggings were the norm for minor infringements; they were unlikely to show much understanding towards Aboriginal peoples. In South Africa and North America, we can speculate that centuries of hatred and killing must have imbued settlers with a particular world view that made killing permissible, even desirable.

Livestock were the target of Indigenous attacks, in Australia, North America and South Africa. In Australia, Aboriginal people in Victoria in the 1830s were known to have killed hundreds if not thousands of sheep.[2] In South Africa, on the other hand, the Xhosa and the Boers were more likely to take than kill each other's livestock. In North America, particularly during the Muscogee Civil War, invader livestock was killed in favour of Indigenous animals, even as settlers took Indigenous American resources, or troops would destroy fruit trees and crops. The burning of villages and towns was part and parcel of the kind of warfare that we have witnessed, contributing enormously to the social instability and eventual malnutrition of Indigenous populations. Women and children were raped and taken captive, people were scalped, and others were mutilated. Anyone familiar with the European colonizing enterprise will know that the massacre of Indigenous peoples around the world continued until well into the twentieth century. Before drawing some conclusions about the nature of violence in the Revolutionary Age, it is worth reminding people what happened next in our four regions.

The Killing Continues

The Continuing Destruction of the San in South Africa

In South Africa, commando activity continued into the 1820s and beyond. As the northern Cape became settled by colonists, colonial frontiersmen and their families moved onwards, over the Orange River into what would become the Orange Free State. As Stockenstrom noted quite frankly: 'Here I wish it to be particularly noticed and remembered, how as early as 1823, we colonists were desirous of migrating across the Orange River and possessing ourselves of that part of Bushman or Hottentot Land as we and our fathers had done with the more southern parts.'[3] In the west, colonists continued their expropriation of the trekveld of Bushmanland (the land between the north of the colony and the Gariep River, now known as the Orange River). More massacres would follow, many committed by the Griqua and Bergenaars of Trans-Orania and many committed by the settlers and 'Bastaards' of the northern Cape frontier zone. For each man, woman or child who became a servant there was probably one who was killed, or starved to death, because they would not submit. These were, however, mopping up operations. The real damage to the San had been done between about 1770 and 1828.

The new Acting Governor of the Cape, Major–General Richard Bourke, who replaced Somerset in 1826 and who would later be Governor of New South Wales, made one last attempt to protect the San from destruction. In 1828 he despatched Dr Andrew Smith, a man with a reputation for knowledge of the border tribes, to the northern frontier of the colony on a confidential mission. Smith's task was to seek out the colonists, 'Bastaards', Khoikhoi and San of the northwestern Cape frontier zone to 'obtain information in reference to their views, and in reference to what was going on among them with regard to the Bushmen; to ascertain whether the colonial policy was correctly understood by them'.[4]

What he discovered was that the region was in an unsettled state, largely on account of the murderous depredations of the Bergenaars, a group of Griqua rebels especially hostile towards the San. The San were, however, few in number, being 'thinly scattered over the extensive flat which lies between the colony and the Orange River'. They were, reported Smith, regarded as 'the determined enemy of every peaceable community around them, and they in turn regarded all such as equally hostile to them'. Smith suggested that the colonial frontier should be advanced to the Orange River and that the San should be regarded as colonial subjects under British law and British protection. He further suggested that both they and the Khoikhoi group, the Korana, should be given land, and their property secured for them by law and entailed so that they could not alienate it to colonists for trifling sums. Sadly, Smith noted his prevailing impression: 'every stranger was to the Bushmen an actual enemy'.[5]

Smith's report, if it was ever delivered, seems to have been lost or 'pigeonholed' in some obscure file as no official copy of it exists and it was never acted upon. This was probably the result of the change in governorship that occurred while Smith was still on his travels. Bourke handed over his office to Sir Lowry Cole and the new governor lacked the reforming zeal of his predecessor.[6] In the northwestern Cape, the Orange River only became the official colonial boundary in 1848 and, even then, no attention was paid to the rights of the San.

In retrospect, 1828 now appears close to the highwater mark of the missionaries' ability to initiate humanitarian policies in southern Africa, particularly in so far as the Khoisan were concerned. In August 1828, the British parliament passed a resolution that all the natives of South Africa under British government should enjoy the same freedom and protection as any other British subjects. Two days later Acting Governor Richard Bourke, on advice from both the newly arrived Superintendent of the LMS, Dr John Philip, and Stockenstrom, declared essentially the same thing in what was called Ordinance 50 at the Cape, which attempted to regulate the mobility of Khoisan in the labour market. No special mention was made, however, concerning the rights of the San – unless they may be considered to be among the 'other free people of colour' mentioned besides the Khoikhoi – and Philip did not seem to think such specific attention to be necessary. Perhaps this was because he was confident that the Report of the Commission of Enquiry would be acted on, or perhaps he was satisfied that Ordinance 50 covered the San as well as the Khoikhoi, a people he believed to be essentially the same.

Significantly, Philip declined after 1828 to republish his *Researches in South Africa*, a work that had been aimed at revealing and combating the iniquities of the Caledon Code. It was an indication that Philip thought the book had done its job.[7]

Whether or not Ordinance 50 helped the Khoikhoi is the topic of some debate in South African historiography.[8] But it certainly failed to help the San, except in so far as they were now considered to be identical to colonial Khoikhoi. There were, in any event, new challenges for Philips and the humanitarians to face after 1828 that made the struggle to protect the San seem less important. As the abolition of slavery loomed in 1834 the threat of a settler driven Anti-Vagrancy Law had to be combated and defeated. When the Sixth Frontier War broke out in 1834 the humanitarian cause became less and less able to counter the growth of colonial racism. The Great Trek of Dutch farmers out of the colony now threatened to destabilize not just Griqua polities over the colonial boundaries but the entire region of southern Africa. Liberal-minded or humanitarian missionaries became more and more unpopular and Dr Philip himself was the most reviled figure in the colony.[9] Accompanying this decline in humanitarian influence was the almost continuous and unremarked destruction of the San. Whereas before 1828 the British government at the Cape had declared itself to be dedicated to the preservation of the San, there was no official concern for them thereafter. It is unlikely, however, that this later neglect proved to be decisive. The real damage to San societies had been inflicted much earlier and some of it, incontestably, under the ineffectual protection of a supposedly benevolent government.

The Violent Dispossession of Indigenous Americans

In North America, the killing of Indigenous peoples continued with increasing disregard for human life throughout the nineteenth century and was always carried out with impunity.[10] The 1820s saw the beginning of a new litany of atrocities committed against the traditional owners of the lands of the North American continent. According to the Constitution, Indigenous 'Tribes' were among the 'foreign Nations' with whom the government could negotiate, here in pursuit of land through treaty powers. This description was modified by the

'Marshall Trilogy' of US Supreme Court rulings. In *Johnson v. M'Intosh* (1823), the Supreme Court decided that the United States owned the land under the 'Doctrine of Discovery' and declared Indigenous Americans an 'inferior race of people, without the privilege of citizens', so that they did not really own the land but merely had rights of 'occupancy'.[11] In *Cherokee Nation v. Georgia* (1831), the Court mystifyingly declared the Indigenous nations 'domestic dependent nations', turning them into subject peoples, internally at least, while they were still considered domestic sovereign treaty partners.[12] Finally, in *Worcester v. Georgia* (1832), the Court found that the federal government alone, as opposed to state governments, controlled 'Indian Affairs'.

As European settlers pushed westwards, they openly and violently dispossessed many Indigenous American peoples of their land. In 1830, the US government introduced what was known as the Indian Removal Act. It authorized the deportation of Indigenous peoples from east of the Mississippi River to lands west of the river, which were still occupied by the original Indigenous inhabitants. All eastern nations were subjected to Removal, with the most-often discussed by Western historians being the 'Five Civilized Tribes' – the Cherokee, Choctaw, Chickasaw, Seminole and Muscogee nations – who were forcibly deported along what became known as the 'Trail of Tears', a 1,300-kilometre nightmare during which as many as 8,000 died.[13] A recent review places Choctaw fatalities at up to 30 per cent of those removed.[14] The 25 per cent of diehards who hid out to remain behind on ancestral lands were officially declared to have chosen to 'expatriate themselves' from their nations, their existence thereafter obviated in a new form of violence since dubbed 'documentary genocide'.[15]

The 'Trail of Tears' was one of the first instances of the modern death march. Between 1830 and 1844, around 70,000 Indians were removed from their homes east of the Mississippi and driven west of the Mississippi River.[16] The resulting hardship and the brutality of the process meant that nearly one-third of those people died along the way. Thus began what is a peculiarly modern phenomenon, states 'managing' unwanted Indigenous as well as 'hostile' civilian populations by forcibly deporting, isolating and interning them. From the 1850s to the 1870s, forced relocation took place over smaller distances, as a policy of 'elimination' gave way to another form of violence, that of 'civilizing the Indian'. Nevertheless, Indigenous resistance to US government efforts to regulate where and how they could live, sporadic but violent, continued well into the last quarter of the nineteenth century.

We do not yet have an accurate picture of the number of Indigenous American killed by Europeans during conquest and invasion. As with Australia and South Africa, it is difficult to know the total population of Indigenous peoples on the North American Continent before contact. Population summaries always depended upon extrapolations from old civilian and military head counts, which were never much more than guestimates. We do know, however, that within a short space of time, in North America and Australia, the number of settlers far surpassed the number of local Indigenous peoples. By 1770, for example, there were probably only about 150,000 Indigenous Americans between the Mississippi and the Appalachians, while there were already about two million settlers.[17] Overall estimates for the decline in Indigenous populations vary enormously although demographic trends for individual nations are better known.[18] What we can say with a degree of certainty is that a number of related factors – warfare, enslavement, disease, malnutrition – led to severe population declines. One assessment has placed the 'rate of extermination pertaining to Native North America during the conquest as having been 98 to 99 per cent overall'.[19] It is impossible to know how many Indigenous Americans died of disease and malnutrition, and how many died as a direct result of violent conflict, but it is clear that war and forced relocation greatly increased incidents of disease and malnutrition.

The 'Lost Cause' of Aboriginal Peoples in Australia

When Governor Macquarie and his entourage departed New South Wales in 1822, the colonial population had skyrocketed to 39,968, while the Aboriginal population on the Cumberland Plain had declined from about 5,000 to fewer than 300.[20] The impact of the colonial wars was unmistakable. Small Aboriginal communities of up to sixty people were located at Botany Bay, at Kissing Point on the northern side of the Parramatta River, at Parramatta, at Milperra near Liverpool and Windsor on the Hawkesbury. Other communities were known to live on the other side of Nepean River near Camden. Some of them resided on their own lands, which now occupied by settlers. The local people were no longer considered dangerous and some of them would intermarry with labourers. The *Sydney Gazette* considered them beyond redemption. They had not willingly sought to convert to Christianity. Rather they had adopted the worst aspects of British society, drinking alcohol, smoking, gambling, and swearing, and relied on British foodstuffs such as tea and flour for their survival. 'Real Aboriginal people' lived beyond the Blue Mountains west of Sydney.[21] Throughout the European imperial world, the unwillingness or the inability of Indigenous and local people either to assimilate into European societies or to submit to the depredations of European settlers was increasingly interpreted throughout the nineteenth century as evidence of an inferior racial character.[22]

Apart from people like William Shelley, the colonial clergy considered Aboriginal people on the Cumberland Plain and their counterparts in Tasmania to be a lost cause. The Native Institution that had been established at Parramatta would close in the mid-1820s and some of the former residents would take up small farms at present-day Blacktown. Individual Aboriginal people, some brought up by colonists, would find employment as seamen and stockmen, but in almost every case, they do not appear to have married or left offspring.[23] This very sensitive issue requires further exploration.

After the amnesty of November 1816, the colonial population of NSW increased more than two and half times, indicating that the colony was on a new trajectory. Small self-sufficient farms were being gobbled up by large stations requiring vast swathes of Aboriginal homelands to run sheep for wool for export to England. The arrival of vast numbers of transported convicts meant that harsher measures were required to control them, and more prisons to hold the recidivists. In this new environment, Aboriginal people were no longer expected to become part of colonial society. Instead, more violent measures would be imposed against them, including martial law, and the survivors removed to islands and other remote locations where they were expected to die out.[24] That belief appears to have been there from the beginning. The first Aboriginal heads were despatched to Sir Joseph Banks in 1789; he would continue to receive many more up to 1820. They would include the heads of Pemulwuy, the parents of Robert Hobart May in Tasmania, the warriors who challenged the British at Port Dalrymple and some of the victims of the Appin massacre. The British fetish for the trophy heads of Indigenous people would continue unabated until the mid-twentieth century.[25]

The small British population to 1820 struggled to kill Aboriginal people in great numbers. Soldiers patrolled in small groups and were often under-resourced in weaponry and the ability to fire the Brown Bess musket. This changed after 1820 when greater numbers of settlers and convicts arrived in NSW and Tasmania, along with greater numbers of British soldiers. The British population more than doubled in less than five years. Analysis of the data on colonial massacres carried out in Australia between 1794 and 1820 indicates that the vast majority of the massacres were reprisals or pre-emptive strike massacres. The number of massacres for our period were, however, limited in scope. Eight massacres took place in NSW and Tasmania. Of those, five were reprisals and three were pre-emptive strikes. Seven were carried out by soldiers from serving British regiments, and the other by sealers on the

Table 1 Violent encounters between Aboriginal people and colonists, 1794–1824

Estimated Date	Location	Language Group	Estimated Killed
1 Sep 1794	Hawkesbury (1)	Bediagal	7
7 Jun 1795	Hawkesbury (2)	Bediagal	7
3 May 1804	Risdon Cove, River Derwent	Oyster Bay [Pydairrererme; Moomairremener]	30
27 Apr 1805	Yarramundi, Hawkesbury River	Bediagal/Darug	7
1 Mar 1806	Twofold Bay, South Coast	Thawa or Djirringany	9
1 November 1815 to 30 Nov 1815	Scantlands Plains	Oyster Bay	17
17 Apr 1816	Appin	Gundungurra	14
1 Oct 1818	Minnamurra River, South Coast	Dharawal	6
1 June 1823 to 2 Jun 1824	Eight Mile Swamp Creek, Bathurst	Wiradjuri	6

Source: Colonial Frontier Massacres in Australia, 1788–1930: https://c21ch.newcastle.edu.au/colonialmassacres/timeline.php

far south coast of NSW, 480 kilometres south of Sydney. Five of the seven massacres led by British soldiers were assisted by male settlers and their male employees. In all, we think about eighty-nine Aboriginal people were killed, although many more may have been killed in numbers of less than five or six at a time, thereby not technically meeting the criteria for a massacre. Australia was a fledgling colony, with fewer Indigenous peoples and fewer settlers compared to South Africa or North America, where significant populations were involved. We cannot give figures for the number of Indigenous and local people killed in the other three regions of the world with the same degree of accuracy, but of the massacres we know of, much larger numbers of people were involved.

The French Proving Ground in Africa

The Napoleonic Empire came to an end in 1815, but the legacies of the colonial-imperial wars would endure. When the French launched on another colonial enterprise, this time in North Africa during the reign of Louis-Philippe (1830–48), they would use much the same approach as they had used in Europe during the Revolutionary and Napoleonic Wars to conquer extra-European territories to quell any resistance they met along the way. This was particularly the case in Algeria, which was a proving ground for young officers coming up the ranks, but which was also led by men who had fought in the Napoleonic Wars. The French use of violence, atrocities and massacres during the colonial conquest of North, West and North-Central Africa was common and frequent, and about which quite a lot has been written.[26] They were carried out in an attempt to regenerate French 'glory', something that had been tarnished by the defeat of Napoleon in 1815. There was too an acceptance of the mass killing of Indigenous peoples by the French political elites, as seen in Alexis de Tocqueville's calls to brutally supress revolts in the North African colony of Algeria, despite being a liberal and despite having experienced first-hand French colonial rule.[27] Put another way, by the 1830s, French liberal elites had come to accept extreme violence as a means by which 'civilized rule' could be introduced to the Indigenous peoples of the world.[28]

Global Connections, Violent Attributes

What then have we learned of the complex interlocking processes at work involving colonial violence at a global level at the end of the eighteenth and the beginning of the nineteenth century? It is worth pointing to a number of commonalities regarding the types of violence used in English-speaking settler societies as well as in the French empire, an empire of colonial domination, as well as the manner in which Indigenous and local communities repelled, accommodated and appropriated the colonial encounter.[29]

We think it now evident that what was happening in Europe directly influenced what was happening in those corners of the world where the European imperial powers had planted their flags. To paraphrase Dierk Walter, Western imperial regimes were a knowledge community in which information, military techniques and technology were shared.[30] This certainly continued into the nineteenth century. That said, the competing empires they had been during the eighteenth century – an extension of great power politics onto the world stage – changed after the defeat of Napoleon and the Congress of Vienna in 1814 and 1815. Once the European powers had more or less agreed on a new security system that brought relative political stability to the European Continent, the imperial powers agreed, somewhat grudgingly, to not only tolerate each other's imperial ambitions overseas but assist each other when needed.[31] The French invasion of Algeria is a case in point; it was shaped by the Congress system.[32]

All the violence in these pages resulted from dominant European powers attempting to impose their rule on peoples other than their own. In all of these societies, the colonizers were in the process of profoundly transforming every aspect of the lives of the inhabitants. The bulk of the violence was necessarily perpetrated by the occupiers against the occupied, by the colonizers against the colonized, empowered by the knowledge and attitudes of empire. During that process, the colonizer created Otherness to justify the treatment of the inhabitants. Moreover, because of European concepts of ownership as well as techniques used to exploit the land, Europeans invariably clashed with Indigenous relations to the land thus creating tensions that often led to violence. The two were a heady mix. The willingness of Europeans to use violence to dispossess Indigenous populations or to control territory is striking. Indigenous and local populations also used violence, but generally as a means of protecting local customs and rights. Violence often led to deaths, but invariably many more deaths were incurred among the Indigenous and local inhabitants than among the invading forces.

Moreover, as we have seen across all four regions, when colonial conquerors arrived and waged war on local populations, they did not distinguish between combatants and non-combatants. This could of course work both ways. Indigenous and local groups were known to kill European non-combatants, but certainly not in the numbers that Europeans killed Indigenous non-combatants. It was characteristic of the viciousness of the violence on the frontier. Given that, however, Europeans generally prevailed over Indigenous and local people because settlers outnumbered Indigenous communities, were better supplied, especially in weapons, and in many instances their troops were better trained. At the local level, colonial war could mean total war.[33]

More comparative studies need to be undertaken, but from the evidence presented here, a systematic approach appears to have been adopted towards Indigenous and local peoples who resisted the incursion of settlers and or the state, regardless of the European occupying power and regardless of the Indigenous and local peoples involved. In some respects, there was nothing out of the ordinary. The destructive impulses of European warfare were waged with equal savagery in Europe and in the colonies.[34] The French political and military elite, for example, ordered rebel villages to be burnt to the ground and often all those who lived in them killed, but one can find the same situation in Ireland, in India, in Venezuela and in the Yucatán Peninsula, almost everywhere the European colonizer/settler encountered the original inhabitants of the land they were occupying.[35] Violence was a tool of intimidation, at least in the European mindset. That tactic often worked in Europe, that is, if the survivors of a besieged town were put to death, it was in the hope that other towns and garrisons would capitulate without a fight. They often did. Outside of Europe, scorched-earth tactics and punitive expeditions were standard strategies used by colonial forces to cower recalcitrant local and Indigenous populations across European empires. In settler colonies, however, Indigenous inhabitants were part of the land; capitulation to European settlers meant the annihilation of their way of life.

Massacre was but one tool of colonial control in a repertory that also included forced displacement and hunger. The reality of colonialism on the ground was that it was maintained and buoyed by violence, in spite of prevailing discourses on humanitarianism, civilization and progress.[36] Indeed, the very discourses that aimed to incorporate Indigenous peoples into the European worlds in which they lived reinforced the structures of exclusion. In understanding that, we need to revise our view of the European-colonial perpetrator. In settler societies, those who killed were sometimes in the military or were part of a local militia, as in North America, but in South Africa the bulk of the killing appears to have been carried out by mounted militia units, dubbed commandos, made up of farmers and their armed Black servants.[37] In revisionist studies on colonialism, to the extent that there is an understanding that killings took place on the colonial frontier at all, perpetrators are often portrayed as valiant settlers protecting their homesteads from the incursions of Indigenous peoples. This myth, such that it persists in some quarters of former colonial societies, needs to be turned on its head. The European settler was the invader who attacked and dispossessed Indigenous populations wherever they lived.[38]

Generally speaking, the colonizer killed Indigenous and local peoples with impunity. In all regions under consideration, the state was often aware of what was happening on the frontier but often turned a blind eye to the killing. In Europe, instructions were sometimes sent to commanders in the field to carry out reprisals and to burn villages to set an example, as we have seen, but often the initiative to massacre was made on the ground and was typically portrayed as part of a cycle of retaliation and retribution within irregular warfare. This is also true for the other three regions of the world studied here. Soldiers and settler militias, whether acting on the orders of the colonial government or not, perpetrated most of the massacres. In the few cases where settlers were known to have perpetrated massacre – what can be called decentralized killings – the perpetrators were sometimes tried and even convicted of murder by a jury but in almost all instances they were set free.[39] Similarly, no white man was ever convicted for the rape of a Khoikhoi or a slave woman.[40] That is,

Europeans literally often got away with murder when they killed Indigenous peoples on the frontier – they were often placed above the law. In North America and South Africa, murders that took place in Indian Country or in San territory were considered to be outside of the purview of the courts so that the law was never applied. In the penal colony of New South Wales, the local state worked very hard to assert control over everyone under its control within a defined territory even if in reality the frontier was a chaotic, lawless zone. Settlers who killed Indigenous peoples were brought to trial during this period but never hanged.

Indigenous peoples, on the other hand, were always punished, and often collectively, for the death of a settler. Thus, when James Stirling invaded the Avon Valley in Western Australia in the 1830s and killed the Noongar people who resisted those incursions, there were no sanctions for the violence and murder committed.[41] In Australia, settlers knew the massacres they sometimes carried out were beyond the law. When twelve men were put on trial for the massacre of twenty-eight Wirrayaraay men, women and children at Myall Creek in New South Wales in June 1838, and seven were actually hanged, settlers began to close ranks and continued to perpetrate massacres in a culture of silence.[42]

Many of the conflicts that ensued between Europeans and local populations were tit-for-tat killings, although the jovial mood in which 'punitive expeditions' were sometimes undertaken by militias in North America is not always consistent with an explanation of cold retaliation. In Indigenous cultures, like those of the San and Aboriginal people of the Australian eastern coast, the killing of a member of the group called for a revenge killing of a member of the perpetrator's group. For Woodlanders of the American Eastern coast, on the other hand, there were elaborate mechanisms in place designed to avoid revenge killings, such as wampum penalties.[43] When this broke down, the death of a member of the clan was also an occasion for young men to show their courage and to prove themselves in battle. In North America, this custom was enormously complicated by the political and diplomatic dealings of particular Indian nations with the Europeans, when they often used European alliances to try to outmanoeuvre rival nations.

Massacres were meant to be public knowledge, were meant to instil fear in others, and yet it was rare in the early part of the nineteenth century for the participants to brag about their bloody feats. The exception to this rule appears to be North America, where boasting of one's kills took place. It was only when this kind of swagger was likely to cast vilification on the government that such accounts were suppressed, as was the formal documentation of Colonel David Williamson's Goschochking (Gnadenhütten) expedition, which, shortly after having been received by Congress, mysteriously disappeared from the records.[44] In Europe, on the other hand, there was an implicit understanding that it was not talked about. True, some of the memoirs from this period, often written many years after the event, describe the massacres, sometimes in vivid detail, and more often than not the difficulties – what today we would refer to as post-traumatic stress disorder – experienced by the witnesses and the participants. The noise of cutting metal against flesh and bone, the smell of burning or rotting corpses, the memories of the screams of those being raped or killed and the sight of mangled and mutilated bodies are recalled. However, these were often 'moral' examples given to demonstrate just how difficult was war, colonization and the civilizing process. The implication is that massacre was not 'normal' even if widely practised, for the atrocities committed were so horrific that the perpetrators and the witnesses became incapable of expressing and articulating the horrors they had either committed or were witness to.[45] A sort of stupor overcame them, if you will. This is one argument that may help explain why descriptions of atrocities are at best oblique and never direct. It is also possible that people were prudish or did not yet possess the vocabulary to articulate what they were seeing and feeling at the end of the eighteenth and the beginning of the nineteenth century; that would come later.

In the European colonial empires, settlers, abetted by the authorities, killed and dispossessed Indigenous peoples to acquire access to land, resources and slaves. The extent to which massacres constituted a distinct system of violence varied in intensity across the regions under study but lies behind what we believe to be a fundamental characteristic of the colonial enterprise, namely, that wherever the colonizer met with resistance, violence was used to overcome it. That violence was always preceded by settler propaganda against the Indigenous inhabitants in the press of the day, at least in North America. In Europe, but also in Australia and North America, the military commanders and the political elites who either ordered or were complicit in the massacres that took place often justified their actions by arguing for a higher good: they were bringing enlightenment and civilization to a superstitious and barbarous people.

Throughout the rest of the nineteenth and into the twentieth century, Aboriginal people, San, Khoikhoi, Xhosa and Indigenous Americans would continue to be murdered and massacred or displaced from their land, largely out of sight of the public eye. In South Africa, the San would almost completely disappear, while in Australia and North America dozens of Indigenous nations would cease to exist having been killed on paper, if not on the ground. What is not common, however, is the memory of these atrocities committed against subjected peoples by European colonizers. Colonial settler societies like France, Britain, Australia and the United States have yet to fully recognize the extent of the violent destruction wrought against Indigenous and local peoples in the creation of their respective empires.

The legacies of violence continued for many generations. The silence surrounding the massacres on the colonial frontier in colonial societies is profound. Lyndall Ryan's research into the extent and number of massacres throughout Australian history is testimony to the fact that most of these massacres have been forgotten in history.[46] The kind of digital mapping exercise that has brought the Australian frontier wars into greater public consciousness is slowly being picked up in other parts of the world. For the moment, the forgetting that has occurred in Australia persists in South Africa, North America, and Europe where only a few of the most notorious examples of massacres might be remembered. We are hopeful that books like this one might lead to a deeper understanding of the violence inherent in any colonial project, and lead to a better understanding of the suffering inflicted by Europeans on Indigenous populations.

Notes

A Note on the Use of Names

1   See, for example, James Merrell, 'Second Thoughts on Colonial Historians and American Indians', *William and Mary Quarterly* 69, no. 3 (2012): 473–6.

Introduction

1   Before 1793, Britain had twenty-six colonies; by 1816, it had forty-three. See Bruce Lenman, 'British Colonial Politics in an Age of European War and Creole Rebellion', in *The Cambridge History of the Napoleonic Wars, Vol. 1, Politics and Diplomacy*, ed. Michael Broers and Philip Dwyer (Cambridge: Cambridge University Press, 2022), 64.

2   See Lorenzo Veracini, *Settler Colonialism: A Theoretical Overview* (Houndmills: Palgrave Macmillan, 2010), 3–11.

3   See, Christy Pichichero, *The Military Enlightenment: War and Culture in the French Empire from Louis XIV to Napoleon* (Ithaca, NY: Cornell University Press, 2017), 106–7.

4   For a wider discussion on the term 'Age of Revolution', see Michael A. McDonnell, 'Rethinking the Age of Revolution', *Atlantic Studies* 13, no. 3 (2016): 301–14. Kate Fullagar and Michael A. McDonnell, 'Introduction: Empire, Indigeneity, and Revolution', in *Facing Empire: Indigenous Experiences in a Revolutionary Age, 1760–1840*, ed. Kate Fullagar and Michael A. McDonnell (Baltimore, MD: Johns Hopkins University Press, 2018), 11–12, write that the term is not just a European construct.

5   David Armitage and Sanjay Subrahmanyam, 'Introduction: The Age of Revolutions, c.1760–1840 – Global Causation, Connection, and Comparison', in *The Age of Revolutions in Global Context, c. 1760–1840*, ed. David Armitage and Sanjay Subrahmanyam (New York: Palgrave Macmillan, 2010), xii–xxxii; C. A. Bayly, 'The First Age of Global Imperialism, c. 1760–1830', *The Journal of Imperial and Commonwealth History* 26, no. 2 (1998): 28–47.

6   Beatrice Heuser, 'Small Wars in the Age of Clausewitz: The Watershed between Partisan War and People's War', *Journal of Strategic Studies* 33, no. 1 (2010): 139–62.

7   C. A. Bayly, *Imperial Meridian: The British Empire and the World 1780–1830* (London: Longman, 1989), 196.

8   Linda Colley, *Britons: Forging the Nation, 1707–1837* (New Haven, CT: Yale University Press, 1992).

9   Bayly, *Imperial Meridian*, 6–7.

10 Alexander Mikaberidze, *The Napoleonic Wars: A Global History* (Oxford: Oxford University Press, 2020).

11 See, R. Douglas Hurt, *The Indian Frontier, 1763–1846* (Albuquerque: University of New Mexico Press, 2002), xii–xiii.

12 On the concept of the 'borderlands', see Paul Readman, Cynthia Radding and Chad Bryant, 'Introduction: Borderlands in a Global Perspective', in *Borderlands in World History, 1700–1914*, ed. Paul Readman, Cynthia Radding and Chad Bryant (Basingstoke: Palgrave Macmillan 2014), 14; and Andrew K. Frank and A. Glenn Crothers, 'Introduction', in *Borderlands Narratives: Negotiation and Accommodation in North America's Contested Spaces, 1500–1850*, ed. Andrew K. Frank and A. Glenn Crothers (Gainesville: University Press of Florida, 2017), 1–17. For the borderlands in American historiography, see Erik Altenbernd and Alex Trimble Young, 'Introduction: The Significance of the Frontier in an Age of Transnational History', *Settler Colonial Studies* 4, no. 2 (2014): 127–50. For Australia see, Frank Bongiorno, '"The Men Who Made Australia Federated Long Ago": Australian Frontiers and Borderlands', in *Borderlands in World History*, ed. Paul Readman, Cynthia Radding and Chad Bryant (Basingstoke: Palgrave Macmillan, 2014), 46–62. For South Africa, see Nigel Penn, 'The Northern Cape Frontier Zone in South African Historiography', in *Colonial Frontiers: Indigenous-European Encounters in Settler Societies*, ed. Lynette Russell (Manchester: Manchester University Press, 2001), 19–46.

13 See Vincent O'Malley, *Beyond the Imperial Frontier: The Contest for Colonial New Zealand* (Wellington: Bridget Williams Books, 2014), 11–14; and Howard Lamar and Leonard Thompson, 'Comparative Frontier History', in *The Frontier in History: North America and Southern Africa Compared*, ed. Howard Lamar and Leonard Thompson (New Haven, CT: Yale University Press, 1981), 3–5, and Hermann Giliomee, 'Process Development of the Southern African Frontier', in *The Frontier in History: North America and Southern Africa Compared*, ed. Howard Lamar and Leonard Thompson (New Haven, CT: Yale University Press, 1981), 3–5, and 76–119.

14 For an example of this in the Australian context. see Amanda Nettelbeck, 'Proximate Strangers and Familiar Antagonists: Violence on an Intimate Frontier', *Australian Historical Studies* 47, no. 2 (2016): 209–24.

15 This problem has been raised in another context by Omer Bartov, 'Genocide and the Holocaust: Arguments over History and Politics', in *Lessons and Legacies*, ed. Karl

Schleunes and Hilary Earl, Vol. XI (Evanston, IL: Northwestern University Press, 2014), 5–28; Omer Bartov, 'Communal Genocide: Personal Accounts of the Destruction of Buczacz, Eastern Galicia, 1941–44', in *Shatterzone of Empires: Coexistence and Violence in the German, Habsburg, Russian, and Ottoman Borderlands*, ed. Omer Bartov and Eric D. Weitz (Bloomington: Indiana University Press, 2013), 399–421.

16 See, for example, the discussion in Karl Jacoby, 'Indigenous Empires and Native Nations: Beyond History and Ethnohistory in Pekka Hämäläinen's', *The Comanche Empire*', *History and Theory* 52, no. 1 (2013): 60–6; and Daniel Richter, 'Whose Indian History?' *William and Mary Quarterly* 50, no. 2 (1993): 379–93.

17 See Philippa Levine, 'Is Comparative History Possible?' *History and Theory* 53, no. 3 (2014): 331–47.

18 John Connor, *The Australian Frontier Wars 1788–1838* (Sydney: UNSW Press, 2002), 1–7; Dierk Walter, *Colonial Violence: European Empires and the Use of Force*, trans. Peter Lewis (London: Hurst, 2017), 47–50.

19 Se, for example, Niall Ferguson, *Empire: How Britain Made the Modern World* (London: Allen Lane, 2003); and Nigel Biggar, *Colonialism: A Moral Reckoning* (London: William Collins, 2023).

20 Caroline Elkins, *Legacy of Violence a History of the British Empire* (New York: Alfred A. Knopf, 2022), 6–8; and Patricia M. E. Lorcin, 'Nostalgias for Empire', *History and Theory* 57, no. 2 (2018): 269–85.

Chapter 1

1 Christoph Kamissek and Jonas Kreienbaum, 'An Imperial Cloud? Conceptualising Interimperial Connections and Transimperial Knowledge', *Journal of Modern European History* 14, no. 2 (2016): 164–82.

2 For South Africa, although for the later nineteenth century, see Alan Lester, *Imperial Networks: Creating Identities in Nineteenth-Century South Africa and Britain* (London: Routledge, 2001). See also David Lambert and Alan Lester, 'Introduction: Imperial Spaces, Imperial Subjects', in *Colonial Lives across the British Empire: Imperial Careering in the Long Nineteenth Century*, ed. David Lambert and Alan Lester (Cambridge: Cambridge University Press, 2006), 1–31, who talk about 'imperial careering' to describe the 'servants of empire' who travelled across British imperial spaces.

3 Philip D. Morgan, 'Encounters between British and "Indigenous" Peoples, c.1500–c.1800', in *Empire and Others: British Encounters with Indigenous Peoples, 1600–1850*, ed. Martin Daunton and Rick Halpern (Philadelphia: University of Pennsylvania Press, 1999), 56–62; Nicholas Canny, *The Elizabethan Conquest of*

Ireland: A Pattern Established 1565–76 (Hassocks: Harvester Press, 1976), 159–63; Joyce E. Chaplin, 'The British Atlantic', in *The Oxford Handbook of the Atlantic World, 1450–1850*, ed. Nicholas Canny and Philip Morgan (Oxford: Oxford University Press, 2011), 223.

4   On the Australian connection, see Christine Wright, *Wellington's Men in Australia: Peninsular War Veterans and the Making of Empire c.1820–40* (Basingstoke: Palgrave Macmillan, 2011). It is important not to overlook leaders of the Irish rebellion. A rank-and-file Irish rebel, Edward White, who was convicted of treason and transported to Australia, was a key witness to a massacre of Tasmanian Aboriginal people by British soldiers, settlers and convicts in 1804. See Phillip John Tardif, *John Bowen's Hobart: The Beginning of European Settlement in Tasmania* (Hobart: Tasmanian Historical Research Association, 2003), 2, 3, 144, 145–6.

5   Karin Racine, 'Message by Massacre: Venezuela's War to the Death, 1810–1814', *Journal of Genocide Research* 15, no. 2 (2013): 201–17; C. I. Archer, 'The Cutting Edge: The Historical Relationship between Insurgency, Counterinsurgency and Terrorism during Mexican Independence, 1810–1821', in *Terrorism: Roots, Impact, Responses*, ed. Lawrence Howard (New York: Praeger, 1992), 29–45; Anthony McFarlane, 'Breaking the Pax Hispanica: Collective Violence in Colonial Spanish America', in *A Global History of Early Modern Violence*, ed. Erica Charters, Marie Houllemare, and Peter H. Wilson (Manchester: Manchester University Press, 2020), 115; and Anthony McFarlane, *War and Independence in Spanish America* (New York: Routledge, 2014).

6   Olivier Le Cour Grandmaison, *Coloniser, Exterminer – Sur la guerre et l'Etat colonial* (Paris: Fayard, 2005), 18–19. On Algeria, see William Gallois, *A History of Violence in the Early Algerian Colony* (Houndmills: Palgrave Macmillan, 2013).

7   William Gallois, 'Genocide in Nineteenth-Century Algeria', *Journal of Genocide Research* 15, no. 1 (2013): 72, f. 17. See also Fergus Robson, 'French Soldiers and the Revolutionary Origins of the Colonial Mind', in *Militarized Cultural Encounters in the Long Nineteenth Century: Making War, Mapping Europe*, ed. Joseph Clarke and John Horne (Cham: Palgrave Macmillan, 2018), 28.

8   Serna, 'Pour un épilogue: Le massacre au XVIIIe siècle', 9–10; and Ivan Burel, 'From Egypt to Algeria: General Pierre Boyer's Counter-Insurgent and Imperial Career', in *From the Napoleonic Empire to the Age of Empire: Empire after the Emperor*, ed. Thomas Dodman and Aurélien Lignereux (Cham: Springer, 2023), 253–69. For a recent work that places raiding at the forefront of European and Indigenous conflict, see Lauren Benton, *They Called It Peace: Worlds of Imperial Violence* (Princeton, NJ: Princeton University Press, 2024).

9   See Stephen Gapps, *The Sydney Wars Conflict in the Early Colony 1788–1817* (Sydney: NewSouth Publishing, 2018), 89. The punitive raid was the 'classic instrument of power on the militarized frontier' and was also used in South Africa and North America (Walter, *Colonial Violence*, 122).

10 Armitage and Subrahmanyam, 'Introduction', xxxi, suggest that there are two ways of conceptualizing the interconnected histories of the period: identifying networks that existed by rediscovering past actors, or constructing connections that contemporaries may have been unaware of.

11 Perpetrator studies have blossomed in recent years, often to the detriment of the victims of violence, although there have been attempts to incorporate the categories 'victims' and 'bystanders' into studies of mass killings. Most of the scholarship is centred on the Holocaust, but it has since moved on from the classical triad of perpetrator-victim-bystander that emerged in the 1980s. See, for example, David Cesarani and Paul A. Levine (eds), *'Bystanders' to the Holocaust: A Re-Evaluation* (London: Routledge, 2002); Michael Rothberg, *The Implicated Subject: Beyond Victims and Perpetrators* (Stanford: Stanford University Press, 2019); Kjell Anderson and Erin Jessee (eds), *Researching Perpetrators of Genocide* (Madison: University of Wisconsin Press, 2020); and Susanne C. Knittel and Zachary J. Goldberg (eds), *The Routledge International Handbook of Perpetrator Studies* (London: Routledge, 2020).

12 Benjamin Valentino, *Final Solutions: Mass Killing and Genocide in the Twentieth Century* (Ithaca, NY: Cornell University Press, 2004), 71, 77–80.

13 The term is of course a reference to the killing capacity of 'ordinary' men in Christopher Browning, *Ordinary Men: Reserve Police Battalion 101 and the Final Solution in Poland* (New York: HarperPerennial, 1993).

14 On the definition of mass killing, see Valentino, *Final Solutions*, 10–15.

15 Mark Mazower, 'Violence and the State in the Twentieth Century', *American Historical Review* 107, no. 4 (2002): 1162.

16 Timothy Snyder, *Bloodlands: Europe between Hitler and Stalin* (New York: Basic Books, 2010), 413.

17 The literature is too extensive to cite here. Some of the more prominent advocates of the 'colonialism = genocide thesis' in Australia are Colin Tatz, 'Confronting Australian Genocide', *Aboriginal History* 25 (2001): 16–36; A. Dirk Moses, 'Empire, Colony, Genocide: Keywords and the Philosophy of History', in *Empire, Colony, Genocide: Conquest, Occupation, and Subaltern Resistance in World History*, ed. A. Dirk Moses (New York: Berghahn, 2008), 4–54. Patrick Wolfe, 'Settler Colonialism and the Elimination of the Native', *Journal of Genocide Research* 8, no. 4 (2006): 388–403, and Veracini, *Settler Colonialism*, 16–17, both have slightly more nuanced approaches. Wolfe wrote of the 'logic of elimination' but argued that settler colonialism is not always genocidal. Veracini writes of the elimination of Indigenous peoples through various means, including 'extermination, expulsion, incarceration, containment and assimilation'. Lorenzo Veracini, 'Colonialism, Frontiers, Genocide: Civilian-Driven Violence in Settler Colonial Situations', in *Civilian-Driven Violence and the Genocide of Indigenous Peoples in Settler Societies*, ed. Mohamed Adhikari (London: Routledge, 2021), 267, contends that those who argue settler colonialism is genocidal have the sequence wrong: 'it is not that settler colonialism is genocidal,

it is genocide that is settler colonial'. For a recent summary of the genocide debates in Australia, see Thomas James Rogers and Stephen Bain, 'Genocide and Frontier Violence in Australia', *Journal of Genocide Research* 18, no. 1 (2016): 83–100, who come down on the side of genocide. For North America, see Jeffrey Ostler, *Surviving Genocide: Native Nations and the United States from the American Revolution to Bleeding Kansas* (New Haven, CT: Yale University Press, 2019), 383–7.

18   On the Black Line, see the articles by Lyndall Ryan, Nick Clements and Eleanor Cave in 'Themed Section: The Black Line in Tasmania – A Reconsideration', *Journal of Australian Studies* 37, no. 1 (2013): 1–47. See also Rebe Taylor, 'Genocide in Van Diemen's Land (Tasmania), 1803–1871', in *Cambridge World History of Genocide*, ed. Ned Blackhawk, Ben Kiernan, Benjamin Madley, and Rebe Taylor, Vol. 2 (Cambridge: Cambridge University Press, 2023), 481–507.

19   The case studies for our period are limited but one can consult Gregory A. Waselkov, *A Conquering Spirit: Fort Mims and the Redstick War of 1813–1814* (Tuscaloosa: University of Alabama Press, 2006); Jane Lydon and Lyndall Ryan (eds), *Remembering the Myall Creek Massacre* (Sydney: NewSouth Publishing, 2018). For massacre during the period under consideration, see the Special Issue of the *Journal of Genocide Research* 15, no. 2 (2013).

20   One of the few examples, based on a conference in France, were published in the *Revue Internationale de Politique Comparée* (January 2001). See also Jacques Sémelin, 'In Consideration of Massacres', *Journal of Genocide Research* 3, no. 3 (2001): 377–89; and Ben Kiernan, *Blood and Soil: Modern Genocide 1500–2000* (New Haven, CT: Yale University Press, 2007), 13–16, refers to 'limited episodes of killing directed at a specific local or regional community' as 'genocidal massacres', a term first used by Leo Kuper. Barbara Alice Mann, 'Fractal Massacres in the Old Northwest: the example of the Miamis', *Journal of Genocide Research* 15, no. 2 (2013): 167–82, has hit on the idea of 'fractal massacres' to describe the successive waves of attack against Indigenous Americans.

21   For an attempt to theorize massacre, see Jacques Sémelin, *Purify and Destroy: The Political Uses of Massacre and Genocide*, trans. Cynthia Schoch (New York: Columbia University Press, 2007).

22   Stathis Kalyvas provides the most helpful framework for understanding massacres, although his work focuses on civil war. See Stathis N. Kalyvas, 'Aspects méthodologiques de la recherche sur les massacres: le cas de la guerre civile Grecque', *Revue internationale de politique comparée*, 8 (2001): 23–42; and Stathis N. Kalyvas, *The Logic of Violence in Civil War* (Cambridge: Cambridge University Press, 2006), 146–72. For a broader perspective, see Philip Dwyer and Lyndall Ryan, 'The Massacre and History', in *Theatres of Violence: Massacre, Mass Killing and Atrocity Throughout History*, ed. Philip Dwyer and Lyndall Ryan (New York: Berghahn, 2012), ix–xxv; and Mark Levene, 'Introduction', in *The Massacre in History*, ed. Mark Levene and Penny Roberts (New York: Berghahn Books, 1999), 1–38; Allan Tulchin, 'Massacres during the French Wars of Religion', *Past & Present*, 7 (2012): 100–26.

23 See, for example, Alain Corbin, *The Village of Cannibals: Rage and Murder in France, 1870*, trans. Arthur Goldhammer (Cambridge, MA: Harvard University Press, 1992).

24 Jacques Sémelin, 'Du crime de masse', in *Faut-il s'accommoder de la violence?* Ed. Thomas Ferenczi (Paris: Complexe, 2000), 375–91.

25 Levene and Roberts (eds), *The Massacre in History*, 1, 4, 5.

26 See Lyndall Ryan, 'Settler Massacres on the Australian Colonial Frontier, 1836–1851', in *Theatres of Violence: Massacre, Mass Killing and Atrocity Throughout History*, ed. Philip Dwyer and Lyndall Ryan (New York: Berghahn, 2012), 99; Lyndall Ryan, 'Establishing a Code of Silence: Civilian and State Complicity in Genocidal Massacres on the New South Wales Frontier, 1788–1859', in *Civilian-Driven Violence and the Genocide of Indigenous Peoples in Settler Societies*, ed. Mohamed Adhikari (London: Routledge, 2021), 121; Ian D. Clark, *Scars in the Landscape: A Register of Massacre Sites in Western Victoria* (Canberra: Australian Institute of Aboriginal and Torres Strait Islander Studies, 1995), 7; Ben Kiernan, 'Australia's Aboriginal Genocide', *Yale Journal of Human Rights* 1, no. 1 (2000): 52.

27 Jacques Sémelin, 'Analysis of a Mass Crime: Ethnic Cleansing in the Former Yugoslavia, 1991–1999', in *Specter of Genocide: Mass Murder in Historical Perspective*, ed. Robert Gellately and Ben Kiernan (Cambridge: Cambridge University Press, 2003), 355–6.

28 Jacques Sémelin, 'From Massacre to the Genocidal Process', *International Social Science Journal* 54, no. 174 (2002): 435–6.

29 Mazower, 'Violence and the State in the Twentieth Century', 1165.

30 A question posed by Rob Harper, 'State Intervention and Extreme Violence in the Eighteenth-Century Ohio Valley', *Journal of Genocide Research* 10, no. 2 (2008): 234.

31 Pierre Serna, 'Pour un épilogue: Le massacre au XVIIIe siècle ou comment écrire une histoire de l'inhumain des Lumières aux Révolutions, puis à la conquête de l'Algérie', *La Révolution française*, 3 (2011): 3; Nicolas Cadet, *Honneur et violences de guerre au temps de Napoléon: la Campagne de Calabre* (Paris: Vendémiaire, 2015), 296.

32 Barbara Alice Mann, *George Washington's War on Native America* (Westport, CT: Praeger, 2005), 94, 100, 115–16, 183 (note 18). For an extended historical documentation of scalp bounties in North America, see Ward Churchill, *A Little Matter of Genocide: Holocaust and Denial in the Americas, 1492 to the Present* (San Francisco, CA: City Lights Books, 1997), 181–5.

33 Lisa Ford, *Settler Sovereignty: Jurisdiction and Indigenous People in America and Australia, 1788–1836* (Cambridge, MA: Harvard University Press, 2010), 85–6.

34 Jonathan Leader Maynard, *Ideology and Mass Killing: The Radicalized Security Politics of Genocides and Deadly Atrocities* (Oxford: Oxford University Press, 2022), 4.

35 Roger Chickering, 'Total War: The Use and Abuse of a Concept', in Manfred F. Boemeke, Roger Chickering and Stig Förster (eds), *Anticipating Total War: The German and American Experiences, 1871–1914* (Cambridge: Cambridge University Press, 1999), 23.

36 David A. Bell, 'The French Revolution, the Vendée, and Genocide', *Journal of Genocide Research* 22, no. 1 (2020): 19–25.

37 Jean-Clément Martin, *La Vendée et la France* (Paris: Seuil, 1987); Roger Dupuy, *La République jacobine. Terreur, guerre et government révolutionnaire (1792–1794)* (Paris: Seuil, 2005), 267–69; Peter McPhee, 'A Vicious Civil War in the French Revolution: "The Vendée," 1793–1795', in *The Cambridge World History of Genocide*, ed. Ned Blackhawk, Ben Kiernan, Benjamin Madley, and Rebe Taylor, Vol. 2 (Cambridge: Cambridge University Press, 2023), 312–34.

38 David A. Bell, *The First Total War: Napoleon's Europe and the Birth of Warfare as We Know It* (Boston, MA: Houghton Mifflin, 2007), 154–85; and Mark Levene, *Genocide in the Age of the Nation-State*, Vol. 2 (London: I. B. Tauris, 2005), 103–61. This dramatic escalation in levels of state violence is, according to Bell, part of the conditions of 'total war', something that was part of French revolutionary ideology.

39 Joseph Clarke, 'A "Theatre of Bloody Carnage": The Revolt of Cairo and Revolutionary Violence', in *A Global History of Early Modern Violence*, ed. Erica Charters, Marie Houllemare and Peter H. Wilson (Manchester: Manchester University Press, 2020), 218–34, takes a different approach and argues that far from being unambiguously modern, the experience of violence is a complex interplay between the present and the past.

40 Religion did have a role to play in resistance to the colonizer, especially among Indigenous populations who remained faithful to traditional religious practices. For the French, see Philip Dwyer, 'Religion and Violence during the French Revolutionary and Napoleonic Wars: Between Tradition and Modernity' in Eveline G. Bouwers (ed.), *Catholics and Violence in the Nineteenth-Century Global World* (London: Routledge, 2024), 33–55. It could also play a role in Indigenous resistance to imperial domination. See Walter, *Colonial Violence*, 144; Armstrong Starkey, *European and Native American Warfare, 1675–1815* (New York: Routledge, 1998), 66.

41 For an overview of Anglo-American racial thought in the late eighteenth and early nineteenth centuries, see Audrey Smedley, *Race in North America: Origin and Evolution of a Worldview* (Boulder, CO: Westview Press, 2012), 171–88. For an argument that British colonists racialized Indians in the seventeenth century, see Joyce E. Chaplin, *Subject Matter: Technology, the Body, and Science on the Anglo-American Frontier, 1500–1676* (Cambridge, MA: Harvard University Press, 2001).

42 See, for example, Gustav Jahoda, *Images of Savages: Ancient Roots of Modern Prejudice in Western Culture* (New York: Routledge, 1999), 15–35, 36–50; and George M. Fredrickson, *Racism: A Short History* (Princeton, NJ: Princeton University Press, 2015), 56–72.

43 Anthony Pagden, *European Encounters with the New World: From Renaissance to Romanticism* (New Haven, CT: Yale University Press, 1993), 14.

44 See, Madeleine Dobie, *Trading Places: Colonization and Slavery in Eighteenth-Century French Culture* (Ithaca, NY: Cornell University Press, 2010), 136–7.

45 Wulf D. Hund, '"It Must Come from Europe": The Racisms of Immanuel Kant', in Wulf D. Hund, Christian Koller and Moshe Zimmermann (eds), *Racisms Made in Germany* (Berlin: LIT Verlag, 2011), 69–98; Harvey Chisick, 'Ethics and History in Voltaire's Attitudes toward the Jews', *Eighteenth-Century Studies* 35, no. 4 (2002): 577–600; and Avram Alpert, 'Philosophy's Systemic Racism', *Aeon*, 24 September 2020: https://aeon.co/essays/racism-is-baked-into-the-structure-of-dialectical-philosophy

46 Marie-Jean-Antoine-Nicolas de Condorcet, *Outlines of an Historical View of the Progress of the Human Mind* (Philadelphia, PA: M. Carey, 1795), 253–54, 256–7.

47 Michael Mann, 'Have Wars and Violence Declined?' *Theory and Society* 47, no. 2 (2018): 38.

48 Andrew S. Curran, *The Anatomy of Blackness: Science & Slavery in an Age of Enlightenment* (Baltimore, MD: Johns Hopkins University Press, 2011), 23–24; Claudia Bruns, 'Antisemitism and Colonial Racism', in *Racisms Made in Germany*, ed. Wulf D. Hund, Christian Koller and Moshe Zimmermann (Berlin: LIT Verlag, 2011), 99–122.

49 Jonathan Israel, *Enlightenment Contested: Philosophy, Modernity, and the Emancipation of Man, 1670–1752* (Oxford: Oxford University Press, 2006), 591–92.

50 A similar view is expressed by Mohammed Adhikari, '"We Are Determined to Exterminate Them": The Genocidal Impetus behind Commercial Stock Farmer Invasions of Hunter-Gatherer Territories', in *Genocide on Settler Frontiers: When Hunter-Gatherers and Commercial Stock Farmers Clash*, ed. Mohammed Adhikari (Cape Town: UCT Press, 2014), 13.

51 Alan Forrest, 'The Ubiquitous Brigand: The Politics and Language of Repression', in *Popular Resistance in the French Wars: Patriots, Partisans and Land Pirates*, ed. Charles J. Esdaile (New York: Palgrave Macmillan, 2005), 39–40.

52 This is something that most social psychologists recognize. See David Livingstone Smith, *Less Than Human: Why We Demean, Enslave, and Exterminate Others* (New York: St. Martin's Press, 2011); and Siniša Malešević, *Why Humans Fight: The Social Dynamics of Close-Range Violence* (Cambridge: Cambridge University Press, 2022), 84–6, 89–90.

53 For the Australian context, see Nicholas Clements and Andrew Gregg, '"I Am Frightened out of My Life": Black War, White Fear', *Settler Colonial Studies* 7, no. 2 (2017): 221–40. For South Africa see, Margot Winer, 'Landscapes, Fear and Land Loss on the Nineteenth-Century South African Colonial Frontier', in *Contested Landscapes: Movement, Exile and Place*, ed. Barbara Bender and Margot Winer (London: Routledge, 2020), 257–72. For the American experience, although for a later date, see Brendan C. Lindsay, *Murder State: California's Native American Genocide, 1846–1873*

(Lincoln: University of Nebraska Press, 2012), 18, 19, 109–23. Lindsay uses the framework established by Daniel Chirot and Clark McCauley, *Why Not Kill Them All?: The Logic and Prevention of Mass Political Murder* (Princeton, NJ: Princeton University Press, 2010), 19–44, who propose four overlapping motivational factors leading to genocide – convenience, revenge, simple fear and fear of (racial) pollution.

54 Joanna Bourke, *Fear: A Cultural History* (London: Virago, 2005), 391, writes that 'Fear has been one of the most significant driving forces in history'.

55 See, for example, Ruth Leys, 'How Did Fear Become a Scientific Object and What Kind of Object Is It?' *Representations* 110, no. 1 (2010): 66–104.

56 On mutual incomprehension in intercultural warfare, see Stephen Morillo, 'A General Typology of Transcultural Wars – The Early Middle Ages and Beyond', in *Transcultural Wars: From the Middle Ages to the 21st Century*, ed. Hans-Henning Kortüm (Berlin: Akademie Verlag, 2006), 29–42; and Walter, *Colonial Violence*, 230–4.

57 For the role of fear in French revolutionary violence, see David P. Jordan, 'Rumor, Fear, and Paranoia in the French Revolution', in *The Fundamentalist Mindset: Psychological Perspectives on Religion, Violence, and History*, ed. Charles B. Strozier, David M. Terman, James W. Jones and Katherine A. Boyd (New York: Oxford University Press, 2010), 175–94; and Haim Burstin, 'Pour une phénoménologie de la violence révolutionnaire: réflexions autour du cas parisie', *Historical Reflections/ Réflexions Historiques* 29, no. 3 (2003): 395–6, 406.

Chapter 2

1 Who these people were is contested. Perhaps they were Bantu-speakers who originated in West Africa and then dispersed southwards or perhaps they were Nilo-Hamitic people from the northeast of Africa.

2 Elphick and Malherbe estimate that there were perhaps about 50,000 Khoisan in the southwestern Cape at the time of European contact. Richard Elphick and V.C. Malherbe, 'The Khoisan to 1828', in *The Shaping of South African Society, 1652–1840*, ed. Richard Elphick and Hermann Giliomee (Cape Town: Maskew Miller Longman, 1989), 3.

3 David Lewis-Williams and David Pearce, *San Spirituality: Roots, Expression, and Social Consequences* (Cape Town: Double Storey, 2004), 102–3.

4 John Parkington and Simon Hall, 'The Appearance of Food Production in Southern Africa', in *The Cambridge History of South Africa, Vol 1, From Early Times to 1885*, ed. Carolyn Hamilton, Bernard K. Mbenga and Robert Ross (Cambridge: Cambridge University Press, 2016), 99–111.

5   Andrew Smith, *First People: The Lost History of the Khoisan* (Cape Town: Jonathan Ball, 2022), 123–44.

6   See John E. Parkington, 'Soaqua and Bushmen: Hunters and Robbers', in *Past and Present in Hunter Gatherer Studies*, ed. Carmel Schrire (New York: Routledge, 2016), 151–74.

7   Nigel Penn, *The Forgotten Frontier: Colonist and Khoisn on the Cape's Northern Frontier in the 18th Century* (Cape Town: Double Storey and Ohio University Press, 2005), chs. 1–4; and Nigel Penn, '"Fated to Perish": The Destruction of the Cape San', in *Miscast: Negotiating the Presence of the Bushmen*, ed. Pippa Skotnes (Cape Town: University of Cape Town Press, 1996), 81–92.

8   Penn, *Forgotten Frontier*, 187–91.

9   Noel Mostert, *Frontiers: The Epic of South Africa's Creation and the Tragedy of the Xhosa People* (London: Pimlico, 1992).

10 For the influence of Turner in shaping the frontier tradition in South African historiography, see Penn, 'The Northern Cape Frontier Zone', in *Colonial Frontiers*, ed. Russell, 19–46.

11 For an overview of the historiography of the eastern frontier zone, see Martin Legassick, *The Struggle for the Eastern Cape 1800–1854* (Johannesburg: KMM Review Publishing Company, 2010), 1–4. See also Hermann Giliomee, 'The Eastern Frontier, 1770–1812', in *The Shaping of South African* Society, ed. Elphick and Giliomee, 421–71, for a concise account of the early history of the frontier.

12 The alliteration was that of W. M. Macmillan in his *Bantu, Boer and Britain* (London: Faber, 1929).

13 Christopher Saunders, 'The Hundred Years' War: Some Reflections on African Resistance on the Cape-Xhosa Frontier', in *Profiles of Self-Determination: African Responses to European Colonialism in Southern Africa, 1652–Present*, ed. David Chainawa (Northridge: California State University, 1976), 55–77.

14 I. D. MacCrone, *Race Attitudes in South Africa: Historical, Experimental and Psychological Studies* (Johannesburg: Oxford University Press, 1937).

15 For a survey of Xhosa prehistory, see J. B. Peires, *The House of Phalo: A History of the Xhosa People in the Days of Their Independence* (Johannesburg: Ravan Press, 1981).

16 Peires, *House of Phalo*.

17 Peires, *House of Phalo*.

18 Hazel Crampton, Jeff Peires and Carl Vernon (eds), *Into the Hitherto Unknown: Ensign Beutler's Expedition to the Eastern Cape, 1752* (Cape Town: Van Riebeeck Society, 2013), 75.

19 Ben MacLennan, *A Proper Degree of Terror: John Graham and the Cape's Eastern Frontier* (Johannesburg: Ravan Press, 1986), 58.

20 According to Pekka Hämäläinen, *Indigenous Continent: The Epic Contest for North America* (New York: Liveright, 2022), 325.

21 Doug Georg-Kanentiio and Bruce E. Johansen, 'Land Area of the Haudenosaunee in New York State', in *Encyclopedia of the Haudenosaunee (Iroquois Confederacy)*, ed. Bruce E. Johansen and Barbara Alice Mann (Westport, CT: Greenwood Press, 2000), 191–94.

22 For the Muscogee Confederacy, see Willard B. Walker, 'Creek Confederacy before Removal', in *Southeast, Handbook of North American Indians*, Vol. 14 (Washington, DC: Smithsonian Institution, 2004), 373. For the Natchez, see J. J. Bauxar, 'Ethnohistorical Reconstructions', in *The Prehistory of the Chickamauga Basin in Tennessee*, ed. Thomas M. N. Lewis, Madeleine D. Kneberg Lewis and Lynne Sullivan, Vol. 1 (Knoxville: University of Tennessee Press, 1995), 262–64.

23 Tony Hall, 'Native Limited Identities and Newcomer Metropolitanism in Upper Canada, 1814–1867', in *Old Ontario: Essays in Honour of J. M. S. Careless*, ed. David Keane and Colin Read (Toronto: Dundurn Press, 1990), 152–3.

24 For the Seneca, see Arthur Caswell Parker, *The Constitution of the Five Nations or The Iroquois Book of the Great Law* (Albany, NY: University of the State of New York, 1916). For the Tuscarora scholar, see John Napoleon Brinton Hewitt, 'A Constitutional League of Peace in the Stone Age of America: The League of the Iroquois and Its Constitution', *Smithsonian Institution Series* (1920), 527–45.

25 John Napoleon Brinton Hewitt, 'Some Esoteric Aspects of the League of the Iroquois', *Proceedings of the International Congress of Americanists* 19 (1915): 325; idem., 'Ethnological Studies among the Iroquois Indians', *Smithsonian Miscellaneous Collections* 78, no. 7 (1927): 240–1.

26 Barbara Alice Mann, *Spirits of Blood, Spirits of Breath: The Twinned Cosmos of Indigenous America* (New York: Oxford, 2016); idem., 'A Failure to Communicate: How Christian Missionary Assumptions Ignore Binary Patterns of Thinking within Native American Communities', in *Remembering Jamestown: Hard Questions about Christian Mission*, ed. Barbara Brown Zikmund and Amos Yong (Eugene, OR: Pickwick Publications, 2010), 37–42.

27 John Reed Swanton, *Creek Religion and Medicine* (1928; Lincoln: University of Nebraska Press, 2000), 482.

28 Jean-Bernard Bossu, *Nouveau Voyages aux Indies Occidentales* (Paris: Le Jay, 1768), 225.

29 'Harmony Ethic, Cherokee', in *The Encyclopedia of Native American Legal Tradition*, ed. Bruce Elliott Johansen (Westport, CT: Greenwood Press, 1998), 111.

30 Barbara Alice Mann, *Iroquoian Women: The Gantowisas* (New York: Lang, 2000), 107–8, 228, 254, 286.

31 Mann, *Iroquoian Women*, 149, 170, 172, 178–9.

32 Mann, *Iroquoian Women*, 170, 175-7; Mann, *George Washington's War*, 17-18.

33 Mann, *Iroquoian Women*, 155-82.

34 Mann, *Iroquoian Women*, 165-70.

35 See, for example, Elisabeth Tooker, *An Iroquois Source Book* (New York: Garland Publishing, 1985-1986), 139.

36 Mann, *Iroquoian Women*, 179-82. For an example of Grandmothers working for peace, see John Heckewelder, *History, Manners, and Customs of the Indian Nations Who Once Inhabited Pennsylvania and the Neighboring States* (1820; New York: Arno Press, 1971), 57-8. For three warnings, see Parker, *The Constitution of the Five Nations*, 54. See also Mann, *George Washington's War*, 150; and Paul A. W. Wallace (ed.), *The Travels of John Heckewelder in Frontier America* (Pittsburgh: University of Pittsburgh Press, 1958), 158-9, 167-8.

37 Wampum was a writing system consisting of beads knotted into characters that had specific meanings. When a law was breached, a penalty wampum was conveyed to the victim's family as soon as possible to diffuse the situation. See Barbara Alice Mann, *Native American Speakers of the Eastern Woodlands: Selected Speeches and Critical Analyses* (Westport, CT: Praeger, 2001), 38-9.

38 Mann, *Iroquoian Women*, 179-82; Mann, 'Fractal Massacres', 169.

39 Joseph François Lafitau, *Customs of the American Indians Compared with the Customs of Primitive Times*, ed. and trans. William N. Fenton and Elizabeth M. Moore, Vol. 2 (1724; Toronto: The Champlain Society, 1974), 99; Carl Benn, *The Iroquois in the War of 1812* (Toronto: University of Toronto Press, 1998), 58-9.

40 Mann, 'Fractal Massacres', 169.

41 That said, archaeologists have found heavily palisaded towns in eastern North America in the late fifteenth and early sixteenth centuries. See Jennifer Birch and Victor D. Thompson (eds), *The Archaeology of Villages in Eastern North America* (Gainesville: University Press of Florida, 2018).

42 Mann, *Spirits of Blood, Spirits of Breath*; and Mann, 'A Failure to Communicate', 29-48.

43 Indian consensus philosophy requires singular pronouns to refer to entire groups. John Napoleon Brinton Hewitt, *Notes on the Creek Indians* (Washington, DC: Government Printing Office, 1939), 124, n. 2.

44 Barbara Alice Mann, 'The Greenville Treaty of 1795: Pen-and-Ink Witchcraft in the Struggle for the Old Northwest', in *Enduring Legacies: Native American Treaties and Contemporary Controversies*, ed. Bruce E. Johansen (Westport, CT: Praeger, 2004), 137, 141-2; Francis Jennings, *The Invasion of America: Indians, Colonialism, and the Cant of Conquest* (New York: W. W. Norton, 1976), 67, 71; Robbie Ethridge, *Creek Country: The Creek Indians and Their World* (Chapel Hill: University of North Carolina Press, 2003), 136.

45 Arthur Caswell Parker, *Iroquois Uses of Maize and Other Food Plants* (Albany, NY: New York State Museum, 1910), 22; Heckewelder, *History, Manners, and Customs*, 101, 149, 181–2, 328; Ethridge, *Creek Country*, 108–9.

46 For historical descriptions of early-contact Indigenous groups trying to make gifting work with Europeans, see Barbara Alice Mann, 'The Mother-Suckling Child Principle of the Gift in Indigenous North American Culture', *Canadian Woman Studies/les cahiers de la femme* 34, nos. 1–2 (2020): 23–30.

47 Heckewelder, *History, Manners, and Customs*, 149.

48 Louis LeClerc Milfort, *Memoirs, or a Quick Glance at My Various Travels and My Sojourn in the Creek Nation*, trans. and ed. Ben C. McCary (1802; Kennesaw, GA: Continental Book Company, 1959), 17–18.

49 George Stiggins, *Creek Indian History: A Historical Narrative of the Genealogy, Traditions and Downfall of the Ispocoga or Creek Indian Tribe of Indians by One of the Tribe*, ed. Virginia Pounds Brown (Birmingham, AL: Birmingham Public Library Press, 1989), 52.

50 Wallace, *Travels of John Heckewelder*, 136–7.

51 Daniel S. Murphree, *Native America: A State-by-State Historical Encyclopedia* (Santa Barbara, CA: Greenwood Press, 2012), 636–38.

52 Wilbur R. Jacobs, *Wilderness Politics and Indian Gifts: The Northern Colonial Frontier* (Norman: University of Oklahoma Press, 1950); Wilbur R. Jacobs, *Dispossessing the American Indian: Indians and Whites on the Colonial Frontier* (Norman: University of Oklahoma Press, 1985), 12–17; Colin G. Calloway, *The Scratch of a Pen: 1763 and the Transformation of North America* (New York: Oxford University Press, 2006), 67–9; Richard White, *The Middle Ground: Indians, Empires, and Republics in the Great Lakes Region, 1650–1815* (New York: Cambridge University Press, 2010), 112–19.

53 Wallace, *Travels of John Heckewelder*, 184; Barbara Alice Mann, 'I Hope You Will Not Destroy What I Have Saved': Hopocan before the British Tribunal in Detroit, 1781', in *Native American Speakers of the Eastern Woodlands: Selected Speeches and Critical Analyses*, ed. Barbara Alice Mann (Westport, CT: Greenwood Press, 2001), 150–1.

54 White, *The Middle Ground*, 258 (n. 68).

55 Walter Scott Dunn, Jr., *Profit and Loss: The British Army and the Fur Traders, 1760–1764* (Westport, CT: Greenwood Press, 1998), 38.

56 William Stone (ed.), *The Life and Times of Sir William Johnson, Bart.*, Vol. 2 (Albany, NY: H. Munsell, 1865), 136–7.

57 United States, *Statutes at Large*, 1st Congress, Sess. II, Chapter 33 (Philadelphia, PA: John Fenno, 1790), 137–8: https://en.wikisource.org/wiki/United_States_Statutes_at_Large/Volume_1/1st_Congress/2nd_Session/Chapter_33

58 Ethridge, *Creek Country*, 131.

59 Some photos from the early twentieth century lend a sense of the extent of goods proffered in gifting rituals, although Westerners still insist on viewing gifting through an exchange lens, in Sevda Sparks, 'Incited to Potlatch', Library and Archives Canada Blog, 7 December 2017, accessed 14 August 2023: https://thediscoverblog.com/tag/aboriginal/

60 William S. Coker, 'The Papers and History of Panton, Leslie and Company, and John Forbes', *Florida Historical Quarterly* 13 (April 1935): 132, 134–40.

61 Thomas Foster, II, ed., *The Collected Works of Benjamin Hawkins, 1796–1810* (Tuscaloosa: University of Alabama Press, 2003), 408–10; Florette Henri, *The Southern Indians and Benjamin Hawkins, 1796–1816* (Norman: University of Oklahoma Press, 1986), 235.

62 *The Writings of Thomas Jefferson*, ed. Albert Ellery Bergh, Vol. 10 (Washington, DC: The Thomas Jefferson Memorial Association, 1907), 369–70. For a solid analysis of federal Indian policies, see Robert J. Miller, *Reservation 'Capitalism:' Economic Development in Indian Country* (Santa Barbara, CA: ABC-CLIO, 2012), especially, 34–5.

63 *Writings of Thomas Jefferson*, 375.

64 Milfort, *Memoirs*, 126.

65 Ethridge, *Creek County*, 181.

66 William Thomas Hagan, *The Sac and Fox Indians* (Norman: University of Oklahoma Press, 1958), 134.

67 Val Attenbrow, *Sydney's Aboriginal Past: Investigating the Archaeological and Historical Records* (Sydney: UNSW Press, 2003), 37; Lyndall Ryan, *Tasmanian Aborigines A History since 1803* (Sydney: Allen & Unwin, 2012), 5.

68 Chris Clarkson, Zenobia Jacobs, Ben Marwick, et al., 'Human occupation of northern Australia by 65,000 years ago', *Nature* 547, no. 7663 (2017): 306–10.

69 Attenbrow, *Sydney's Aboriginal Past*, 3.

70 R. M. Berndt, *Australian Aboriginal Religion*, Vol. 1 (Leiden: Brill, 1974), 9–10.

71 Attenbrow, *Sydney's Aboriginal Past*, 57.

72 Attenbrow, *Sydney's Aboriginal Past*, 57–8.

73 Attenbrow, *Sydney's Aboriginal Past*, 58.

74 Grace Karskens, *The Colony: A History of Early Sydney* (Sydney: Allen & Unwin, 2008), 37.

75 Attenbrow, *Sydney's Aboriginal Past*, 58.

76 In 1806, Governor King reinforced British sovereignty in the region by appointing Justices of the Peace in Fiji and Tahiti and insisting that masters of ships clearing

Sydney for the Southern Fisheries sign good behaviour bonds stipulating that they must keep within the 'Limits of the Territory' defined in Governor Phillip's instructions in 1787. David Collins, *An Account of the English Colony of New South Wales by David Collins*, ed. Brian Fletcher, Vol. 1 (Sydney: The Royal Australian Historical Society and A.H. &A.W. Reed, 1975), 463–4.

77 N. J. B. Plomley (ed.), *Friendly Mission: The Tasmanian Journals of George August Robinson 1829-1834* (Hobart: Queen Victoria Museum and Art Gallery and Quintus Publishing, 2008), 411.

78 J. C. Beaglehole (ed.), *The Journals of Captain James Cook*, Vol. 1, and Vo. 3 (London: Hakluyt Society, 1955-1974), 399, and 52.

79 Karskens, *The Colony*, 37–41.

80 Karskens, *The Colony*, 496.

81 Karskens, *The Colony*, 37.

82 For the Darkinyung, see Umilliko Darkinyung Research Working Group, *Darkinyungur Voices, Our Place* (Newcastle: School of Aboriginal Studies, University of Newcastle, 2003); Attenbrow, *Sydney's Aboriginal Past*, 17–22. For the Awabakal see John Turner and Greg Blyton, *The Aboriginals of Lake Macquarie: A Brief History* (Toronto, New South Wales: Lake Macquarie City Council, 1995).

83 For slightly different figures, see Attenbrow, *Sydney's Aboriginal Past*, 17, who estimates between 4,000 and 8,000 people for the greater Sydney area.

84 Nicolas Peterson, 'The natural and cultural areas of Aboriginal Australia: a preliminary analysis of population groupings with adaptive significance', in *Tribes and Boundaries in Australia*, ed. Nicolas Peterson (Canberra: Australian Institute of Aboriginal Studies, 1976), 50–71; Attenbrow, *Sydney's Aboriginal Past*, 30–5; Michael Powell and Rex Hesline, 'Making tribes? Constructing Aboriginal tribal entities in Sydney and coastal NSW from the early colonial period to the present', *Journal of the Royal Australian Historical Society* 96, part 2 (2011): 115–48.

85 For colonial drawings of major ceremonies, see Fletcher, *An Account of the English Colony*, 452–513.

86 Ryan, *Tasmanian Aborigines*, 41–2.

87 Attenbrow, *Sydney's Aboriginal Past*, 17–36.

88 Ryan, *Tasmanian Aborigines*, 13–19.

89 Ryan, *Tasmanian Aborigines*, 50–1.

90 Ryan, *Tasmanian Aborigines*, 7; Attenbrow, *Sydney's Aboriginal Past*, 128.

91 Berndt, *Australian Aboriginal Religion*, Vol. 1, 9–10.

92 Attenbrow, *Sydney's Aboriginal Past*, p. 129.

93 Ryan, *Tasmanian Aborigines*, 7.

94 Attenbrow, *Sydney's Aboriginal Past*, plate 25.

95 Taiaiake Alfred, *Peace, Power, Righteousness: An Indigenous Manifesto* (Oxford: Oxford University Press, 2008).

96 David Lewis-Williams and David Pearce, *San Spirituality*, 154–6.

97 Vine Deloria, Jr., *God Is Red: A Native View of Religion* (Golden, CO: Fulcrum Publishing, 1994), 68, 71–73; George E. Tinker, *American Indian Liberation: A Theology of Sovereignty* (Maryknoll, NY: Orbis Books, 2008), 70–74; and George E. Tinker, 'American Indians and the Arts of the Land: Spatial Metaphors and Contemporary Existence', *Voices from the Third World* 14, no. 2 (1992): 170–93.

98 Mann, *Spirits of Blood, Spirits of Breath*, 173.

99 Mann, *Spirits of Blood, Spirits of Breath*, 51–9, 75–7.

100 Anthony J. Marsella, Jeanette L. Johnson, Patricia Watson and Jan Gryczynski, *Ethnocultural Perspectives on Disasters and Trauma: Foundations, Issues, and Applications* (New York: Springer, 2008), 89.

101 Marguelonne Toussaint-Samat, *A History of Food* (Malden, MA: Wiley-Blackwell, 2009), 155.

102 Mann, *George Washington's War*, 72; Lyman Butterfield, 'History at the Headwaters', *New York History* 51, no. 2 (1970): 135.

103 Parker, *Iroquois Uses of Maize*, 36; Barbara Alice Mann, 'Mound Cultures of North America', in *Encyclopedia of American Indian History*, ed. Bruce Elliot Johansen and Barry M. Pritzker, Vol. 1 (Santa Barbara, CA: ABC-CLIO, 2008), i. 435.

104 Parker, *Iroquois Uses of Maize*, 27.

105 Mann, *Iroquoian Women*, 220.

106 Parker, *Iroquois Uses of Maize*, 25–7; Conrad E. Heidenreich, 'Huron', in *Handbook of North American Indians*, vol. 15, *Northeast*, ed. Bruce G. Trigger (Washington, DC: Smithsonian Institution, 1978), 380.

107 Sharon O'Brien, *American Indian Tribal Governments* (Norman: University of Oklahoma Press, 1993), 21.

108 Mann, *Iroquoian Women*, 220.

109 Heidenreich, 'Huron', 381.

110 Jennings, *Invasion of America*, 65.

111 Swanton, *Creek Religion and Medicine*, 568–69.

112 This section is based on Collins; Tench; Kohen and Lampert; Attenbrow; Karskens; Willey; and Keith Vincent Smith.

Chapter 3

1. On what is referred to as 'primitive warfare' – 'primitive' in the sense of early, see Azar Gat, *War in Human Civilization* (Oxford: Oxford University Press, 2006), 116–27.

2. In 1673 a group of Dutch hippopotami hunters were killed by some San, allegedly under the patronage of Gonnema, the Khoikhoi leader of the Cochoqua. The incident sparked the Second Khoikhoi-Dutch war of 1673–7 in which the Cochoqua lost 1,765 cattle and 4,930 sheep to the VOC. See Penn, *Forgotten Frontier*, 32.

3. See Robert Ross, 'Khoesan and Immigrants: The Emergence of Colonial Society in the Cape, 1500–1800', in *Cambridge History of South Africa*, Vol. 1, ed. Carolyn Hamilton, Bernard K. Mbenga and Robert Ross (Cambridge: Cambridge University Press, 2016), 171–3.

4. Gerrit Harinck, 'Interaction between Xhosa and Khoi: Emphasis on the Period 1620–1750', in *African Societies in Southern Africa*, ed. Leonard Thompson (London: Heinemann, 1969), 145–70; and Simon Hall, 'Farming Communities of the Second Millennium: Internal Frontiers, Identity, Continuity and Change', in *Cambridge History of South Africa, Vol. 1*, ed. Carolyn Hamilton, Bernard K. Mbenga and Robert Ross (Cambridge: Cambridge University Press, 2016), 164–5.

5. See for instance Yiming Cao, Benjamin Enke, Armin Falk, Paola Giuliano and Nathan Nunn, 'Herding, Warfare, and a Culture of Honor: Global Evidence', *National Bureau of Economic Research Working Paper Series, Working Paper 29250*, 1–66: https://www-nber-org.ezproxy.newcastle.edu.au/system/files/working_papers/w29250/w29250.pdf

6. Penn, *Forgotten Frontier*, 117–42.

7. Penn, *Forgotten Frontier*, 104–5.

8. Moodie, *The Record*, Part, III, 35–7.

9. Penn, *Forgotten Frontier*, 125.

10. For the required warning as articulated in the Iroquois Constitution, Arthur C. Parker, 'The Constitution of the Five Nations', *New York State Museum Bulletin* 184 (April 1916): 34, 41–42, 46–47, 55. All nations had a version of this. On Indigenous American warfare, see Starkey, *European and Native American Warfare*; Timothy Shannon, 'Iroquoia', in *The Oxford Handbook of American Indian History*, ed. Frederick E. Hoxie (New York: Oxford University Press, 2016), 199–216; and Patrick M. Malone, *The Skulking Way of War: Technology and Tactics among the New England Indians* (New York: Madison Books, 2000); Wayne E. Lee, *Barbarians and Brothers: Anglo-American Warfare, 1500–1865* (Oxford: Oxford University Press, 2011); David J. Silverman, *Thundersticks: Firearms and the Violent Transformation of Native America* (Cambridge, MA: Belknap Press, 2016); and Wayne E. Lee, *The Cutting-Off Way: Indigenous Warfare in Eastern North America, 1500–1800* (Chapel Hill: University of North Carolina Press, 2023).

11 For typical instances of 'friendly Indians' delivering warnings, see Francis Whiting Halsey, *The Old New York Frontier, Its Wars with Indians and Tories, Its Missionary Schools, Pioneers and Land Titles, 1614–1800* (Port Washington, NY: Ira Friedman, 1901), 175, 205.

12 'Some Esoteric Aspects of the League of the Iroquois', 325; Hewitt, 'Ethnological Studies among the Iroquois Indians', 240–1.

13 Pierre de Charlevoix, *Journal of a Voyage to North America*, Vol. 2 (1761; Ann Arbor, MI: University Microfilms, Inc., 1966), 26; Mann, *Iroquoian Women*, 164.

14 Johansen and Mann, *Encyclopedia*, 125.

15 For a view of the southeastern Creek male-female interface, see Jean-Bernard Bossu, *New Travels in North America by Jean-Bernard Bossu, 1770–1771*, ed. Samuel Dorris Dickinson (Natchitoches, LA: Northwestern State University Press, 1982), 92–3. For an Iroquoian discussion of the northeastern system, see Mann, *Iroquoian Women*, 115–84.

16 [Garcilasco de la Vega], *La Florida del Ynca: Historia del Adelantado de Hernando de Soto, Gouenador y capitan general del Reyno de la Florida* (Lisbon: Pedro Crossbeek, 1605), 161–4; Edward Gaylord Bourne, *Narratives of the Career of Hernando de Soto*, Vol. 2 (London: David Nutt, 1905), 13–14, 99–101.

17 For Jigonsaseh's grave, Pete Jemison, 'Mother of Nations: The Peace Queen, a Neglected Tradition', *Akwe:kon* 5 (1988): 69; for pearls of *Cofitachequi*, Vega, *La Florida del Ynca*, 163.

18 Mann, *Iroquoian Women*, 37, 132, 135.

19 For *la femme Chef*, see Joseph François Lafitau, *Moeurs des sauvages Ameriquains, comparées aux moeurs des premiers temps*, Vol. 2 (Paris: Saugrain, 1724), 410; for *cacica*, see John Tate Lanning, *Spanish Missions of Georgia* (Chapel Hill: University of North Carolina Press, 1935), 17; and Maynard J. Geiger, *The Franciscan Conquest of Florida, 1573–1618* (Washington, DC: Catholic University of America, 1937), 162.

20 Arthur C. Parker, 'Notes on the Ancestry of Cornplanter', *Researches and Transactions of the New York State Archaeological Association* (1927; New York: Times Presses, 1970), 10; Louise Wells Murray, *A History of Old Tioga Point and Modern Athens, Pennsylvania* (Wilkes-Barre, PA: Raeder Press, 1908), 110–12.

21 Mann, *Iroquoian Women*, 179–82.

22 Reuben Gold Thwaites (ed. and trans.), *Les Relations de Jésuites, or The Jesuit Relations: Travels and Explorations of the Jesuit Missionaries in New France, 1610–1791*, Vol. 53 (New York: Pageant Book Company, 1959), 251.

23 Heckewelder, *History, Manners, and Customs*, xxxviii.

24 Milfort, *Memoirs*, 150; Bossu *Travels in the Interior of North America*, 62.

25 Lafitau, *Moeurs des sauvages Ameriquains*, Vol. 2, 186–7.

26 Louis Armand de Lom d'Arce, baron de Lahontan, *New Voyages to North America*, ed. Reuben Gold Thwaites, Vol. 2 (1703; Chicago, IL: A. C. McClurg, 1905), 507.

27 Milfort, *Memoirs*,153.

28 Milfort, *Memoirs*, 152–3; Colin G. Calloway, *The Victory with No Name: The Native American Defeat of the First American Army* (New York: Oxford University Press, 2015), 112.

29 Charles Christopher Trowbridge, *Meearmeear Traditions*, ed. Vernon Kinietz (Ann Arbor: University of Michigan Press, 1938), 14.

30 White, *The Middle Ground*, 346, 356.

31 Johansen and Mann, *Encyclopedia of the Haudenosaunee*, 127; Mann, *Iroquoian Women*, 116–17, 181. For the annoyance over 'unreliable' Indian allies see, Robert L. Yaple, 'Braddock's Defeat: The Theories and a Reconsideration', *Journal of the Society for Army Historical Research* 46, n. 188 (1968): 194–201; Colin G. Calloway, *One Vast Winter Count: The Native American West before Lewis and Clark* (Lincoln: University of Nebraska Press, 2003), 340.

32 Johansen and Mann, *Encyclopedia of the Haudenosaunee*, 127; Mann, *Iroquoian Women*, 141; Arthur C. Parker, *The Life of Ely S. Parker, Last Grand Sachem of the Iroquois and General Grant's Military Secretary* (Buffalo, NY: Buffalo Historical Society, 1919), 46.

33 Mann, *George Washington's War*, 90–1.

34 For female-led Oka action, see David P. Ball, 'Women Warriors: 5 Standout Indigenous Female Leaders in Canada', *Indian Country Today*, 8 March 2014, http://indiancountrytodaymedianetwork.com/2014/03/08/women-warriors-5-standout-indigenous-female-leaders-canada-153921. For grandmother-led Circle Mound action, see Barbara Alice Mann, *Native Americans, Archaeologists, and the Mounds* (New York: Peter Lang, 2003), 302–3.

35 Heckewelder, *History, Manners, and Customs*, 136, n. 1, 338.

36 Frederick Cook, *Journals of the Military Expedition of Major General John Sullivan against the Six Nations of Indians in 1779* (1887; Freeport, NY: Books for Libraries, 1972), 287, 363, 366; Barbara Alice Mann, 'War Women of the Eastern Woodlands', in *Women Waging War in the American Revolution*, ed. Holly A. Mayer (Charlottesville: University of Virginia Press, 2022), 62–4.

37 See, for instance, *American State Papers, Indian Affairs*, Vol. 1 (Washington, DC: Gales & Seaton, 1832), 571, 573. On the wider, geo-political significance of the battle, see John C. Kotruch, 'The Battle of Fallen Timbers: An Assertion of U.S. Sovereignty in the Atlantic World along the Banks of the Maumee River', in *Between Sovereignty and Anarchy: The Politics of Violence in the American Revolutionary Era*, ed. Patrick Griffin, Robert G. Ingram, Peter S. Onuf and Brian Schoen (Charlottesville: University of Virginia Press, 2015), 263–84.

38 Barbara Alice Mann, *The Tainted Gift: The Disease Method of Frontier Advance* (Santa Barbara, CA: Praeger, 2009), 3–5.

39 *American State Papers, Indian Affairs*, Vol. 1, 564.

40 The use of Indians as 'proxies' in imperial warfare is now acknowledged. See Jane T. Merritt, 'Native Peoples in the Revolutionary War', in *The Oxford Handbook of the American Revolution*, ed. Edward G. Gray and Jane Kamensky (New York: Oxford University Press, 2013), 243. As early as 1781, the Lenape holy man Hopocan rebuked the British for the practice in a speech to the commandant at Detroit, saying, 'You should not compel your children, the Indians, to expose themselves to danger for *your sakes*', in Heckewelder, *History, Manners, and Customs*, 135, italics in the original.

41 Georg Friederici, *Skalpieren und ähnliche Kriegsgebräuche in Amerika* (Braunschweig: Druck von Friedrich Vieweg und Sohn, 1906), 5, 17.

42 James L. Axtell and William C. Sturtevant, 'The Unkindest Cut, or Who Invented Scalping', *William and Mary Quarterly* 37, no. 3 (1980): 451–72; Thomas S. Abler, 'Scalping, Torture, Cannibalism and Rape: An Ethnohistorical Analysis of Conflicting Cultural Values in War', *Anthropologica* 34, no. 1 (1992): 3–20. See also Helen F. Donohoe, 'Dancing with Scalps: Native North American Women, White Men and Ritual Violence in the Eighteenth Century' (PhD thesis, University of Glasgow, 2013).

43 For the archaeological evidence, see George R. Milner, Eve Anderson and Virginia G. Smith, 'Warfare in Late Prehistoric West-Central Illinois', *American Antiquity* 56, n. 4 (1991): 581–603; Patricia Marie Lambert, 'The Archaeology of War: A North American Perspective', *Journal of Archaeological Research* 10, no. 3 (2002): 207–41; and Christopher W. Schmidt and Amber E. Osterhol, 'Middle and Late Archaic Trophy-Taking in Indiana', in *Violence and Warfare among Hunter-Gatherers*, ed. Mark W. Allen and Terry L. Jones (Walnut Creek, CA: Left Coast Press, 2014), 241–56.

44 Mark van de Logt, '"The Powers of the Heavens Shall Eat of My Smoke": The Significance of Scalping in Pawnee Warfare', *Journal of Military History* 72, no. 1 (2007): 104–71.

45 *Teiohonwé:thon* in Jacob E. Thomas and Terry Boyle, *Teachings from the Longhouse* (Toronto: Stoddart, 1994), 127.

46 Chief Elias Johnson, 'The Iroquois Are Not Savages', in *Native Heritage: Personal Accounts by American Indians, 1790 to Present*, ed. Arlene Hirschfelder (New York: Macmillan, 1995), 238–40.

47 Edward Rondthaler, *Life of John Heckewelder*, ed. B. H. Coates (Philadelphia, PA: Townsend Ward, 1847), 50.

48 John Heckewelder, *A Narrative of the Mission of the United Brethren among the Delaware and Mohegan Indians from Its Commencement in the Year 1740, to the Close of the Year 1808* (Philadelphia, PA: M'Carthy & Davis, 1820), 178.

49 Wallace, *Travels of John Heckewelder*, 148, note *, and 194, note *.

50 W. Vernon Kienitz, *Delaware Culture Chronology* (Indianapolis: Indiana Historical Society, 1946), 69.

51 Various traditions of this event are named and discussed in context, in Mann, *Iroquoian Women*, 134–42.

52 Paul Radin, *Winnebago Hero Cycles: A Study in Aboriginal Literature* (Baltimore, MD: Waverly Press, 1948), 123–29.

53 Nathaniel Knowles, 'The Torture of Captives by the Indians of Eastern North America', *Proceedings of the American Philosophical Society* 82, no. 2 (1940): 151–225; and William Fitzhugh Brundage, *Civilising Torture: An American Tradition* (Cambridge, MA: Harvard University Press, 2018), 13–52.

54 For examples of the rituals involved in the 'mourning war', see Thwaites (ed.), *The Jesuit Relations and Allied Documents*, Vol. 44, 253–5; and Vol. 51, 213–15. See also Daniel K. Richter, 'War and Culture: The Iroquois Experience', *William and Mary Quarterly* 40, no. 4 (1983): 528–59; Daniel K. Richter, *The Ordeal of the Longhouse: The Peoples of the Iroquois League in the Era of European Colonization* (Chapel Hill: University of North Carolina, 1992), 35–6; Lee, *Barbarians and Brothers*, 155–6.

55 In Australia, ritual cannibalism was part of the interment ceremony among Aboriginals in the Gulf of Carpentaria, in Arnhem Land, in the northern Kimberleys and in northeast South Australia. On the Americas and cannibalism, see Francisco Bethencourt, *Racisms: From the Crusades to the Twentieth Century* (Princeton, NJ: Princeton University Press, 2014), 101–13.

56 Thwaites, *Jesuit Relations*, 34: 27–31. For a discussion of the purpose of Indigenous ritualized cannibalism, see Peggy Reeves Sandy, *Divine Hunger: Cannibalism as a Cultural System* (New York: Cambridge University Press, 1986).

57 William Arens, *The Man-Eating Myth* (New York: Oxford University Press, 1979), 127–8.

58 Kathryn Zabelle Derounian-Stodola and James Arthur Levernier, *The Indian Captivity Narrative, 1500–1900* (New York: Twayne Publishers, 1993), 68, underlines that captivity writers were quick to accuse Indians of cannibalism. For settler cannibalism, see William M. Kelso, *Jamestown: The Truth Revealed* (Charlottesville: University of Virginia Press, 2017), 185–203.

59 R. David Edmunds, *The Shawnee Prophet* (Lincoln: University of Nebraska Press, 1983), 48.

60 James E. Seaver, *A Narrative of the Life of Mrs. Mary Jemison* (1823; Syracuse, NY: Syracuse University Press, 1990), 116.

61 Trina N. Seitz, 'A History of Execution Methods in the United States', in *Handbook of Death and Dying, Vol. 1: The Presence of Death*, ed. Clifton D. Bryant (Thousand Oaks, CA: Sage Publications, 2003), 357.

62 Chaplin, *Subject Matter*, 268–9.

63 Connor, *Australian Frontier Wars*, 2.

64 Collins, *An Account of the English Colony*, 3.

65 Henry Reynolds, *The Other Side of the Frontier: Aboriginal Resistance to the European Invasion of Australia* (1982, Sydney: UNSW Press, 2006), 56–8. For a different interpretation, Karskens, *The Colony*, 47–9.

66 Collins, *An Account of the English Colony*, 110–112.

67 Connor, *Australian Frontier Wars*, 2.

68 Connor, *Australian Frontier Wars*, 3. See also Karskens, *The Colony*, 448–516; Ray Kerkhove, *How They Fought: Indigenous Tactics and Weaponry of Australia's Frontier Wars* (Tingalpa, Qld: Boolarong Press, 2023).

69 Connor, *Australian Frontier Wars*, 3.

70 Reynolds, *The Other Side of the Frontier*, 139–41.

71 Watkin Tench, *Sydney's First Four Years* being a reprint of *A Narrative of the Expedition to Botany Bay* and *A Complete Account of the Settlement at Port Jackson*, with an introduction and annotation by L. F. Fitzhardinge (Sydney: Library of Australian History, 1970), 51.

72 Collins, *An Account of the English Colony*, i. 18.

73 Collins, *An Account of the English Colony*, ii. 20.

74 Connor, *Australian Frontier Wars*, 4.

75 Neil Gunson (ed.), *Australian Reminiscences & Papers of L.E. Threlkeld, Missionary to the Aborigines, 1824–1859*, Vol. 2 (Canberra: Australian Institute of Aboriginal Studies, 1974), 41.

76 Peter Turbet, *The First Frontier: The Occupation of the Sydney Region 1788 to 1816* (Sydney: Rosenberg Publishing, 2011), 102.

77 Collins, *An Account of the English Colony*, 133–5.

78 Connor, *Australian Frontier Wars*, 4.

79 Plomley, *Friendly Mission*, 586.

80 See, Nicholas Clements, *The Black War: Fear, Sex and Resistance in Tasmania* (St Lucia, Qld: University of Queensland Press, 2014), 68–9.

81 Collins, *An Account of the English Colony*, Vol. 1, 122; Vol. 2, 9.

82 Connor, *Australian Frontier Wars*, 4.

83 Collins, *An Account of the English Colony*, 304.

84 Collins, *An Account of the English Colony*, 326.

85 Collins, *An Account of the English Colony*, i. 326.

86 Henry Reynolds, *Frontier: Aborigines, Settlers and Land* (Sydney: Allen & Unwin, 1987), 8.

87 Clem Sargent, *The Colonial Garrison 1817–1824. The 48th Foot: The Northamptonshire Regiment in the Colony of New South Wales* (Canberra: TCS Publications, 1996). See also Ann Beaumont, *A Man of Many Parts: The Life and Times of Edward Charles Close 1790–1866* (Mittagong, NSW: Highland House Publications, 2016), 61–6.

88 Connor, *Australian Frontier Wars*, 40.

89 Connor, *Australian Frontier Wars*, 41.

90 Connor, *Australian Frontier Wars*, 41; *Sydney Gazette*, 2 and 9 June 1805.

91 *Sydney Gazette*, 5, 12 May 1805; Gapps, *The Sydney Wars*, 173–5.

92 Connor, *Australian Frontier Wars*, 43–4.

93 Reynolds, *The Other Side of the Frontier*, 148.

94 Reynolds, *The Other Side of the Frontier*, 223.

95 Sharon Morgan, *Land Settlement in Early Tasmania: Creating an Antipodean England* (Cambridge: Cambridge: University Press, 1992), 155.

96 Connor, *Australian Frontier Wars*, 25.

97 Karskens, *The Colony*, 476–7.

98 Connor, *Australian Frontier Wars*, 49.

99 Connor, *Australian Frontier Wars*, 48.

100 Aurélien Lignereux, 'Accommodation et arrangements dans les départements réunis: l'éclairage paradoxal des rébellions (1800–1813)', in *Le Temps des hommes doubles. Les arrangements face à l'occupation. De la Révolution française à la guerre de 1870*, ed. Annie Crépin, Jean-François Chanet and Christian Windler (Rennes: Presses universitaires de Rennes, 2013), 109–12. Lignereux defines a revolt as a violent or collective rebellion incorporating more than three uprisings against gendarmes or police in one locality, and which come to the attention of the authorities.

101 Stuart Woolf, *Napoleon's Integration of Europe* (London: Routledge, 1991), 231–2.

102 John Lawrence Tone, 'Small Wars and Guerrilla Fighting', in *The Cambridge History of the Napoleonic Wars. Vol. II, Fighting the Napoleonic Wars*, ed. Bruno Colson and Alexander Mikaberidze (Cambridge: Cambridge University Press, 2023), 59.

103 Charles J. Esdaile, 'Popular Resistance to the Napoleonic Empire', in *Napoleon and Europe*, ed. Philip Dwyer (Harlow: Longman, 2001), 144.

104 Alexander Grab, 'State Power, Brigandage and Rural Resistance in Napoleonic Italy', *European History Quarterly* 25, no. 1 (1995): 40.

105 See Forrest, 'The Ubiquitous Brigand', 25–43.

106 Esdaile, 'Popular Resistance to the Napoleonic Empire', 147–8.

107 Charles J. Esdaile, 'Patriots, Partisans and Land Pirates in Retrospect', in *Popular Resistance in the French Wars*, ed. Charles J. Esdaile (Houndmills: Palgrave Macmillan, 2005), 17.

108 Martin Rink, 'The Partisan's Metamorphosis: From Freelance Military Entrepreneur to German Freedom Fighter, 1740-1815', *War in History* 17, no. 1 (2010): 22.

109 See Philip Dwyer, 'Violence and the Revolutionary and Napoleonic Wars: Massacre, Conquest and the Imperial Enterprise', *Journal of Genocide Research* 15, no. 2 (2013): 117–31; Charles J. Esdaile, *Fighting Napoleon: Guerrillas, Bandits and Adventurers in Spain, 1808-1814* (New Haven, CT: Yale University Press, 2004). For the modern era, see Benjamin Valentino, Paul Huth and Dylan Balch-Lindsay, '"Draining the Sea": Mass Killing and Guerrilla Warfare', *International Organization* 58, no. 2 (2004): 375–407.

110 See, for example, Robson, 'French Soldiers and the Revolutionary Origins of the Colonial Mind', *Militarized Cultural Encounters*, ed. Clarke and Horne, 31–5; and Joseph Clarke, 'Encountering the Sacred: British and French Soldiers in the Revolutionary and Napoleonic Mediterranean', in *Militarized Cultural Encounters in the Long Nineteenth Century: Making War, Mapping Europe*, ed. Joseph Clarke and John Horne (Cham: Palgrave Macmillan, 2018), 49–73.

111 T. C. W. Blanning, *The French Revolution in Germany: Occupation and Resistance in the Rhineland: 1792-1802* (Oxford: Clarendon Press, 1986), 207–13.

112 Richard Cobb, *Les armées revolutionaires: instrument de la terreur dans les départments, Avril 1793 - Floreal An II*, Vol. 2 (Paris: Mouton, 1961), 653; Blanning, *The French Revolution in Germany*, 207–54.

113 Nigel Aston, *Christianity and Revolutionary Europe, 1750-1830* (Cambridge: Cambridge University Press, 2002), 230; Blanning, *French Revolution in Germany*, 237.

114 Tone, 'Small Wars and Guerrilla Fighting', 57–8. The same thing happened in Calabria (Esdaile, 'Popular Resistance to the Napoleonic Empire', 144).

115 There are no figures, and indeed no studies on the numbers of women that may have been raped during the wars. The phenomenon is briefly touched on in Alan Forrest, *Napoleon's Men: The Soldiers of the Revolution and Empire* (London: Hambledon Continuum, 2002), 146. It is interesting to note that American Indians on the east coast of north America did not as a general rule rape female captives; Europeans did (Abler, 'Scalping, Torture, Cannibalism and Rape', 13–15).

116 Gilles Avril (ed.), *L'anti-Napoléon: écrits inédits et papiers de Noël-Antoine Apuril du Pontreau, chanoine de la Congrégation de France* (Paris: Nouveau monde éd., 2006), 116–17.

117 Jean-Gabriel Peltier, *Examen de la campagne de Buonaparte en Italie par un témoin oculaire* (Paris: Le Normant, 1814), 82–3.

118 François Bernoyer, *Avec Bonaparte en Egypte et en Syrie, 1798–1800: 19 lettres inédites* (Poet-Laval: Éditions Curandera, 1981), 147–8 (19 April 1799). We do not know how many were killed on this occasion.

119 Pierre Guingret, *Relation historique et militaire de la campagne de Portugal sous le maréchal Masséna* (Limoges: Bargeas, 1817), 123–7.

120 François Lavaux, *Mémoires de Campagnes: 1793–1814* (Paris: Arléa, 2004), 152–3.

121 Esprit Victor Elisabeth Boniface Castellane, *Journal du maréchal Castellane, 1804–1862*, Vol. 1 (Paris: E. Plon, Nourrit et Cie, 1895–97), i. 33.

122 Comte Henri de Vigier, *Davout, maréchal d'empire, duc d'Auerstaedt, prince d'Eckmühl (1770–1823)*, Vol. 1 (Paris: P. Ollendorff, 1898), 51–2.

123 Walter, *Colonial Violence*, 195–6.

Chapter 4

1 Lynn Hunt, *Inventing Human Rights: A History* (New York: W. W. Norton, 2007), 15–34.

2 Penn, *The Forgotten Frontier*, 255.

3 The word 'Kaffir' is deeply offensive today but in the eighteenth and early nineteenth centuries had a different meaning to its later usage. The word originated from the Arabic word meaning 'heathen' and was applied by Muslims to the non-Islamic Africans of Africa's east coast. When such Africans were enslaved, some of them circulated within the trade routes of the Indian Ocean. Here they entered the domain of the slave trading VOC in the East Indies. The personnel of the VOC adopted the Arabic word to refer to Africans in general. At the Cape, however, the word was applied more particularly to the first non-Khoisan Africans that the VOC's settlers encountered – the Xhosa. The word thus implied both 'heathenism' and 'African' but was not, at least initially, racist.

4 Leo Fouché, *Die Evolutie van die Trekboer* (Pretoria: Volkstem, 1909), 1.

5 See, for example, Cook, *Journals of the Military Expedition*, 98; Washington Irving, *A History of New York, form the Beginning of the World to the End of the Dutch Dynasty*, ed. Stanley Williams and Tremaine McDowell (1809; New York: Harcourt, Brace, 1927), 62; and Alexander C. Flick, 'New Sources on the Sullivan-Clinton Campaign in 1779', *Quarterly Journal of the New York State Historical Society* 10 (October, 1929): 310.

6   Jeffrey Ostler, '"To Extirpate the Indians": An Indigenous Consciousness of Genocide in the Ohio Valley and Lower Great Lakes, 1750s-1810', *William and Mary Quarterly* 72, no. 4 (2015): 587-622.

7   Arthur C. Parker, *An Analytical History of the Seneca Indians: Researches and Transactions of the New York State Archeological Association*, Vol. 6 (Canandaigua, NY: The Times Presses, 1926), 126.

8   Jack B. Martin and Margret McKane Mauldin, *A Dictionary of Creek/Muskogee with Notes on the Florida and Oklahoma Seminole Dialects of Creek* (Lincoln: University of Nebraska Press, 2000), 153, 270.

9   For the following, Robert J. Miller, *Native America, Discovered and Conquered: Thomas Jefferson, Lewis & Clark, and Manifest Destiny* (Westport, CT: Praeger, 2006), 92-4; Merrill D. Peterson, *Thomas Jefferson and the New Nation: A Biography* (Norwalk, CT: Easton Press, 1987), 173; Peter S. Onuf, *Jefferson's Empire: The Language of American Nationhood* (Charlottesville: University Press of Virginia, 2000), 47, n. 66.

10 Knox to Washington, 29 December 1794, *American State Papers: Indian Affairs*, 544; David J. Weber, *Bárbaros: Spaniards and their Savages in the Age of Enlightenment* (New Haven, CT: Yale University Press, 2005), 1.

11 Jared Sparks (ed.), *The Writings of George Washington; Being His Correspondence, Addresses, Messages, and Other Papers, Official and Private, Selected and Published from the Original Manuscripts*, Vol. 6 (Boston, MA: Little, Brown, 1855), 264, 265.

12 J. Jefferson Looney (ed.), *The Papers of Thomas Jefferson: Retirement Series, Vol. 7: November 1813 to September 1814* (Princeton, NJ: Princeton University Press, 2010), 91.

13 Looney, *The Papers of Thomas Jefferson*, 91.

14 Looney, *The Papers of Thomas Jefferson*, 91.

15 See, for example, David A. Bell, *Cult of the Nation in France: Inventing Nationalism, 1680-1800* (Cambridge, MA: Harvard University Press, 2001), 78-106.

16 See Bell, *Cult of the Nation in France*, 101-6, for a discussion of contemporary meanings of race.

17 Louis Florimond Fantin des Odoards, *Journal du Général Fantin des Odoards, étapes d'un officier de la Grande Armée, 1800-1830* (Paris: E. Plon, Nourrit et Cie, 1895), 47; Adrien Bourgogne, *Mémoires du sergent Bourgogne* (Paris: Arléa, 1992), 92; Jean Barada, 'Lettres d'Alexandre Ladrix', *Bulletin de la Société d'histoire et d'archéologie du Gers* 28 (1927): 235-6. For French attitudes towards Germans, see Michael Rapport, '"The Germans Are Hydrophobes": Germany and the Germans in the Shaping of French Identity', in *The Bee and the Eagle: Napoleonic France and the End of the Holy Roman Empire, 1806*, ed. Alan Forrest and Peter H. Wilson (Basingstoke: Palgrave Macmillan, 2009), 238-43.

18 Auguste-Julien Bigarré, *Mémoires du Général Bigarré, 1775–1813* (Paris: Grenadier, 2002), 200.

19 *Correspondance de Napoléon Ier, publiée par ordre de l'Empereur Napoléon III*, 32 vols (Paris: Impr. Impériale, 1858–69), Vol. 9, n. 9550 (7 December 1805).

20 Jean-René Aymes, 'La guerre d'Espagne dans la presse impériale (1808–1814)', *Annales historiques de la Révolution française*, 336 (2004): 133–4.

21 Auguste Thirion, *Souvenirs militaires* (Paris: Librairie des Deux Empires, 1998), 30.

22 Robson, 'Insurgent Identities, Destructive Discourses, and Militarized Massacre', 137, 142.

23 Odoards, *Journal*, 211.

24 Robson, 'French Soldiers and the Revolutionary Origins of the Colonial Mind', 30–1.

25 J. Lort Stokes, *Discoveries in Australia; With an Account of the Coasts and Rivers Explored and Surveyed during the Voyage of H.M.S. Beagle 1837*, Vol. 2 (London: T. and W. Boone, 1846), 459.

26 James Bonwick, *The Last of the Tasmanians, Or, The Black War of Van Diemen's Land The Last of the Tasmanians* (London: Sampson Low, Son & Marston, 1870), 59, 61, 66–7.

27 *Colonial Times*, 1 December 1826.

28 Cited in *Copies of All Correspondence between Lieutenant-Governor Arthur and His Majesty's Secretary of State for the Colonies, on the Subject of the Military Operations Lately Carried on against the Aboriginal Inhabitants of Van Diemen's Land*, British Parliamentary Papers, Paper no. 259 (London: House of Commons, 1831), 47.

29 For British views of the Portuguese and the Spanish see, Gavin Daly, 'A Dirty, Indolent, Priest-Ridden City: British Soldiers in Lisbon during the Peninsular War, 1808–1813', *History* 94, no. 316 (2009): 461–82; and Gavin Daly, '"Barbarity More Suited to Savages": British Soldiers' Views of Spanish and Portuguese Violence during the Peninsular War, 1808–1814', *War & Society* 35, no. 4 (2016): 242–58.

30 Leader Maynard, *Ideology and Mass Killing*, 112–15.

31 David A. Bell, 'Jumonville's Death. War Propaganda and National Identity in Eighteenth-Century France', in *The Age of Cultural Revolutions. Britain and France, 1750–1820*, ed. Colin Jones and Dror Wahrman (Berkeley, CA: University of California Press, 2002), 52.

32 Nigel Penn, 'Land, Labour and Livestock in the Western Cape during the Eighteenth Century: The Khoisan and the Colonists', in *The Angry Divide: Social and Economic History of the Western Cape*, ed. Wilmot G. James and Mary Simons (Cape Town: David Philip, 1989), 2–19.

33 Penn, *Forgotten Frontier*, 39, 40.

34 Penn, *Forgotten Frontier*, 53.

35 Penn, *Forgotten Frontier*, 56–78.

36 H. J. Mandelbrote (ed.), *A Geographical and Topographical Description of the Cape of Good Hope by O.F. Mentzel*, Vol. 3 (Cape Town: Van Riebeeck Society, 1944), 309–19.

37 Penn, *Forgotten Frontier*, ch. 4.

38 Heckewelder, *Narrative of the Mission*, 61–2.

39 Michael Leroy Oberg, *Dominion and Civility: English Imperialism and Native America* (Ithaca, NY: Cornell University Press, 2004), 57.

40 Louis M. Waddell (ed.), *The Papers of Henry Bouquet*, Vol. 6 (Harrisburg: The Pennsylvania Historical and Museum Commission, 1994), 304–5.

41 John C. Fitzpatrick, *The Writings of George Washington from the Original Manuscript Sources, 1745–1799*, Vol. 15 (Washington, DC: Government Printing Office, 1938), 190–91.

42 [Alexander McKee], *Minutes of Debates in Council on the Banks of the Ottawa River, (commonly Called the Miamis of the Lake), November 1791* (Philadelphia, PA: William Young, Bookseller, 1792), 13.

43 Ronald Dale Karr, 'Why Should You Be So Furious?': The Violence of the Pequot War', *The Journal of American History*, 85, no. 3 (1998): 876–909; John Mason, 'A Brief History of the Pequot War, 1637', in *The History of the Pequot War: The Contemporary Accounts of Mason, Underhill, and Gardner*, ed. Charles Orr (Cleveland, OH: The Helman-Taylor Company, 1897), 28–9. John Mason puts the death toll at 700. Peter Charles Hoffer, *Sensory Worlds in Early America* (Baltimore, MD: Johns Hopkins University Press, 2003), 277, n. 40, has calculated towards the lower end at 400 deaths.

44 For a reproduction of Underhill's map showing encirclement, see Figure 6 in Jennings, *The Invasion of America*, 224.

45 John Underhill, 'News from America, or a Late and Experimental Discovery of New England', in *The History of the Pequot War: The Contemporary Accounts of Mason, Underhill, and Gardner*, ed. Charles Orr (Cleveland, OH: The Helman-Taylor Company, 1897), 80–1.

46 For Pequots versus Puritans killed, see Jennings, *Invasion of America*, 225.

47 For the economic interpretation, see Katherine Grandjean, 'New World Tempests: Environment, Scarcity, and the Coming of the Pequot War', *William and Mary Quarterly* 68, no. 1 (2011): 76–7, n. 4, 86; Steven T. Katz, 'The Pequot War Reconsidered', *New England Quarterly* 64, no. 2 (1991): 206–224.

48 Philippe Buc, *Holy War, Martyrdom, and Terror: Christianity, Violence, and the West* (Philadelphia: University of Pennsylvania Press, 2015), 276; and William S. Simmons, 'Cultural Bias in the New England Puritans' Perception of Indians', *William and Mary Quarterly* 38, no. 1 (1981): 67–8.

49 Illinois State Historical Library, *Collections of the Illinois State Historical Library* (Springfield: Illinois State Historical Library, 1926), Vol. 8, 144.

50 Edward Duyker, *An Officer of the Blue: Marc-Joseph Marion Dufresne, South Sea Explorer, 1724–1772* (Melbourne: Melbourne University Press, 1994).

51 https://c21ch.newcastle.edu.au/colonialmassacres/map.php

52 Shino Kinoshi, 'The Father Governor: The British Administration of Aboriginal People at Port Jackson, 1788–1972', in *Public Men: Political Masculinities in Modern Britain*, ed. Matthew McCormack (Hampshire: Palgrave Macmillan, 2007), 66.

53 Henry Reynolds, 'Genocide in Tasmania', in *Genocide and Settler Society. Frontier Violence and Stolen Indigenous Children in Australian Society*, ed. A. Dirk Moses (New York: Berghahn, 2005), 135.

54 See, for example, Peter H. Wilson, 'Atrocities in the Thirty Years War', in *Ireland: 1641: Contexts and Reactions*, ed. Micheál Ó Siochrú and Jane Ohlmeyer (Manchester: Manchester University Press, 2013), 153–75.

55 Jean-Philippe Cénat, 'Le ravage du Palatinat: politique de destruction, stratégie de cabinet et propagande au début de la guerre de la Ligue d'Augsbourg', *Revue historique* 307, no. 1 (2005): 97–132; John A. Lynn, 'A Brutal Necessity? The Devastation of the Palatinate, 1688–1689', in *Civilians in the Path of War*, ed. Mark Grimsley and Clifford J. Rogers (Lincoln: University of Nebraska Press, 2002), 79–110; and Emilie Dosquet, 'Between Positional Warfare and "Guerre de Partis": Soldiers and Civilians during the "Desolation of the Palatinate" (1688–89)', in *Civilians under Siege from Sarajevo to Troy*, ed. John Horne and Alex Dowdall (Basingstoke: Palgrave Macmillan, 2018), 107–36.

56 Dan Edelstein, 'War and Terror: The Law of Nations from Grotius to the French Revolution', *French Historical Studies* 31, no. 2 (2008): 248–9; Bell, *The First Total War*, 247.

57 Emilie Dosquet, '"We Have Been Informed that the French Are Carrying Desolation Everywhere": The Desolation of the Palatinate as a News Event', in *New Networks in Early Modern Europe*, ed. Joad Raymond and Noah Moxham (Leiden: Brill, 2016), 641–74.

58 Esdaile, 'Patriots, Partisans and Land Pirates', 13–15.

59 Esdaile, 'Patriots, Partisans and Land Pirates', 14.

60 Rory Muir (ed.), *At Wellington's Right Hand: The Letters of Lieutenant-Colonel Sir Alexander Gordon, 1808–1815* (Phoenix Mill: Sutton, 2003), 174.

61 Reported in Georges Bangofsky, 'Les Étapes de Georges Bangofsky, officier lorrain. Extraits de son journal de campagnes (1797–1815)', *Mémoires de l'Académie de Stanislas* 2 (1905): 291.

62 Léonce Bernard, *Les prisonniers de guerre du Premier Empire* (Paris: Christian, 2000), 227–8.

63 Eugène Labaume, *Relation circonstanciée de la campagne de Russie* (Paris: Pancoucke, 1815), 271, 274.

64 See, Fergus Robson, 'Siege Warfare in Comparative Early Modern Contexts: Norms, Nuances, Myth and Massacre During the Revolutionary Wars', in *Civilians under Siege from Sarajevo to Troy*, ed. John Horne and Alex Dowdall (Basingstoke: Palgrave Macmillan, 2018), 83–105.

65 See, Gavin Daly, '"The Sacking of a Town Is an Abomination": Siege, Sack and Violence to Civilians in British Officers' Writings on the Peninsular War', *Historical Research* 92, no. 255 (2019): 160–82; and Gavin Daly, *Storm and Sack: British Sieges, Violence and the Laws of War in the Napoleonic Era, 1799–1815* (Cambridge: Cambridge University Press, 2022), esp. 234–44 on estimating civilian deaths. Daly estimates that the number of civilian deaths during the sack of Badajoz was considerably lower than previous reports, and probably came to around 120 people. At San Sebastián, about half the population died during the siege, but exactly how many is anyone's guess.

66 *Correspondance de Napoléon Ier*, 69, xii. n. 9744 (4 February 1806).

67 Levene, 'Introduction', in Levene and Roberts (eds), *The Massacre in History*, 18; Robert Gellately and Ben Kiernan, 'The Study of Mass Murder and Genocide', in *The Specter of Genocide*, ed. Gellately and Kiernan, 13.

68 For the Iroquois, see Mann, *George Washington's War on Native America*, 107–11. For the Miamis, see Mann, 'Fractal Massacres', 177–79.

69 There are, for example, memoirs and journals, such as the collected journals of many of Sullivan's 1779 troops, published in preparation for an 1889 celebration of the destruction of Iroquoia (Cook, *Journals of the Military Expedition*).

70 See the 'intelligence' sent to Jackson by a subordinate militia general that was, this time, 'certain' regarding the 'Murder of Six Persons' on the Duck River by Creek 'Indians', indicating the other potential pretexts already sent and dismissed as insufficient. See letter of 27 May 1812, in *The Papers of Andrew Jackson*, ed. Harold D. Moser and Sharon Macpherson, Vol. 2 (Knoxville: The University of Tennessee Press, 1984), 298.

71 Levene, 'Introduction', in Levene and Roberts (eds), *The Massacre in History*, 15.

72 Penn, *Forgotten Frontier*, 35; Mohamed Adhikari, 'A Total Extinction Confidently Hoped For: The Destruction of Cape San Society under Dutch Colonial Rule, 1700–1795', *Journal of Genocide Research* 12, no. 1–2 (2010): 19–44.

73 Paul A. W. Wallace, *Conrad Weiser: Friend of Colonist and Mohawk* (New York: Russell & Russell, 1945), 295.

74 Philip S. Klein and Ari Hoogenboom, *A History of Pennsylvania*, 2nd ed., rev. (University Park: University of Pennsylvania Press, 1980), 80.

75 State of Pennsylvania, *Minutes of the Provincial Council of Pennsylvania from the Organization to the Termination of the Proprietary Government*, Vol. 9 (Harrisburg, PA: Theo. Fenn, 1852), 27–30.

76 Klein and Hoogenboom, *A History of Pennsylvania*, 79–80.

77 *St. Clair Papers*, 6.

78 Sally Roesch Wagner, 'The Root of Oppression Is the Loss of Memory: The Iroquois and the Early Feminist Vision', in *Iroquois Women: An Anthology*, ed. William Guy Spittal (Ontario, CA: Iroquois Publishing and Craft Supplies, 1990), 235; Gregory Evans Dowd, *A Spirited Resistance: North American Indian Struggle for Unity, 1745–1815* (Baltimore, MD: Johns Hopkins University Press, 1992), 9–11; Mann, *Iroquoian Women*, 277–78.

79 Natalie Zemon Davis, 'The Rites of Violence: Religious Riot in Sixteenth-Century France', *Past and Present* 59, no.1 (1973): 57–65. See also Corbin, *The Village of Cannibals*, 87–91.

80 Jacques Sémelin, 'Towards a Vocabulary of Massacre and Genocide', *Journal of Genocide Research*, 5, no. 2 (2003): 207–8.

81 Cadet, *Honneur et violences de guerre*, 306–9, 311–16.

82 Cadet, *Honneur et violences de guerre*, 312.

83 Cited in Cadet, *Honneur et violences de guerre*, 311.

84 [McKee], *Minutes of Debate in Council*, 17.

85 Cook, *Journals of the Military Expedition*, 8, 240, 244, 279, n*.

86 Heckewelder, *A Narrative of the Mission*, 130.

87 Heckewelder, *A Narrative of the Mission*, 342.

88 Jack Weatherford, *Native Roots: How American Indians Enriched America* (New York: Fawcett Books, 1991), 169.

89 Robert Earl, 'Indian Scalping', *Papers Read before the Herkimer County Historical Society during the Years 1896, 1897, and 1898*, Vol. 2 (Herkimer and Ilyon, NY: Citizen Publishing Company, Publishers, 1899), 129.

90 On scalping and scalp bounties see, Mairin Odle, *Under the Skin: Tattoos, Scalps, and the Contested Language of Bodies in Early America* (Philadelphia: University of Pennsylvania Press, 2022), 68–91; Henry J. Young, 'A Note on Scalp Bounties in Pennsylvania', *Pennsylvania History: A Journal of Mid-Atlantic Studies* 24, no. 3 (1957): 207–18; and Margaret Haig Roosevelt Sewall Ball, 'Grim Commerce: Scalp Bounties and the Transformation of Trophy Taking in the Early American Northeast, 1450–1770' (PhD, University of Colorado, 2013).

91 C. Hale Sipe, *The Indian Wars of Pennsylvania: An Account of the Indian Events, in Pennsylvania, of the French and Indian War, Pontiac's War, Lord Dunmore's War, the Revolutionary War and the Indian Uprising from 1789 to 1795* (Harrisburg, PA: The Telegraph Press, 1929), 281–84, 473, 495, 505, 625–26.

92 George Rogers Clark, *George Rogers Clark Papers, 1771–1781*, ed. James Alton James, Vol. 8 (Springfield, IL: Trustees of the Illinois State Historical Library, 1912), 97.

93 Kathrine Wagner Seineke, *The George Rogers Clark Adventure in the Illinois and Selected Documents of the American Revolution at the Frontier Posts* (New Orleans, LA: Polyanthos, 1981), 453.

94 Louise Phelps Kellogg (ed.), *Frontier Retreat on the Upper Ohio, 1779–1781* (1917; Baltimore: Geneaological Publishing, 2003), 379–80, n. 2; Cecil B. Hartley, *The Life and Adventures of Lewis Wetzel, the Virginia Ranger* (Philadelphia, PA: G. G. Evans, 1860).

95 Philip Sturm, 'Lewis Wetzel', *The West Virginia Encyclopedia*, 7 February 2023, accessed 22 August 2023: https://www.wvencyclopedia.org/articles/1161

Chapter 5

1 There has been a recent attempt to reassess the Napoleonic Empire as an important chain in the global history of Empires. See Thomas Dodman and Aurélien Lignereux (eds), *From the Napoleonic Empire to the Age of Empire: Empire after the Emperor* (Cham: Springer, 2023).

2 Stuart Woolf, 'The Construction of a European World-view in the Revolutionary-Napoleonic Years', *Past & Present* 137 (1992): 72–101. Michael Broers, *The Napoleonic Empire in Italy, 1796–1814: Cultural Imperialism in a European Context?* (New York: Palgrave Macmillan, 2005), 275–94, has adopted a similar approach, describing Italy under the French imperium as a 'subaltern society'.

3 For an example of the notion of colonialism being used within Europe in an entirely different context, for the Nazis and the Second World War, see Jürgen Zimmerer, 'Colonialism and the Holocaust. Towards an Archaeology of Genocide', in *Genocide and Settler Society. Frontier Violence and Stolen Indigenous Children in Australian Society*, ed. A. Dirk Moses (New York: Berghahn, 2005), 49–76.

4 See, for example, Paul W. Schroeder, *The Transformation of European Politics, 1763–1848* (Oxford: Clarendon Press, 1994), 394–95.

5 Dwyer, 'Violence and the Revolutionary and Napoleonic Wars', 117–31.

6 Karr, 'Why Should You Be So Furious?', 883.

7 See, for example, Napoleon Bonaparte, *La Correspondance de Napoléon*, Vol. 4 (Paris: Fayard, 2004–2018), 8513 (25 December 1803); Vol. 6, 11392 (4 February 1806),

11506 (19 February 1806), 11740 (27 February 1806), 11881 (11 April 1806), 12111 (13 May 1806), 12613 (30 July 1806), 12742 (17 August 1806).

8   H. L. Wesseling, 'Colonial Wars: An Introduction', in *Imperialism and War: Essays on Colonial Wars in Asia and Africa*, ed. J. A. de Moor and H. L. Wesseling (Leiden: E. J. Brill, 1989), 3–5.

9   Charles Tilly, *Coercion, Capital, and European States, AD 990–1990* (Cambridge, MA: B. Blackwell, 1990).

10   See, for example, Erica Charters, Marie Houllemare and Peter H. Wilson, 'Introduction: Violence in the Early Modern World', in *A Global History of Early Modern Violence*, ed. Charters, Houllemare, and Wilson, 1–16.

11   For an overview of the debates with French history, see William Beik, 'The Absolutism of Louis XIV as Social Collaboration', *Past & Present* 188 (2005): 195–224. See also Benton, *They Called It Peace*, for a new interpretation on the ways in which violence was used by both state and non-state actors on the periphery.

12   For the development of the concept of 'small war' in the eighteenth century, see Sibylle Scheipers, *On Small War: Carl Von Clausewitz and People's War* (Oxford: Oxford University Press, 2018), 27–51; and Beatrice Heuser, 'Small Wars in the Age of Clausewitz: The Watershed between Partisan War and People's War', *Journal of Strategic Studies* 33, no. 1 (2010): 139–62.

13   Rink, 'The Partisan's Metamorphosis', 11; Heuser, 'Small Wars in the Age of Clausewitz', 143.

14   Heuser, 'Small Wars in the Age of Clausewitz', 149–50.

15   Rink, 'The Partisan's Metamorphosis', 10, 20.

16   Pablo Kalmanovitz, *The Laws of War in International Thought* (Oxford: Oxford University Press, 2020), 72, n. 11.

17   Bell, *Total War*, 21–51. See also James Q. Whitman, *The Verdict of Battle: The Law of Victory and the Making of Modern War* (Cambridge, MA: Harvard University Press, 2012), 172–206.

18   Cited in Edelstein, 'War and Terror', 238, and 242 where Vattel had come to the same conclusion.

19   Michel Senellart, 'La qualification de l'ennemi chez Emer de Vattel', *Astérion: philosophie, histoire des idées, pensée politique* 2 (2004): https://doi.org/10.4000/asterion.82

20   Edelstein, 'War and Terror', 244; Pablo Kalmanovitz, 'Regular War, Irregulars, and Savages', in *Concepts and Contexts of Vattel's Political and Legal Thought*, ed. Peter Schröder (Cambridge: Cambridge University Press, 2021), 141–60, who shows that Vattel reserved the harshest punishments in response to the violation of the rules of war to non-European peoples.

21 As recognized by Edelstein, 'War and Terror', 231–47.

22 Not all historians agree that ideology played a role in the violence. Martin, *La Vendée et la France*, 225–46, plays down the role of revolutionary discourse in the massacres that were committed, arguing that there was never a 'unitary logic' and that revolutionary discourse cannot be taken literally.

23 Mona Ozouf, 'War and Terror in French Revolutionary Discourse (1792–1794)', *Journal of Modern History* 56, no. 4 (1984): 579–97.

24 Jacques Godechot, 'Les variations de la politique française à l'égard des pays occupés 1792–1815', in *Occupants-Occupés, 1792–1815* (Brussels: Université libre, Institut de sociologie, 1969), 19–31.

25 Michael Broers, 'Revolt and Repression in Napoleonic Italy, 1796–1814', in *War in an Age of Revolution, 1775–1815*, ed. Roger Chickering and Stig Förster (Washington, DC: German Historical Institute, 2010), 197–217, stresses the economic causes of the anti-French revolts in Italy during what he calls the first invasions, from 1796 to 1799. See also Blanning, *The French Revolution in Germany*, 83–134.

26 According to Alexandre Bellot de Kergorre, *Journal d'un commissaire des guerres pendant le Premier Empire (1806–1821)* (Paris: La Vouivre, 1997), 20, where he cites one unspecified example of villages being 'reduced to ashes' on the frontier with Prussia during the war of 1806–8.

27 On the revolts caused by and against conscription, see Alan Forrest, 'Policing, Rural Revolt and Conscription in Napoleonic France', in *The Napoleonic Empire and the New European Political Culture. War, Culture and Society, 1750–1850*, ed. Michael Broers, Peter Hicks and Augustín Guimerá (Basingstoke: Palgrave Macmillan, 2012), 49–58.

28 Forrest, 'Policing, Rural Revolt and Conscription', 53.

29 Paul Verhaegen, *La Belgique sous la domination française, 3, La guerre des paysans, 1798–1799*, Vol. 2 (Brussels and Paris: Goemaere and Plon, 1926), 285–726; Henri Pirenne, *Histoire de Belgique*, Vol. 6 (Brussels: Lamertin, 1902–1932), 109–17.

30 Yves-Marie Bercé, *Révoltes et révolutions dans l'Europe moderne (XVIe–XVIIIe siècles)* (Paris: Presses universitaires de France, 1980), 238; Georges-Henri Dumont, *Histoire de la Belgique: des origines à 1830* (Brussels: Le Cri édition, 2005), 392.

31 Broers, 'Revolt and Repression in Napoleonic Italy', 199–204.

32 *Correspondance de Napoléon Ier*, vi. n. 4523 (14 January 1800).

33 *Correspondance de Napoléon Ier*, xiii. n. 10573 (30 July 1806).

34 Vincent Haegele (ed.), *Napoléon et Joseph Bonaparte: correspondence intégrale 1784–1818* (Paris: Tallandier, 2007), 284 (8 August 1806).

35 *Correspondance de Napoléon Ier*, xi. n. 9678 (19 January 1806).

36 Gilles Candela, *L'armée d'Italie: des missionnaires armés à la naissance de la guerre napoléonienne* (Rennes: Presses universitaires de Rennes, 2011), 317–18.

37 Haegele (ed.), *Napoléon et Joseph*, 293 (17 August 1806).

38 Haegele (ed.), *Napoléon et Joseph*, 167–8 (8 March 1806); 179 (31 March 1806).

39 Jacques Sémelin, 'Du massacre au processus génocidiare', *Revue internationale des sciences sociales* 174 (2002): 483–92, makes a distinction between 'exhibited' and 'hidden' massacres.

40 Jacques Miot, *Mémoires pour servir à l'histoire des expéditions en Égypte et en Syrie, pendant les années VI, VII et VIII de la république française*, 2nd ed. (Paris: Le Normant, 1814), 145–8.

41 On this point, see Philip Dwyer, '"It Still Makes Me Shudder": Memories of Massacres and Atrocities during the Revolutionary and Napoleonic Wars', *War in History* 16, no. 4 (2009): 381–405. One can note a similar phenomenon for battlefield experiences in Forrest, *Napoleon's Men*, 112–17.

42 Jean-Noël Brégeon, *Napoléon et la guerre d'Espagne: 1808–1814* (Paris: Perrin, 2006), 98. John Lawrence Tone, *The Fatal Knot: The Guerrilla War in Navarre and the Defeat of Napoleon in Spain* (Chapel Hill: University of North Carolina Press, 1994), 50, and 198, n. 23, places the figure at anywhere between 400 and 1,200.

43 Louis-Philippe Gille, *Les Prisonniers de Cabrera, mémoires d'un conscrit de 1808* (Paris: Victor-Havard, 1892), 72; Louis-François-Joseph Bausset, *Mémoires anecdotiques sur l'intérieur du Palais et sur quelques évènemens de l'Empire depuis 1805 jusqu'au 1er mai 1814, pour servir à l'histoire de Napoléon*, Vol. 1 (Paris: Baudouin frères, 1827), 234–36; Charles François, *Le journal d'un officier français ou Les cahiers du capitaine François: 1792–1815* (Paris: Charles Carrington, 1903), 558–61 (2 May 1808).

44 *Moniteur universel*, 11 May 1808; and Napoleon to Fouché, in Léon Lecestre (ed.), *Lettres inédites de Napoléon*, Vol. 1 (Paris: E. Plon, Nourrit et cie, 1897), 194 (21 May 1808).

45 Gunter Rothenberg, 'The Age of Napoleon', in *The Laws of War: Constraints on Warfare in the Western World*, ed. Michael Howard, George J. Andreopoulos and Mark R. Shulman (New Haven, CT: Yale University Press, 1994), 93.

46 *Journal de Paris*, 9 and 10 July 1811.

47 Oscar von Lettow-Vorbeck (ed.), *Der Krieg von 1806 und 1807*, Vol. 2 (Berlin: Ernst Siegfried Mittler und Sohn, 1891–1896), 384–6; Daly, *Storm and Sack*, 181–2.

48 Pierre, vicomte de Pelleport, *Souvenirs militaire et intimes du général vicomte de Pelleport de 1793 à 1853*, Vol. 1 (Paris: Didier, 1857), 238; Bangofsky, 'Les Étapes', 291; Charles de Villers, *Lettre à Madame la Comtesse F… de B…* (Amsterdam: bureau

des arts et d'industrie, 1807), written by Charles François Dominique de Villiers, an émigré writer who had lived in Lübeck for a number of years.

49 Ernest de Hauterive, *La Police secrète du premier Empire, bulletins quotidiens adressés par Fouché à l'Empereur*, Vol. 1 (Paris: Clavreuil, 1908-1964), 260 (29 May 1807).

50 Milton Finley, *The Most Monstrous of Wars: The Napoleonic Guerrilla War in Southern Italy, 1806-1811* (Columbia: University of South Carolina Press, 1994), 49; Jacques Rambaud, *Naples sous Joseph Bonaparte, 1806-1808* (Paris: Plon-Nourrit, 1911), 143.

51 Christopher Duggan, *The Force of Destiny: A History of Italy Since 1796* (London: Allen Lane, 2007), 23 and 55.

52 John A. Davis, *Naples and Napoleon. Southern Italy and the European Revolutions (1780-1860)* (Oxford: Oxford University Press, 2006), 114.

53 Jean-Marc Lafon, 'Justices d'exception napoléoniennes, militaire et civile, dans l'Espagne occupée: l'exemple de l'Andalousie (1810-1812)', *Crime, Histoire & Sociétés/Crime, History & Societies* 13, no. 2 (2009): 74-5; Isabelle Renaudet, 'Mourir en Espagne: "garrot vil" et exécution capitale dans l'Espagne contemporaine', in *L'exécution capitale. Une mort donnée en spectacle XVIe-XXe siècles*, ed. Régis Bertrand and Anne Carol (Aix-en-Provence: Publications de l'Univesité de Provence, 2003), 83-106; Robert Muchembled, *Le temps des supplices. De l'obéissance sous les rois absolus*, XVe-XVIIIe siècles (Paris: Armand Colin, 1992), 115-22.

54 See Howard G. Brown, 'Domestic State Violence: Repression from the Croquants to the Commune', *Historical Journal* 42, no. 3 (1999): 597-622. For Brown 'domestic state violence' is force that is deemed excessive and is hence discredited. He points to the outcry among certain elites when repression was extreme. There is little, however, about the deliberate use of extreme violence by the state to impose authority on recalcitrant peoples.

55 Charles Tilly, 'Routine Conflicts and Peasant Rebellions in Seventeenth Century France', in *Power and Protest in Protest in the Countryside: Studies of Rural Unrest in Asia. Europe, and Latin America*, ed. Robert Weller and Scott E. Guggenheim (Durham, NC: Duke University Press, 1982), 13-41.

56 As an example, Browning's *Ordinary Men.*

57 Leader Maynard, *Ideology and Mass Killing*, is among the leading proponents of this view, although he has a slightly different take on what constitutes 'ideology'. He defines it not in any narrow political sense, but much more broadly as a culture, a way of understanding and seeing.

58 Bernard Gainot, 'Les affrontements militaires sous la Revolution et l'Empire: une "guerre totale"?' *Revue d'histoire moderne & contemporaine* 59, no. 2 (2012): 178-86; and Hervé Drévillon, 'Pratiques et representations de la violence des guerres de la

Convention, 1792–95', in *L'historien-citoyen*, ed. Benjamin Deruelle, Émilie Dosquet and Paul Vo-Ha (Paris: Éditions de la Sorbonne, 2022), 367–68.

59 Tim Blanning, 'The Abortive Crusade', *History Today* 39 (1989): 33–8; and Hervé Leuwers, 'République et relations entre les peuples. Quelques éléments de l'idéal républicain autour de brumaire an VIII', *Annales historiques de la Révolution française* 318 (1999): 677–93.

60 Bell, *First Total War*, 273; Finley, *The Most Monstrous of Wars*, 64–5.

61 All of this is detailed in the report by Berthier in Services Historiques de l'Armée de Terre [SHAT], Correspondence, Armée de Naples, carton C-5, 4, 15 August 1806.

62 SHAT, Corr. Armée de Naples, carton C-5, 4.

63 AN AFIV 1605 (2), Duhesme to Clarke, 29 February 1808.

64 Gunther E. Rothenberg, *The Art of Warfare in the Age of Napoleon* (Bloomington: Indiana University Press, 1978), 120.

65 On this point and the Vendée, see Jean-Clément Martin, 'Le cas de Turreau et des colonnes infernales: réflexion sur une historiographie', in *La plume et le sabre: volume d'hommages offerts à Jean-Paul Bertaud*, ed. Michel Biard, Annie Crépin and Bernard Gainot (Paris: Publications de la Sorbonne, 2002), 244–5.

66 Nicolas Cadet, 'Anatomie d'une "petite guerre," la campagne de Calabre de 1806–1807', *Revue d'histoire du XIXe siècle* 30 (2005): 73–4.

67 Michael Broers, *Napoleon's Other War: Bandits, Rebels and Their Pursuers in the Age of Revolutions* (Oxford: Peter Lang, 2010), 48, 82.

68 Michael Broers, 'Civilians in the Napoleonic Wars', in *Daily Lives of Civilians in Wartime Europe, 1618–1900*, ed. Linda Frey and Marsha Frey (Westport, CT: Greenwood Press, 2007), 150.

69 Guillaume-Philibert Duhesme, *Essai sur l'infanterie légère* (Paris: L.-G. Michaud, 1814), 378. See, for example, AN AFIV, 1621 (1), 9 June 1808.

70 This and the following quote cited in Hervé Drévillon, 'Guerre, violence et Révolution', in *Histoire militaire de la France. I. Des Mérovingiens au Second Empire*, ed. Hervé Drévillon and Olivier Wieviorka (Paris: Perrin, 2018), 519.

71 Dupuy, *La République jacobine*, 268–9.

72 T. C. W. Blanning, 'Liberation or Occupation? Theory and Practice in the French Revolutionaries Treatment of Civilians outside France', in Grimsley and Rogers (eds), *Civilians in the Path of War*, 127–8.

73 Emmanuel de Las Cases, *Le Mémorial de Sainte-Hélène*, Vol. 1 (Paris: Flammarion, 1983), 864; Félix Bouvier, 'La révolte de Pavie (23–6 mai 1796)', *Revue historique de la Revolution française* 2, no. 8 (1911): 519–39.

74 Napoleon Bonaparte, *La Correspondance de Napoléon*, Vol. 1 (Paris: Fayard, 2004), 460–1.

75 Jean-François Boulart, *Mémoires militaires du général Bon Boulart sur les guerres de la république et de l'empire* (Paris: A la librairie illustrée, 1892), 50.

76 Henri Laurens, *L'expédition d'Egypte, 1798–1801* (Paris: Armand Colin, 1989), 148–53; and Juan Cole, *Napoléon's Egypt: Invading the Middle East*. 1st ed. New York: Palgrave Macmillan, 2007); and Clarke, 'A "Theatre of Bloody Carnage,"' 218–34.

77 Nicolas Cadet, 'Violences de guerre et transmission de la mémoire des conflits à travers l'exemple de la campagne de Calabre de 1806–1807', *Annales historiques de la Révolution française* 348, no. 2 (2007): 167; Finley, *The Most Monstrous of Wars*, 26–7, 50, 52–4.

78 Jean-Michel Chevalier, *Souvenirs des guerres napoléoniennes* (Paris: Hachette, 1970), 74.

79 Nicolas Marcel, *Campagnes du capitaine Marcel, du 69e de ligne, en Espagne et en Portugal (1804–1814)* (Paris: Plon-Nourrit, 1913), 37–8.

80 Cited in McPhee, 'A Vicious Civil War in the French Revolution', 321.

81 See, for example, Rothenberg, 'The Age of Napoleon', 87; Franco della Peruta, 'War and Society in Napoleonic Italy: The Armies of the Kingdom of Italy at Home and Abroad', in *Society and Politics in the Age of the Risorgimento. Essays in Honour of Denis Mack Smith*, ed. John Davis and Paul Ginsborg (Cambridge: Cambridge University Press, 1991), 43.

82 See, for example, Le Cour Grandmaison, *Coloniser, exterminer*, esp. 138–43.

Chapter 6

1 Ruling by judge advocate Richard Atkins in, Frederick Watson (ed.), *Historical Records of Australia, Series I. Governors' Despatches to and from England*, Vol. 5 (Sydney: Library Committee of the Commonwealth Parliament, 1914–25), 502–4 (HRA). See also Bruce Kercher, *An Unruly Child. A History of Law in Australia* (St Leonards, NSW: Allen & Unwin, 1995), 16–17.

2 Jan Barkley-Jack, *Hawkesbury Settlements Revealed: A New Look at Australia's Third Mainland Settlement* (Sydney: Rosenberg Publishing, 2009), 16; Karskens, *The Colony*, 122. For sex ratio, see John C. Caldwell, 'Colonial Population 1788–1825', in *Australians, Historical Statistics*, ed. Wray Vamplew (Sydney: Fairfax Syme & Weldon Associates, 1987), 25.

3 Karskens, *The Colony*, 121.

4   Karskens, *The Colony*, 464.

5   James L. Kohen and Ronald Lampert, 'Hunters and Fishers in the Sydney Region', in *Australians to 1788*, ed. D. John Mulvaney and J. Peter White (Sydney: Fairfax, Syme and Weldon Associates, 1987), 345.

6   Kohen and Lampert, 'Hunters and Fishers', 345.

7   Karskens, *The Colony*, 463.

8   Kohen and Lampert, 'Hunters and Fishers', 345; Turbet, *The First Frontier*, 90.

9   Collins, *An Account of the English Colony*, 326.

10 Collins, *An Account of the English Colony*, 327.

11 Turbet, *The First Frontier*, 81.

12 Turbet, *The First Frontier*, 93.

13 Collins, *An Account of the English Colony*, 329.

14 Collins, *An Account of the English Colony*, 341.

15 Collins, *An Account of the English Colony*, 348.

16 Collins, *An Account of the English Colony*, 348.

17 Connor, *Australian Frontier Wars*, 38.

18 Collins, *An Account of the English Colony*, 349.

19 Collins, *An Account of the English Colony*, 349.

20 Connor, *Australian Frontier Wars*, 39.

21 Collins, *An Account of the English Colony*, 371.

22 Collins, *An Account of the English Colony*, Vol. 2, 11.

23 Collins, *An Account of the English Colony*, Vol. 2, 26.

24 Collins, *An Account of the English Colony*, Vol. 2, 45; Hunter to Portland, in *HRA*, Series I, Vol. 2, 24.

25 Turbet, *The First Frontier*, 107.

26 Grace Karskens, *People of the River: Lost Worlds of Early Australia* (Sydney: Allen & Unwin, 2020), 143.

27 Karskens, *The Colony*, 473.

28 Connor, *Australian Frontier Wars*, 39.

29 Connor, *Australian Frontier Wars*, 48.

30 Connor, *Australian Frontier Wars*, 46.

31 Karskens, *The Colony*, 468.

32 Connor, *Australian Frontier Wars*, 46.

33 Caldwell, 'Colonial Population 1788–1825', 25.

34 King to Hobart, 14 August and 20 December 1804, *HRA*, Series I, Vol. 17 and, 166–7.

35 King to Hobart, 20 December 1804, *HRA*, Series I, Vol. 5, 167. *Sydney Gazette*, 30 May 1805.

36 *Sydney Gazette*, 23 June and 7 July 1805.

37 Connor, *Australian Frontier Wars*, 44.

38 A. G. L. Shaw, 'Philip Gidley King (1758–1808)', *Australian Dictionary of Biography*, https://adb.anu.edu.au/biography/king-philip-gidley-2309.

39 David Hainsworth, *The Sydney Traders: Simeon Lord and His Contemporaries, 1788–1821* (Melbourne: Cassell, 1972).

40 Alan Atkinson, *The Europeans in Australia: A History*, Vol. 1 (Melbourne: Oxford University Press, 1998–2004), 212–19.

41 Francis Grose, the Colonel Commanding, had returned to England in 1794 in ill health but remained vitally interested in the Corps and was known to use his patrons, the MPs Henry Phipp, Viscount Normanby and Earl Mulgrave, to protect its interests. T. George Parsons, personal communication.

42 Compiled from Pamela Statham (ed.), *A Colonial Regiment: New Sources Relating to the New South Wales Corps 1789–1810* (Canberra: P. Statham, 1992), 37–75.

43 J. L. Kohen, 'Pemulwuy 1750–1802', in *Australian Dictionary of Biography, Supplementary Volume*, https://adb.anu.edu.au/biography/pemulwuy-13147. See also Karskens, *The Colony*, 474.

44 Collins, *An Account of the English Colony*, 249, 292, 304, 371, 378; Vol. 2, 20, 25.

45 Karskens, *The Colony*, 476; Collins, *An Account of the English Colony*, ii. 66.

46 Karksens. *The Colony*, 476.

47 Karskens, *The Colony*, 476.

48 Karskens, *The Colony*, 478.

49 Karskens, *The Colony*, 478.

50 Collins, *An Account of the English Colony*, Vol. 2, 149.

51 Karskens, *The Colony*, 478.

52 Karksens, *The Colony*, 479.

53 Karskens, *The Colony*, 479–80.

54 King to Hobart, 30 October 1802, *HRA*, Series I, Vol. 4, 867-8.

55 Keith Vincent Smith, 'Australia's oldest murder mystery', *Sydney Morning Herald*, 1 November 2003.

56 Doug Kohlhoff, 'Did Henry Hacking shoot Pemulwuy? A reappraisal', *Journal of the Royal Australian Historical Society* 99, no. 1 (2013): 77-93.

57 Eric Willmot, *Pemulwuy, The Rainbow Warrior* (Sydney: Weldon Publishing, 1987).

58 Atkinson, *Europeans in Australia*, 251.

59 Proclamation in King to Hobart, 9 November 1802, *HRA*, Series I, Vol. 3, 618-21.

60 List of ships entering and leaving Sydney Harbour, January to July 1802, enclosure in King to Hobart, 9 November 1802, *HRA*, Series I, Vol. 3, 618- 21.

61 'Plan of Itinerary for Citizen Baudin', *The Journal of Post Captain Nicolas Baudin*, trans. Christine Cornell (Adelaide: Libraries Board of South Australia, 1974), 1-6.

62 King to Hobart, 9 November 1802, *HRA*, Series I, Vol. 3, 637 and 697.

63 King to Hobart, 9 November 1802, Vol. 3, 637.

64 Edward Duyker, *Francois Peron an Impetuous Life* (Melbourne: Miegunyah Press, 2006), 135-50.

65 King to Hobart, 9 November 1802, *HRA*, Series 1, Vol. 3, 698-9.

66 King to Hobart, 23 November 1802, *HRA*, Series 1, Vol. 3, 737.

67 King to Hobart, 23 November 1802, *HRA*, Series I, Vol. 3, 737-9.

68 Baudin to King, 23 December 1802, in *Historical Records of New South Wales*, ed. Frank Murcot Bladon, Vol. 5 (Sydney: Government Printer 1897), 830-3 (HRNSW).

69 King to Bowen, 28 March 1803, *HRNSW*, Vol. 5, 76-7; Bowen to King, 20 September 1803, *HRA*, Series III, Vol. 1, 198. Risdon Cove was selected because it had been 'discovered' and named by British explorer John Hayes in 1792 and later visited by Matthew Flinders in 1800 who spoke highly of the location.

70 Bowen to King, 20 September 1803, *HRA*, Series III, Vol. 1, 198.

71 Ryan, *Tasmanian Aborigines*, 43.

72 Philip Tardif, *John Bowen's Hobart*, Hobart: Tasmanian Historical Research Association, 2003, 73.

73 Statham, *A Colonial Regiment*, 321; Tardif, 73-4.

74 Collins to King, 28 February 1804, *HRNSW*, v. 312-13.

75 King to Bowen, 12 January 1804, *HRA*, Series I, Vol. 4, 207 and King to Collins, 4 February 1804, *HRA*, Series III, Vol. 1, 55; Collins to King, 24 April 1804, *HRA*,

Series III, Vol. 1, 243–7; Mary Nicholls (ed.), *The Diary of the Reverend Robert Knopwood 1803–1838* (Hobart: Tasmanian Historical Research Association, 1977), 49–50.

76 King to Hobart, 1 March 1804, *HRA*, Series I, Vol. 4, 483–4.

77 Nicholls, *Diary of Reverend Robert Knopwood,* 51.

78 Nicholls, *Diary of Reverend Robert Knopwood,* 51.

79 Moore to Collins, 7 May 1804, Enclosure in Collins to King, 15 May 1804, *HRA*, Series III, Vol. 1, 242–3.

80 Government Order, 8 May 1804, in Collins to King, 15 May 1804, *HRA*, Series III, Vol. 1, 258; Nicholls, *Diary of the Reverend Robert Knopwood*, 51.

81 Collins to King, 15 May 1804, *HRA*, Series III, Vol. 1, 238.

82 *HRA*, Series III, Vol. 1, 809.

83 King to Collins, 30 September 1804, *HRA*, Series III, Vol. 1, 282.

84 *Sydney Gazette,* 2 September 1804.

85 Van Diemen's Land, Correspondence Concerning Military Operations Carried Out against the Aboriginal Inhabitants', *British Parliamentary Papers, House of Commons,* Vol. 19 (London: H.M. Stationery Office, 1831), 50–1.

86 Bonwick, *The Last of the Tasmanians*, 35.

87 King to Paterson, 1 June 1804, *HRNSW*, Vol. 5, 383–5; Proclamation, 11 August 1804, *HRNSW*, Vol. 5, 416–7.

88 Paterson to King, 26 November 1804, *HRNSW*, Vol. 5, 486; *HRA*, Series III, Vol. 1, 605–7, 629, 658–9.

89 Caldwell, 'Colonial Population 1788–1825', 25.

90 *Sydney Gazette*, 7 January and 28 July 1810; Macquarie to Bathurst, 8 October 1814, *HRA*, Series I, Vol. 8, 368.

91 Karskens, *The Colony*, 491.

92 Karksens, *The Colony*, 490–1, 500–1.

93 Macquarie to Goulburn, 7 May 1814, *HRA*, Series I, Vol. 8, 250–1; *Sydney Gazette*, 18 June 1814.

94 Karskens, *The Colony*, 492, 498.

95 *Sydney Gazette*, 18 June 1814.

96 Karskens, *The Colony*, 494.

97 Gunson (ed.), *Australian Reminiscences*, Vol. 1, 11.

98 Karksens, *The Colony*, 501.

99   Karskens, *The Colony*, 502.

100 Karskens, *The Colony*, 503.

101 https://www.nma.gov.au/explore/features/aboriginal-breastplates

102 Karskens, *The Colony*, 504.

103 Karksens, *The Colony*, 504.

104 Karskens, *The Colony*, 504–6; *Sydney Gazette,* 30 March 1816.

105 Karskens, *The Colony*, 506–8; Macquarie to Bathurst, 25 May 1816, *HRA*, Series I, Vol. 9, 139.

106 Karskens, *The Colony*, 508–9.

107 Karskens, *The Colony*, 510–11.

108 Karskens, *The Colony*, 511–13.

109 Karskens, *The Colony*, 511.

110 *Sydney Gazette*, 20, 27 July, 3 August 1816; Karskens, *The Colony*, 512.

111 *Sydney Gazette*, 2, 19, 16 November 1816.

112 *Sydney Gazette*, 4 January 1817.

Chapter 7

1   On the use of treaties as a precursor to violence, see Benton, *They Called It Peace*, 42, 123–4. It is worth noting, however, that while used in South Africa, treaties were never used in Australia.

2   Peter R. Henriques, *Realistic Visionary: A Portrait of George Washington* (Charlottesville: University of Virginia Press, 2006), 6–7.

3   For *Chiningue*, as Shawnee ('Chaouanon') town visited by the Lenape Rueben Gold Thwaites French (ed.), *The Jesuit Relations and Allied Documents,* 73 vols (Cleveland, OH: Burroughs Brothers Publishers, 1896–1901), Vol. 69, 183; George P. Donehoo, 'A Few Facts in the History of Logstown', *Western Pennsylvania Historical Magazine* 1, no. 1 (1918): 259, 260.

4   Brady Krytzer, *Major Washington's Pittsburgh and the Mission to Fort Le Bœuf* (Charleston, SC: History Press, 2011), 43. For the Ohio Union, see Mann, 'The Greenville Treaty of 1795', 153–5, 159.

5   Italics in the original, [McKee], *Minutes of Debates in Council*, 8–9.

6   For quotation, [McKee], *Minutes of Debates in Council*, 9. On the opposition, Richard Butler, 'Gen. Butler's Journal, Continued', *The Olden Time* 2, no. 11 (1847): 518-19.

7   Butler, 'Gen. Butler's Journal', 520. For Shawnee clan behaviour, Erminie Wheeler Voegelin, *Mortuary Customs of the Shawnee and Other Eastern Tribes* (1944; New York: AMS Press, 1980), 256.

8   Butler, 'Gen. Butler's Journal', 520; [McKee], *Minutes of Debates in Council*, 9.

9   [McKee], *Minutes of Debates in Council*, 9.

10 Punctuation as in the original, [McKee], *Minutes of Debates in Council*, 9.

11 Butler, 'Gen. Butler's Journal', 522.

12 Butler, 'Gen. Butler's Journal', 522; [McKee], *Minutes of Debates in Council*, 9.

13 See, for instance, the attempt at a Condolence Speech made by Anthony Wayne at the Greenville Council in 1794, following that by Tarje, the great Wyandot speaker, who properly delivered Condolence speech, *American State Papers, Indian Affairs*, 573; see Tarje's properly delivered speech, *American State Papers, Indian Affairs*, 571. For demands, see Butler, 'Gen. Butler's Journal', 522-3.

14 Butler, 'Gen. Butler's Journal', 523.

15 [McKee], *Minutes of Debates in Council*, 9-10; Ebenezer Denny, 'Denny's Military Journal', *Memoirs of the Historical Society of Pennsylvania* 7 (1860): 277.

16 Butler, 'Gen. Butler's Journal', 523; [McKee], *Minutes of Debate*, 10; Denny, 'A Military Journal', 277.

17 {McKee}, 'Minutes of Debate', 10; Denny, 'A Military Journal', 277.

18 Denny, 'A Military Journal', 277.

19 [McKee], *Minutes of Debates in Council*, 10.

20 Butler, 'Gen. Butler's Journal', 524; Denny, 'Military Journal', 277: [McKee], *Minutes of Debate in Council*, 10.

21 Butler, 'Gen. Butler's Journal', 524-25.

22 Butler, 'Gen. Butler's Journal', 525; Denny, 'Military Journal', 277.

23 Butler, 'Gen. Butler's Journal', 525.

24 Denny, 'Military Journal', 277.

25 Denny, 'Military Journal', 277; C. J. Kappler (ed.), *Indian Treaties, 1778-1883* (1903; New York: Interland Publishing, 1973), 17; [McKee], *Minutes of Debate in Council*, 11. For other examples of fraudulence, see interlineations on the Greenville Treaty, unreliable claims of Indigenous speakership and inclusion of nations not present at the conference, in Mann, 'The Greenville Treaty of 1795', 181-3; Dorothy Libby and

David Bond Stout, 'The Piankashaw and Kaskaskia and the Treaty of Greene Ville', *Piankashaw and Kaskaskia Indians* (New York: Garland, 1974), 351–6.

26   Denny, 'Military Journal', 284.

27   Denny, 'Military Journal', 284–5; William Henry Smith, *The St. Clair Papers: The Life and Public Services of Arthur St. Clair; Soldier of the Revolutionary War; President of the Continental Congress, and Governor of the North-Western Territory; with His Correspondence and Other Papers*, Vol. 2 (Cincinnati, OH: Robert Clark, 1882), 17, n. 1.

28   David W. Miller, *The Forced Removal of American Indians from the Northeast: A History of Territorial Cessions and Relocations, 1620–1854* (Jefferson, NC: McFarland, 2011), 116. For 'banditti', see George Washington, *The Papers of George Washington, July–November 1790*, ed. William Wright Abbott, Philander D. Chase, Dorothy Twohig, Mark A. Mastromarino, Vol. 6 (Charlottesville: University of Virginia Press, 1996), 25, 362, n. 1.

29   Miller, *Forced Removal of American Indians from the Northeast*, 116.

30   United States Congress, *Journals of the American Congress, from 1774 to 1788*, Vol. 4 (Washington, DC: Way and Gideon, 1823), 714.

31   'The Haldiman Papers', *Pioneer Society of Michigan*, Vol. 10, 583–84.

32   For Washington's 1752 introduction to Shingask, David A. Clary, *George Washington's First War: His Early Military Adventures* (New York: Simon and Schuster, 2011), 57.

33   Miller, *Forced Removal of American Indians from the Northeast*, 18.

34   Archer Butler Hulbert, *Historic Highways of America*, vol. 9: *Waterways of Westward Expansion* (Cleveland, OH: Arthur H. Clark, 1903), 59–60.

35   *Collections of the Illinois State Historical Library*, Vol. 19, 112–14; William L. Stone, *Life of Joseph Brant-Thayendanegea: Including the Border Wars of the American Revolution, and Sketches of the Indian Campaign of Gernerals Harmar, St. Clair, and Wayne, and Other Matters Connected with the Indian Relations of the United States and Britain, from the Peace of 1783 to the Indian Peace of 1795*, Vol. 2 (1838; New York: Kraus, 1969), 16.

36   Wiley Sword, *President Washington's Indian War: The Struggle for the Old Northwest, 1790–1795* (Norman: University of Oklahoma Press, 1985), 38.

37   Denny, 'Military Journal', 297; *St. Clair Papers*, Vol. 2, 18–19.

38   *St. Clair Papers*, Vol. 2, 19.

39   *Michigan Pioneer and Historical Society, Historical Collections*, Vol. 24 (Lansing, MI: State Printers, 1908), 34.

40   American prairie grass is thick and can grow up to ten feet tall. William Lytle, 'Logan's Expedition against the Ma-co-chee Towns', in *Historical Collections of Ohio*, ed. Henry Howe, Vol. 2 (Cincinnati, OH: C. J. Krehbiel, 1902), 98.

41 Lytle, 'Logan's Expedition', 98.

42 *Michigan Pioneer*, Vol. 24, 37–8.

43 John Alexander McClung, *Sketches of Western Adventure: Containing an Account of the Most Interesting Incidents Connected with the Settlement of the West from 1755 to 1794* (Cincinnati, OH: U. James, 1839), 118; Kiernan, *Blood and Soil*, 325; Miller, *Forced Removal of American Indians from the Northeast*, 116.

44 *Michigan Pioneer*, Vol. 24, 34.

45 McClung, *Sketches of Western Adventure*, 118; *St. Clair Papers*, Vol. 2, 19. The 'shawl' might have been the flag; reports are unclear.

46 McClung, *Sketches of Western Adventure*, 118.

47 McClung, *Sketches of Western Adventure*, 118; Lytle, 'Logan's Expedition', 99. McClung, *Sketches of Western Adventure*, 118, claimed that McGary used a tomahawk; Denny, 'Military Journal', 298, also claimed that McGary used a tomahawk, while *St. Clair Papers*, Vol. 2, 19, had 'Melanthy' being 'shot down', clearly incorrect based on eye-witness accounts.

48 McClung, *Sketches of Western Adventure*, 118; Lytle, 'Logan's Expedition', 99.

49 McClung, *Sketches of Western Adventure*, 118.

50 *St. Clair Papers*, ii. 19; Denny, 'Military Journal', 298; *Michigan Pioneer*, Vol. 24, 34.

51 Denny, 'Military Journal', 298; *Michigan Pioneer*, Vol. 24, 34.

52 *Michigan Pioneer*, Vol. 24, 34.

53 *Michigan Pioneer*, Vol. 24, 34. The chief was often called '*Shade*' for short.

54 William Palmer (ed.), *Calendar of Virginia State Papers and Other Manuscripts*, 1 January 1785 to 2 July 1789, Vol. 4 (Richmond, VA: R. U. Derr, Superintendent of Public Printing, 1884), 258–60.

55 Patrick Henry and George Rogers Clark, *The Secret Orders & … 'Great Things Have Been Done by a Few Men …'* (Indianapolis: Indiana State Historical Society, 1974), original documents in unnumbered pages.

56 Clark, *The George Rogers Clark Papers*, Vol. 8, 429–30, 151–52; Paul V. Lutz, 'Fact and Myth concerning George Rogers Clark's Grant of Land at Paducah, Kentucky', *Register of the Kentucky Historical Society* 67, no. 3 (1969): 248, 250, 251–2.

57 Edmund Berkeley and Dorothy Smith Berkeley, *Dr. John Mitchell: The Man Who Made the Map of North America* (Chapel Hill: University of North Carolina Press, 1974), 202; map reproduction, 204–5.

58 [McKee], *Minutes of Debates in Council*.

59 *Outpost on the Wabash, 1787–1791*, ed. Gayle Thornbrough (Indianapolis: Indiana Historical Society, 1957), 7, 12–13.

60 Thornbrough, *Outpost on the Wabash*, 57.

61 Thornbrough, *Outpost on the Wabash*, 57, n. 29.

62 *St. Clair Papers*, Vol. 2, 115, 116. In his letter, St. Clair called the Ohio River 'the Mississippi' because Woodlanders defined the Ohio River as a northern leg of the Mississippi River, and settlers had not yet changed geographical designations of the rivers.

63 Mann, 'Fractal Massacres in the Old Northwest', 173.

64 *St. Clair Papers*, Vol. 2, 162.

65 See, for instance, the collated allegations in *American State Papers, Indian Affairs*, 85–98.

66 *American State Papers, Indian Affairs*, 100.

67 Thornbrough, *Outpost on the Wabash*, 114–17.

68 Charles Whittlesey, 'White Men as Scalpers', *Western Reserve and Northern Ohio Historical Society* 22 (1874): 6. The price of land in 1800 was $2 an acre (Anne Mackin, *Americans and Their Land: The House Built on Abundance* (Ann Arbor: University of Michigan Press, 2006), 86).

69 Kellogg (ed.), *Frontier Retreat on the Upper Ohio*, 379–80, n. 2; and Hartley, *The Life and Adventures of Lewis Wetzel*.

70 Thornbrough, *Outpost on the Wabash*, 247, 255.

71 *American State Papers, Indian Affairs*, 98–99.

72 Mann, 'Fractal Massacres in the Old Northwest', 173–74.

73 *American State Papers, Military Affairs*, 21–9, 34, 37; United States casualty statistics, 27; Thornbrough, *Outpost on the Wabash*, 268.

74 *American State Papers, Indian Affairs*, 104; Thornbrough, *Outpost on the Wabash*, 268.

75 *St. Clair Papers*, Vol. 2, 239.

76 *St. Clair Papers*, Vol. 2, 292–3, n. 1.

77 *American State Papers, Indian Affairs*, 131–32; *Michigan Pioneer and Historical Society*, Vol. 24, 261.

78 Scott, 'Report', in *American State Papers, Indian Affairs*, 131.

79 *Michigan Pioneer and Historical Society*, Vol. 24, 273.

80 Scott, 'Report', in *American State Papers, Indian Affairs*, 131–2.

81 Scott, 'Report', in *American State Papers, Indian Affairs*, 132.

82 Scott, 'Report', in *American State Papers, Indian Affairs*, 131.

83 *St. Clair Papers*, Vo. 2, 237; *American State Papers, Indian Affairs*, 131.

84 Winthrop Sargeant, 'Winthrop Sargeant's Diary while with General Arthur St. Clair's Expedition against the Indians', *Ohio Archaeological and Historical Quarterly* 33, no. 2 (July 1924): 261; and Mann, 'The Greenville Treaty of 1795', 135–201.

85 Sargeant, 'Diary', 260; Alan Axelrod, *Chronicle of the Indian Wars from Colonial Times to Wounded Knee* (New York: Prentice Hall, 1993), 125; James M. Perry, *Arrogant Armies: Great Military Disasters and the Generals behind Them* (New York: John Wiley, 1996), 58.

86 *St. Clair Papers*, Vol. 2, 188, 190; Alexrod, *Chronicle*, 125.

87 *St. Clair Papers*, Vol. 2, 282–6.

88 The United States, *Laws of the United States, Resolutions of Congress under the Confederation, Treaties, Proclamations, and Other Documents Having Operation and Respect to Public Lands* (Washington, DC: Jonathan Elliot, 1817), 63–71.

89 *St. Clair Papers*, ii. 228.

90 Mann, 'Fractal Massacres', 179.

91 A 1788 male Western Miami census (1/4 of population) was 1,290, yielding 5,160, all told, plus the 500 in Kekionga, for a grand total of 5,660. For the 1788 census, see Thornbrough, *Outpost on the Wabash*, 80. Kekionga was a large trading town with many non-Miamis and no Miami census in this period found, but 500 permanent Miami residents is not an unreasonable approximation. For the 1840 census, see Melissa A. Rinehart and Kate A. Berry, 'Kansas and the Exodus of the Miami Tribe', in *Tribes and the States: Geographies of Intergovernmental Interaction*, ed. Brad A. Bays and Erin Higan Fouberg (New York: Roman and Littlefield, 2002), 33.

92 Albert James Pickett, *History of Alabama, and Incidentally of Georgia and Mississippi, from the Earliest Period*, Vol. 1 (Charleston, SC: Walker and James, 1851), 311–16.

93 *American State Papers, Indian Affairs*, Vol. 1, 15, 29, 66, 81–2, 184, 197, 378, 458; Milfort, *Memoirs*, 91, 92; Claudio Saunt, *A New Order of Things: Property, Power, and the Transformation of the Creek Indians, 1733–1816* (New York: Cambridge University Press, 1999), 192, 196.

94 Francis Paul Prucha (ed.), 'Ordinance for the Regulation of Indian Affairs, 7 August 1786', *Documents of United States Indian Policy*, 3rd ed. (1975; Lincoln: University of Nebraska Press, 2000), 8–9.

95 Foster, *Collected Works of Benjamin Hawkins*, 24; Benjamin Hawkins, *Letters of Benjamin Hawkins* (Savannah, GA: The Morning News, 1916), 10.

96 Foster, *Collected Works of Benjamin Hawkins*, 102.

97 Foster, *Collected Works of Benjamin Hawkins*, 57–58.

98 Hewitt, *Notes on the Creek Indians*, 125; James Adair, *Adair's History of the American Indians*, ed. Samuel Cole Williams (New York: Promontory Press, 1930), 49.

99 For the concept and operation of the Twinned Cosmos, see Mann, *Spirits of Blood, Spirits of Breath*.

100 Buckner F. Melton Jr., *Aaron Burr: Conspiracy to Treason* (New York: Wiley & Sons, 2002); and Mann, *President by Massacre*, 8–13 and 131–38.

101 Jackson letters of 25 September 1806 and of 4 October 1806, in *Papers of Andrew Jackson*, Vol 2, 110-11.

102 Henry Adams, *John Randolph* (1882; New York: Houghton Mifflin Company, 1910), 218–19.

103 Indications of Jackson's involvement abound throughout the *Papers of Andrew Jackson*, Vol. 2, 110, 114, n. 14, 115–16, 116–17, 147–50, 309, 322, 398–9.

104 As plantation owner, slaver and slave dealer, see *Papers of Andrew Jackson*, Vol. 2, 40–1, 59–60, 96, 106–107, 225–6, 261–3, 269, 271, 273, 277–9, 281, 286–90, 293. As land speculator, Adams, *John Randolph*, letter of 30 April 1805, John Randolph to James Nicholson, 156.

105 Jessica Buckelew, 'The Man Who Sold the World: The Long Con of Discovery', *American Indian Law Journal* 3, no. 2 (2015): 363, 365, 365, n. 49, 427, n. 13; Miller, *Native America*, 4–5, 36, 40–1, 46, 66.

106 Henry deLeon Southerland, $1 Jerry Elijah Brown, *The Federal Road through Georgia, the Creek Nation, and Alabama, 1806-1836* (Tuscaloosa: University of Alabama Press, 1989), 1–2, 17.

107 Clarence Edwin Carter, *The Territorial Papers of the United States, Vol. 6: The Territory of Mississippi, 1809-1817* (Washington, DC: Government Printing Office, 1938), 213.

108 James F. Doster, 'Early Settlements on the Tombigbee and Tensaw Rivers', *The Alabama Review* 12, no. 2 (1959): 91, n. 14.

109 *American State Papers, Indian Affairs*, 811.

110 *American State Papers, Indian Affairs*, 811.

111 *Papers of Andrew Jackson*, letter of 27 May 298, 301.

112 *American State Papers, Indian Affairs*, 814; Henri, *The Southern Indians and Benjamin Hawkins*, 272.

113 Waselkov, *A Conquering Spirit*, 98; Carter, *The Territorial Papers of the United States*, 396.

114 Carter, *The Territorial Papers of the United States*, 396–7; Stiggins, *Creek Indian History*, 13, 100–1; Waselkov, *A Conquering Spirit*, 100 and 304, n. 12; Sean Michael O'Brien, *In Bitterness and in Tears: Andrew Jackson's Destruction of the Creek and Seminoles* (Westport, CT: Praeger, 2003), 41.

115 Waselkov, *A Conquering Spirit*, 102.

116 Stiggins, *Creek Indian History*, 114, was himself Creek and got his number of 726 attackers from Creek survivors. Henry S. Halbert and Timothy H. Ball, *The Creek War of 1813 and 1814* (Chicago, IL: Donohue & Henneberry, 1895), 153, figured that there were 1,000 Red Sticks, but they apparently threw in the 200 Red Sticks send to size up a second fort, Waselkov, *A Conquering Spirit*, 112.

117 Waselkov, *Conquering Spirit*, 106, and Table 2, 192. Writing in 1830, the Creek memorialist Stiggins, *Creek Indian History*, 112–33, inaccurately cited the settler tally of 303 dead in the Fort, but Waselkov's research completely belies the old statistics. See also Halbert and Ball, *The Creek War of 1813 and 1814*, 148.

118 Waselkov, *A Conquering Spirit*, 192–93, 229–57.

119 Carter, *The Territorial Papers of the United States*, 265.

120 *Papers of Andrew Jackson*, Vol. 2, 433, n. 2; David Crockett, *A Narrative of the Life of David Crockett of the State of Tennessee* (1834. Knoxville: The University of Tennessee Press, 1973), 75.

121 John Francis Hamtramck Claiborne, *The Life and Times of Gen. Sam Dale, the Mississippi Partisan* (New York: Harper & Brothers, 1860), 51.

122 John Brannan (ed.), *Official Letters of the Military and Naval Officers of the United States during the War with Great Britain in the Years 1812, 13, 14, & 15* (Washington City: Way & Gideon, 1823), passim; Crockett, *Life of David Crockett*, 87–99; Gregory A. Waselkov and Brian M. Wood, 'The Creek War of 1813–1814: Effects on Creek Society and Settlement Pattern', *Journal of Alabama Archaeology* 32, no. 1 (1986): 12–14. For a full recital of the entire Creek War, see Mann, *President by Massacre*, 158–210.

123 *Report on Indians Taxed and Indians Not Taxed in the United States (Except Alaska) at the Eleventh Census: 1890* (Washington, DC: Government Printing Office, 1894), 639.

124 S. Putnam Waldo, *Memoirs of Andrew Jackson, Major-General in the Army of the United States; and Commander in Chief of the Division of the South*, 5th ed. (Hartford, CT: J. & W. Russell, 1820), 73–74.

125 Crockett, *Life of David Crockett*, 88. 'Squaw' is the Iroquoian particle for genitals, used by settlers as a slur against Indigenous women. See Mann, *Iroquoian* Women, 19–24.

126 Crockett, *Life of David Crockett*, 88.

127 Crockett, *Life of David Crockett*, 89–90.

128 Coffee cites 200 dead in Brannan, *Official Letters*, 256; *Report on Indians Taxed and Indians Not Taxed*, 639; *Papers of Andrew Jackson*, Vol. 2, 444, 466, Jackson asserted 'there is no doubt but 200 was killed', but in his later official report to Pinckney, Jackson cited 186 dead and eighty (80) taken prisoner. Used here is Coffee's direct head count in his official report of eighty-four as prisoners.

129 Stiggins, *History of the Creek*, 123.

130 *Papers of Andrew Jackson*, Vol. 2, 456–7.

131 Williams, *Sketches of the War*, 241.

132 Brannan, *Official Letters*, 298–305; *Papers of Andrew Jackson*, Vol. 2, 462.

133 *Papers of Andrew Jackson*, Vol. 3, 12.

134 Thomas Woodward [*Chulatarla Emathla*], *Reminiscences of the Creek, or Muscogee Indians* (Montgomery, AL: Barret & Wimish, 1859), 89.

135 *Papers of Andrew Jackson*, Vol. 3, 54–55.

136 Woodward, *Reminiscences*, 88–9.

137 *Papers of Andrew Jackson*, Vol. 3, 38, 39 (note 4).

138 *Papers of Andrew Jackson*, Vol. 3, 52.

139 *Papers of Andrew Jackson*, Vol. 3, 53.

140 *Papers of Andrew Jackson*, Vol. 3, 54–55.

141 *Papers of Andrew Jackson*, Vol. 3, 53; Jackson upped his prisoner count to 347 in April, 54–55.

142 For a blow-by-blow account of the 'Creek War', see Mann, *President by Massacre*, 189–207.

Chapter 8

1 For an overview, see Richard Elphick and Hermann Giliomee, 'The Origins and Entrenchment of European Dominance at the Cape, 1652–c. 1840', in *The Shaping of South African Society, 1652–1840*, ed. Richard Elphick and Hermann Giliomee (Cape Town: Maskew Miller Longman, 1989), 521–66.

2 Penn, *The Forgotten Frontier*; and Martin Legassick, *The Politics of a South African Frontier: The Griqua, the Sotho-Tswana, and the Missionaries, 1780–1840* (Basel: Basler Afrika Bibliographien, 2010).

3 A pioneering study was that of P. J. Van der Merwe, *Die Noordwaartse Beweging van die Boere Voor die Groot Trek* (The Hague: W. P. Van Stockum and Son, 1937).

4 Nigel Penn, 'Pastoralists and Pastoralism in the Northern Cape Frontier Zone during the Eighteenth Century', *South Africa Archaeological Bulletin, Goodwin Series* 5 (1986): 62–8.

5 See, P. E. Roux, 'Die Verdedigingstelsel aan die Kaap onder die Hollands-Oosindiese Kompanjie, 1652–1795' (M.A., Stellenbosch University, 1925).

6   Penn, *Forgotten Frontier*, 108–12.

7   Penn, *Forgotten Frontier*, 112.

8   Donald Moodie, *The Record: Or A Series of Official Papers Relative to the Condition and Treatment of the Native Tribes of South Africa* (1838, 1842; Amsterdam and Cape Town: A.A. Balkema, 1960, 1966), part 3, 20.

9   Penn, *Forgotten Frontier*, 108–25.

10 Penn, *Forgotten Frontier*, 117.

11 Quoted by Jared McDonald, 'Stolen Childhoods: Cape San Child Captives and the Raising of Colonial Subjects in the Nineteenth Century Cape Colony', *Historia* 68, no. 2 (2023): 12. On the subject of San child captives, see also Jared McDonald, '"Like a Wild Beast, He Can be Got for the Catching": Child Forced Labour and the "Taming" of the San along the Cape's North-Eastern Frontier, c. 1806–1830', in *Genocide on Settler Frontiers: When Hunter-Gatherers and Commercial Stock Farmers Clash*, ed. Mohammed Adhikari (Cape Town: UCT Press, 2014), 60–87; and Lance van Sittert and Thierry Rousset, '"An Unbroken Line of Crime and Blood": Settler Militia and the Extermination and Enslavement of San in the Graaf-Reinet District of the Cape Colony, c. 1776–1825', in *Civilian Driven Violence and the Genocide of Indigenous Peoples in Settler Societies*, ed. M. Adhikari (Cape Town: UCT Press, 2020).

12 Penn, *Forgotten Frontier*, 117–42.

13 Van Sittert and Rousset, 'Unbroken Line', 95–6, estimate over a thousand San killed per decade from 1774 to c.1804.

14 For British peace initiatives regarding the San, see Nigel Penn, 'The British and the "Bushmen": The Massacre of the Cape San, 1795 to 1828', *Journal of Genocide Research* 15, no. 2 (2013): 183–200; and Nigel Penn, '"Civilising" the San: The First Mission to the San, 1791–1806', in *Claim to the Country: The Archive of Wilhelm Bleek and Lucy Lloyd*, ed. Pippa Skotness (Athens: Ohio, Ohio University Press, 2007), 90–117. See also Miklós Szalay, *The San and the Colonisation of the Cape, 1770–1789: Conflict, Incorporation, Acculturation* (Cologne: Rudiger Köppe, 1995).

15 Mostert, *Frontiers*; and John Laband, *The Land Wars: The Dispossession of the Khoisan and Ama Xhosa in the Cape Colony* (Cape Town: Penguin, 2020). and Laband, *The Land Wars*. See also Leo Switzer, *Power and Resistance in an African Society: The Ciskei Xhosa and the Making of South Africa* (Madison: University of Wisconsin Press, 1993); and Clifton Crais, *White Supremacy and Black Resistance in Pre-Industrial South Africa: The Making of the Colonial Order in the Eastern Cape, 1770–1865* (Cambridge: Cambridge University Press, 1992).

16 For the early history of the Xhosa, see Peires, *House of Phalo*.

17 For the implications of thinking in terms of boundaries, see Denver A. Webb, 'Further Beyond the Pale: Decolonisation, Historians and Military Discourse in the 18th and 19th Centuries on the Eastern Cape "Frontier"', *Journal of Southern African Studies* 43, no. 4 (2017): 681–97.

18. For the origins and consequences of the Third Frontier War, see Denver A. Webb, '"The War Took Its Origins in a Mistake": The Third War of Dispossession and Resistance in The Cape Of Good Hope Colony', *Scientia Militaria: South African Journal of Military Studies* 42, no. 2 (2014): 54–83.

19. Susan Newton-King and Vertrees Canby Malherbe, *The Khoikhoi Rebellion in the Eastern Cape (1799–1803)* (Cape Town: Centre for African Studies, University of Cape Town, 1993).

20. As notes Giliomee, 'The Eastern Frontier, 1770–1812', 438–9 and note.

21. For an excellent recent account of these wars, see Laband, *The Land Wars*, 105–50.

22. Giliomee, 'Eastern Frontier', 437.

23. G. E. Cory, *The Rise of South Africa, Volume One: From the Earliest Times to the Year 1820* (Cape Town: Stuik, 1965), 221; Giliomee, 'Eastern Frontier', 445.

24. Julie C. Wells, *The Return of Makhanda: Exploring the Legend* (Scottsville: University of KwaZulu-Natal Press, 2012), 93.

25. Collins' Report is contained in Moodie, *The Record*, Part V, 1808–1819, 1–60.

26. Moodie, *The Record*, Part V, 16–17.

27. John Milton, *The Edges of War: A History of Frontier Wars (1702–1878)* (Cape Town: Juta, 1983), 59–60.

28. MacLennan, *A Proper Degree of Terror*, 71.

29. For Cuyler's request, see Cory, *The Rise of South Africa*, 232.

30. MacLennan, *A Proper Degree of Terror*, 73; Cory, *The Rise of South Africa*, 234.

31. MacLennan, *A Proper Degree of Terror*, 73–4.

32. Bayly, *Imperial Meridian*; and Linda Colley, *Britons*.

33. MacLennan, *A Proper Degree of Terror*, 76–7.

34. For Graham see MacLennan, *A Proper Degree of Terror*.

35. Cory, *The Rise of South Africa*, 236–7.

36. Cory, *The Rise of South Africa*, 243.

37. Thomas Pringle, *Narrative of a Residence in South Africa* (London: Moxon, 1835), 274–5.

38. MacLennan, *A Proper Degree of Terror*, 80.

39. MacLennan, *A Proper Degree of Terror*, 118–19.

40. George Thompson, *Travels and Adventures in Southern Africa*, Vol. 2 (London: Henry Colburn, 1827), 195.

41 Pringle, *Narrative of a Residence in South Africa*, 275; MacLennan, *A Proper Degree of Terror*, 119.

42 Cory, *The Rise of South Africa*, 245.

43 John Campbell, *Travels in South Africa Travels in South Africa: Undertaken at the Request of the Missionary Society* (London: Black and Parry, 1815), 100–1.

44 MacLennan, *A Proper Degree of Terror*, 128–9.

45 Milton, *Edges of War*, 74. Peter Anderson has elaborated on the significance of this in P. R. Anderson, 'The Fish River Bush and the Place of History', *South African Historical Journal* 53, no. 1 (2005): 23–49.

46 MacLennan, *A Proper Degree of Terror*, 156–7.

47 C. W. Hutton (ed.), *The Autobiography of the Late Sir Andries Stockenström*, Vol. II (Cape Town: Jutta, 1887), 152–3.

48 Hutton, *Autobiography of Stockenstrom*, 138.

49 The core provisions of the Code were that all Khoikhoi should be in colonial employment, have a fixed place of residence and carry a pass if they wished to travel within the colony. See Elizabeth Elbourne, *Blood Ground: Colonialism, Missions, and the Contest for Christianity in the Cape Colony and Britain, 1799–1853* (Montreal: McGill-Queen's University Press, 2002), 165–5.

50 For the influence and significance of Slagtersnek on the construction of Afrikaner identity, see J. A. Heese, *Slagtersnek en sy Mense* (Cape Town: Tafelberg, 1973).

51 These ideas have a great deal in common with the millenarian message of Nongqawuse, the prophetess behind the Great Cattle Killing of the Xhosa in 1856. The classic account ahead of a burgeoning historiography is Jeffrey B. Peires, *The Dead Will Arise: Nongqawuse and the Great Xhosa Cattle-killing Movement of 1856* (Johannesburg: Ravan Press, 1989).

52 Wells, *Return of Makhanda*, ch. 2, is extremely sceptical about the traditional accounts of Makhanda's prophetic message. See also Peires, *House of Phalo*, ch. 5.

53 Janet Hodgson, Ntsikana's Great Hymn: A Xhosa Expression of Christianity in the Early 19th Century (Cape Town: Centre for African Studies, University of Cape Town, 1982).

54 Wells, *Makhanda*, 101–54.

55 Tim Couzens has lively accounts of both the battles of amaLinde and Grahamstown in his *South African Battles* (Johannesburg: Jonathan Ball, 2013).

56 MacLennan, *A Proper Degree of Terror*, 169–84.

57 Cory, *The Rise of South Africa*, 377–8.

58 One of the main sources of information about the battle is Pringle, *Narrative of a Residence in South Africa*, 282-3. See also Wells, *Makhanda*, 168-79; MacLennan, *A Proper Degree of Terror*, 190-9; and Cory, *The Rise of South Africa*, 386-91.

59 MacLennan, *A Proper Degree of Terror*, 183.

60 Cory, *The Rise of South Africa*, 390; MacLennan, *A Proper Degree of Terror*, 197.

61 MacLennan, *A Proper Degree of Terror*, 212.

62 MacLennan *A Proper Degree of Terror*, 207; Pringle, *Narrative of a Residence in South Africa*, 284.

63 Makhanda would subsequently drown in escaping from Robben Island in August 1820. He escaped in the company of Khoikhoi rebels David Stuurman and Hans Trompeter, who survived to be recaptured, the former eventually being transported to New South Wales. Stuurman, who had escaped from Robben Island before, was recaptured during the war of 1819. See Wells, *Makhanda*, 215-39.

64 MacLennan, *A Proper Degree of Terror*, 218.

65 Jeffrey B. Peires, 'The British and the Cape 1814-1834', in *The Shaping of South African Society*, ed. Elphick and Giliomee, 483.

66 For Maqoma see Timothy J. Stapleton, *Maqoma: The Legend of a Great Xhosa Warrior* (Kuilsrivier: Amava Heritage Publishing, 2016).

67 See Mostert, *Frontiers*; Crais, *White Supremacy*; Andrew Bank, 'The Return of the Noble Savage: The Changing Image of Africans in Cape Colonial Art, 1800-1850', *South African Historical Journal* 39 (1998): 17-43; Andrew Bank, 'Of "Native Skulls" and "Noble Caucasians": Phrenology in Colonial South Africa', *Journal of Southern African Studies* 22, no. 3 (1996): 387-403.

68 For Barrow, see Nigel Penn, 'Mapping the Cape: John Barrow and the First British Occupation of the Cape Colony, 1795-1803', *Pretexts* 4, no. 2 (1993): 20-43. For Daniell, see Michael Stevenson, *Samuel Daniell: An Enigmatic Life in Southern Africa and Ceylon, 1799-1811* (Cape Town: Jonathan Ball, 2025).

Epilogue

1 Connor, *Australian Frontier Wars*, 49-51.

2 Connor, *Australian Frontier Wars*, 115-17.

3 Hutton (ed.), *Autobiography of Stockenstrom*, Vol. 1, 213-14.

4 In Percival R. Kirby, *Sir Andrew Smith, M.D., K.C.B. His Life Letters and Works, 1797-1850* (Cape Town: Balkema, 1965), 66.

5   Kirby, *Sir Andrew Smith*, 67–75.

6   Kirby, *Sir Andrew Smith*, 76. According to Kirby, Smith's report exists only in the form of his rough notes in the Cape Archives.

7   Penn, 'The British and the "Bushmen"', 197.

8   See Jay Naidoo, 'Was the 50th Ordinance a Charter of Khoi Liberties?' in *Tracking Down Historical Myths: Eight South African Cases*, ed. Jay Naidoo (Johannesburg: Ravan Press, 1989); Robert Ross, 'The Cape Economy and the Cape Gentry', in *Beyond the Pale: Essays on the History of Colonial South Africa*, ed. Robert Ross (Middletown, CT: Wesleyan University Press, 1993), 13–49; Robert Ross, 'Rather Mental Than Physical: Emancipations and the Cape Economy', in Breaking the Chains: Slavery and its Legacy in the Nineteenth Century Cape Colony, ed. Nigel Worden and Clifton Crais (Johannesburg: University of the Witwatersrand Press, 1994), 145–68; Peires, 'The British and the Cape 1814–1834', in *The Shaping of South African Society*, ed. Elphick and Giliomee, 472–518; and Elbourne, *Blood Ground*, 254–8.

9   Andrew Bank, 'Losing faith in the civilizing mission: the premature decline of humanitarian liberalism at the Cape, 1840–60', in *Empire and Others: British Encounters with Indigenous Peoples, 1600–1850*, ed. Martin Daunton and Rick Halpern (Philadelphia: University of Pennsylvania Press, 1999), 364–83. For the debate over the decline of Cape Liberalism see also Timothy Keegan, *Colonial South Africa and the Origins of the Racial Order* (Cape Town: David Philip, 1996), ch. 4; Crais, *White Supremacy*; and Legassick, *The Struggle for the Eastern Cape*.

10 For a comparison of the Irish and North American colonial situation, see Katie Kane, 'Nits Make Lice: Drogheda, Sand Creek and the Poetics of Colonial Extermination', *Cultural Critique*, 42 (Spring, 1999): 81–103. For recent works on the killing of North American Indians, see Ned Blackhawk, *Violence over the Land: Indians and Empires in the Early American West* (Cambridge, MA: Harvard University Press, 2006); Benjamin Madley, *An American Genocide: The United States and the California Indian Catastrophe, 1846–1873* (New Haven, CT: Yale University Press, 2017); and Ostler, *Surviving Genocide*.

11 Elizabeth Furse and Robert J. Miller, 'American Indian Nations, Indian Treaties, and Tribal Sovereignty', *Government, Law and Policy Journal* 8, no. 1 (2006): 10–11; Jane Burbank and Frederick Cooper, *Empires in World History: Power and the Politics of Difference* (Princeton, NJ: Princeton University Press, 2011), 263.

12 Walter, *Colonial Violence*, 80.

13 Robert V. Remini, *Andrew Jackson and His Indian Wars* (Harmondsworth: Penguin Books, 2002), 269; Walter, *Colonial Violence*, 138.

14 Donna Akers, 'Removing the Heart of the Choctaw People: Indigenous Removal from a Native Perspective', *American Indigenous Culture and Research Journal* 23, no. 3 (1999): 74.

15 United States, Department of the Interior, *Annual Report of the Commissioner of Indian Affairs for the Fiscal Year Ended 30 June 1898* (Washington, DC: Government Printing Office, 1898), 485; J. David Smith, *The Eugenic Assault on America: Scenes in Red, White, and Black* (Fairfax, VA: George Mason University, 1993), 89, 100, 111.

16 Ronald Takaki, 'The Metaphysics of Civilization: Indians and the Age of Jackson', in *From Different Shores: Perspectives on Race and Ethnicity in America*, ed. Ronald Takaki (New York: Oxford University Press, 1987), 61–3.

17 Walter, *Colonial Violence*, 66.

18 See the population trend in individual nations in Ostler, *Surviving Genocide*.

19 M. Annette Jaimes, 'Introduction: Sand Creek: The Morning After', in *The State of Native America: Genocide, Colonization, and Resistance*, ed. M. Annette Jaimes (Boston, MA: South End Press, 1992), 6–7.

20 Caldwell, 'Colonial Population 1788–1825', 25.

21 *Sydney Gazette*, February 1822.

22 For the North American experience, Smedley, *Race in North America*, 165–6.

23 Ryan, *Tasmanian Aborigines*, 68–9.

24 See, for example, Mark Finnane, 'Law and Regulation', in *The Cambridge History of Australia*, ed. Alison Bashford and Stuart Macintyre, Vol. 1 (Cambridge: Cambridge University Press, 2013), 391–3.

25 Tom Lawson, *The Last Man: A British Genocide in Tasmania* (London: I. B. Taurus, 2014), 200–2.

26 See Gallois, *A History of Violence in the Early Algerian Colony*; Benjamin Claude Brower, *A Desert Named Peace: The Violence of France's Empire in the Algerian Sahara, 1844-1902* (New York: Columbia University Press, 2009); Bertrand Taithe, *The Killer Trail: A Colonial Scandal in the Heart of Africa* (Oxford: Oxford University Press, 2009).

27 See, for example, Cheryl B. Welch, 'Colonial Violence and the Rhetoric of Evasion: Tocqueville on Algeria', *Political Theory* 31, no. 2 (2003): 235–64; Cheryl B. Welch, 'Out of Africa: Tocqueville's Imperial Voyages', *Review of Middle East Studies* 45, no. 1 (2011): 53–61; Roger Boesche, 'The Dark Side of Tocqueville: On War and Empire', *Review of Politics* 67, no. 4 (2005): 737–52; and more broadly on Tocqueville in Algeria, Jeremy Jennings, *Travels with Tocqueville beyond America* (Harvard: Harvard University Press, 2023), 169–212.

28 Michael Shurkin, 'French Liberal Governance and the Emancipation of Algeria's Jews', *French Historical Studies* 33, no. 2 (2010): 265–9.

29 To use an expression by Fullagar and McDonnell, 'Introduction: Empire, Indigeneity, and Revolution', 6.

30 Walter, *Colonial Violence*, 256.

31 According to Beatrice de Graaf, *Fighting Terror After Napoleon: How Europe Became Secure after 1815* (Cambridge: Cambridge University Press, 2020), 31–3. See also John M. MacKenzie, 'European Imperialism: A Zone of Cooperation Rather than Competition?' in *Imperial Co-Operation and Transfer, 1870–1930: Empires and Encounters*, ed. Volker Barth and Roland Cvetkovski (London: Bloomsbury, 2015), 39–40. A somewhat different view is propounded by Edward Ingram, 'Bellicism as Boomerang. The Eastern Question during the Vienna System', in *The Transformation of European Politics, 1763–1848: Episode or Model in Modern History?* ed. Peter Krüger and Paul W. Schroeder (Münster: LIT Verlag, 2002), 205–26, who argues that 'the [European] core reposed in equilibrium only because it exported to the periphery its previous bellicist style'.

32 Erik de Lange, 'The Congress System and the French Invasion of Algiers, 1827–1830', *Historical Journal* 64, no. 4 (2021): 940–62.

33 Walter, *Colonial Violence*, 136–40, 149–50; A. Dirk Moses, *The Problems of Genocide: Permanent Security and the Language of Transgression* (Cambridge: Cambridge University Press, 2021), 252.

34 Beatrice Heuser, *War: A Genealogy of Western Ideas and Practices* (Oxford: Oxford University Press, 2021), 48.

35 For Central America see, Robert W. Patch, 'Culture, Community, and "Rebellion" in the Yucatec Maya Uprising of 1761', in *Native Resistance and the Pax Colonial in New Spain*, ed. Susan Schroeder (Lincoln: University of Nebraska Press, 1998), 67–83; and Robert W. Patch, *Maya Revolt and Revolution in the Eighteenth Century* (2nd ed., London: Routledge, 2015). Alexander Downes, *Targeting Civilians in War* (Ithaca, NY: Cornell University Press, 2008), 1–9, argues that targeting non-combatants was a military strategy chosen by the political and military elites. He is, admittedly, talking about the twentieth century, but the same rationale can be applied to earlier polities dealing with 'potentially troublesome populations dwelling on land that expansionist states seek to annex'.

36 For the Australian example of humanitarian discourse and the tensions with those who propounded terror and punishment, see Anna Johnston, *The Antipodean Laboratory: Making Colonial Knowledge, 1770–1870* (Cambridge: Cambridge University Press, 2023).

37 Van Sittert and Rousset, 'An Unbroken Line of Crimes and Blood', 86–113.

38 On the denial of settler violence in the Australian context, see Bain Attwood, 'Denial in a Settler Society: The Australian Case', *History Workshop Journal* 84 (Autumn 2017): 24–43.

39 See, for example, Ford, *Settler Sovereignty*, 97–9, for the case of the murder of two Aboriginal boys on the Hawkesbury in 1799.

40 See, for example, Nigel Penn, 'Casper, Crebis and the Knegt: Rape, Homicide and Violence in the Eighteenth-Century Rural Western Cape', *South African Historical Journal* 66, no. 4 (2014): 611–34.

41 Jeremy Martens, '"In a State of War": Governor James Stirling, Extrajudicial Violence and the Conquest of Western Australia's Avon Valley, 1830–1840', *History Australia* 19, no. 4 (2022): 668–86.

42 Jane Lydon and Lyndall Ryan, 'Remembering Myall Creek', in *c*, 1–15; and Ryan, 'Establishing a Code of Silence'.

43 Mann takes exception to the explanations surrounding revenge killings provided by historians such as Wayne E. Lee, 'Peace Chiefs and Blood Revenge: Patterns of Restraint in Native American Warfare, 1500–1800', *Journal of Military History* 71, no. 3 (2007): 701–2, believing that their views are 'culturally confused'.

44 Documents logged as received, *Minutes of the Supreme Executive Council of Pennsylvania from Its Organization to the Termination of the Revolution*, Vol. 13 (Harrisburg, PA: Theo. Fenn, 1853), 297; documents as disappearing, Wilshire Consul Butterfield, *Washington-Irvine Correspondence, the Official Letters* (Madison, WI: David Atwood, 1882), 245, n. 3.

45 Jean-Clément Martin, 'Les mots de la violence: les guerres révolutionnaires', in *La Violence de guerre 1914–1945: approches comparées des deux conflits mondiaux*, ed. Stéphane Audoin-Rouzeau et al. (Paris: Éd. Complexe, 2002), 34.

46 https://c21ch.newcastle.edu.au/colonialmassacres/introduction.php

Bibliography

Printed primary sources

American State Papers, Indian Affairs, 1815–1827, 2 Vols. Washington, DC: Gales & Seaton, 1832.

Annual Report of the Commissioner of Indian Affairs for the Fiscal Year Ended June 30, 1898. Washington, DC: Government Printing Office, 1898.

Bangofsky, Georges. 'Les Étapes de Georges Bangofsky, officier lorrain. Extraits de son journal de campagnes (1797–1815)', *Mémoires de l'Académie de Stanislas* 2 (1905): 241–340.

Barada, Jean. 'Lettres d'Alexandre Ladrix', *Bulletin de la Société d'histoire et d'archéologie du Gers* 28 (1927): 231–8.

Baudin, Nicholas. *The Journal of Post Captain Nicolas Baudin. Commander-in-Chief of the Corvettes Géographe and Naturaliste, Assigned by Order of the Government to a Voyage of Discovery*, trans. Christine Cornell. Adelaide: Libraries Board of South Australia, 1974.

Bausset, Louis-François-Joseph. *Mémoires anecdotiques sur l'intérieur du Palais et sur quelques évènemens de l'Empire depuis 1805 jusqu'au 1er mai 1814, pour servir à l'histoire de Napoléon*, 2 Vols. Paris: Baudouin frères, 1827.

Beaglehole, John Cawte, ed. *The Journals of Captain James Cook*, 3 Vols. London: Hakluyt Society, 1955–1974.

Bergh, Albert Ellery, ed. *The Writings of Thomas Jefferson*, 20 Vols. Washington, DC: The Thomas Jefferson Memorial Association, 1907.

Bernard, Léonce. *Les prisonniers de guerre du Premier Empire*. Paris: Christian, 2000.

Bernoyer, François. *Avec Bonaparte en Egypte et en Syrie, 1798–1800: 19 lettres inédites*. Poet-Laval: Éditions Curandera, 1981.

Bigarré, Auguste-Julien. *Mémoires du Général Bigarré, 1775–1813*. Paris: Grenadier, 2002.

Bladon, Frank Murcot, ed. *Historical Records of New South Wales*, 7 Vols. Sydney: Government Printer, 1897.

Bonaparte, Napoleon. *Correspondance de Napoléon Ier, publiée par ordre de l'Empereur Napoléon III*, 32 Vols. Paris: Impr. Impériale, 1858–69.

Bonaparte, Napoleon. *La Correspondance de Napoléon*, 15 Vols. Paris: Fayard, 2004–2018.

Bonwick, James. *The Last of the Tasmanians: Or, The Black War of Van Diemen's Land The Last of the Tasmanians*. London: Sampson Low, Son & Marston, 1870.

Bossu, Jean-Bernard. *Nouveau Voyages aux Indies Occidentales; contenant une relation des differens peuples qui habitent les environs du grand fleuve Saint-Louis, appelle vulgairement le Mississippi; leur religion; leur gouvernement; leurs murs; leurs guerres & leur commerce, Premiere Partie*. Paris: Le Jay, 1768.

Bossu, Jean-Bernard. *New Travels in North America by Jean-Bernard Bossu, 1770–1771*, ed. Samuel Dorris Dickinson. Natchitoches, LA: Northwestern State University Press, 1982.

Boulart, Jean-François. *Mémoires militaires du général Bon Boulart sur les guerres de la république et de l'empire*. Paris: A la librairie illustrée, 1892.

Bourgogne, Adrien. *Mémoires du sergent Bourgogne*. Paris: Arléa, 1992.

Bourne, Edward Gaylord. *Narratives of the Career of Hernando de Soto*, 2 Vols. London: David Nutt, 1905.

Brannan, John, ed. *Official Letters of the Military and Naval Officers of the United States during the War with Great Britain in the Years 1812, 13, 14, & 15*. Washington City: Way & Gideon, 1823.

British Parliamentary Papers, House of Commons. London: H. M. Stationery Office, 1831.

Butterfield, Wilshire Consul. *Washington-Irvine Correspondence, the Official Letters*. Madison, WI: David Atwood, 1882.

Campbell, John. *Travels in South Africa Travels in South Africa: Undertaken at the Request of the Missionary Society*. London: Black and Parry, 1815.

Carter, Clarence Edwin. *The Territorial Papers of the United States, Vol. 6: The Territory of Mississippi, 1809–1817*. Washington, DC: Government Printing Office, 1938.

Castellane, Esprit Victor Elisabeth Boniface. *Journal du maréchal Castellane, 1804–1862*, 5 Vols. Paris: E. Plon, Nourrit et Cie, 1895–97.

Charlevoix, Pierre de. *Journal of a Voyage to North America*, 2 Vols. 1761 reprint. Ann Arbor, MI: University Microfilms, 1966.

Chevalier, Jean-Michel. *Souvenirs des guerres napoléoniennes*. Paris: Hachette, 1970.

Clark, George Rogers. *The George Rogers Clark Papers, 1771–1781*, ed. Clarence Walworth Alvord, Vol. 8. Springfield, IL: Trustees of the Illinois State Historical Library, 1912.

Collections of the Illinois State Historical Library. Springfield, IL: Illinois State Historical Library, 1926.

Collins, David. *An Account of the English Colony of New South Wales by David Collins*, ed. Brian Fletcher. 2 Vols. Sydney: The Royal Australian Historical Society and A.H. & A.W. Reed, 1975.

Condorcet, Marie-Jean-Antoine-Nicolas de. *Outlines of an Historical View of the Progress of the Human Mind*. Philadelphia, PA: M. Carey, 1795.

Cook, Frederick. *Journals of the Military Expedition of Major General John Sullivan against the Six Nations of Indians in 1779*. 1887 reprint. Freeport, NY: Books for Libraries, 1972.

Copies of All Correspondence between Lieutenant-Governor Arthur and His Majesty's Secretary of State for the Colonies, on the Subject of the Military Operations Lately Carried on Against the Aboriginal Inhabitants of Van Diemen's Land, British Parliamentary Papers, Paper no. 259. London: House of Commons, 1831.

Crockett, David. *A Narrative of the Life of David Crockett of the State of Tennessee*, 1834 reprint. Knoxville: The University of Tennessee Press, 1973.

Denny, Ebenezer. 'Denny's Military Journal', *Memoirs of the Historical Society of Pennsylvania* 7 (1860): 237–409.

Des Odoards, Fantin, Louis Florimond. *Journal du Général Fantin des Odoards, étapes d'un officier de la Grande Armée, 1800–1830*. Paris: E. Plon, Nourrit et Cie, 1895.

Duhesme, Guillaume-Philibert. *Essai sur l'infanterie légère, ou Traité des petites opérations de la guerre, à l'usage des jeunes officiers*. Paris: L.-G. Michaud, 1814.

Fitzpatrick, John C., ed. *The Writings of George Washington from the Original Manuscript Sources, 1745–1799*, 39 Vols. Washington, DC: Government Printing Office, 1938.

Foster, Thomas, ed. *The Collected Works of Benjamin Hawkins, 1796–1810*. Tuscaloosa: University of Alabama Press, 2003.

François, Charles. *Le journal d'un officier français ou Les cahiers du capitaine François: 1792–1815*. Paris: Charles Carrington, 1903.

Gille, Louis-Philippe. *Les Prisonniers de Cabrera, mémoires d'un conscrit de 1808*. Paris: Victor-Havard, 1892.

Guingret, Pierre. *Relation historique et militaire de la campagne de Portugal sous le maréchal Masséna*. Limoges: Bargeas, 1817.

Gunson, Neil, ed. *Australian Reminiscences & Papers of L.E. Threlkeld, Missionary to the Aborigines, 1824–1859*, 2 Vols. Canberra: Australian Institute of Aboriginal Studies, 1974.

Haegele, Vincent, ed. *Napoléon et Joseph Bonaparte: correspondence intégrale 1784–1818*. Paris: Tallandier, 2007.

Hartley, Cecil B. *The Life and Adventures of Lewis Wetzel, the Virginia Ranger*. Philadelphia, PA: G. G. Evans, 1860.

Hauterive, Ernest de. *La Police secrète du premier Empire, bulletins quotidiens adressés par Fouché à l'Empereur*, 5 Vols. Paris: Clavreuil, 1908–1964.

Hawkins, Benjamin. *Letters of Benjamin Hawkins*. Savannah: The Morning News, 1916.

Heckewelder, John. *A Narrative of the Mission of the United Brethren among the Delaware and Mohegan Indians from Its Commencement in the Year 1740, to the Close of the Year 1808*. Philadelphia, PA: M'Carthy & Davis, 1820.

Heckewelder, John. *History, Manners, and Customs of the Indian Nations Who Once Inhabited Pennsylvania and the Neighboring States*. 1820 reprint. New York: Arno Press, 1971.

Henry, Patrick and George Rogers Clark. *The Secret Orders & … 'Great Things Have Been Done by a Few Men …'*. Indianapolis, IN: Indiana State Historical Society, 1974.

Hutton, C. W. ed. *The Autobiography of the Late Sir Andries Stockenström*, 2 Vols. Cape Town: Jutta, 1887.

Irving, Washington. *A History of New York, from the Beginning of the World to the End of the Dutch Dynasty*, ed. Stanley Williams and Tremaine McDowell. 1809 reprint. New York: Harcourt, Brace, 1927.

Journals of the American Congress, from 1774 to 1788, 4 Vols. Washington, DC: Way and Gideon, 1823.

Kergorre, Alexandre Bellot de. *Journal d'un commissaire des guerres pendant le Premier Empire (1806–1821)*. Paris: La Vouivre, 1997.

Kirby, Percival R. *Sir Andrew Smith, M.D., K.C.B. His Life Letters and Works, 1797–1850*. Cape Town: Balkema, 1965.

Labaume, Eugène. *Relation circonstanciée de la campagne de Russie*. Paris: Pancoucke, 1815.

Lafitau, Joseph François. *Moeurs des sauvages Ameriquains, comparées aux moeurs des premiers temps*, 2 Vols. Paris: Saugrain, 1724.

Lafitau, Joseph François. *Customs of the American Indians Compared with the Customs of Primitive Times*, ed. and trans. William N. Fenton and Elizabeth M. Moore, 2 Vols. 1724 reprint. Toronto: The Champlain Society, 1974.

Lahontan, Louis Armand de Lom d' Arce, Baron de. *New Voyages to North America*, ed. Reuben Gold Thwaites, 2 Vols. 1703 reprint. Chicago, IL: A. C. McClurg, 1905.

Las Cases, Emmanuel de. *Le Mémorial de Sainte-Hélène*, 2 Vols. Paris: Flammarion, 1983.

Lavaux, François. *Mémoires de Campagnes: 1793–1814*. Paris: Arléa, 2004.

Laws of the United States, Resolutions of Congress under the Confederation, Treaties, Proclamations, and Other Documents Having Operation and Respect to Public Lands. Washington, DC: Jonathan Elliot, 1817.

Lecestre, Léon ed. *Lettres inédites de Napoléon*, 2 Vols. Paris: E. Plon, Nourrit et cie, 1897.

Lettow-Vorbeck, Oscar von, ed. *Der Krieg von 1806 und 1807*, 3 Vols. Berlin: Ernst Siegfried Mittler und Sohn, 1891–1896.

Looney, J. Jefferson, ed. *The Papers of Thomas Jefferson: Retirement Series, Vol. 7: November 1813 to September 1814*. Princeton, NJ: Princeton University Press, 2010.

Mandelbrote, H. J., ed. *A Geographical and Topographical Description of the Cape of Good Hope by O.F. Mentzel*, 3 Vols. Cape Town: Van Riebeeck Society, 1944.

Marcel, Nicolas. *Campagnes du capitaine Marcel, du 69e de ligne, en Espagne et en Portugal (1804–1814)*. Paris: Plon-Nourrit, 1913.

McKee, Alexander. *Minutes of Debates in Council on the Banks of the Ottawa River (Commonly Called the Miamis of the Lake), November 1791*. Philadelphia, PA: William Young, Bookseller, 1792.

Michigan Pioneer and Historical Society, Historical Collections, 40 Vols. Lansing, MI: State Printers, 1887–1912.

Milfort, Louis LeClerc. *Memoirs, or a Quick Glance at My Various Travels and My Sojourn in the Creek Nation*, trans. and ed. Ben C. McCary. 1802 reprint. Kennesaw, GA: Continental Book, 1959.

Minutes of the Provincial Council of Pennsylvania from the Organization to the Termination of the Proprietary Government, 10 Vols. Harrisburg: Theo. Fenn, 1852.

Minutes of the Supreme Executive Council of Pennsylvania from Its Organization to the Termination of the Revolution, 16 Vols. Harrisburg, PA: Theo. Fenn, 1853.

Miot, Jacques. *Mémoires pour servir à l'histoire des expéditions en Égypte et en Syrie, pendant les années VI, VII et VIII de la république française*, 2nd ed. Paris: Le Normant, 1814.

Moodie, Donald. *The Record: Or A Series of Official Papers Relative to the Condition and Treatment of the Native Tribes of South Africa*. 1838, 1842 reprint. Amsterdam and Cape Town: A.A. Balkema, 1960, 1966.

Moser, Harold D. and Sharon Macpherson, ed. *The Papers of Andrew Jackson*, 6 Vols. Knoxville: The University of Tennessee Press, 1984.

Muir, Rory, ed. *At Wellington's Right Hand: The Letters of Lieutenant-Colonel Sir Alexander Gordon, 1808–1815*. Phoenix Mill: Sutton, 2003.

Nicholls, Mary, ed. *The Diary of the Reverend Robert Knopwood 1803–1838*. Hobart: Tasmanian Historical Research Association, 1977.

Orr, Charles. *The History of the Pequot War: The Contemporary Accounts of Mason, Underhill, and Gardner*. Cleveland, OH: The Helman-Taylor, 1897.

Palmer, William, ed. *Calendar of Virginia State Papers and Other Manuscripts, January 1, 1785 to July 2, 1789*, 11 Vols. Richmond, VA: R. U. Derr, Superintendent of Public Printing, 1884.

Pelleport, Pierre, Vicomte de. *Souvenirs militaire et intimes du général vicomte de Pelleport de 1793 à 1853*, 2 Vols. Paris: Didier, 1857.

Peltier, Jean-Gabriel. *Examen de la campagne de Buonaparte en Italie par un témoin oculaire*. Paris: Le Normant, 1814.

Pickett, Albert James. *History of Alabama, and Incidentally of Georgia and Mississippi, from the Earliest Period*, 3rd ed., 2 Vols. Charleston, SC: Walker and James, 1851.

Plomley, N. J. B., ed. *Friendly Mission: The Tasmanian Journals of George August Robinson 1829–1834*. Hobart: Queen Victoria Museum and Art Gallery and Quintus Publishing, 2008.

Pringle, Thomas. *Narrative of a Residence in South Africa*. London: Moxon, 1835.

Prucha, Francis Paul, ed. *Documents of United States Indian Policy*, 3rd ed. 1975 reprint. Lincoln: University of Nebraska Press, 2000.

Report on Indians Taxed and Indians Not Taxed in the United States (Except Alaska) at the Eleventh Census: 1890. Washington, DC: Government Printing Office, 1894.

Rondthaler, Edward. *Life of John Heckewelder*, ed. B. H. Coates. Philadelphia, PA: Townsend Ward, 1847.

Seaver, James E. *A Narrative of the Life of Mrs. Mary Jemison*. 1823 reprint. Syracuse, NY: Syracuse University Press, 1990.

Seineke, Kathrine Wagner. *The George Rogers Clark Adventure in the Illinois and Selected Documents of the American Revolution at the Frontier Posts*. New Orleans, LA: Polyanthos, 1981.

Sipe, C. Hale. *The Indian Wars of Pennsylvania: An Account of the Indian Events, in Pennsylvania, of the French and Indian War, Pontiac's War, Lord Dunmore's War, the Revolutionary War and the Indian Uprising from 1789 to 1795*. Harrisburg, PA: The Telegraph Press, 1929.

Smith, William Henry. *The St. Clair Papers: The Life and Public Services of Arthur St. Clair; Soldier of the Revolutionary War; President of the Continental Congress, and Governor of the North-Western Territory; with His Correspondence and Other Papers*, 2 Vols. Cincinnati, OH: Robert Clark, 1882.

Sparks, Jared, ed. *The Writings of George Washington; Being His Correspondence, Addresses, Messages, and Other Papers, Official and Private, Selected and Published from the Original Manuscripts*, 12 Vols. Boston, MA: Little, Brown, 1855.

Stokes, J. Lort. *Discoveries in Australia: With an Account of the Coasts and Rivers Explored and Surveyed during the Voyage of H.M.S. Beagle 1837*, 2 Vols. London: T. and W. Boone, 1846.

Stone, William, ed. *The Life and Times of Sir William Johnson, Bart*. 2 Vols. Albany, NY: H. Munsell, 1865.

Stone, William L. *Life of Joseph Brant-Thayendanegea: Including the Border Wars of the American Revolution, and Sketches of the Indian Campaign of Gernerals Harmar, St. Clair, and Wayne, and Other Matters Connected with the Indian Relations of the United

States and Britain, from the Peace of 1783 to the Indian Peace of 1795. 2 Vols. 1838 reprint. New York: Krause, 1969.
Tench, Watkin. *Sydney's First Four Years* being a reprint of *A Narrative of the Expedition to Botany Bay* and *A Complete Account of the Settlement at Port Jackson*, with an introduction and annotation by L. F. Fitzhardinge. Sydney: Library of Australian History, 1970.
Thirion, Auguste. *Souvenirs militaires*. Paris: Librairie des Deux Empires, 1998.
Thompson, George. *Travels and Adventures in Southern Africa*, 2 Vols. London: Henry Colburn, 1827.
Thornbrough, Gayle, ed. *Outpost on the Wabash, 1787–1791, Letters of Brigadier General Josiah Harmar and Major John Francis Hamtramck, and Other Letters and Documents Selected from the Harmar Papers in the William L. Clements Library*. (Indianapolis, IN: Indiana Historical Society, 1957),
Thwaites, Reuben Gold, ed. and trans. *Les Relations de Jésuites, or The Jesuit Relations: Travels and Explorations of the Jesuit Missionaries in New France, 1610–1791*, 73 Vols. New York: Pageant Book, 1959.
Vega, Garcilasco de la. *La Florida del Ynca: Historia del Adelantado de Hernando de Soto, Gouenador y capitan general del Reyno de la Florida*. Lisbon: Pedro Crossbeek, 1605.
Vigier, Comte Henri de. *Davout, maréchal d'empire, duc d'Auerstaedt, prince d'Eckmühl (1770–1823)*, 2 Vols. Paris: P. Ollendorff, 1898.
Villers, Charles de. *Lettre à Madame la Comtesse F ... de B ... [Fanny de Beauharnais], contenant un récit des événemens qui se sont passés à Lubeck dans la journée du ... 6 novembre 1806 et les suivantes*. Amsterdam: bureau des arts et d'industrie, 1807.
Waddell, Louis M., ed. *The Papers of Henry Bouquet*, 6 Vols. Harrisburg, PA: The Pennsylvania Historical and Museum Commission, 1994.
Waldo, S. Putnam. *Memoirs of Andrew Jackson, Major-General in the Army of the United States and Commander in Chief of the Division of the South*, 5th ed. Hartford, CT: J. & W. Russell, 1820.
Washington, George. *The Papers of George Washington, July-November 1790*, ed. William Wright Abbott, Philander D. Chase, Dorothy Twohig, Mark A. Mastromarino, Vol. 6. Charlottesville: University of Virginia Press, 1996.
Watson, Frederick, ed. *Historical Records of Australia. Series I. Governors' despatches to and from England*, 33 Vols. Sydney: Library Committee of the Commonwealth Parliament, 1914–25.
Woodward, Thomas [*Chulatarla Emathla*]. *Reminiscences of the Creek, or Muscogee Indians*. Montgomery, AL: Barret & Wimish, 1859.

Unpublished dissertations

Ball, Margaret. 'Grim Commerce: Scalps, Bounties, and the Transformation of Trophy-Taking in the Early American Northeast, 1450–1770'. PhD thesis, University of Colorado Boulder, 2013.

Donohoe, Helen F. 'Dancing with Scalps: Native North American Women, White Men and Ritual Violence in the Eighteenth Century', PhD thesis, University of Glasgow, 2013.

Roux, P. E. 'Die Verdedigingstelsel aan die Kaap onder die Hollands-Oosindiese Kompanjie, 1652–1795'. M.A., Stellenbosch University, 1925.

Secondary literature

Abler, Thomas S. 'Scalping, Torture, Cannibalism and Rape: An Ethnohistorical Analysis of Conflicting Cultural Values in War', *Anthropologica* 34, no. 1 (1992): 3–20.

Adair, James. *Adair's History of the American Indians*, ed. Samuel Cole Williams. New York: Promontory Press, 1930.

Adams, Henry. *John Randolph*, 1882 reprint. New York: Houghton Mifflin, 1910.

Adhikari, Mohamed. 'A Total Extinction Confidently Hoped For: The Destruction of Cape San Society under Dutch Colonial Rule, 1700–1795', *Journal of Genocide Research* 12, no. 1–2 (2010): 19–44.

Adhikari, Mohamed. '"We Are Determined to Exterminate Them": The Genocidal Impetus behind Commercial Stock Farmer Invasions of Hunter-Gatherer Territories'. In *Genocide on Settler Frontiers: When Hunter-Gatherers and Commercial Stock Farmers Clash*, ed. Mohammed Adhikari, 1–31. Cape Town: UCT Press, 2014.

Adhikari, Mohamed, ed. *Civilian-Driven Violence and the Genocide of Indigenous Peoples in Settler Societies*. London: Routledge, 2021.

Akers, Donna. 'Removing the Heart of the Choctaw People: Indigenous Removal from a Native Perspective', *American Indigenous Culture and Research Journal* 23, no. 3 (1999): 63–76.

Alfred, Taiaiake. *Peace, Power, Righteousness: An Indigenous Manifesto*. Oxford: Oxford University Press, 2008.

Alpert, Avram. 'Philosophy's Systemic Racism', *Aeon*, 24 September 2020: https://aeon.co/essays/racism-is-baked-into-the-structure-of-dialectical-philosophy.

Altenbernd, Erik and Alex Trimble Young. 'Introduction: The Significance of the Frontier in an Age of Transnational History', *Settler Colonial Studies* 4, no. 2 (2014): 127–50.

Anderson, Kjell and Erin Jessee, eds. *Researching Perpetrators of Genocide*. Madison: University of Wisconsin Press, 2020.

Anderson, P. R. 'The Fish River Bush and the Place of History', *South African Historical Journal* 53, no. 1 (2005): 23–49.

Archer, C. I. 'The Cutting Edge: The Historical Relationship between Insurgency, Counterinsurgency and Terrorism during Mexican Independence, 1810–1821'. In *Terrorism: Roots, Impact, Responses*, ed. Lawrence Howard, 29–45. New York: Praeger, 1992.

Arens, William. *The Man-Eating Myth*. New York: Oxford University Press, 1979.

Armitage, David and Sanjay Subrahmanyam. 'Introduction: The Age of Revolutions, c. 1760–1840 – Global Causation, Connection, and Comparison'. In *The Age of Revolutions in Global Context, c. 1760–1840*, ed. David Armitage and Sanjay Subrahmanyam, xii–xxxii. New York: Palgrave Macmillan, 2010.

Aston, Nigel. *Christianity and Revolutionary Europe, 1750–1830*. Cambridge: Cambridge University Press, 2002.

Atkinson, Alan. *The Europeans in Australia: A History*, 3 Vols. Melbourne: Oxford University Press, 1998–2004.

Attenbrow, Val. *Sydney's Aboriginal Past: Investigating the Archaeological and Historical Records*. Sydney: UNSW Press, 2003.

Attwood, Bain. 'Denial in a Settler Society: The Australian Case', *History Workshop Journal* 84, no. 1 (Autumn 2017): 24–43.

Avril, Gilles, ed. *L'anti-Napoléon: écrits inédits et papiers de Noël-Antoine Apuril du Pontreau, chanoine de la Congrégation de France*. Paris: Nouveau monde éd., 2006.

Axelrod, Alan. *Chronicle of the Indian Wars from Colonial Times to Wounded Knee*. New York: Prentice Hall, 1993.

Axtell, James L. and William C. Sturtevant. 'The Unkindest Cut, or Who Invented Scalping', *William and Mary Quarterly* 37, no. 3 (1980): 451–72.

Ball, David P. 'Women Warriors: 5 Standout Indigenous Female Leaders in Canada', *Indian Country Today*, 8 March 2014: http://indiancountrytodaymedianetwork.com/2014/03/08/women-warriors-5-standout-indigenous-female-leaders-canada-153921.

Bank, Andrew. 'Of "Native Skulls" and "Noble Caucasians": Phrenology in Colonial South Africa', *Journal of Southern African Studies* 22, no. 3 (1996): 387–403.

Bank, Andrew. 'The Return of the Noble Savage: The Changing Image of Africans in Cape Colonial Art, 1800–1850', *South African Historical Journal* 39, no. 1 (1998): 17–43.

Bank, Andrew. 'Losing Faith in the Civilizing Mission: The Premature Decline of Humanitarian Liberalism at the Cape, 1840–60'. In *Empire and Others: British Encounters with Indigenous Peoples, 1600–1850*, ed. Martin Daunton and Rick Halpern, 364–83. Philadelphia: University of Pennsylvania Press, 1999.

Barkley-Jack, Jan. *Hawkesbury Settlements Revealed: A New Look at Australia's Third Mainland Settlement*. Sydney: Rosenberg Publishing, 2009.

Bartov, Omer. 'Communal Genocide: Personal Accounts of the Destruction of Buczacz, Eastern Galicia, 1941–44'. In *Shatterzone of Empires: Coexistence and Violence in the German, Habsburg, Russian, and Ottoman Borderlands*, ed. Omer Bartov and Eric D Weitz, 399–421. Bloomington: Indiana University Press, 2013.

Bartov, Omer. 'Genocide and the Holocaust: Arguments over History and Politics'. In *Lessons and Legacies*, ed. Karl Schleunes and Hilary Earl, Vol. XI, 5–28. Evanston, IL: Northwestern University Press, 2014.

Bauxar, J. J. 'Ethnohistorical Reconstructions'. In *The Prehistory of the Chickamauga Basin in Tennessee*, ed. Thomas M. N. Lewis, Madeleine D. Kneberg Lewis and Lynne Sullivan, Vol. 1, 262–4. Knoxville: University of Tennessee Press, 1995.

Bayly, Christopher Alan. *Imperial Meridian: The British Empire and the World 1780–1830*. London: Longman, 1989.

Bayly, Christopher Alan. 'The First Age of Global Imperialism, c. 1760–1830', *The Journal of Imperial and Commonwealth History* 26, no. 2 (1998): 28–47.

Beaumont, Ann. *A Man of Many Parts: The Life and Times of Edward Charles Close 1790–1866*. Mittagong: Highland House Publications, 2016.

Beik, William. 'The Absolutism of Louis XIV as Social Collaboration', *Past & Present* 188, no. 1 (2005): 195–224.

Bell, David A. *Cult of the Nation in France: Inventing Nationalism, 1680–1800*. Cambridge, MA: Harvard University Press, 2001.

Bell, David A. 'Jumonville's Death. War Propaganda and National Identity in Eighteenth-Century France'. In *The Age of Cultural Revolutions. Britain and France, 1750–1820*, ed. Colin Jones and Dror Wahrman, 33–61. Berkeley, CA: University of California Press, 2002.

Bell, David A. *The First Total War: Napoleon's Europe and the Birth of Warfare as We Know It*. Boston, MA: Houghton Mifflin, 2007.

Bell, David A. 'The French Revolution, the Vendée, and Genocide'. *Journal of Genocide Research* 22, no. 1 (2020): 19–25.

Benn, Carl. *The Iroquois in the War of 1812*. Toronto: University of Toronto Press, 1998.

Benton, Lauren. *They Called It Peace: Worlds of Imperial Violence*. Princeton, NJ: Princeton University Press, 2024.

Bercé, Yves-Marie. *Révoltes et révolutions dans l'Europe moderne (XVIe-XVIIIe siècles)*. Paris: Presses universitaires de France, 1980.

Berkeley, Edmund and Dorothy Smith Berkeley. *Dr. John Mitchell: The Man Who Made the Map of North America*. Chapel Hill: University of North Carolina Press, 1974.

Berndt, Ronald Murray. *Australian Aboriginal Religion*, 2 Vols. Leiden: Brill, 1974.

Bethencourt, Francisco. *Racisms: From the Crusades to the Twentieth Century*. Princeton, NJ: Princeton University Press, 2014.

Biggar, Nigel. *Colonialism: A Moral Reckoning*. London: William Collins, 2023.

Birch, Jennifer and Victor D. Thompson, eds. *The Archaeology of Villages in Eastern North America*. Gainesville: University Press of Florida, 2018.

Blackhawk, Ned. *Violence over the Land: Indians and Empires in the Early American West*. Cambridge, MA: Harvard University Press, 2006.

Blanning, Timothy Charles William. *The French Revolution in Germany: Occupation and Resistance in the Rhineland: 1792–1802*. Oxford: Clarendon Press, 1986.

Blanning, Timothy Charles William. 'The Abortive Crusade', *History Today* 39 (1989): 33–8.

Blanning, Timothy Charles William. 'Liberation or Occupation? Theory and Practice in the French Revolutionaries Treatment of Civilians outside France'. In *Civilians in the Path of War*, ed. Mark Grimsley and Clifford J. Rogers, 111–35. Lincoln: University of Nebraska Press, 2002.

Boemeke, Manfred F., Roger Chickering and Stig Förster, eds. *Anticipating Total War: The German and American Experiences, 1871–1914*. Cambridge: Cambridge University Press, 1999.

Boesche, Roger. 'The Dark Side of Tocqueville: On War and Empire', *Review of Politics* 67, no. 4 (2005): 737–52.

Bongiorno, Frank. '"The Men Who Made Australia Federated Long Ago": Australian Frontiers and Borderlands'. In *Borderlands in World History, 1700–1914*, ed. Paul Readman, Cynthia Radding and Chad Bryant, 46–62. Basingstoke: Palgrave Macmillan 2014.

Bourke, Joanna. *Fear: A Cultural History*. London: Virago, 2005.
Bouvier, Félix. 'La révolte de Pavie (23–26 mai 1796)', *Revue historique de la Revolution française* 2, no. 8 (1911): 519–39.
Bouwers, Eveline G., ed. *Catholics and Violence in the Nineteenth-Century Global World*. London: Routledge, 2024.
Brégeon, Jean-Noël. *Napoléon et la guerre d'Espagne: 1808–1814*. Paris: Perrin, 2006.
Broers, Michael. *The Napoleonic Empire in Italy, 1796–1814: Cultural Imperialism in a European Context?* New York: Palgrave Macmillan, 2005.
Broers, Michael. 'Civilians in the Napoleonic Wars'. In *Daily Lives of Civilians in Wartime Europe, 1618–1900*, ed. Linda Frey and Marsha Frey, 133–74. Westport, CT: Greenwood Press, 2007.
Broers, Michael. *Napoleon's Other War: Bandits, Rebels and Their Pursuers in the Age of Revolutions*. Oxford: Peter Lang, 2010.
Broers, Michael. 'Revolt and Repression in Napoleonic Italy, 1796–1814'. In *War in an Age of Revolution, 1775–1815*, ed. Roger Chickering and Stig Förster, 197–217. Washington, DC: German Historical Institute, 2010.
Brower, Benjamin Claude. *A Desert Named Peace: The Violence of France's Empire in the Algerian Sahara, 1844–1902*. New York: Columbia University Press, 2009.
Brown, Howard G. 'Domestic State Violence: Repression from the Croquants to the Commune', *Historical Journal* 42, no. 3 (1999): 597–622
Browning, Christopher. *Ordinary Men: Reserve Police Battalion 101 and the Final Solution in Poland*. New York: HarperPerennial, 1993.
Brundage, William Fitzhugh. *Civilising Torture: An American Tradition*. Cambridge, MA: Harvard University Press, 2018.
Bruns, Claudia. 'Antisemitism and Colonial Racism'. In *Racisms Made in Germany*, ed. Wulf D. Hund, Christian Koller and Moshe Zimmermann, 99–122. Berlin: LIT Verlag, 2011.
Buc, Philippe. *Holy War, Martyrdom, and Terror: Christianity, Violence, and the West*. Philadelphia: University of Pennsylvania Press, 2015.
Buckelew, Jessica. 'The Man Who Sold the World: The Long Con of Discovery', *American Indian Law Journal* 3, no. 2 (2015): 358–80.
Burbank, Jane and Frederick Cooper. *Empires in World History: Power and the Politics of Difference*. 1st ed. Princeton: Princeton University Press, 2011.
Burel, Ivan. 'From Egypt to Algeria: General Pierre Boyer's Counter-Insurgent and Imperial Career'. In *From the Napoleonic Empire to the Age of Empire: Empire after the Emperor*, ed. Thomas Dodman and Aurélien Lignereux, 253–69. Cham: Springer, 2023.
Burstin, Haim. 'Pour une phénoménologie de la violence révolutionnaire: réflexions autour du cas parisie', *Historical Reflections / Réflexions Historiques* 29, no. 3 (2003): 389–407.
Butler, Richard. 'Gen. Butler's Journal, Continued', *The Olden Time: a Monthly Publication, Devoted to the Preservation of Documents and Other Authentic Information in Relation to the Early Explorations, and the Settlement and Improvement of the Country Around the Head of the Ohio (1846–1847)* 2, no. 11 (1847): 481–528.
Butterfield, Lyman. 'History at the Headwaters', *New York History* 51, no. 2 (1970): 126–46.

Cadet, Nicolas, 'Anatomie d'une "petite guerre," la campagne de Calabre de 1806–1807', *Revue d'histoire du XIXe siècle* 30, no. 1 (2005): 65–84.

Cadet, Nicolas. 'Violences de guerre et transmission de la mémoire des conflits à travers l'exemple de la campagne de Calabre de 1806–1807', *Annales historiques de la Révolution française* 348, no. 2 (2007): 147–63.

Cadet, Nicolas. *Honneur et violences de guerre au temps de Napoléon: la Campagne de Calabre*. Paris: Vendémiaire, 2015.

Caldwell, John C. 'Colonial Population 1788–1825'. In *Australians, Historical Statistics*, ed. Wray Vamplew, 23–41. Sydney: Fairfax Syme & Weldon Associates, 1987.

Calloway, Colin G. *One Vast Winter Count: The Native American West before Lewis and Clark*. Lincoln: University of Nebraska Press, 2003.

Calloway, Colin G. *The Scratch of a Pen: 1763 and the Transformation of North America*. New York: Oxford University Press, 2006.

Calloway, Colin G. *The Victory with No Name: The Native American Defeat of the First American Army*. New York: Oxford University Press, 2015.

Candela, Gilles. *L'armée d'Italie: des missionnaires armés à la naissance de la guerre napoléonienne*. Rennes: Presses universitaires de Rennes, 2011.

Canny, Nicholas. *The Elizabethan Conquest of Ireland: A Pattern Established 1565–76*. Hassocks: Harvester Press, 1976.

Cao, Yiming, Benjamin Enke, Armin Falk, Paola Giuliano and Nathan Nunn, 'Herding, Warfare, and a Culture of Honor: Global Evidence', *National Bureau of Economic Research Working Paper Series, Working Paper 29250*, 1–66: https://www-nber-org. ezproxy.newcastle.edu.au/system/files/working_papers/w29250/w29250.pdf

Cénat, Jean-Philippe. 'Le ravage du Palatinat: politique de destruction, stratégie de cabinet et propagande au début de la guerre de la Ligue d'Augsbourg', *Revue historique* 307, no. 1 (2005): 97–132.

Cesarani, David and Paul A. Levine, eds. *'Bystanders' to the Holocaust: A Re-Evaluation*. London: Routledge, 2002.

Chaplin, Joyce E. *Subject Matter: Technology, the Body, and Science on the Anglo-American Frontier, 1500–1676*. Cambridge, MA: Harvard University Press, 2001.

Chaplin, Joyce E. 'The British Atlantic'. In *The Oxford Handbook of the Atlantic World, 1450–1850*, ed. Nicholas Canny and Philip Morgan, 219–34. Oxford: Oxford University Press, 2011.

Charters, Erica, Marie Houllemare and Peter H. Wilson, eds. *A Global History of Early Modern Violence*. Manchester: Manchester University Press, 2020.

Chickering, Roger. 'Total War: The Use and Abuse of a Concept'. In *Anticipating Total War: The German and American Experiences, 1871–1914*, ed. Manfred F. Boemeke, Roger Chickering and Stig Förster, 13–28. Cambridge: Cambridge University Press, 1999.

Chirot, Daniel and Clark McCauley, *Why Not Kill Them All?: The Logic and Prevention of Mass Political Murder*. Princeton: Princeton University Press, 2010.

Chisick, Harvey. 'Ethics and History in Voltaire's Attitudes toward the Jews', *Eighteenth-Century Studies* 35, no. 4 (2002): 577–600.

Churchill, Ward. *A Little Matter of Genocide: Holocaust and Denial in the Americas, 1492 to the Present*. San Francisco, CA: City Lights Books, 1997.

Claiborne, John Francis Hamtramck. *The Life and Times of Gen. Sam Dale, the Mississippi Partisan*. New York: Harper & Brothers, 1860.

Clark, Ian D. *Scars in the Landscape: A Register of Massacre Sites in Western Victoria*. Canberra: Australian Institute of Aboriginal and Torres Strait Islander Studies, 1995.

Clarke, Joseph. 'Encountering the Sacred: British and French Soldiers in the Revolutionary and Napoleonic Mediterranean'. In *Militarized Cultural Encounters in the Long Nineteenth Century: Making War, Mapping Europe*, ed. Joseph Clarke and John Horne, 49–73. Cham: Palgrave Macmillan, 2018.

Clarke, Joseph. 'A "theatre of bloody carnage": The revolt of Cairo and Revolutionary violence'. In *A Global History of Early Modern Violence*, ed. Erica Charters, Marie Houllemare and Peter H. Wilson, 218–34. Manchester: Manchester University Press, 2020.

Clarke, Joseph and John Horne, eds. *Militarized Cultural Encounters in the Long Nineteenth Century: Making War, Mapping Europe*. Cham: Palgrave Macmillan, 2018.

Clarkson, Chris, Zenobia Jacobs, Ben Marwick, et al., 'Human occupation of northern Australia by 65,000 years ago', *Nature* 547, no. 7663 (2017): 306–310.

Clary, David A. *George Washington's First War: His Early Military Adventures*. New York: Simon and Schuster, 2011.

Clements, Nicholas. *The Black War: Fear, Sex and Resistance in Tasmania*. St Lucia: University of Queensland Press, 2014.

Cobb, Richard. *Les armées revolutionaires: instrument de la terreur dans les départments, Avril 1793 – Floreal An II*, 2 Vols. Paris: Mouton, 1961.

Coker, William S. 'The Papers and History of Panton, Leslie, and John Forbes', Florida Historical Quarterly 13 (April 1935): 130-2, 133-4.

Cole, Juan. *Napoléon's Egypt: Invading the Middle East*. New York: Palgrave Macmillan, 2007.

Colley, Linda. *Britons*. New Haven, CT: Yale University Press, 1992.

Connor, John. *The Australian Frontier Wars 1788–1838*. Sydney: UNSW Press, 2002.

Corbin, Alain. *The Village of Cannibals: Rage and Murder in France, 1870*. Trans. Arthur Goldhammer. Cambridge, MA: Harvard University Press, 1992.

Cory, George. *The Rise of South Africa, Volume One: From the Earliest Times to the Year 1820*. Cape Town: Stuik, 1965.

Couzens, Tim. *South African Battles*. Johannesburg: Jonathan Ball, 2013.

Crais, Clifton C. *White Supremacy and Black Resistance in Pre-Industrial South Africa: The Making of the Colonial Order in the Eastern Cape, 1770–1865*. Cambridge: Cambridge University Press, 1992.

Crampton, Hazel, Jeff Peires and Carl Vernon, eds. *Into the Hitherto Unknown: Ensign Beutler's Expedition to the Eastern Cape, 1752*. Cape Town: Van Riebeeck Society, 2013.

Curran, Andrew S. *The Anatomy of Blackness: Science & Slavery in an Age of Enlightenment*. Baltimore, MD: Johns Hopkins University Press, 2011.

Daly, Gavin. 'A Dirty, Indolent, Priest-Ridden City: British Soldiers in Lisbon during the Peninsular War, 1808–1813', *History* 94, no. 316 (2009): 461–82.

Daly, Gavin. '"Barbarity more suited to Savages": British Soldiers' Views of Spanish and Portuguese Violence during the Peninsular War, 1808–1814', *War & Society* 35, no. 4 (2016): 242–58.

Daly, Gavin. '"The Sacking of a Town is an Abomination": Siege, Sack and Violence to Civilians in British Officers' Writings on the Peninsular War', *Historical Research* 92, no. 255 (2019): 160–82.

Daly, Gavin. *Storm and Sack: British Sieges, Violence and the Laws of War in the Napoleonic Era, 1799–1815*. Cambridge: Cambridge University Press, 2022.

Davis, John A. *Naples and Napoleon. Southern Italy and the European Revolutions (1780–1860)*. Oxford: Oxford University Press, 2006.

Davis, Natalie Zemon, 'The Rites of Violence: Religious Riot in Sixteenth-Century France'. *Past and Present* 59, no. 1 (1973): 51–91.

De Graaf, Beatrice. *Fighting Terror after Napoleon: How Europe Became Secure after 1815*. Cambridge: Cambridge University Press, 2020.

De Lange, Erik. 'The Congress System and the French Invasion of Algiers, 1827–1830'. *Historical Journal* 64, no. 4 (2021): 940–62.

Deloria, Jr., Vine. *God Is Red: A Native View of Religion*. Golden, CO: Fulcrum Publishing, 1994.

Derounian-Stodola, Kathryn Zabelle and James Arthur Levernier, *The Indian Captivity Narrative, 1500–1900*. New York: Twayne Publishers, 1993.

Dobie, Madeleine. *Trading Places: Colonization and Slavery in Eighteenth-Century French Culture*. Ithaca, NY: Cornell University Press, 2010.

Dodman, Thomas and Aurélien Lignereux, eds. *From the Napoleonic Empire to the Age of Empire: Empire after the Emperor*. Cham: Springer, 2023.

Donehoo, George P. 'A Few Facts in the History of Logstown'. *Western Pennsylvania Historical Magazine* 1, no. 1 (1918): 259–64.

Dosquet, Emilie. '"We have been Informed that the French are Carrying Desolation Everywhere": The Desolation of the Palatinate as a News Event'. In *New Networks in Early Modern Europe*, ed. Joad Raymond and Noah Moxham, 641–74. Leiden: Brill, 2016.

Dosquet, Emilie. 'Between Positional Warfare and "Guerre de Partis": Soldiers and Civilians during the "Desolation of the Palatinate" (1688–89)'. In *Civilians under Siege from Sarajevo to Troy*, ed. John Horne and Alex Dowdall, 107–136. Basingstoke: Palgrave Macmillan, 2018.

Doster, James F. 'Early Settlements on the Tombigbee and Tensaw Rivers'. *The Alabama Review* 12, no. 2 (1959): 83–94.

Downes, Alexander. *Targeting Civilians in War*. Ithaca, NY: Cornell University Press, 2008.

Drévillon, Hervé. 'Guerre, violence et Révolution'. in *Histoire militaire de la France. I. Des Mérovingiens au Second Empire*, ed. Hervé Drévillon and Olivier Wieviorka, 507–35. Paris: Perrin, 2018.

Drévillon, Hervé. 'Pratiques et représentations de la violence des guerres de la Convention, 1792–95', in *L'historien-citoyen*, ed. Benjamin Deruelle, Émilie Dosquet and Paul Vo-Ha, 367–86. Paris: Éditions de la Sorbonne, 2022.

Duggan, Christopher. *The Force of Destiny: A History of Italy Since 1796*. London: Allen Lane, 2007.

Dumont, Georges-Henri. *Histoire de la Belgique: des origines à 1830*. Brussels: Le Cri édition, 2005.

Dunn, Jr., Walter Scott. *Profit and Loss: The British Army and the Fur Traders, 1760–1764*. Westport, CT: Greenwood Press, 1998.

Dupuy, Roger. *La République jacobine. Terreur, guerre et government révolutionnaire (1792–1794)*. Paris: Seuil, 2005.

Duyker, Edward. *An Officer of the Blue: Marc-Joseph Marion Dufresne, South Sea Explorer, 1724–1772*. Melbourne: Melbourne University Press, 1994.

Duyker, Edward. *Francois Peron an Impetuous Life*. Melbourne: Miegunyah Press, 2006.

Dwyer, Philip. '"It Still Makes Me Shudder": Memories of Massacres and Atrocities during the Revolutionary and Napoleonic Wars'. *War in History* 16, no. 4 (2009): 381–405.

Dwyer, Philip. 'Violence and the Revolutionary and Napoleonic Wars: Massacre, Conquest and the Imperial Enterprise', *Journal of Genocide Research* 15, no. 2 (2013): 117–31.

Dwyer, Philip. 'Religion and Violence during the French Revolutionary and Napoleonic Wars: Between Tradition and Modernity'. In *Catholics and Violence in the Nineteenth-Century Global World*, ed. Eveline G. Bouwers, 33–55. London: Routledge, 2024.

Dwyer, Philip and Lyndall Ryan. 'The Massacre and History'. In *Theatres of Violence: Massacre, Mass Killing and Atrocity Throughout History*, ed. Philip Dwyer and Lyndall Ryan, ix–xxv. New York: Berghahn, 2012.

Earl, Robert. 'Indian Scalping'. *Papers Read before the Herkimer County Historical Society during the Years 1896, 1897, and 1898*, Vol. 2, 128–35. Herkimer and Ilyon, NY: Citizen Publishing, Publishers, 1899.

Edelstein, Dan. 'War and Terror: The Law of Nations from Grotius to the French Revolution'. *French Historical Studies* 31, no. 2 (2008): 229–62.

Edmunds, R. David. *The Shawnee Prophet*. Lincoln: University of Nebraska Press, 1983.

Elbourne, Elizabeth. *Blood Ground: Colonialism, Missions, and the Contest for Christianity in the Cape Colony and Britain, 1799–1853*. Montreal: McGill-Queen's University Press, 2002.

Elkins, Caroline. *Legacy of Violence A History of the British Empire*. New York: Alfred A. Knopf, 2022.

Elphick, Richard and Hermann Giliomee, 'The Origins and Entrenchment of European Dominance at the Cape, 1652-c. 1840'. In *The Shaping of South African Society, 1652–1840*, ed. Richard Elphick and Hermann Giliomee, 521–66. Cape Town: Maskew Miller Longman, 1989.

Elphick, Richard and V. C. Malherbe. 'The Khoisan to 1828'. In *The Shaping of South African Society, 1652–1840*, ed. Richard Elphick and Hermann Giliomee, 3–65. Cape Town: Maskew Miller Longman, 1989.

Esdaile, Charles J. 'Popular Resistance to the Napoleonic Empire'. In *Napoleon and Europe*, ed. Philip Dwyer, 136–52. Harlow: Longman, 2001.

Esdaile, Charles J. *Fighting Napoleon: Guerrillas, Bandits and Adventurers in Spain, 1808–1814*. New Haven, CT: Yale University Press, 2004.

Esdaile, Charles J. 'Patriots, Partisans and Land Pirates in Retrospect'. In *Popular Resistance in the French Wars*, ed. Charles J. Esdaile, 1–24. Houndmills: Palgrave Macmillan, 2005.

Esdaile, Charles J., ed. *Popular Resistance in the French Wars: Patriots, Partisans and Land Pirates*. New York: Palgrave Macmillan, 2005.

Ethridge, Robbie. *Creek Country: The Creek Indians and Their World*. Chapel Hill: University of North Carolina Press, 2003.

Ferguson, Niall. *Empire: How Britain Made the Modern World*. London: Allen Lane, 2003.

Finley, Milton. *The Most Monstrous of Wars: The Napoleonic Guerrilla War in Southern Italy, 1806-1811*. Columbia: University of South Carolina Press, 1994.

Finnane, Mark. 'Law and Regulation'. In *The Cambridge History of Australia*, ed. Alison Bashford and Stuart Macintyre, Vol. 1, 391-413. Cambridge: Cambridge University Press, 2013.

Flick, Alexander C. 'New Sources on the Sullivan-Clinton Campaign in 1779', *Quarterly Journal of the New York State Historical Society* 10, no. 3 (1929): 185-224, 265-317.

Ford, Lisa. *Settler Sovereignty: Jurisdiction and Indigenous People in America and Australia, 1788-1836*. Cambridge, MA: Harvard University Press, 2010.

Forrest, Alan. *Napoleon's Men: The Soldiers of the Revolution and Empire*. London: Hambledon Continuum, 2002.

Forrest, Alan. 'The Ubiquitous Brigand: The Politics and Language of Repression'. In *Popular Resistance in the French Wars: Patriots, Partisans and Land Pirates*, ed. Charles J. Esdaile, 25-43. New York: Palgrave Macmillan, 2005.

Forrest, Alan. 'Policing, Rural Revolt and Conscription in Napoleonic France'. In *The Napoleonic Empire and the New European Political Culture. War, Culture and Society, 1750-1850*, ed. Michael Broers, Peter Hicks, and Augustín Guimerá, 49-58. Basingstoke: Palgrave Macmillan, 2012.

Foster, II, Thomas, ed. *The Collected Works of Benjamin Hawkins, 1796-1810*. Tuscaloosa: University of Alabama Press, 2003.

Frank, Andrew K. and A. Glenn Crothers. 'Introduction'. In *Borderlands Narratives: Negotiation and Accommodation in North America's Contested Spaces, 1500-1850*, ed. Andrew K. Frank and A. Glenn Crothers, 1-17. Gainesville: University Press of Florida, 2017.

Fredrickson, George M. *Racism: A Short History*. Princeton, NJ: Princeton University Press, 2015.

Friederici, Georg. *Skalpieren und ähnliche Kriegsgebräuche in Amerika*. Braunschweig: Druck von Friedrich Vieweg und Sohn, 1906.

Fullagar, Kate and Michael A. McDonnell, eds. *Facing Empire: Indigenous Experiences in a Revolutionary Age, 1760-1840*. Baltimore: Johns Hopkins University Press, 2018.

Furse, Elizabeth and Robert J. Miller. 'American Indian Nations, Indian Treaties, and Tribal Sovereignty', *Government, Law and Policy Journal* 8, no. 1 (2006): 9-13.

Gainot, Bernard, 'Les affrontements militaires sous la Revolution et l'Empire: une "guerre totale"?'. *Revue d'histoire moderne & contemporaine* 59, no. 2 (2012): 178-86.

Gallois, William. *A History of Violence in the Early Algerian Colony*. Houndmills: Palgrave Macmillan, 2013.

Gallois, William. 'Genocide in Nineteenth-Century Algeria', *Journal of Genocide Research* 15, no. 1 (2013): 69-88.

Gapps, Stephen. *The Sydney Wars Conflict in the Early Colony 1788-1817*. Sydney: NewSouth Publishing, 2018.

Gat, Azar. *War in Human Civilization*. Oxford: Oxford University Press, 2008.

Geiger, Maynard J. *The Franciscan Conquest of Florida, 1573–1618*. Washington, DC: Catholic University of America, 1937.

Gellately, Robert and Ben Kiernan. 'The Study of Mass Murder and Genocide'. In *The Specter of Genocide: Mass Murder in Historical Perspective*, ed. Robert Gellately and Ben Kiernan, 3–26. Cambridge: Cambridge University Press, 2003.

Georg-Kanentiio, Doug and Bruce E. Johansen. 'Land Area of the Haudenosaunee in New York State'. In *Encyclopedia of the Haudenosaunee (Iroquois Confederacy)*, ed. Bruce E. Johansen and Barbara Alice Mann, 191–94. Westport, CT: Greenwood Press, 2000.

Giliomee, Hermann. 'Process Development of the Southern African Frontier'. In *The Frontier in History: North America and Southern Africa Compared*, ed. Howard Lamar and Leonard Thompson, 76–119. New Haven, CT: Yale University Press, 1981.

Giliomee, Hermann. 'The Eastern Frontier, 1770–1812'. In *The Shaping of South African Society, 1652–1840*, ed. Richard Elphick and Hermann Giliomee, 421–71. Cape Town: Maskew Miller Longman, 1989.

Godechot, Jacques. 'Les variations de la politique française à l'égard des pays occupés 1792–1815'. In *Occupants-Occupés, 1792–1815*, 19–31. Brussels: Université libre, Institut de sociologie, 1969.

Grab, Alexander. 'State Power, Brigandage and Rural Resistance in Napoleonic Italy', *European History Quarterly* 25, no. 1 (1995): 39–70.

Grandjean, Katherine. 'New World Tempests: Environment, Scarcity, and the Coming of the Pequot War', *William and Mary Quarterly* 68, no. 1 (2011): 75–100.

Gregg, Andrew. '"I am frightened out of my life": Black War, White Fear', *Settler Colonial Studies* 7, no. 2 (2017): 221–40.

Hagan, William Thomas. *The Sac and Fox Indians*. Norman: University of Oklahoma Press, 1958.

Hainsworth, David. *The Sydney Traders: Simeon Lord and His Contemporaries, 1788–1821*. Melbourne: Cassell, 1972.

Halbert, Henry S. and Timothy H. Ball. *The Creek War of 1813 and 1814*. Chicago: Donohue & Henneberry, 1895.

Hall, Simon. 'Farming Communities of the Second Millennium: Internal Frontiers, Identity, Continuity and Change'. In *The Cambridge History of South Africa, Vol. 1, From Early Times to 1885*, ed. Carolyn Hamilton, Bernard K. Mbenga and Robert Ross, 112–67. Cambridge: Cambridge University Press, 2016.

Hall, Tony. 'Native Limited Identities and Newcomer Metropolitanism in Upper Canada, 1814–1867'. In *Old Ontario: Essays in Honour of J. M. S. Careless*, ed. David Keane and Colin Read, 148–73. Toronto: Dundurn Press, 1990.

Halsey, Francis Whiting. *The Old New York Frontier, Its Wars with Indians and Tories, Its Missionary Schools, Pioneers and Land Titles, 1614–1800*. Port Washington, NY: Ira Friedman, 1901.

Hämäläinen, Pekka. *Indigenous Continent: The Epic Contest for North America*. New York: Liveright, 2022.

Harinck, Gerrit. 'Interaction between Xhosa and Khoi: Emphasis on the Period 1620–1750'. In *African Societies in Southern Africa*, ed. Leonard Thompson, 145–70. London: Heinemann, 1969.

Harper, Rob. 'State Intervention and Extreme Violence in the Eighteenth-Century Ohio Valley'. *Journal of Genocide Research* 10, no. 2 (2008): 233–48.

Heese, J. A. *Slagtersnek en sy Mense*. Cape Town: Tafelberg, 1973.

Heidenreich, Conrad E. 'Huron'. In *Handbook of North American Indians*, Vol. 15, *Northeast*, ed. Bruce G. Trigger, 368–88. Washington, DC: Smithsonian Institution, 1978.

Henri, Florette. *The Southern Indians and Benjamin Hawkins, 1796–1816*. Norman: University of Oklahoma Press, 1986.

Henriques, Peter R. *Realistic Visionary: A Portrait of George Washington*. Charlottesville: University of Virginia Press, 2006.

Heuser, Beatrice. 'Small Wars in the Age of Clausewitz: The Watershed between Partisan War and People's War'. *Journal of Strategic Studies* 33, no. 1 (2010): 139–62.

Heuser, Beatrice. *War: A Genealogy of Western Ideas and Practices*. Oxford: Oxford University Press, 2022.

Hewitt, John Napoleon Brinton. 'Some Esoteric Aspects of the League of the Iroquois'. *Proceedings of the International Congress of Americanists* 19 (1915): 322–6.

Hewitt, John Napoleon Brinton. 'A Constitutional League of Peace in the Stone Age of America: The League of the Iroquois and Its Constitution'. *Smithsonian Institution Series* (1920): 527–45.

Hewitt, John Napoleon Brinton. 'Ethnological Studies among the Iroquois Indians'. *Smithsonian Miscellaneous Collections* 78, no. 7 (1927): 237–43.

Hewitt, John Napoleon Brinton. *Notes on the Creek Indians*, Anthropological Papers No. 10, Smithsonian Institution, Bureau of American Ethnology. Washington, DC: Government Printing Office, 1939.

Hodgson, Janet. Ntsikana's Great Hymn: A Xhosa Expression of Christianity in the Early 19th Century. Cape Town: Centre for African Studies, University of Cape Town, 1982.

Hoffer, Peter Charles. *Sensory Worlds in Early America*. Baltimore, MD: Johns Hopkins University Press, 2003.

Hughes, Brian and Fergus Robson, eds. *Unconventional Warfare from Antiquity to the Present Day*. Cham: Palgrave Macmillan, 2017.

Hulbert, Archer Butler. *Historic Highways of America, Vol. 9: Waterways of Westward Expansion*. Cleveland: Arthur H. Clark, 1903.

Hund, Wulf D. '"It must come from Europe": The Racisms of Immanuel Kant'. In *Racisms Made in Germany*, ed. Wulf D. Hund, Christian Koller and Moshe Zimmermann, 69–98. Berlin: LIT Verlag, 2011.

Hunt, Lynn. *Inventing Human Rights: A History*. New York, NY: W.W. Norton & Co., 2007.

Hurt, R. Douglas. *The Indian Frontier, 1763–1846*. Albuquerque: University of New Mexico Press, 2002.

Ingram, Edward. 'Bellicism as Boomerang. The Eastern Question during the Vienna System'. In *The Transformation of European Politics, 1763–1848: Episode or Model in Modern History?* ed. Peter Krüger and Paul W. Schroeder, 205–26. Münster: LIT Verlag, 2002.

Israel, Jonathan. *Enlightenment Contested: Philosophy, Modernity, and the Emancipation of Man, 1670–1752*. Oxford: Oxford University Press, 2006.

Jacobs, Wilbur R. *Wilderness Politics and Indian Gifts: The Northern Colonial Frontier*. Norman: University of Oklahoma Press, 1950.

Jacobs, Wilbur R. *Dispossessing the American Indian: Indians and Whites on the Colonial Frontier*. Norman: University of Oklahoma Press, 1985.

Jacoby, Karl. 'Indigenous Empires and Native Nations: Beyond History and Ethnohistory in Pekka Hämäläinen's *The Comanche Empire*'. *History and Theory* 52, no. 1 (2013): 60–6.

Jahoda, Gustav. *Images of Savages: Ancient Roots of Modern Prejudice in Western Culture*. New York: Routledge, 1999.

Jaimes, M. Annette. 'Introduction: Sand Creek: The Morning After'. In *The State of Native America: Genocide, Colonization, and Resistance*, ed. M. Annette Jaimes, 1–12. Boston: South End Press, 1992.

Jemison, Pete. 'Mother of Nations: The Peace Queen, a Neglected Tradition', *Akwe:kon* 5 (1988): 68–70.

Jennings, Jeremy. *Travels with Tocqueville beyond America*. Cambridge, MA: Harvard University Press, 2023.

Johnson, Chief Elias. 'The Iroquois Are Not Savages'. In *Native Heritage: Personal Accounts by American Indians, 1790 to Present*, ed. Arlene Hirschfelder, 238–40. New York: Macmillan, 1995.

Johnston, Anna. *The Antipodean Laboratory: Making Colonial Knowledge, 1770–1870*. Cambridge: Cambridge University Press, 2023.

Jordan, David P. 'Rumor, Fear, and Paranoia in the French Revolution'. In *The Fundamentalist Mindset: Psychological Perspectives on Religion, Violence, and History*, ed. Charles B. Strozier, David M. Terman, James W. Jones and Katherine A. Boyd, 175–94. New York: Oxford University Press, 2010.

Kalmanovitz, Pablo. *The Laws of War in International Thought*. Oxford: Oxford University Press, 2020.

Kalmanovitz, Pablo. 'Regular War, Irregulars, and Savages'. In *Concepts and Contexts of Vattel's Political and Legal Thought*, ed. Peter Schröder, 141–60. Cambridge: Cambridge University Press, 2021.

Kalyvas, Stathis N. 'Aspects méthodologiques de la recherche sur les massacres: le cas de la guerre civile Grecque', *Revue internationale de politique comparée* 8, no. 1 (2001): 23–42.

Kalyvas, Stathis N. *The Logic of Violence in Civil War*. Cambridge: Cambridge University Press, 2006.

Kamissek, Christoph, and Jonas Kreienbaum. 'An Imperial Cloud? Conceptualising Interimperial Connections and Transimperial Knowledge'. *Journal of Modern European History* 14, no. 2 (2016): 164–82.

Kane, Katie. 'Nits Make Lice: Drogheda, Sand Creek and the Poetics of Colonial Extermination', *Cultural Critique* 42 (Spring, 1999): 81–103.

Karr, Ronald Dale. '"Why Should You Be So Furious?": The Violence of the Pequot War', *Journal of American History* 85, no. 3 (1998): 876–909.

Karskens, Grace. *The Colony: A History of Early Sydney*. Sydney: Allen & Unwin, 2008.

Karskens, Grace. *People of the River: Lost Worlds of Early Australia*. Sydney: Allen & Unwin, 2020.

Katz, Steven T. 'The Pequot War Reconsidered', *New England Quarterly* 64, no. 2 (1991): 206–24.

Keegan, Timothy. *Colonial South Africa and the Origins of the Racial Order*. Cape Town: David Philip, 1996.

Kellogg, Louise Phelps, ed. *Frontier Retreat on the Upper Ohio, 1779–1780*, 1917 reprint. Baltimore, MD: Genealogical Publishing, 2003.

Kelso, William M. *Jamestown: The Truth Revealed*. Charlottesville: University of Virginia Press, 2017.

Kercher, Bruce. *An Unruly Child. A History of Law in Australia*. St Leonards, NSW: Allen & Unwin, 1995.

Kerkhove, Ray. *How They Fought: Indigenous Tactics and Weaponry of Australia's Frontier Wars*. Tingalpa: Boolarong Press, 2023.

Kienitz, W. Vernon. *Delaware Culture Chronology*. Indianapolis, IN: Indiana Historical Society, 1946.

Kiernan, Ben. 'Australia's Aboriginal Genocide', *Yale Journal of Human Rights* 1, no. 1 (2000): 49–56.

Kiernan, Ben. *Blood and Soil: Modern Genocide 1500–2000*. New Haven, CT: Yale University Press, 2007.

Kinoshi, Shino. 'The Father Governor: The British Administration of Aboriginal People at Port Jackson, 1788–1972'. In *Public Men: Political Masculinities in Modern Britain*, ed. Matthew Mccormack, 54–72. Hampshire: Palgrave Macmillan, 2007.

Klein, Philip S. and Ari Hoogenboom, *A History of Pennsylvania*. University Park: University of Pennsylvania Press, 1980.

Knittel, Susanne C. and Zachary J. Goldberg, eds. *The Routledge International Handbook of Perpetrator Studies*. London: Routledge, 2020.

Knowles, Nathaniel. 'The Torture of Captives by the Indians of Eastern North America', *Proceedings of the American Philosophical Society* 82, no. 2 (1940): 151–225.

Kohen, James L. 'Pemulwuy 1750–1802', In *Australian Dictionary of Biography, Supplementary Volume*: https://adb.anu.edu.au/biography/pemulwuy-13147.

Kohen, James L. and Ronald Lampert. 'Hunters and Fishers in the Sydney Region'. In *Australians to 1788*, ed. D. John Mulvaney and J. Peter White, 343–68. Sydney: Fairfax, Syme and Weldon Associates, 1987.

Kohlhoff, Doug. 'Did Henry Hacking shoot Pemulwuy? A reappraisal', *Journal of the Royal Australian Historical Society* 99, no. 1 (2013): 77–93.

Kotruch, John C. 'The Battle of Fallen Timbers: An Assertion of U.S. Sovereignty in the Atlantic World along the Banks of the Maumee River'. In *Between Sovereignty and Anarchy: The Politics of Violence in the American Revolutionary Era*, ed. Patrick Griffin, Robert G. Ingram, Peter S. Onuf and Brian Schoen, 263–84. Charlottesville: University of Virginia Press, 2015.

Krytzer, Brady. *Major Washington's Pittsburgh and the Mission to Fort Le Bœuf*. Charleston, SC: History Press, 2011.

Laband, John. *The Land Wars: The Dispossession of the Khoisan and Ama Xhosa in the Cape Colony*. Cape Town: Penguin, 2020.

Lafon, Jean-Marc. 'Justices d'exception napoléoniennes, militaire et civile, dans l'Espagne occupée: l'exemple de l'Andalousie (1810–1812)', *Crime, Histoire & Sociétés / Crime, History & Societies* 13, no. 2 (2009): 69–87.

Lamar, Howard and Leonard Thompson. 'Comparative Frontier History'. In *The Frontier in History: North America and Southern Africa Compared*, ed. Howard Lamar and Leonard Thompson, 3–13. New Haven, CT: Yale University Press, 1981.

Lambert, David and Alan Lester. 'Introduction: Imperial Spaces, Imperial Subjects'. In *Colonial Lives across the British Empire: Imperial Careering in the Long Nineteenth Century*, ed. David Lambert and Alan Lester, 1–31. Cambridge: Cambridge University Press, 2006.

Lambert, Patricia Marie. 'The Archaeology of War: A North American Perspective', *Journal of Archaeological Research* 10, no. 3 (2002): 207–41.

Lanning, John Tate. *Spanish Missions of Georgia*. Chapel Hill: University of North Carolina Press, 1935.

Laurens, Henri. *L'expédition d'Egypte, 1798–1801*. Paris: Armand Colin, 1989.

Lawson, Tom. *The Last Man: A British Genocide in Tasmania*. London: I. B. Tauris, 2014.

Le Cour Grandmaison, Olivier. *Coloniser, Exterminer – Sur la guerre et l'Etat colonial*. Paris: Fayard, 2005.

Leader Maynard, Jonathan. *Ideology and Mass Killing: The Radicalized Security Politics of Genocides and Deadly Atrocities*. Oxford: Oxford University Press, 2022.

Lee, Wayne E. 'Peace Chiefs and Blood Revenge: Patterns of Restraint in Native American Warfare, 1500–1800', *Journal of Military History* 71, no. 3 (2007): 701–41.

Lee, Wayne E. *Barbarians and Brothers: Anglo-American Warfare, 1500–1865*. Oxford: Oxford University Press, 2011.

Lee, Wayne E. *The Cutting-Off Way: Indigenous Warfare in Eastern North America, 1500–1800*. Chapel Hill: University of North Carolina Press, 2023.

Legassick, Martin. *The Struggle for the Eastern Cape 1800–1854*. Johannesburg: KMM Review Publishing, 2010.

Legassick, Martin. *The Politics of a South African Frontier: The Griqua, the Sotho-Tswana, and the Missionaries, 1780–1840*. Basel: Basler Afrika Bibliographien, 2010.

Lenman, Bruce. 'British Colonial Politics in an Age of European War and Creole Rebellion'. In *The Cambridge History of the Napoleonic Wars, Vol. 1, Politics and Diplomacy*, ed. Michael Broers and Philip Dwyer, 45–66. Cambridge: Cambridge University Press, 2022.

Lester, Alan. *Imperial Networks: Creating Identities in Nineteenth-Century South Africa and Britain*. London: Routledge, 2001.

Leuwers, Hervé. 'République et relations entre les peuples. Quelques éléments de l'idéal républicain autour de brumaire an VIII', *Annales historiques de la Révolution française* 318 (1999): 677–93.

Levene, Mark. 'Introduction', In *The Massacre in History*, ed. Mark Levene and Penny Roberts, 1–38. New York: Berghahn Books, 1999.

Levene, Mark. *Genocide in the Age of the Nation-State*, 2 Vols. London: I. B. Tauris, 2005.

Levine, Philippa. 'Is Comparative History Possible?' *History and Theory* 53, no. 3 (2014): 331–47.

Lewis-Williams, David and David Pearce. *San Spirituality: Roots, Expression, and Social Consequences*. Cape Town: Double Storey, 2004.

Leys, Ruth. 'How Did Fear Become a Scientific Object and What Kind of Object Is It?' *Representations* 110, no. 1 (2010): 66–104.

Libby, Dorothy and David Bond Stout. *Piankashaw and Kaskaskia Indians*. New York: Garland, 1974.

Lignereux, Aurélien. 'Accommodation et arrangements dans les départements réunis: l'éclairage paradoxal des rébellions (1800–1813)'. In *Le Temps des hommes doubles. Les arrangements face à l'occupation. De la Révolution française à la guerre de 1870*, ed. Annie Crépin, Jean-François Chanet and Christian Windler, 107–26. Rennes: Presses universitaires de Rennes, 2013.

Lindsay, Brendan C. *Murder State: California's Native American Genocide, 1846–1873*. Lincoln: University of Nebraska Press, 2012.

Lorcin, Patricia M. E. 'Nostalgias for Empire', *History and Theory* 57, no. 2 (2018): 269–85.

Lutz, Paul V. 'Fact and Myth Concerning George Rogers Clark's Grant of Land at Paducah, Kentucky', *Register of the Kentucky Historical Society* 67, no. 3 (1969): 248–53.

Lydon, Jane and Lyndall Ryan, eds. *Remembering the Myall Creek Massacre*. Sydney: NewSouth Publishing, 2018.

Lynn, John A. 'A Brutal Necessity? The Devastation of the Palatinate, 1688–1689'. In *Civilians in the Path of War*, ed. Mark Grimsley and Clifford J. Rogers, 79–110. Lincoln: University of Nebraska Press, 2002.

Lytle, William. 'Logan's Expedition against the Ma-co-chee Towns'. In *Historical Collections of Ohio*, ed. Henry Howe, Vol. 2, 98–102. Cincinnati, OH: C. J. Krehbiel, 1902.

MacCrone, Ian Douglas. *Race Attitudes in South Africa: Historical, Experimental and Psychological Studies*. Johannesburg: Oxford University Press, 1937.

MacKenzie, John M. 'European Imperialism: A Zone of Cooperation Rather than Competition?' In *Imperial Co-Operation and Transfer, 1870–1930: Empires and Encounters*, ed. Volker Barth and Roland Cvetkovski, 35–53. London: Bloomsbury, 2015.

Mackin, Anne. *Americans and Their Land: The House Built on Abundance*. Ann Arbor: University of Michigan Press, 2006.

MacLennan, Ben. *A Proper Degree of Terror: John Graham and the Cape's Eastern Frontier*. Johannesburg: Ravan Press, 1986.

Macmillan, William Miller. *Bantu, Boer and Britain*. London: Faber, 1929.

Madley, Benjamin. *An American Genocide: The United States and the California Indian Catastrophe, 1846–1873*. New Haven, CT: Yale University Press, 2017.

Malešević, Siniša. *Why Humans Fight: The Social Dynamics of Close-Range Violence*. Cambridge: Cambridge University Press, 2022.

Malone, Patrick M. *The Skulking Way of War: Technology and Tactics among the New England Indians*. New York: Madison Books, 2000.

Mann, Barbara Alice. *Iroquoian Women: The Gantowisas*. New York: Lang, 2000.

Mann, Barbara Alice. '"I Hope You Will Not Destroy What I Have Saved": Hopocan before the British Tribunal in Detroit, 1781'. In *Native American Speakers of the Eastern Woodlands: Selected Speeches and Critical Analyses*, ed. Barbara Alice Mann, 145–64. Westport, CT: Greenwood Press, 2001.

Mann, Barbara Alice. *Native American Speakers of the Eastern Woodlands: Selected Speeches and Critical Analyses*. Westport, CT: Praeger, 2001.

Mann, Barbara Alice. *Native Americans, Archaeologists, and the Mounds*. New York: Peter Lang, 2003.

Mann, Barbara Alice. 'The Greenville Treaty of 1795: Pen-and-Ink Witchcraft in the Struggle for the Old Northwest'. In *Enduring Legacies: Native American Treaties and Contemporary Controversies*, ed. Bruce E. Johansen, 136–201. Westport, CT: Praeger, 2004.

Mann, Barbara Alice. *George Washington's War on Native America*. Westport, CT: Praeger, 2005.

Mann, Barbara Alice. 'Mound Cultures of North America'. In *Encyclopedia of American Indian History*, ed. Bruce Elliot Johansen and Barry M. Pritzker, Vol. 1, 435–8. Santa Barbara, CA: ABC-CLIO, 2008.

Mann, Barbara Alice. *The Tainted Gift: The Disease Method of Frontier Advance*. Santa Barbara, CA: Praeger, 2009.

Mann, Barbara Alice. 'A Failure to Communicate: How Christian Missionary Assumptions Ignore Binary Patterns of Thinking within Native American Communities'. In *Remembering Jamestown: Hard Questions about Christian Mission*, ed. Barbara Brown Zikmund and Amos Yong, 29–48. Eugene, OR: Pickwick Publications, 2010.

Mann, Barbara Alice. *Spirits of Blood, Spirits of Breath: The Twinned Cosmos of Indigenous America*. New York: Oxford University Press, 2016.

Mann, Barbara Alice. 'The Mother-Suckling Child Principle of the Gift in Indigenous North American Culture', *Canadian Woman Studies/les cahiers de la femme* 34, nos. 1–2 (2020): 23–30.

Mann, Barbara Alice. 'War Women of the Eastern Woodlands'. In *Women Waging War in the American Revolution*, ed. Holly A. Mayer, 56–75. Charlottesville: University of Virginia Press, 2022.

Mann, Michael. 'Have Wars and Violence Declined?' *Theory and Society* 47, no. 2 (2018): 37–60.

Marsella, Anthony J., Jeanette L. Johnson, Patricia Watson and Jan Gryczynski. *Ethnocultural Perspectives on Disasters and Trauma: Foundations, Issues, and Applications*. New York: Springer, 2008.

Martens, Jeremy. '"In a State of War": Governor James Stirling, Extrajudicial Violence and the Conquest of Western Australia's Avon Valley, 1830–1840', *History Australia* 19, no. 4 (2022): 668–86.

Martin, Jack B. and Margret McKane Mauldin. *A Dictionary of Creek/Muskogee with Notes on the Florida and Oklahoma Seminole Dialects of Creek*. Lincoln: University of Nebraska Press, 2000.

Martin, Jean-Clément. *La Vendée et la France*. Paris: Seuil, 1987.

Martin, Jean-Clément. 'Le cas de Turreau et des colonnes infernales: réflexion sur une historiographie'. In *La plume et le sabre: volume d'hommages offerts à Jean-Paul Bertaud*, ed. Michel Biard, Annie Crépin and Bernard Gainot, 237–48. Paris: Publications de la Sorbonne, 2002.

Martin, Jean-Clément. 'Les mots de la violence: les guerres révolutionnaires'. In *La Violence de guerre 1914–1945: approches comparées des deux conflits mondiaux*, ed. Stéphane Audoin-Rouzeau et al., 27–42. Paris: Éd. Complexe, 2002.

Mazower, Mark. 'Violence and the State in the Twentieth Century', *American Historical Review* 107, no. 4 (2002): 1158-78.

McClung, John Alexander. *Sketches of Western Adventure: Containing an Account of the Most Interesting Incidents Connected with the Settlement of the West from 1755 to 1794*. Cincinnati, OH: U. James, 1839.

McDonald, Jared. '"Like a Wild Beast, He Can Be Got for the Catching": Child Forced Labour and the "Taming" of the San along the Cape's North-Eastern Frontier, c. 1806-1830'. In *Genocide on Settler Frontiers: When Hunter-Gatherers and Commercial Stock Farmers Clash*, ed. Mohammed Adhikari, 60-87. Cape Town: UCT Press, 2014.

McDonald, Jared. 'Stolen Childhoods: Cape San Child Captives and the Raising of Colonial Subjects in the Nineteenth Century Cape Colony', *Historia* 68, no. 2 (2023): 3-23.

McDonnell, Michael A. 'Rethinking the Age of Revolution', *Atlantic Studies* 13, no. 3 (2016): 301-14.

McFarlane, Anthony. *War and Independence in Spanish America*. New York: Routledge, 2014.

McFarlane, Anthony. 'Breaking the Pax Hispanica: Collective Violence in Colonial Spanish America'. In *A Global History of Early Modern Violence*, ed. Erica Charters, Marie Houllemare and Peter H. Wilson, 105-23. Manchester: Manchester University Press, 2020.

McPhee, Peter. 'A Vicious Civil War in the French Revolution: "The Vendée," 1793-1795'. In *The Cambridge World History of Genocide*, ed. Ned Blackhawk, Ben Kiernan, Benjamin Madley and Rebe Taylor, Vol. 2, 312-34. Cambridge: Cambridge University Press, 2023.

Melton, Jr., Buckner F. *Aaron Burr: Conspiracy to Treason*. New York: Wiley & Sons, 2002.

Merrell, James. 'Second Thoughts on Colonial Historians and American Indians', *William and Mary Quarterly* 69, no. 3 (2012): 451-512.

Merritt, Jane T. 'Native Peoples in the Revolutionary War'. In *The Oxford Handbook of the American Revolution*, ed. Edward G. Gray and Jane Kamensky, 234-49. New York: Oxford University Press, 2013.

Mikaberidze, Alexander. *The Napoleonic Wars: A Global History*. Oxford: Oxford University Press, 2020.

Miller, David W. *The Forced Removal of American Indians from the Northeast: A History of Territorial Cessions and Relocations, 1620-1854*. Jefferson, NC: McFarland, 2011.

Miller, Robert J. *Native America, Discovered and Conquered: Thomas Jefferson, Lewis & Clark, and Manifest Destiny*. Westport, CT: Praeger, 2006.

Miller, Robert J. *Reservation 'Capitalism:' Economic Development in Indian Country*. Santa Barbara, CA: ABC-CLIO, 2012.

Milner, George R., Eve Anderson and Virginia G. Smith. 'Warfare in Late Prehistoric West-Central Illinois', *American Antiquity* 56, no. 4 (1991): 581-603.

Milton, John. *The Edges of War: A History of Frontier Wars (1702-1878)*. Cape Town: Juta, 1983.

Morgan, Philip D. 'Encounters between British and "Indigenous" peoples, c.1500-c.1800'. In *Empire and Others: British Encounters with Indigenous Peoples, 1600-1850*, ed.

Martin Daunton and Rick Halpern, 56–62. Philadelphia: University of Pennsylvania Press, 1999.

Morgan, Sharon. *Land Settlement in Early Tasmania: Creating an Antipodean England*. Cambridge: Cambridge University Press, 1992.

Morillo, Stephen. 'A General Typology of Transcultural Wars – The Early Middle Ages and Beyond'. In *Transcultural Wars: From the Middle Ages to the 21st Century*, ed. Hans-Henning Kortüm, 29–42. Berlin: Akademie Verlag, 2006.

Moses, A. Dirk, ed. *Empire, Colony, Genocide: Conquest, Occupation, and Subaltern Resistance in World History*. New York: Berghahn, 2008.

Moses, A. Dirk. 'Empire, Colony, Genocide: Keywords and the Philosophy of History'. In *Empire, Colony, Genocide: Conquest, Occupation, and Subaltern Resistance in World History*, ed. A. Dirk Moses, 4–54. New York: Berghahn, 2008.

Moses, A. Dirk. *The Problems of Genocide: Permanent Security and the Language of Transgression*. Cambridge: Cambridge University Press, 2021.

Mostert, Noel. *Frontiers: The Epic of South Africa's Creation and the Tragedy of the Xhosa People*. London: Pimlico, 1992.

Muchembled, Robert. *Le temps des supplices. De l'obéissance sous les rois absolus*, XVe-XVIIIe siècles. Paris: Armand Colin, 1992.

Murphree, Daniel S. *Native America: A State-by-State Historical Encyclopedia*. Santa Barbara, CA: Greenwood Press, 2012.

Murray, Louise Wells. *A History of Old Tioga Point and Modern Athens, Pennsylvania*. Wilkes-Barre, PA: Raeder Press, 1908.

Naidoo, Jay. 'Was the 50th Ordinance a Charter of Khoi Liberties?' In *Tracking Down Historical Myths: Eight South African Cases*, ed. Jay Naidoo, 35–48. Johannesburg: Ravan Press, 1989.

Nettelbeck, Amanda. 'Proximate Strangers and Familiar Antagonists: Violence on an Intimate Frontier', *Australian Historical Studies* 47, no. 2 (2016): 209–24.

Newton-King, Susan and Vertrees Canby Malherbe. *The Khoikhoi Rebellion in the Eastern Cape (1799–1803)*. Cape Town: Centre for African Studies, University of Cape Town, 1993.

O'Brien, Sean Michael. *In Bitterness and in Tears: Andrew Jackson's Destruction of the Creek and Seminoles*. Westport, CT: Praeger, 2003.

O'Brien, Sharon. *American Indian Tribal Governments*. Norman: University of Oklahoma Press, 1993.

O'Malley, Vincent. *Beyond the Imperial Frontier: The Contest for Colonial New Zealand*. Wellington: Bridget Williams Books, 2014.

Oberg, Michael Leroy. *Dominion and Civility: English Imperialism and Native America*. Ithaca, NY: Cornell University Press, 2004.

Odle, Mairin. *Under the Skin: Tattoos, Scalps, and the Contested Language of Bodies in Early America*. Philadelphia: University of Pennsylvania Press, 2022.

Onuf, Peter S. *Jefferson's Empire: The Language of American Nationhood*. Charlottesville: University Press of Virginia, 2000.

Ostler, Jeffrey. '"To Extirpate the Indians": An Indigenous Consciousness of Genocide in the Ohio Valley and Lower Great Lakes, 1750s–1810', *William and Mary Quarterly* 72, no. 4 (2015): 587–622.

Ostler, Jeffrey. *Surviving Genocide: Native Nations and the United States from the American Revolution to Bleeding Kansas*. New Haven, CT: Yale University Press, 2019.
Ozouf, Mona. 'War and Terror in French Revolutionary Discourse (1792-1794)', *Journal of Modern History* 56, no. 4 (1984): 579-97.
Pagden, Anthony. *European Encounters with the New World: From Renaissance to Romanticism*. New Haven, CT: Yale University Press, 1993.
Parker, Arthur C. *Iroquois Uses of Maize and Other Food Plants*. Albany, NY: New York State Museum, 1910.
Parker, Arthur C. 'The Constitution of the Five Nations', *New York State Museum Bulletin* 184 (April 1916): 7-158.
Parker, Arthur C. *The Constitution of the Five Nations or The Iroquois Book of the Great Law*. Albany, NY: University of the State of New York, 1916.
Parker, Arthur C. *The Life of Ely S. Parker, Last Grand Sachem of the Iroquois and General Grant's Military Secretary*. Buffalo, NY: Buffalo Historical Society, 1919.
Parker, Arthur C. *An Analytical History of the Seneca Indians: Researches and Transactions of the New York State Archeological Association*, Vol. 6. Canandaigua, NY: The Times Presses, 1926.
Parker, Arthur C. 'Notes on the Ancestry of Cornplanter'. *Researches and Transactions of the New York State Archaeological Association*, 1927 reprint. New York: Times Presses, 1970.
Parkington, John and Simon Hall. 'The Appearance of Food Production in Southern Africa'. In *The Cambridge History of South Africa, Vol 1, From Early Times to 1885*, ed. Carolyn Hamilton, Bernard K. Mbenga and Robert Ross, 99-111. Cambridge: Cambridge University Press, 2016.
Parkington, John E. 'Soaqua and Bushmen: Hunters and Robbers'. In *Past and Present in Hunter Gatherer Studies*, ed. Carmel Schrire, 151-74. New York: Routledge, 2016.
Patch, Robert W. 'Culture, Community, and "Rebellion" in the Yucatec Maya Uprising of 1761'. In *Native Resistance and the Pax Colonial in New Spain*, ed. Susan Schroeder, 67-83. Lincoln: University of Nebraska Press, 1998.
Patch, Robert W. *Maya Revolt and Revolution in the Eighteenth Century*. 2nd ed. Oxford: Routledge, 2015.
Peires, Jeffrey B. *The House of Phalo: A History of the Xhosa People in the Days of Their Independence*. Berkeley: University of California Press, 1981.
Peires, Jeffrey B. *The House of Phalo: A History of the Xhosa People in the Days of Their Independence*. Johannesburg: Ravan Press, 1981.
Peires, Jeffrey B. 'The British and the Cape 1814-1834'. In *The Shaping of South African Society, 1652-1840*, ed. Richard Elphick and Hermann Giliomee, 472-518. Cape Town: Maskew Miller Longman, 1989.
Peires, Jeffrey B. *The Dead Will Arise: Nongqawuse and the Great Xhosa Cattle-killing Movement of 1856-7*. Johannesburg: Ravan Press, 1989.
Penn, Nigel. 'Pastoralists and Pastoralism in the Northern Cape Frontier Zone during the Eighteenth Century', *South Africa Archaeological Bulletin, Goodwin Series* 5 (1986): 62-8.
Penn, Nigel. 'Land, Labour and Livestock in the Western Cape during the Eighteenth Century: The Khoisan and the Colonists'. In *The Angry Divide: Social and Economic*

History of the Western Cape, ed. Wilmot G. James and Mary Simons, 2–19. Cape Town: David Philip, 1989.

Penn, Nigel. 'Mapping the Cape: John Barrow and the First British Occupation of the Cape Colony, 1795–1803', *Pretexts* 4, no. 2 (1993): 20–43.

Penn, Nigel. '"Fated to Perish": The Destruction of the Cape San'. In *Miscast: Negotiating the Presence of the Bushmen*, ed. Pippa Skotnes, 81–92. Cape Town: University of Cape Town Press, 1996.

Penn, Nigel. 'The Northern Cape Frontier Zone in South African Historiography'. In *Colonial Frontiers: Indigenous-European Encounters in Settler Societies*, ed. in Lynette Russell, 19–46. Manchester: Manchester University Press, 2001.

Penn, Nigel. *The Forgotten Frontier: Colonist and Khoisn on the Cape's Northern Frontier in the 18th Century*. Cape Town: Double Storey and Ohio University Press, 2005.

Penn, Nigel. '"Civilising" the San: The First Mission to the San, 1791–1806'. In *Claim to the Country: The Archive of Wilhelm Bleek and Lucy Lloyd*, ed. Pippa Skotness, 90–117. Athens: Ohio, Ohio University Press, 2007.

Penn, Nigel. 'The British and the "Bushmen": The Massacre of the Cape San, 1795 to 1828', *Journal of Genocide Research* 15, no. 2 (2013): 183–200.

Penn, Nigel. 'Casper, Crebis and the Knegt: Rape, Homicide and Violence in the Eighteenth-Century Rural Western Cape', *South African Historical Journal* 66, no. 4 (2014): 611–34.

Perry, James M. *Arrogant Armies: Great Military Disasters and the Generals behind Them*. New York: John Wiley, 1996.

Peruta, Franco della. 'War and Society in Napoleonic Italy: The Armies of the Kingdom of Italy at Home and Abroad'. In *Society and Politics in the Age of the Risorgimento: Essays in Honour of Denis Mack Smith*, ed. John Davis and Paul Ginsborg, 26–48. Cambridge: Cambridge University Press, 1991.

Peterson, Merrill D. *Thomas Jefferson and the New Nation: A Biography*. Norwalk, CT: Easton Press, 1987.

Peterson, Nicolas. 'The Natural and Cultural Areas of Aboriginal Australia: A Preliminary Analysis of Population Groupings with Adaptive Significance'. In *Tribes and Boundaries in Australia*, ed. Nicolas Peterson, 50–71. Canberra: Australian Institute of Aboriginal Studies, 1976.

Pichichero, Christy. *The Military Enlightenment: War and Culture in the French Empire from Louis XIV to Napoleon*. Ithaca, NY: Cornell University Press, 2017.

Pirenne, Henri. *Histoire de Belgique*, 7 Vols. Brussels: Lamertin, 1902–1932.

Powell, Michael and Rex Hesline. 'Making Tribes? Constructing Aboriginal Tribal Entities in Sydney and Coastal NSW from the Early Colonial Period to the Present', *Journal of the Royal Australian Historical Society* 96, part 2 (2011): 115–48.

Racine, Karin. 'Message by Massacre: Venezuela's War to the Death, 1810–1814', *Journal of Genocide Research* 15, no. 2 (2013): 201–17.

Radin, Paul. *Winnebago Hero Cycles: A Study in Aboriginal Literature*. Baltimore, MD: Waverly Press, 1948.

Rambaud, Jacques. *Naples sous Joseph Bonaparte, 1806–1808*. Paris: Plon-Nourrit, 1911.

Rapport, Michael. '"The Germans Are Hydrophobes": Germany and the Germans in the Shaping of French Identity'. In *The Bee and the Eagle: Napoleonic France and the*

End of the Holy Roman Empire, 1806, ed. Alan Forrest and Peter H. Wilson, 234–5. Basingstoke: Palgrave Macmillan, 2009.

Readman, Paul, Cynthia Radding and Chad Bryant. 'Introduction: Borderlands in a Global Perspective'. In *Borderlands in World History, 1700–1914*, ed. Paul Readman, Cynthia Radding and Chad Bryant, 1–17. Basingstoke: Palgrave Macmillan 2014.

Remini, Robert V. *Andrew Jackson and His Indian Wars*. Harmondsworth: Penguin Books, 2002.

Renaudet, Isabelle. 'Mourir en Espagne: "garrot vil" et exécution capitale dans l'Espagne contemporaine'. In *L'exécution capitale. Une mort donnée en spectacle XVIe-XXe siècles*, ed. Régis Bertrand and Anne Carol, 83–106. Aix-en-Provence: Publications de l'Univesité de Provence, 2003.

Reynolds, Henry. *Frontier: Aborigines, Settlers and Land*. Sydney: Allen & Unwin, 1987.

Reynolds, Henry. 'Genocide in Tasmania'. In *Genocide and Settler Society: Frontier Violence and Stolen Indigenous Children in Australian Society*, ed. A. Dirk Moses, 127–49. New York: Berghahn, 2005.

Reynolds, Henry. *The Other Side of the Frontier: Aboriginal Resistance to the European Invasion of Australia*. 1982 reprint. Sydney: UNSW Press, 2006.

Richter, Daniel K. 'War and Culture: The Iroquois Experience', *William and Mary Quarterly* 40, no. 4 (1983): 528–59.

Richter, Daniel K. *The Ordeal of the Longhouse: The Peoples of the Iroquois League in the Era of European Colonization*. Chapel Hill: University of North Carolina, 1992.

Richter, Daniel K. 'Whose Indian History?' *William and Mary Quarterly* 50, no. 2 (1993): 379–93.

Rinehart, Melissa A. and Kate A. Berry. 'Kansas and the Exodus of the Miami Tribe'. In *Tribes and the States: Geographies of Intergovernmental Interaction*, ed. Brad A. Bays and Erin Higan Fouberg, 29–50. New York: Roman and Littlefield, 2002.

Rink, Martin. 'The Partisan's Metamorphosis: From Freelance Military Entrepreneur to German Freedom Fighter, 1740–1815', *War in History* 17, no. 1 (2010): 6–36.

Robson, Fergus. 'Insurgent Identities, Destructive Discourses, and Militarized Massacre: French Armies on the Warpath against Insurgents in the Vendée, Italy, and Egypt'. In *Unconventional Warfare from Antiquity to the Present Day*, ed. Brian Hughes and Fergus Robson, 133–54. Cham: Palgrave Macmillan, 2017.

Robson, Fergus. 'French Soldiers and the Revolutionary Origins of the Colonial Mind'. In *Militarized Cultural Encounters in the Long Nineteenth Century: Making War, Mapping Europe*, ed. Joseph Clarke and John Horne, 25–47. Cham: Palgrave Macmillan, 2018.

Robson, Fergus. 'Siege Warfare in Comparative Early Modern Contexts: Norms, Nuances, Myth and Massacre during the Revolutionary Wars'. In *Civilians under Siege from Sarajevo to Troy*, ed. Alex Dowdall and John Horne, 83–105. London: Palgrave Macmillan, 2018.

Rogers, Thomas James and Stephen Bain. 'Genocide and Frontier Violence in Australia', *Journal of Genocide Research* 18, no. 1 (2016): 83–100.

Ross, Robert. 'The Cape Economy and the Cape Gentry'. In *Beyond the Pale: Essays on the History of Colonial South Africa*, ed. Robert Ross, 13–49. Middletown, CT: Wesleyan University Press, 1993.

Ross, Robert. 'Rather Mental than Physical: Emancipations and the Cape Economy'. In *Breaking the Chains: Slavery and Its Legacy in the Nineteenth Century Cape Colony*, ed. Nigel Worden and Clifton Crais, 145–68. Johannesburg: University of the Witwatersrand Press, 1994.

Ross, Robert. 'Khoesan and Immigrants: The Emergence of Colonial Society in the Cape, 1500–1800'. In *The Cambridge History of South Africa, Vol. 1, From Early Times to 1885*, ed. Carolyn Hamilton, Bernard K. Mbenga and Robert Ross, 168–210. Cambridge: Cambridge University Press, 2016.

Rothberg, Michael. *The Implicated Subject: Beyond Victims and Perpetrators*. Stanford, CA: Stanford University Press, 2019.

Rothenberg, Gunter. *The Art of Warfare in the Age of Napoleon*. Bloomington: Indiana University Press, 1978.

Rothenberg, Gunter. 'The Age of Napoleon'. In *The Laws of War: Constraints on Warfare in the Western World*, ed. Michael Howard, George J. Andreopoulos and Mark R. Shulman, 86–97. New Haven, CT: Yale University Press, 1994.

Russell, Lynette. *Colonial Frontiers: Indigenous–European Encounters in Settler Societies*. Manchester: Manchester University Press, 2001.

Ryan, Lyndall. 'Settler Massacres on the Australian Colonial Frontier, 1836–1851'. In *Theatres of Violence: Massacre, Mass Killing and Atrocity Throughout History*, ed. Philip Dwyer and Lyndall Ryan, 94–109. New York: Berghahn, 2012.

Ryan, Lyndall. *Tasmanian Aborigines: A History since 1803*. Sydney: Allen & Unwin, 2012.

Ryan, Lyndall. 'Establishing a Code of Silence: Civilian and State Complicity in Genocidal Massacres on the New South Wales Frontier, 1788–1859'. In *Civilian-Driven Violence and the Genocide of Indigenous Peoples in Settler Societies*, ed. Mohamed Adhikari, 114–38. London: Routledge, 2021.

Ryan, Lyndall, Jennifer Debenham, Bill Pascoe, Robyn Smith, Chris Owen, Jonathan Richards, Stephanie Gilbert, Robert J. Anders, Kaine Usher, Daniel Price, Jack Newley, Mark Brown and Hugh Craig. 'Colonial Frontier Massacres in Australia, 1788–1930', https://c21ch.newcastle.edu.au/colonialmassacres/introduction.php.

Sandy, Peggy Reeves. *Divine Hunger: Cannibalism as a Cultural System*. New York: Cambridge University Press, 1986.

Sargeant, Winthrop. 'Winthrop Sargeant's Diary while with General Arthur St. Clair's Expedition against the Indians', *Ohio Archaeological and Historical Quarterly* 33, no. 2 (July 1924): 237–73.

Sargent, Clem. *The Colonial Garrison 1817–1824. The 48th Foot: The Northamptonshire Regiment in the Colony of New South Wales*. Canberra: TCS Publications, 1996.

Saunders, Christopher. 'The Hundred Years' War: Some Reflections on African Resistance on the Cape-Xhosa Frontier'. In *Profiles of Self-Determination: African Responses to European Colonialism in Southern Africa, 1652–Present*, ed. David Chainawa, 55–77. Northridge: California State University, 1976.

Saunt, Claudio. *A New Order of Things: Property, Power, and the Transformation of the Creek Indians, 1733–1816*. New York: Cambridge University Press, 1999.

Scheipers, Sibylle. *On Small War: Carl Von Clausewitz and People's War*. Oxford: Oxford University Press, 2018.

Schmidt, Christopher W. and Amber E. Osterhol. 'Middle and Late Archaic Trophy-Taking in Indiana'. In *Violence and Warfare among Hunter-Gatherers*, ed. Mark W. Allen and Terry L. Jones, 241–56. Walnut Creek, CA: Left Coast Press, 2014.

Schroeder, Paul W. *The Transformation of European Politics, 1763–1848*. Oxford: Clarendon Press, 1994.

Seitz, Trina N. 'A History of Execution Methods in the United States'. In *Handbook of Death and Dying, Vol. 1: The Presence of Death*, ed. Clifton D. Bryant, 357–67. Thousand Oaks, CA: Sage Publications, 2003.

Sémelin, Jacques. 'Du crime de masse'. In *Faut-il s'accommoder de la violence?* ed. Thomas Ferenczi, 375–91. Paris: Complexe, 2000.

Sémelin, Jacques. 'In Consideration of Massacres', *Journal of Genocide Research* 3, no. 3 (2001): 377–89.

Sémelin, Jacques. 'Du massacre au processus génocidiare', *Revue internationale des sciences sociales* 174, no. 4 (2002): 483–92

Sémelin, Jacques. 'From Massacre to the Genocidal Process', *International Social Science Journal* 54, no. 174 (2002): 433–42.

Sémelin, Jacques. 'Analysis of a Mass Crime: Ethnic Cleansing in the Former Yugoslavia, 1991–1999'. In *Specter of Genocide: Mass Murder in Historical Perspective*, ed. Robert Gellately and Ben Kiernan, 353–70. Cambridge: Cambridge University Press, 2003.

Sémelin, Jacques. 'Towards a Vocabulary of Massacre and Genocide', *Journal of Genocide Research* 5, no. 2 (2003): 193–210.

Sémelin, Jacques. *Purify and Destroy: The Political Uses of Massacre and Genocide*. Trans. Cynthia Schoch. New York: Columbia University Press, 2007.

Senellart, Michel. 'La qualification de l'ennemi chez Emer de Vattel', *Astérion: philosophie, histoire des idées, pensée politique* 2 (2004): https://doi.org/10.4000/asterion.82.

Serna, Pierre. 'Pour un épilogue: Le massacre au XVIIIe siècle ou comment écrire une histoire de l'inhumain des Lumières aux Révolutions, puis à la conquête de l'Algérie', *La Révolution française* 3 (2011): 1–12.

Shannon, Timothy. 'Iroquoia'. In *The Oxford Handbook of American Indian History*, ed. Frederick E. Hoxie, 199–216. New York: Oxford University Press, 2016.

Shaw, Alan George Lewers. 'Philip Gidley King (1758–1808)', *Australian Dictionary of Biography*: https://adb.anu.edu.au/biography/king-philip-gidley-2309.

Shurkin, Michael. 'French Liberal Governance and the Emancipation of Algeria's Jews', *French Historical Studies* 33, no. 2 (2010): 259–80.

Silverman, David J. *Thundersticks: Firearms and the Violent Transformation of Native America*. Cambridge, MA: Belknap Press, 2016.

Simmons, William S. 'Cultural Bias in the New England Puritans' Perception of Indians', *William and Mary Quarterly* 38, no. 1 (1981): 56–72.

Smedley, Audrey. *Race in North America: Origin and Evolution of a Worldview*. Boulder, CO: Westview Press, 2012.

Smith, Andrew. *First People: The Lost History of the Khoisan*. Cape Town: Jonathan Ball, 2022.

Smith, David Livingstone. *Less than Human: Why We Demean, Enslave, and Exterminate Others*. New York: St. Martin's Press, 2011.

Smith, J. David. *The Eugenic Assault on America: Scenes in Red, White, and Black*. Fairfax, VA: George Mason University, 1993.

Snyder, Timothy. *Bloodlands: Europe between Hitler and Stalin*. New York: Basic Books, 2010.

Southerland, Jr., Henry deLeon and Jerry Elijah Brown. *The Federal Road through Georgia, the Creek Nation, and Alabama, 1806–1836*. Tuscaloosa: University of Alabama Press, 1989.

Stapleton, Timothy J. *Maqoma: The Legend of a Great Xhosa Warrior*. Kuilsrivier: Amava Heritage Publishing, 2016.

Starkey, Armstrong. *European and Native American Warfare, 1675–1815*. New York: Routledge, 1998.

Statham, Pamela, ed. *A Colonial Regiment: New Sources Relating to the New South Wales Corps 1789–1810*. Canberra: P. Statham, 1992.

Stevenson, Michael. *Samuel Daniell: An Enigmatic Life in Southern Africa and Ceylon, 1799–1811*. Cape Town: Jonathan Ball, 2025.

Stiggins, George. *Creek Indian History: A Historical Narrative of the Genealogy, Traditions and Downfall of the Ispocoga or Creek Indian Tribe of Indians by One of the Tribe*, ed. Virginia Pounds Brown. Birmingham, AL: Birmingham Public Library Press, 1989.

Strozier, Charles B., David M Terman, James W. Jones and Katherine A Boyd, eds. *The Fundamentalist Mindset: Psychological Perspectives on Religion, Violence, and History*. New York: Oxford University Press, 2010.

Sturm, Philip. 'Lewis Wetzel', *The West Virginia Encyclopedia*, 7 February 2023: https://www.wvencyclopedia.org/entries/1119.

Swanton, John Reed. *Creek Religion and Medicine*. 1928 reprint. Lincoln: University of Nebraska Press, 2000.

Switzer, Leo. *Power and Resistance in an African Society: The Ciskei Xhosa and the Making of South Africa*. Madison: University of Wisconsin Press, 1993.

Sword, Wiley. *President Washington's Indian War: The Struggle for the Old Northwest, 1790–1795*. Norman: University of Oklahoma Press, 1985.

Szalay, Miklós. *The San and the Colonisation of the Cape, 1770–1789: Conflict, Incorporation, Acculturation*. Cologne: Rudiger Köppe, 1995.

Taithe, Bertrand. *The Killer Trail: A Colonial Scandal in the Heart of Africa*. Oxford: Oxford University Press, 2009.

Takaki, Ronald. 'The Metaphysics of Civilization: Indians and the Age of Jackson'. In *From Different Shores: Perspectives on Race and Ethnicity in America*, ed. Ronald Takaki, 52–66. New York: Oxford University Press, 1987.

Tardif, Phillip John. *John Bowen's Hobart: The Beginning of European Settlement in Tasmania*. Hobart: Tasmanian Historical Research Association, 2003.

Tatz, Colin. 'Confronting Australian Genocide', *Aboriginal History* 25 (2001): 16–36.

Taylor, Rebe. 'Genocide in Van Diemen's Land (Tasmania), 1803–1871'. In *The Cambridge World History of Genocide*, ed. Ned Blackhawk, Ben Kiernan, Benjamin Madley and Rebe Taylor, Vol. 2, 481–507. Cambridge: Cambridge University Press, 2023.

Thomas, Jacob E. and Terry Boyle. *Teachings from the Longhouse*. Toronto: Stoddart, 1994.

Tilly, Charles. 'Routine Conflicts and Peasant Rebellions in Seventeenth Century France'. In *Power and Protest in Protest in the Countryside: Studies of Rural Unrest in Asia*.

Europe, and Latin America, ed. Robert Weller and Scott E. Guggenheim, 13–41. Durham, NC: Duke University Press. 1982.

Tilly, Charles. *Coercion, Capital, and European States, AD 990–1990*. Cambridge, MA: B. Blackwell, 1990.

Tinker, George E. 'American Indians and the Arts of the Land: Spatial Metaphors and Contemporary Existence', *Voices from the Third World* 14, no. 2 (1992): 170–93.

Tinker, George E. *American Indian Liberation: A Theology of Sovereignty*. Maryknoll, NY: Orbis Books, 2008.

Tone, John Lawrence. *The Fatal Knot: The Guerrilla War in Navarre and the Defeat of Napoleon in Spain*. Chapel Hill: University of North Carolina Press, 1994.

Tone, John Lawrence. 'Small Wars and Guerrilla Fighting'. In *The Cambridge History of the Napoleonic Wars. Vol. II, Fighting the Napoleonic Wars*, ed. Bruno Colson and Alexander Mikaberidze, 47–64. Cambridge: Cambridge University Press, 2023.

Tooker, Elisabeth. *An Iroquois Source Book*. New York: Garland Publishing, 1985–1986.

Toussaint-Samat, Marguelonne. *A History of Food*. Malden, MA: Wiley-Blackwell, 2009.

Trowbridge, Charles Christopher. *Meearmeear Traditions*, ed. Vernon Kinietz. Ann Arbor: University of Michigan Press, 1938.

Tulchin, Allan. 'Massacres during the French Wars of Religion', *Past & Present* 214, no. 7 (2012): 100–26.

Turbet, Peter. *The First Frontier: The Occupation of the Sydney Region 1788 to 1816*. Sydney: Rosenberg Publishing, 2011.

Turner, John and Greg Blyton. *The Aboriginals of Lake Macquarie: A Brief History*. Toronto, New South Wales: Lake Macquarie City Council, 1995.

Valentino, Benjamin. *Final Solutions: Mass Killing and Genocide in the Twentieth Century*. Ithaca, NY: Cornell University Press, 2004.

Valentino, Benjamin, Paul Huth and Dylan Balch-Lindsay. '"Draining the Sea": Mass Killing and Guerrilla Warfare', *International Organization* 58, no. 2 (2004): 375–407.

Van de Logt, Mark. '"The Powers of the Heavens Shall Eat of My Smoke": The Significance of Scalping in Pawnee Warfare', *Journal of Military History* 72, no. 1 (2007): 104–71.

Van der Merwe, Petrus Johannes. *Die Noordwaartse Beweging van die Boere Voor die Groot Trek*. The Hague: W.P. Van Stockum and Son, 1937.

Van Sittert, Lance and Thierry Rousset. '"An Unbroken Line of Crime and Blood": Settler Militia and the Extermination and Enslavement of San in the Graaf-Reinet District of the Cape Colony, c. 1776–1825'. In *Civilian Driven Violence and the Genocide of Indigenous Peoples in Settler Societies*, ed. Mohamed Adhikari, 86–113. Cape Town: UCT Press, 2020.

Veracini, Lorenzo. *Settler Colonialism: A Theoretical Overview*. Houndmills: Palgrave Macmillan, 2010.

Veracini, Lorenzo. 'Colonialism, Frontiers, Genocide: Civilian-Driven Violence in Settler Colonial Situations'. In *Civilian-Driven Violence and the Genocide of Indigenous Peoples in Settler Societies*, ed. Mohamed Adhikari, 266–84. London: Routledge, 2021.

Verhaegen, Paul. *La Belgique sous la domination française, 3, La guerre des paysans, 1798–1799*, 5 Vols. Brussels and Paris: Goemaere and Plon, 1926.

Voegelin, Erminie Wheeler. *Mortuary Customs of the Shawnee and Other Eastern Tribes*, 1944 reprint. New York: AMS Press, 1980.

Wagner, Sally Roesch. 'The Root of Oppression Is the Loss of Memory: The Iroquois and the Early Feminist Vision'. In *Iroquois Women: An Anthology*, ed. William Guy Spittal, 223–9. Ontario, CA: Iroquois Publishing and Craft Supplies, 1990.

Walker, Willard B. 'Creek Confederacy before Removal'. In *Handbook of North American Indians, Vol. 14, Southeast*, ed. Raymond D. Fogelson, 373. Washington, DC: Smithsonian Institution, 2004.

Wallace, Paul A. W. *Conrad Weiser: Friend of Colonist and Mohawk*. New York: Russell & Russell, 1945.

Wallace, Paul A. W., ed. *The Travels of John Heckewelder in Frontier America*. Pittsburgh: University of Pittsburgh Press, 1958.

Walter, Dierk. *Colonial Violence: European Empires and the Use of Force*, trans. Peter Lewis. London: Hurst, 2017.

Waselkov, Gregory A. and Brian M. Wood. 'The Creek War of 1813–1814: Effects on Creek Society and Settlement Pattern', *Journal of Alabama Archaeology* 32, no. 1 (1986): 1–24.

Waselkov, Gregory A. *A Conquering Spirit: Fort Mims and the Redstick War of 1813–1814*. Tuscaloosa: University of Alabama Press, 2006.

Weatherford, Jack. *Native Roots: How American Indians Enriched America*. New York: Fawcett Books, 1991.

Webb, Denver A. '"The War Took Its Origins in a Mistake": The Third War of Dispossession and Resistance in The Cape Of Good Hope Colony'. *Scientia Militaria: South African Journal of Military Studies* 42, no. 2 (2014): 54–83.

Webb, Denver A. 'Further beyond the Pale: Decolonisation, Historians and Military Discourse in the 18th and 19th Centuries on the Eastern Cape "Frontier"', *Journal of Southern African Studies* 43, no. 4 (2017): 681–97.

Weber, David J. *Bárbaros: Spaniards and Their Savages in the Age of Enlightenment*. New Haven, CT: Yale University Press, 2005.

Welch, Cheryl B. 'Colonial Violence and the Rhetoric of Evasion: Tocqueville on Algeria', *Political Theory* 31, no. 2 (2003): 235–64.

Welch, Cheryl B. 'Out of Africa: Tocqueville's Imperial Voyages', *Review of Middle East Studies* 45, no. 1 (2011): 53–61.

Wells, Julie C. *The Return of Makhanda: Exploring the Legend*. Scottsville: University of KwaZulu-Natal Press, 2012.

Wesseling, Henk L. 'Colonial Wars: An Introduction'. In *Imperialism and War: Essays on Colonial Wars in Asia and Africa*, ed. J. A. de Moor and H. L. Wesseling, 1–11. Leiden: E. J. Brill, 1989.

White, Richard. *The Middle Ground: Indians, Empires, and Republics in the Great Lakes Region, 1650–1815*. New York: Cambridge University Press, 2010.

Whitman, James Q. *The Verdict of Battle: The Law of Victory and the Making of Modern War*. Cambridge, MA: Harvard University Press, 2012.

Whittlesey, Charles. 'White Men as Scalpers', *Western Reserve and Northern Ohio Historical Society* 22 (1874): 5–6.

Willmot, Eric. *Pemulwuy: The Rainbow Warrior*. Sydney: Weldon Publishing, 1987.

Wilson, Peter H. 'Atrocities in the Thirty Years War'. In *Ireland: 1641: Contexts and Reactions*, ed. Micheál Ó Siochrú and Jane Ohlmeyer, 153–75. Manchester: Manchester University Press, 2013.

Winer, Margot. 'Landscapes, Fear and Land Loss on the Nineteenth-Century South African Colonial Frontier'. In *Contested Landscapes: Movement, Exile and Place*, ed. Barbara Bender and Margot Winer, 257–2. London: Routledge, 2020.

Wolfe, Patrick. 'Settler Colonialism and the Elimination of the Native', *Journal of Genocide Research* 8, no. 4 (2006): 388–403.

Woolf, Stuart. *Napoleon's Integration of Europe*. London: Routledge, 1991.

Woolf, Stuart. 'The Construction of a European World-View in the Revolutionary-Napoleonic Years', *Past & Present* 137, no. 1 (1992): 72–101.

Wright, Christine. *Wellington's Men in Australia: Peninsular War Veterans and the Making of Empire c.1820–40*. Basingstoke: Palgrave Macmillan, 2011.

Yaple, Robert L. 'Braddock's Defeat: The Theories and a Reconsideration', *Journal of the Society for Army Historical Research* 46, no. 188 (1968): 194–201.

Young, Henry J. 'A Note on Scalp Bounties in Pennsylvania', *Pennsylvania History: A Journal of Mid-Atlantic Studies* 24, no. 3 (1957): 207–18.

Zimmerer, Jürgen. 'Colonialism and the Holocaust: Towards an Archaeology of Genocide'. In *Genocide and Settler Society: Frontier Violence and Stolen Indigenous Children in Australian Society*, ed. A. Dirk Moses, 49–76. New York: Berghahn, 2005.

Index

Aboriginal people. *See also* Indigenous people
   in Australia 212, 217–20
   and British 80–1
   New South Wales and Tasmania 43–51, 101, 150–2, 155–6
   revenge attack 77–80
Adhikari, Mohamed 184
Adventure Bay 45
Age of Revolutions 2–3
Algeria 14, 220–1
American Revolution 3, 41, 69–70, 91, 107, 110, 112, 171
Amherst, Jeffrey 41
ancien régime 82, 115, 128–9, 133–4
apartheid 33
Appin massacre 159–62
Armitage, David 231 n.10
Atkinson, Alan 149
atrocities
   and dehumanization 126–7
   on the frontier 108–13
Attenbrow, Val 44–5, 50
Australia 211–12, 217, 224, 226
   Aboriginal people in 217–20
   frontier massacre 18–21
   Indigenous attitudes 57–9, 93–4
   Native Institution 157, 160–2, 218
   New Holland xiv
   policy of terror 101–2
Awabakal people 46, 77

Baird, David 188
Banks, Joseph 146, 154–5, 218
Bantu peoples 28–9, 63, 185
Barère, Bertrand 102
Barrow, John 90–1, 210
Battle of Blue Licks 168–70
Battle of Burnt Corn 178
Baudin, Nicolas 149–51
Bayly, Christopher 193
Bediagal (Bidjigal) 9, 46, 78–80, 137–44
Belgium 123, 130
Bell, David A. 22–3, 120
Bennelong 74, 77, 148
Berndt, Ronald 50
Berthier, Louis-Alexandre 125
Bezuidenhout, Frederick 201
Bird, Henry 11, 192
Black Line 17
Black War 78
Bligh, William 137, 156
Boers 33, 89–90, 97, 187, 194, 197–9, 201–2, 205, 208, 210, 212
Bonaparte, Joseph 85, 123, 124
Bonaparte, Napoleon 86, 102–5, 116–18, 123–5, 129, 132, 220–1
Bonwick, James 93
borderland 5, 228 n.12
Botany Bay 45–6, 57, 217
Boulart, Jean François 132
Bouquet, Henry 99
Bourke, Richard 213–14
Bowen, John 151–2
Boyer, Pierre François 14
Brereton Raid 205
brigandage/brigands 82–3, 120–1, 123–4, 130
British Crown 41, 106–7
Brown, Patrick 172

Brune, Guillaume 123
Budbury, David 159–60
Bugeaud, Thomas Robert 14
Bunbury, Charles 198
Bungaree 158–9
Burr, Aaron 176
Burr Conspiracy 176–7
Bushmen. *See* San peoples/Bushmen
Butler, Richard 164–8

Cacica 68
Calabria 82–3, 102, 105, 109, 129
Caley, George 150
Campbell, John 197
Cape 90–1, 95–8, 181–2, 184–9, 210, 213–15
Cape Colony 33, 181, 186
Cape Frontier Wars 33, 90, 97–8, 106, 188–9, 210, 213
Cape Regiment 191, 194–5, 198, 201, 208–9
Caribbean 2, 113, 115, 136
    Saint-Domingue 2
    sugar islands 3
Castellane, Esprit 87
cattle theft and massacre 95–8, 112, 187, 192, 202
Cherokee 70, 167, 170, 179
    'The Harmony Ethic' 38
Cherokee Nation v. Georgia 216
Choctaw 42, 216
Christianity 24, 38, 89, 92, 157, 176, 203, 206, 218
civilization 24, 73, 93, 116, 126, 130, 135, 174, 226
Clark, George Rogers 101, 112, 168, 170
Classical massacres 133
Clausewitz, Carl von 117, 119, 128
Clauzel, Bertrand 14
Clements, Nicholas 77
Coffee, John 178–9
Colebee 74
Collins, David 45, 51, 140–2, 145, 152–4, 188, 191
Colonial Frontier massacre 18–23

colonialism 1, 4, 11, 17, 24, 115, 133, 223
colonial violence 5–6, 78, 221
commando 21, 32, 65–7, 87, 97–8, 106, 190–2, 194–6, 199–200, 202, 204, 206, 208, 213, 223
    Boer 97
    General Commando 66, 183–5
    trekboer 182
Condorcet, Nicolas de 24
Confederacy
    Indian 37, 70, 173
    Indigenous 39–40
    Iroquois 37–8
    Muscogee 37–8
Connor, John 74–80, 141–3
corroboree 48, 76, 139, 158
Cradock, John 14, 193–9, 201
Creek War 178
Crockett, Davy 178–9
Croghan, George 106–7
Cumberland Plain War 138–9, 158, 162, 217–18
Cuyler, J. G. 190–2, 194, 198

Daniell, Samuel 30, 210
Darug 9, 46, 57–8, 76–81, 139, 146, 148
Davis, Natalie Zemon 109
Dawe, Charles 160
dehumanization 25, 94–5, 112, 126–8
deidentification 94–5
Denny, Ebenezer 164, 166–7
D'Entrecasteaux Channel 49, 149–50
Dharawal people 46, 80–1
du Fresne, Marc-Joseph Marion 101
Dutch 8, 10, 31, 54, 89, 102, 106, 181–2, 187–90, 210
Duyker, Edward 101

eastern Cape 29, 33, 35, 63–4, 106
Egushawa 100, 164–7
Egypt 2, 14, 124, 193
eliminationist violence 16–17, 23–4, 83, 94–5, 99, 105
elimination, politics of 122–6
Elphick, Richard 28–9, 236 n.2

Enlightenment 11, 23–5, 52, 89, 93, 120, 126, 134–6
Europe
    English language, use of 92–3
    French-occupied 81–5
    massacres in 11, 20, 102
    policy of terror 101–2
    powers 221–2
    Revolutionary Wars, outbreak of 2–4
    sackings and scorched earth 102–8
    Wars of Religion 102, 109–10

fear, notion of 25
fire (instrument of war) 131–2
First British Occupation 182
Fish River 36, 192, 196–8, 204, 206–7
Fort Mims 177–8
Foveaux, Joseph 145
France 102, 107, 113, 115, 124, 126, 133–6, 155–6, 193
Fraser, George Sackville 199, 204, 208
French
    in Africa 220
    in Australia 101
    British and 94
    in Canada 111
    Empire 2, 10, 115–17, 132, 221
    Lübeck attack 125
    Naturaliste 149–50
    -occupied Europe 81–5
    rule 15, 118, 122–4, 136
    storming of Tarragona 125
    in Syria 86, 124–5
    troops, Hasselt, capture of 123
    Wars of Religion 109–10, 126
French Revolution 3, 9, 82, 84, 89, 110, 117, 133–4, 150, 193
Friederici, Georg 71
frontier wars 9, 32, 78, 96–8, 105, 138, 157
    Cape 33, 90, 97–8, 106, 188–9, 210, 213
    Eastern 185–8
    Fifth Frontier War 205–10
    Fourth Frontier War 198
    Sixth Frontier War 209–10, 215
    Third Frontier War 187, 203

Gandangara people 80–1
Gayanashagowa (Great Law of Peace) 38–9
generosity 40, 59
genocide 16–17, 22, 51, 91, 128
Germany 24, 87, 93, 103, 124, 130
Gerrit Maritz 89–90
Goodall, William 142
gooroobeera 81
Goya, Francisco (Francisco de Goya y Lucientes) 111
Graham, John 194–8
Grahamstown 205–7
Grande Armée 116
Great Dividing Range 46, 48
Great Law 38–9
Grey, Henry 192–3
Griqua 213, 215
Grose, Francis 137–9, 267 n.41
Guingret, Pierre 86
Guringai people 46

Hamelin, Jacques Felix Emmanuel 149
Hamilton, Henry 112
Hamtramck, John Francis 172–3
Harmar, Josiah 107, 172–3
Harrison, William Henry 42, 73
Haudenosaunee ("Iroquois") 37, 99
    Iroquoia 56, 69–70, 91, 105, 110
    Iroquois 37–9, 68–9, 72–3, 92, 99, 105
Hawkes, Abiather 192
Hawkesbury River 9, 44–6, 78–80, 101, 137–46, 160, 217
Hawkins, Benjamin 175–6
Heckewelder, John 40, 72
Hisagitamisi ('Master of Breath') 38
Hobart 77, 93–4, 151–4
Hobart, Robert 148
Hottentot Code (Caledon Code) 201
Hottentot Regiment 187
Hottentots 31, 90, 187
Hughes, John 99
humanity 11, 25, 94–5, 129, 134
hunter-gatherers 28–33, 52–3, 57, 62–4, 66, 139, 182
Hunter, John 142, 147

Index

ideology/ideological pattern 3, 21, 23, 92, 94, 112–13, 128–32, 134–5, 193, 263 n.57
imperial cloud 13
Indian Ocean 3
Indigenous Americans 7–9, 20, 40, 42, 55, 59, 71, 73, 110–12
   Indian Removal Act ("Jacksonian Removal") 92, 216
   Trail of Tears 216–17
   violent dispossession 215–17
   warfare 67–71
   Woodlands
      American farmers 56
      Eastern 37–40, 71–2
      gift economy 40–3
      Indigenous nations of 37–40
Indigenous Australians 7–9, 52
   warfare 74–81, 87
Indigenous people 6–11, 17, 20–5, 27. *See also* Aboriginal people
   Australia 57–9
   North America 55–7
      Clan Mothers 39–41, 67–9
   South Africa 52–5, 61–7
      Khoikhoi and the San 28–32
      Xhosa 33–7
indiscriminate violence (reprisals) 17
Intercourse Act of 1790 41–2
Iroquois. *See* Haudenosaunee ("Iroquois")
Italy 14, 82, 84, 104, 109, 122–3, 127, 129, 132, 261 n.25

Jackson, Andrew 42, 105, 176–9, 277 n.128
jacquerie 82
Jefferson, Thomas 42, 91–2, 176
Johnson v. M'Intosh 216
Johnson, William 41, 106
Johnston, George 145, 156
Jourdan Law 123
Junot, Jean-Andoche 104, 123

Kaffir 192, 196–7, 200, 252 n.3
Kalyvas, Stathis 17, 232 n.22

Karskens, Grace 45, 139
Kei River 34–5, 208
Keiskamma River 36–7, 204–5, 207–9
Kekewepellethy 164–8
Kemp, Anthony Fenn 145
Kentucky 11, 168–9, 172–4
Khoikhoi (Khoisan) 28–37, 52–5, 61–6, 90, 95–8, 106, 112, 182, 185, 187, 190, 201, 206, 209–10, 213–15, 223
King, Philip Gidley 9, 137–8, 144–6, 148–52, 154, 241 n.76
Knox, Henry 91, 172

Lauria attack 129–30
Lavaux, Sergeant 87
Leader Maynard, Jonathan 263 n.57
Levene, Mark 19
Lignereux, Aurélien 82
Logan, Benjamin 168–9
Louis-Philippe 220
Louis XIV 102
Louis XVI 145
Lycett, Joseph 48

Macarthur, John 145
Macartney, Earl 90
Macquarie, Lachlan 144, 156–62, 211, 217
Makhanda 202–5, 207–8, 282 n.63
Malherbe, Vertrees Canby 236 n.2
Mann, Barbara Alice 286 n.43
Maqoma 204, 207, 209–10
Mason, John 100
massacre 15–18, 132–6, 219–20, 223–6
   in Australia, policy of terror 101–2
   colonial frontier 18–21
   in Europe, sackings and scorched earth 102–8
   February-April 1816 159–62
   in North America, terror tactics 98–101
   reprisal 25
   in South Africa, cattle theft 95–8
Masséna, André 129–30

mass killing 5, 15–16, 21, 94–5, 105, 128–30, 135, 163, 220
Mazower, Mark 16
McGary, Hugh 168–70
McGillivray, Alexander (Hoboi-Hili-Miko) 175–6
Melunathe 167–70
Meredith, Thomas 177
Meshikinokwak 174
Miami of Indiana 170–5
Milfort, Louis LeClerc 40, 69
Mill, John Stuart 24
Milton, John 198
Miot, Jacques 124
Moore, William 151–5
Moowattin, Daniel 157
Morgan, Sharon 80
Mother Earth 38, 55–6
Mountgarrett, Jacob 151–5
Muscogee
    of Alabama 175–9
    assimilant *versus* 'Red Stick' traditionals 178–9
    Civil War 212
    Confederacy 37–8
    Italwalgi and *Kipayalgi* 40
    War of 1813–14 105
mutilation 108–10, 127

Napier, Governor 200
Napoleonic Code 116
Napoleonic Wars 2, 4, 11, 14, 18, 81, 83, 102–5
    sexual assault in 85–7
Ndlambe 190, 194–7, 202–5, 207–9
Nepean River 46, 80–1, 157, 159, 217
Netherlands 32, 122
New South Wales (NSW) 14–15, 43–51
    in 1802 144–6
    Appin massacre 159–62
    Corps 137–8, 141, 145–7, 150–1, 155–6
    Hawkesbury River frontier 138–44
    Pemulwuy's war 76, 138, 146–51
    Risdon Cove 152–9
    Van Diemen's Land 149–52

Ngqika 190, 194, 197, 202–5, 207–10
Nguni people 29, 54, 63, 185
North Africa 220
North America 1, 11, 73–4
    British in 17
    Europeans in 59
    extirpate and exterminate 91
    Indian depredations alleged 163, 168, 172, 177
    Indigenous attitudes 55–7
    Indigenous Clan Mothers 39–41, 67–9
    Miami of Indiana 170–5
    militia armies 21
    Muscogee Civil War 212
    Muscogee of Alabama 175–9
    scalping 8, 21, 71–3, 111–12, 169–72
    Shawnee of Ohio 164–70
    terror tactics 98–101
    Young Men 39, 67–70
Northern Frontier 181–5

Oglethorpe, James Edward 175
Ohio 37, 70, 92, 99, 164–70, 172
Oneidas 68
Orange River 28, 213–14
Ordinance 50 214–15

Padua 127
Palatinate 102
Parker, Arthur C. 91
Parramatta 46, 76, 81, 139, 145–7, 149, 151, 157–8, 162, 217–18
Paterson, William 141, 145, 155
Pawnee 71
Peabody, Sue 24
Peasants War 123
Pemulwuy 9, 76, 81, 138, 146–51, 154, 157, 218
Peninsular War 10, 212
Peron, François 150
petite guerre/irregular warfare 82
Philip, John, *Researches in South Africa* 214–15
Phillip, Arthur 74, 77, 102, 137, 148

Piper, John 145
Pringle, Thomas 195

race and racism 23–6, 36, 65, 77, 92, 113, 121, 200, 215
rape 4, 7, 85, 87, 104, 108, 122, 125, 132–3, 157, 206, 212, 223, 225, 251 n.115
Read, James 203
religion 23–4, 83
Revolutionary Wars
　American 112
　in Britain 2
　in Europe 2–4, 11, 18, 81, 102, 113, 135, 220
　French 82, 84, 110, 116–17, 121, 133–5
　in North America 14–15
Reynier, Jean 132
Reynolds, Henry 75–6, 80
Risdon Cove 9, 50, 138, 151–9, 268 n.69
ritual torture 8, 71, 73
Roberts, Penny 19
Robinson, G. A. 77
Roggeveld 36, 66–7, 89, 182
Ryan, Lyndall 226

Sanfedisti 123
San peoples/Bushmen 21, 28–32, 34–6, 52–4, 61–7, 90, 182–5, 213–15, 226
Savary, Anne-Jean-Marie 14
Scharnhorst, Gerhard von 117
Schaw, William 160
schepsel (creature) 32, 90
scorched-earth tactics 10, 91, 102–8, 113, 131, 187, 195, 222
Scott, Charles 173–4
Second British Occupation 188–92
Semelin, Jacques 18–19
Seven Years' War 2, 41, 107, 112, 164
sexual assault 85–7
Shawnee of Ohio 164–70
Shelley, William 157, 218
Sherwin, John 94
Shingask 164

Sixth Frontier War 209–10, 215
Slagtersnek Rebellion of 1815 201–2
slavery 23–4, 99, 118, 174, 211, 215
Smith, Andrew 213–14
Smith, John 99
Somerset, Charles Henry 201–2, 204–5, 209, 213
South Africa 2–9
　cattle theft 95–8, 112
　destruction of the San 213–15
　Eastern Frontier 185–8
　frontier massacre 18–21
　Indigenous people of 28–37, 52–5, 61–7
　Third Frontier War 187, 203
Spain 14
　French in 127
　guerrilla bands 83
　Napoleonic Wars 105, 109
spirits 38, 50–1, 57–8, 61, 100, 124, 151
spoor law 202–4
state violence 16, 23, 117–22, 128, 134
St. Clair, Arthur 172–4
Stockenstrom, Anders 191, 194, 199–201, 207–9, 213–14
Subrahmanyam, Sanjay 231 n.10
Sullivan, John 91–2, 99
Sundays River 36, 194
Sydney 43–51, 74–8, 80–1, 139, 145, 149–52, 154, 156, 159, 161, 218
Sydney Gazette 154, 218
Syria 86, 124, 127

Tasman, Abel 150
Tasmania 17, 43–51, 77–80, 101–2, 108, 138, 149–52, 155–6, 218–19
Tecumseh 92
Teiohonwé:thon 72
Tench, Watkin 14–15
Tenskwatawa 92
terror
　policy of 101–2
　tactics 98–101
Thirty Years' War 102, 104
Thompson, Andrew 80

Threlkeld, L. E. 76–7
Tocqueville, Alexis de 220
trekboers 32, 36, 66, 98, 106, 182, 184–5
Turbet, Peter 140
Turner, Frederick Jackson 33
Turreau, Louis-Marie 131
Tuscarora sachem 72
Tyrol 82–3

Underhill, John 100
United States, the 1–2, 42, 70, 92, 100, 107, 145, 163–78, 216
Upper Kaffir Drift 207

Van der Kemp 203
Van Dieman's Land (Tasmania) 149–52
Vattel, Emer de 120–1, 261 n.20
veldkos 29
veldwagtmeester/veldcorporaal 32, 89, 182–3
Vendée 14, 23, 102, 119, 129, 131–2, 135
Vereenigde Oost-Indische Compagnie (VOC) 32, 36, 95–7, 181–3, 185, 187, 252 n.3

Wallis, James 160–1
Walter, Dierk 221
wampum 39, 166–7, 224, 239 n.37

wanton attacks 172
warfare
    Aboriginal 76–8, 80
    colonial frontier 22–3
    guerrilla 9, 65, 78, 80, 117, 138, 147, 187
    Indigenous Americans 67–71
Washington, George 91–2, 99, 105, 164, 173
Wellesley, Arthur 103
Wells, Julia 203
West Virginia 110, 168
Wetzel, Lewis 112, 173
White, James 179
Wilkinson, James 176
Williamson, David 225
Willshire, Thomas 205–8
Wilmot, Eric 148
Wilson, James 77
Worcester v. Georgia 216

Xhosa 29, 33–7, 54–5, 61, 63–4, 90–1, 98, 185–210, 212

Yutana Nire 72

Zuurveld 10, 36, 64, 181, 188–91, 193–203, 205, 208–9